CAMBRIDGE STUDIES
IN ENGLISH LEGAL HISTORY

Edited by
D. E. C. YALE
Fellow of Christ's College and
Reader in English Legal History at the University of Cambridge

MARRIAGE LITIGATION IN MEDIEVAL ENGLAND

R. H. HELMHOLZ

Associate Professor of Law and History
Washington University, St Louis

CAMBRIDGE UNIVERSITY PRESS

Published by the Syndics of the Cambridge University Press
Bentley House, 200 Euston Road, London NW1 2DB
American Branch: 32 East 57th Street, New York, N.Y. 10022

© Cambridge University Press 1974

Library of Congress Catalogue Card Number: 73-93395

ISBN 0 521 20411 9

First published 1974

Photoset and Printed in Malta
by St Paul's Press, Ltd

CONTENTS

Preface		vii
Abbreviations		ix
Introduction		1
I	The sources	6
II	Suits to enforce marriage contracts	25
III	Suits for divorce and incidental marriage causes	74
IV	Procedure in marriage cases	112
V	Judges, lawyers, witnesses and litigants	141
VI	Changes and variations in practice	165
Conclusion		187
Appendix	Extracts from marriage cases	190
Bibliography		233
Index		242

PREFACE

In its original version, this study of canonical practice was presented as a Ph.D. thesis at the University of California, Berkeley. I know that it retains, after two revisions, many faults. But it would be a worse book than it is without the help of several people, and I want to express my appreciation to them publicly. Professor John T. Noonan, Jr first interested me in the subject of the history of marriage law. My work owes much to his continued thoughtful guidance and criticism. Professors Peter Herde and Robert Brentano also guided me in the early stages of my work in canon law, and their advice and encouragement I have valued greatly. Mr G. D. G. Hall was kind enough to read the entire text, parts of it more than once. His excellent and penetrating criticism has greatly improved the final product. Professors Charles Donahue and Peter Riesenberg also read through earlier versions of the work, making many helpful suggestions which I have incorporated in the text.

I want also to thank the Keeper of Manuscripts and the Archivist of the Library of the Dean and Chapter, Canterbury, successively Dr William Urry and Miss Anne Oakley, and the Director of the Borthwick Institute of Historical Research in York, Mrs N. K. M. Gurney, for permission to reproduce substantial portions of the MSS. in their care. I am very grateful for the help which they, and the many other archivists I have troubled with queries about documents, unfailingly offered to me.

R. H. H.

ABBREVIATIONS

Citation of manuscript records of the ecclesiastical courts is given by diocese, rather than by the archive repository where they are kept today. The reader should refer to the first section of the bibliography for the latter.

Medieval Legal Texts

D. 1 c. 1	Decretum Gratiani, Distinctio 1, canon 1.
C. 1 q. 1 c. 1	Decretum Gratiani, Causa 1, quaestio 1, canon 1.
X 1.1.1	Decretales Gregorii IX, Liber 1, tit. 1, CANON 1.
Sext. 1.1.1	Liber Sextus, Liber 1, tit. 1, CANON 1.
Clem. 1.1.1	Clementines, Liber 1, tit. 1, CANON 1.
Cod. 1.1.1	Codex Justinianus, Liber 1, tit. 1, lex 1.
Dig. 1.1.1	Digestum, Liber 1, tit. 1, fragmentum 1.

Other Abbreviations

Bracton	Bracton, H. de, *De Legibus et Consuetudinibus Angliae* ed. G. E. Woodbine (4 vols, New Haven and London, 1915–42).
Ch. Ant.	Chartae Antiquae (Canterbury)
Conset, *Practice*	Conset, H., *The Practice of the Spiritual or Ecclesiastical Courts* (London, 1708).
D.D.C.	*Dictionnaire de droit canonique* (7 vols, Paris, 1935–65).
Ecc. Suit	Ecclesiastical Suit Roll (Canterbury)
Esmein	Esmein, A., *Le Mariage en droit canonique* (2 vols, Paris, 1891).
Gl. ord.	*Glossa ordinaria*
Jo. And.	Joannes Andreae

John of Acton,   John of Acton, *Constitutiones Legatinae*
   Constitutiones   *Othonis et Othoboni, cum annotationibus*
                  Johannis de Athonis (Oxford, 1679).

L.Q.R.   *Law Quarterly Review*

Lyndwood, *Provinciale*   Lyndwood, W., *Provinciale (seu Con-*
                  stitutiones Angliae) (Oxford, 1679).

Pollock and Maitland,   Pollock, F. and Maitland, F. W., *History*
   HEL   *of English Law*, 2nd ed. (2 vols,
                  Cambridge, 1898; reissued, 1968).

P.R.O.   Public Record Office, London

Reg.   Register

Sede Vacante S.B.   Sede Vacante Scrapbook (Canterbury)

Spec. Iud.   Durantis, *Speculum Iudiciale* (Lyons,
                  1543).

Swinburne, *On Spousals*   *Treatise of Spousals or Matrimonial*
                  Contracts (London, 1686).

T.R.H.S.   *Transactions of the Royal Historical*
                  Society

Wilkins, *Concilia*   *Concilia Magnae Britanniae et Hiberniae*,
                  ed. D. Wilkins (4 vols, London, 1737).

Woodcock   Woodcock, B. L., *Medieval Ecclesiastical*
                  Courts in the Diocese of Canterbury
                  (Oxford, 1952).

INTRODUCTION

There was, in the late thirteenth century, an extensive system of ecclesiastical courts in England. In theory it was an ordered system, with archdeacon, bishop, archbishop, even pope, having a recognized sphere of authority and appellate jurisdiction. The reality was slightly more confused. Piecemeal growth of the numerous courts, disputes over jurisdiction, and resulting *ad hoc* compromises, had led to a more mottled picture.[1] But it is roughly accurate to say that the bishop of every diocese had a Consistory court, presided over by a judge, called his official, and also a court of audience which exercised concurrent, and occasionally appellate, jurisdiction. Below this, each archdeacon had a court, and many lesser clerics, rural deans, monastic houses and cathedral canons, for example, also held courts of varying competence. Appeal from the lower courts lay to the bishop's court, and from there to the archbishop's court (in the Southern Province the Court of Arches in London, in the Northern the Provincial Court at York). From there, appeal could go to the Papal court. There was, in other words, a large number of courts of ecclesiastical jurisdiction in medieval England. They were a normal and ubiquitous part of English life, as they were throughout Western Christendom.

One of the most significant parts of the law administered in these courts dealt with the matrimonial disputes of the laity. Proof and

---

[1] For accounts of the organization of the courts, see A. H. Thompson, *The English Clergy and Their Organization in the Later Middle Ages* (Oxford, 1947), 40–71; W. Stubbs, 'Report on Ecclesiastical Courts, 1883', Historical Appendix No. 1 to Vol. 1 (*Parliamentary Papers*, 1883, Vol. XXIV). For specific dioceses, although sometimes for the post-medieval period, see Woodcock, 6–29; R. A. Marchant, *The Church Under the Law: Justice, Administration, and Discipline in the Diocese of York, 1560–1640* (Cambridge, 1969); R. M. Haines, *The Administration of the Diocese of Worcester in the First Half of the Fourteenth Century* (London, 1965), 104–14; C. A. Ritchie, *The Ecclesiastical Courts of York* (Arbroath, 1956); M. Aston, *Thomas Arundel, A Study of Church Life in the Reign of Richard II* (Oxford, 1967), 53–82; F. S. Hockaday, 'The Consistory Court of the Diocese of Gloucester', *Transactions of the Bristol and Gloucestershire Archaeological Society*, 46 (1924).

enforcement of marriage contracts, annulment of invalid marriages, punishment of adultery, were all within the exclusive competence of the Church. Everything, that is, having to do with marriage, except questions of property settlement and inheritance, came within the purview of the canon law courts. I have tried, in the pages which follow, to describe the practice of the Church courts in dealing with this marriage litigation.

The study extends from the second half of the thirteenth century through the end of the fifteenth, a convenient if perhaps artificial stopping point. It is based largely on the surviving court records, which are spread throughout the ecclesiastical archives of England, and still almost entirely unprinted. It is my hope that this work will indicate incidentally something of the richness of these records, for other areas of ecclesiastical jurisdiction deserve close study. The records are described in some detail in the first chapter.

This is, above all, a history of actual litigation. The emphasis is on practice, rather than on legal doctrine or theory. I have occasionally covered the writing of the canonists in detail, when it seemed necessary to make clear some of the problems faced by the Church courts. And I have always sought to provide enough information about the formal law to make the practice intelligible to the reader. But for a comprehensive summary of marriage law, one must go elsewhere. Fortunately, this is easily done. There are several scholarly works on the subject, the best of which is Esmein's *Le mariage en droit canonique*.[2] In such works, the interested reader will find discussion on, say, marriages contracted by proxy, a subject much discussed by medieval canonists. But no cases of such marriages appear in the remaining court records. Therefore they find no place in this study.

In his excellent monograph on the medieval courts of the diocese of Canterbury, Brian Woodcock concluded that 'no adequate basis exists for the correlation of the practice of particular courts with the injunctions of the Canon Law'.[3] For the marriage law this judgment has happily proved to be mistaken. Quite a bit can be learned about

---

[2] Besides Esmein's work, see J. Dauvillier, *Le mariage dans de droit classique de l'église* (Paris, 1933); J. Freisen, *Geschichte des canonischen Eherechts* (Paderborn, 1893); G. H. Joyce, *Christian Marriage: An Historical and Doctrinal Study*, 2nd edn (London, 1948); T. A. Lacey, *Marriage in Church and State*, rev. and suppl. by R. C Mortimer (London, 1947). And see the remarks on the approaches of study needed in the history of Christian marriage by C. N. L. Brooke, 'Problems of the Church Historian', *Studies in Church History*, eds. C. W. Dugmore and Charles Duggan, I (London, 1964), 1–19.

[3] Woodcock, 4.

the way the law was put into practice. The different sorts of litigation, the procedure, and the persons involved in marriage causes, can all be described in some detail. Enough complete records have survived for a full background to be available in many cases, far more so than for most secular litigation of the Middle Ages. The cases give substance and life to the doctrines of the canonists. Occasionally, they contradict the dictates of the written law. And the records provide much incidental information about the history of marriage in medieval times. In few places do legal and social history so clearly overlap.

Above all, the records which are the source of this study provide a not unimportant chapter in the history of English law. It was with good reason that Maitland devoted considerable attention to the Church's law of marriage in the *History of English Law*.[4] There was never an English law of marriage apart from that administered by the Church courts. There was some skirmishing at the edges, such as the dispute over jurisdiction to determine questions of bastardy in disputes over inheritance of land.[5] But for the most part, the marriage law of the Church was the law of England. There is, therefore, little to be said in this study about the 'Stubbs–Maitland Controversy', the dispute over the extent to which the medieval English Church considered itself free to deviate from the law of the Western Church.[6] Neither King, Parliament, nor English clergy desired to establish customs or rules at conflict with the formal law of marriage.

The canon law of marriage was, it is worth remembering, also the law of England for a very long time. Ecclesiastical jurisdiction over marriage disputes survived the Reformation. Some alterations in the law were made at that time. And others followed. But there were no sweeping alterations in the substance of the law; there was no real disruption. Only in 1857 was marriage jurisdiction withdrawn from the Church. Even then the secular courts administered much the same law, until the new popular attitude towards divorce of the present century brought about more fundamental legal changes.

---

[4] Pollock and Maitland, *HEL* II, 364–99.

[5] See D. E. Engdahl, 'English Marriage Conflicts Law Before the Time of Bracton', *American J. of Comparative Law*, 15 (1967), 109–35; R. H. Helmholz, 'Bastardy Litigation in Medieval England', *American J. of Legal History*, 13 (1969), 360–83.

[6] For a summary of this controversy, with judicious remarks about the nature of the canon law, see E. W. Kemp, *An Introduction to Canon Law in the Church of England* (London, 1957), 11–32. Maitland's remarks about the binding nature of the canon law of marriage on the English courts are found in *Roman Canon Law in the Church of England* (London, 1898, repr. 1968), 38–41.

The study begins, it has already been said, with litigation of the later thirteenth century. The organization of the ecclesiastical courts in England and the formulation of the Church's law of marriage had already been accomplished by that time. We have to deal with a functioning system. However, a brief note about the history of marriage in the early Middle Ages will not be out of place. It provides part of the context in which the law must be understood, and it helps explain many of the attitudes and habits we shall find in the actual litigation.

In Roman law, marriage was a relatively private matter.[7] No special formula or ceremony was required to contract a valid marriage. There was no requirement of intervention by any sort of a public official, and there was no registration of marriages. Divorce was allowed without a decree by any court. There were, of course, laws which defined and regulated relations between husband and wife. But no action by a public officer was a necessary part of the formation and dissolution of the marriage bond. This was left to the parties directly concerned.

It was against this background of freedom in marriage practice that the Christian religion grew. Christianity, from the start, contained the seeds of more detailed regulation of marriage. But at no time in late antiquity or in the early Middle Ages did the Church achieve, or even seek, complete control over marriage. Certain supplementary rules existed. Churchmen were occasionally drawn to determine controversies about marriage. But the church did not have exclusive competence over matrimonial questions. And of an organized system of enforcement there was nothing. Esmein accurately called it 'une juridiction purement disciplinaire'.[8]

The extent of general compliance with the precepts of Christian marriage in this early period is problematical. It doubtless varied from place to place and from time to time. But we know that the rules in favor of indissolubility and against marriage between kin were not always obeyed. Repudiation of wives was practised. And it was often tolerated. This is not to say that marriage remained exactly as it had been in the Roman Republic. There was some assimilation of new and stricter ideas about marriage. But the movement was far from complete. People retained a control over their matrimonial

---

[7] For a detailed account see P. E. Corbett, *The Roman Law of Marriage* (Oxford, 1930).

[8] Esmein, I, 28. And see, for a recent account, J. Gaudemet, 'Le lien matrimonial: les incertitudes du haut moyen-âge', *Le Lien Matrimonial* (Strasbourg, 1970), 81–105.

affairs which was compatible only with the notion that marriage was a personal matter, one which could not be absolutely regulated by Church or State.

The establishment of the Church's exclusive control over marriage was a long and disputed process. Fixing the date it occurred has exercised scholarly minds.[9] But in my view the effort is wasted: worse, it is misleading. The struggle was not between competing court systems. It was not a question of competition between secular and ecclesiastical jurisdictions. The problem was to ensure that ordinary marriage disputes went to any court at all. The real hurdle was the persistent idea that people could regulate marriages for themselves. The disappearance of this notion occurred gradually, over a very long period of time. It had not been accomplished by the time our study begins. Nor had it been fully realized at the end. But to deal with the problem there did exist regular, professional courts and a relatively complete, uniform body of canon law. Neither of these had existed in the early Middle Ages. This study describes the way in which the English courts applied the canon law of marriage.

[9] See, for example, P. Daudet, *L'Établissement de la compétence de l'église en matière de divorce et consanguinité* (Paris, 1941).

I

THE SOURCES

The volume of records available for the study of later medieval marriage litigation is considerable. The survival rate of the Church court records is far below that of the royal courts, for which plea rolls in virtually unbroken sequence exist from the end of the twelfth century. But what does remain is not inconsequential. At least some pre-1500 court records have come down from the dioceses of Canterbury, York, Bath and Wells, Ely, Hereford, Lichfield, Lincoln, London, Norwich and Rochester. The two metropolitan sees, Canterbury and York, have quite extensive collections. Some of the other dioceses, Norwich for example, are represented in only a scrappy way. But, taken together, the records are good enough to tell us a great deal about the practice of the courts.

Students of law and history are only beginning to give these records the attention they deserve. Brian Woodcock's excellent introductory monograph on the diocesan courts at Canterbury appeared over twenty years ago. Unfortunately, that careful scholar did not live to continue his work, or even to see his book through the press. And only in recent years has a considerable number of studies on the English Church courts begun to appear.[1] All of them show something of the richness of the surviving court records.

---

[1] Among the recent works on the subject are: R. Dunning, 'The Wells Consistory Court in the Fifteenth Century', *Proceedings of the Somersetshire Archaeological and Natural History Society*, 106 (1962), 46–61; C. Morris, 'A Consistory Court in the Middle Ages', *Journal of Ecclesiastical History*, 14 (1963), 150–9; *idem*, 'The Commissary of the Bishop in the Diocese of Lincoln', *ibid.*, 10 (1959), 50–65; *An Episcopal Court Book for the Diocese of Lincoln, 1514–1520*, ed. M. Bowker, Lincoln Record Soc., 61 (1967); D. M. Owen, *The Records of the Established Church of England, Excluding Parochial Records* (Cambridge, 1970); M. M. Sheehan, 'The Formation and Stability of Marriage in Fourteenth-century England: Evidence of an Ely Register', *Mediaeval Studies*, 33 (1971), 228–63; an older account is F. S. Hockaday, 'The Consistory Court of the Diocese of Gloucester', *Transactions of the Bristol and Gloucestershire Archaeological Society*, 46 (1924). Miss Jane Sayers' monograph, *Papal Judges Delegate in the Province of Canterbury, 1198–1254* (Oxford, 1971), treats an important aspect of ecclesiastical jurisdiction for a period before any regular series of English records survive.

Those records will be a rich store for legal and social historians for many years to come.

Where they are complete, particularly when they include the depositions of witnesses, the records provide vivid pictures of life in medieval England. For example, in one York case, we find the cries of a woman being abducted, relevant in the later attempt to dissolve her marriage because of coercion:

Oh, men! What do you mean to do with me? Alas, that I left the city of York today! Alas, that I arose from my bed today, or that my father begot me, or that my mother brought me into the world.[2]

Or, in a quieter scene, this confession of love, relevant in a suit to enforce a marriage contract between the man and woman:

She said to him, 'There is something I would like to say if it is not displeasing'. And the man said, 'Speak'. And then she said, 'There is no man in the world whom I love more'. And he said, 'I am grateful to you. And I love you'.[3]

Not all the records, of course, produce such stories. Sometimes they give procedure in the courts, and nothing more. But even that yields valuable information about the course of marriage litigation. It is invaluable in a work on legal history. It is appropriate, therefore, to begin with a look at the documents which are the basis for this study.

ACT BOOKS

The most frequent surviving court record is the Act book. By canon law, every court was bound to employ a notary or two other suitable men to record all the acts of that court: the citations, the constitution of proctors, the petitions, the exceptions, and so forth.[4] This was

---

[2] York C. P. F 37 (1410): 'O homines, quid mecum proponitis facere? Heu quod hodie de civitate Ebor' exivi. Heu quod hodie de meo lecto surrexi, aut quod pater me genuit, seu mater in mundum me produxit'.

[3] Canterbury Y.1.5, f. 170r (1456): 'Ipsa dixit sibi, "Vellem aliquid dicere vobis si non displiceretur." Et vir dixit, "Dicatis". Et tunc ipsa dixit quod, "non est vir in mundo quem magis diligo". Et ipse dixit, "Regracior vobis, et ego diligo vos."'

[4] X 2.19.11; Innocent IV, *Apparatus* ad X 2.20.28, noted that the judge at one time compiled the records, but that lately notaries had always been used. An application of the rule is found in Rochester DRb Pa 4, f. 197r (1486): 'Et quia iudex non habet notarium pupplicum prontum ad manus, ideoque adsumptis secum duobus honestis et probis sacerdotibus, videlicet magistro Thoma Newel vicario de Malling et domino vicario de Alysforde tanquam in assessores et scribas   '

done to preclude later questioning of the formal validity of the action of the courts. It was also meant to settle possible future doubts about what had been decided. The Fourth Lateran Council, which enacted this rule, laid down no set form for recording the *acta*. And the Act books we have do differ, both over the course of time and between dioceses. But this much may be said of almost all of them. They were day-to-day records of procedure in the cases heard by the courts. They were compiled in codex form, and divided internally into sessions, usually called consistories. Under the heading for each session was recorded the title for each case heard on that day and the action taken in it. For a particular case, for example, under the first recorded session we may find the constitution of proctors and the giving of the libel by the plaintiff.[5] Under the second the defendant's answer to the libel may be recorded; under the third, the plaintiff's introduction of articles and his production of several witnesses. And so on through to the final sentence. Thus, tracing the full hearing of a specific action often requires a search through many folios of an Act book.

The headings of each court session and title of each case were normally written in advance of each sitting. The action taken was recorded at the time of hearing, or later, under the appropriate case title. This is obvious because in most instances the individual cases were usually laid out regularly on each folio of the Act book. Every case was, in other words, given a set amount of space in advance. Entries of the actual procedure taken appear sometimes in a different ink from that used for the heading, and often not enough was done to fill the space which had been left under the heading. For this reason, blank areas appear on many folios. Occasionally, too much was done in a session to be fitted into the space available. The entry for one case then spilled over onto a following folio, inserted

---

[5] The modern terms 'plaintiff' and 'defendant' are used throughout this study to describe the parties to litigation. No solution is ideal, but the terms used in the records, *pars actrix* and *pars rea*, have no very good modern equivalents, so that it seemed to me that the general familiarity of these terms would compensate in some measure for any inaccuracy resulting from their use. 'Plaintiff' and 'defendant' are also the terms used by the seventeenth-century English canonist, Henry Conset. I have also noted cases in the present-day fashion, e.g. *Jones* v. *Smith*, and referred to 'cases' rather than to ecclesiastical court 'causes' for the same reason of familiarity to the modern reader. In describing the documents, however, the English equivalent of the Latin words has been used throughout, e.g. 'libel' for *libellus*, 'positions' for *positiones*, since there are no more familiar terms used in modern litigation which accurately describe these documents.

by the scribe in the blank space left from a less active case.[6]

Not all Act books, it should be said, were compiled in precisely like fashion, even within the same diocese. At Hereford, for instance, the headings for each case were not set down in advance of the court session. They were recorded at the same time as the *acta*, either during the session or later from the scribe's notes. At York, each case was identified by a notation in the left-hand margin or above the normal entry giving the names of the parties. No explicit record was made of the case's subject. At Canterbury, on the other hand, each case was identified by the parish of the parties, and the subject was almost invariably stated expressly. A few Act books were not kept chronologically. The remaining book from Bath and Wells, for example, does not have its entries arranged on a strictly day-by-day basis. The cases recorded in it also cover a long period of time, from 1458 to 1498, so that it may have been put together at the latter date from existing materials.[7] Some Act books combine instance litigation, that is actions begun on the initiative of private parties, with *ex officio* business.[8] A few books contain depositions of witnesses. Most do not. There are, in other words, no absolutely firm rules about Act books. But, in general, it is fair to think of them as systematic records of procedural steps taken in all the cases which came before a particular court, arranged chronologically and individually for each case.

The history of the standards of completeness in recording within the Act books from our period is one of decline and deterioration.[9] It is a virtual rule that the earlier the Act book, the more useful information is to be found in it. I found that the middle of the fifteenth century marks a turning point of sorts. At least it does for marriage cases. In the Act books from before that time, the scribe

---

[6] E.g. Rochester DRb Pa 1, f. 115v (1439), where the note, 'Continetur ad tale signum', followed by a particular symbol, allows the reader to trace the case more easily. In Canterbury Y.1.6, however, so many cases had to be continued that it sometimes becomes quite confusing to follow any particular case, which may have its *acta* recorded in four or more separate spaces.

[7] See R. Dunning, 'The Wells Consistory Court', for a description of this Act book.

[8] E.g. Rochester, DRb Pa 1, f. 50r (1438), where the scribe noted beside an action initially entered in the wrong place: 'Continetur in registro correctionis.' But, it is true that most instance books do contain some office cases, and vice versa.

[9] See the description in G. R. Elton, *England 1200–1640* (Ithaca and London, 1969), 105 '. . . among the more strikingly repulsive of all the relics of the past'.

usually recorded each case fairly thoroughly. He gave the opening steps and followed the suit through to its final disposition, whether sentence, dismissal, or flight by one party. After the middle of the century, however, cases were often left incompletely recorded. Certainly most cases where the Act book records only one or two hearings were settled at once. No witnesses were available or the parties agreed, so that the judge could give sentence by oral decree. But this is not invariably true. The recording of cases was sometimes simply dropped in the middle, so that there is no way to tell whether a sentence was given or not. For example, the case of *Malyn* v. *Adam and Neme*, heard in the court at Canterbury from 13 May 1471 through 29 July in that same year, was not recorded in the Act book for any procedure after the production of witnesses.[10] There would be no way of telling what final disposition was made of the case, except that it happens that the *ex officio* Act book from the period has also survived. In it, we find one party being cited for disobedience to the final sentence of the court.[11] The instance action must, therefore, have gone through to a sentence. The scribe simply did not record the fact in the Act book.

The gradual decline in standards is most discouraging for the historian in the amount of factual material he can find for each case. In fourteenth-century books which survive from Canterbury, Ely, and York, the detailed substance of the claim was almost invariably recorded. For example, we can learn that a plaintiff sought a decree of nullity because he had been coerced into marriage. Often, some of the actual evidence was recorded in the Act book. For instance, in such a case it might be set down that the witnesses expressly denied that there had been any weapons visible at the time of the contract. Likewise, the substance of the court's sentence was usually recorded in the book itself, and sometimes it was given in full. Early fifteenth-century Act books continued to give fairly full details of the actions heard, though with somewhat greater abbreviation.[12] After the 1450s however, only the barest of procedural steps were normally recorded. Instead of knowing what the

---

[10] Y.1.8, fols, 217v–218r.

[11] Y.1.11, fols. 128v, 160r, 163r. A similar instance is *Morton* v. *Swattman*, Lichfield B/C/1/1, fols. 231v, 256r (1468–9), in which the litigation was dropped from the Act book on 13 December 1468 after two brief hearings, then recorded again in the session of 4 July 1469 in the term for taxation of expenses.

[12] The early fifteenth-century records from York are an exception. There is little substantive information to be found in them. And see Owen, *Records of the Established Church*, 40–1.

exact claim was in a marriage case, we learn simply that some sort of marriage suit had begun between two parties. Of its substance nothing was set down. There are some exceptions. An occasional case was more fully recorded in the second half of the century. But, in general, the concrete information about the facts behind each case which can be taken from these late Act books is very small.[13]

The standard of handwriting also deteriorated markedly over the course of the fifteenth century. It is interesting to compare it with that of the royal court plea rolls. At the start of the century, both courts had readable, regular records. At the end, the royal court hand had changed recognizably, but it was still regular and legible, the product of training and vital tradition. The records of the Church courts, on the other hand, had become messy and hurried scrawls. Many of the entries are quite illegible. Abbreviation became extreme, unintelligible to those without experience in reading earlier Act books. The entry, 'h꜀ ꝑ ꝯ iii f꜀ c'c ec̄,' for example, is the abbreviated form of 'habetur pro confesso; tres fustigationes circa ecclesiam'.[14]

This is not to say that the later Act books are without value. They can normally be deciphered. They almost always give the names of the parties, the general type of case, each party's parish, and the action taken by the court. We can learn much about procedure in marriage cases from them. And they provide, as I hope to show, some incidental information, not without value for the history of marriage law. But of the facts and exact points of law at issue in each case, they tell us little. For these, we must turn, where we can, to Deposition books and to Cause papers.

CAUSE PAPERS

The phrase 'Cause papers' seems to have originated with Canon Purvis, who used it to describe the court records under his care at the Borthwick Institute in York.[15] It is, in fact, an excellent description, though so far as I know, the phrase has nothing medieval about

---

[13] These remarks should not be taken to imply that there was an absolute decline in the regularity with which the Church court records were compiled. The Cause papers, described below, were the principal records of the courts; they set out the issues of each case, so that the fuller treatment in the earlier Act books was to some extent simple duplication.

[14] Hereford o/2, 18 (1442). It should perhaps also be said that most post-Reformation Act books were neater and more regular in composition than those of the fifteenth century although, as stated above, they rarely give much of the substance of each case, being confined to procedure.

[15] See J. S. Purvis, *An Introduction to Ecclesiastical Records* (London, 1953), 64–95.

it. Cause papers were the documents used in the course of litigation. Unlike Act books, they were written on separate pieces of paper or parchment.[16] And they were not day-to-day records of the procedural steps taken by the court. They were fuller, formal documents submitted to or issued by the court. They were used by the parties to introduce their arguments, and by the court to embody its findings and rulings. Thus, taken together, Cause papers contain all the issues put before the court, the evidence used to prove each side's contentions, and the judge's decisions. They are the most valuable single set of documents available for the study of marriage litigation.

It is regrettable that the only sizable collections of surviving Cause papers come from York and Canterbury. And for Canterbury, there are only those of the thirteenth century, retained from periods of archiepiscopal vacancies, when metropolitan jurisdiction devolved on the Prior and Chapter. York has the fullest set, about six hundred cases of all kinds from the fourteenth and fifteenth centuries. It is likely that Cause papers were preserved systematically in other diocesan courts during the Middle Ages, but that they have since been lost. From Bath and Wells, we find notations in the Act book to documents from a case being kept 'in a file'.[17] There are similar references to collection of Cause papers in the remaining Act books from Rochester.[18] In these dioceses, and in others, we find the actual documents used in the cases only occasionally, usually when they were copied into formularies or episcopal registers. But what does remain of the actual Cause papers is not insignificant.

It is helpful in understanding marriage litigation to have the nature and function of the principal documents firmly in mind. There are among the Cause papers clearly defined classes of documents which had technical names, and particular uses in canonical court actions. For that reason, I have (with the help of the commentaries of medieval canonists) set out the definitions and characteristics of the Cause

---

[16] With the exception of the witness's depositions, which were sometimes recorded in separate books.

[17] D/D/C A1, 301 (1460): 'Vide attestationes et sentenciam una cum confessionibus partium principalium in filarcio ix diei mensi Januarii.' And see ibid., 271 (1463); 138 (1491).

[18] DRb Pa 1, f. 5v (1437): 'Proposuit quandam materiam in scriptis in philatorio remanentem'; ibid., f. 357v (1443), where there is reference to material, 'prout inter acta manualia eiusdem diei plenius continetur'; Pa 4, f. 264r (1495): reference to a sentence 'ut in cedula plenius continetur'. And see for Canterbury in the fifteenth century, Y.1.4, f. 115r (1423): 'Que quidem depositiones testium et sentencia diffinitiva in dicta causa lata pendent inter exhibita eiusdem anni.' Hereford, I/1, 231 (1495), where reference is made to a document 'penes acta remanens'.

papers as found at York and Canterbury. Not every type of document described will be found today for every case; there has been loss over the centuries, and certain documents could be omitted or combined with others. In some cases, more than those detailed here can be found. But the following were the basic ingredients of a marriage case, and they are the most frequent surviving documents.

(i) *The libel*

As described by the thirteenth-century canonist Guillelmus Durantis, the libel was 'a small sheet, containing the plaintiff's petition, its cause and action'.[19] Usually the first document introduced after the constitution of proctors, the libel gave, in general terms, the allegations on which the suit was based. It closed with a request for a specific order by the court. In a typical suit to enforce a contract of marriage, for example, a libel contained three or four allegations: first, that the parties had contracted marriage by words of present or future consent; second (if appropriate), that it had been followed by sexual relations; third, that the defendant had openly and publicly confessed the existence of the contract; and fourth, that the truth of the allegations was public, notorious and manifest in the places where the parties lived. The libel ended with a demand that the defendant be adjudged the plaintiff's legitimate husband and be required to treat her with marital affection. Durantis summed up the necessary elements of a libel: 'Who, what, before whom, by what right, and from whom'.[20]

To this libel, the defendant gave a general answer. He usually made what amounts to English law's general denial: 'narrata prout narrantur vera non esse'. Alternatively, the defendant could admit the facts alleged in the libel, but counter with a specific exception (unless he did not wish to contest the action at all). For example, he might admit that a claim of the existence of a clandestine marriage was true, but allege by way of exception that it was barred by pro-

[19] Durantis, *Spec. Iud.* IV, tit. *de libellorum conceptione*, § *quid sit libellus*, no. 1: 'brevis membrana actoris petitionem et eius causam et actionem complectens'. Three copies were normally made, one for the judge, one for the opposing party, and one to be retained by the plaintiff; see Durantis, *Spec. Iud.* II, tit. *de libelli oblatione*, no. 3; Conset, 'A brief discourse on the libel' in *Practice*, 400–05. It should also be noted that the remarks made here about the plaintiff apply as well to the defendant where he introduced an affirmative defense. He used the same documents to allege and prove his own case.

[20] *Spec. Iud.* IV, tit. *de lib. concep.* § *libellus quid continere debeat*, no. 1: 'Quis, quid, coram quo, quo iure petat, et a quo.'

hibited degrees of consanguinity or by the existence of a prior marriage contract binding one of the parties.[21] Either a libel or an
exception could legally be amended after it had been introduced. In
one York action, for instance, the name Agnes, wrongly used in the
libel, was replaced by the correct name Alice, with the permission of
the judge.[22] Misnomer of the opposing party was no bar to prosecution
of a marriage case.

There was some controversy among canonists about whether the
libel was a necessary part of a canonical action; whether it was 'de
substantia iudicii'. The answer given by the *glossa ordinaria*, Innocent
IV, and Durantis, was that it was not required.[23] A written libel could
be omitted, and the claim made orally. The eighteenth-century English
canonist, Thomas Oughton, made the same observation: an oral allegation *apud acta* was sufficient.[24] In medieval practice such oral
demands were frequently made. Usually, in the English records, they
were referred to as petitions.[25] Which was used seems to have depended
largely on the wishes of the parties, although in some courts, Rochester
in the 1480s for example, it was the almost invariable practice for an
oral petition to be reduced later to written form.[26]

(ii) *The positions*

Formal positions are easily identifiable. They consist of a number of
positive statements of the plaintiff's case (or of a defendant's affirmative defense) grouped together and each beginning: 'Item pono
quod . . .'.[27] Introduced after the libel, they contained the plaintiff's

---

[21] In Hereford I/3, 41, 42 (1500), for instance, the defendant admitted she had entered
into a contract of marriage with the plaintiff, but added that both she and the plaintiff had
'pre-contracted' with others so that the claimed marriage could not stand.

[22] Cons. A B 1, f. 90r (1418). Another interesting example comes from a defamation
case, Ely EDR D/2/1, f. 128r (1370): 'Pars actrix allegat quod ex inadvertencia erravit
de nomine partis ree vocando ipsum Willelmum in libello cum vocetur Johannes; et de
persona satis liquet et decernimus dictum proprium nomen fore addendum et corrigendum in
libello.' See also Rochester DRb Pa 1, f. 253v (1442). York M 2(i) c, f. 4r (1372). The
other documents described here could also be amended if necessary; for instance, the
depositions in York Cons. A B 1, f. 97r (1418), where the surname Carow was changed to
Cayrok.

[23] *Gl. ord.* ad X 2.3.1 s.v. *libellum reclamationis*; Innocent IV, *Apparatus* ad X 2.3.1,
no. 4; Durantis, *Spec. Iud.* IV, tit. *de lib. concep.*, § *an libellus sit de substantia*, no. 3.

[24] *Ordo Judiciorum* (London, 1738) I, 89. He here refers only to summary procedure, but
marriage cases were included under this heading.

[25] E.g. Canterbury Y.1.3, f. 98v (1419): 'proposita petitione viva voce, datur ad proponendum in scriptis in proximo'.

[26] See DRb Pa 4, fols. 212v, 218v, 221r.

[27] See *gl. ord.* ad Sext 2.9.1 s.v. *statuimus*.

case separated into its several parts. What was set out briefly and generally in the libel was elaborated and divided into separate issues in the positions. Surviving positions vary considerably in length and in specificity. Some are verbose and repetitious, and may contrive to separate a single claim into as many as sixty separate statements.[28] Others simply restate the libel in as few as three.[29] Most positions, even the longer ones, did not, however, state exactly what events the plaintiff relied on. That is, positions might allege that X and Y had legitimately contracted marriage. They did not normally give the exact day and circumstances of the contract.

The purpose of the introduction of positions was to elicit areas of agreement between the parties, so that proof would have to be made only for disputed points of fact. As Durantis wrote, 'The onus of proof by witnesses is heavy . . . , and confessions are carried out more easily than the production of witnesses.'[30] To this end the defendant had to answer each of the positions. His answers were often recorded directly on the document which contained the positions, each statement being separately answered. Those he answered affirmatively were held as proved; only those he denied had to be proved by witnesses. Thus, in a York case of 1338, there were nineteen positions introduced by the plaintiff. On the basis of the defendant's answers to them, the number of issues was reduced to three. Only three questions of fact had to be submitted to the witnesses.[31]

The effectiveness of the use of positions, as found in this York suit, does not however, appear to have been normal in marriage litigation. Almost invariably positions were answered, 'non credit' or 'non credit ut ponitur'. Against this second form of answer, the post-Reformation canonist John Ayliffe protested. He vigorously, and rightly, objected to its 'great uncertainty'.[32] It was not a 'clear and certain' denial. Nor was it an admission. It accomplished no reduction in the scope of proof, and the qualification with which it was expressed avoided any danger of a later charge of perjury. However, no exception to it was taken in medieval practice. Sometimes, in fact,

---

[28] E.g. York C.P. E 248 (1345–6).
[29] E.g. York C.P. F 22 (1402).
[30] *Spec. Iud.* II, tit. *de positionibus*, no. 2:2: 'Grave est onus probandi per testes, . . . , et facilius fiunt confessiones quam testium productiones'.
[31] C.P. E 37.
[32] See *Parergon* s.v. *answers*, 65–7.

defendants used even vaguer phrases: 'dependet' or 'nescit' or even, 'vult deliberare'.[33]

Very likely, the reason for this normal refusal to admit any of the positions is that the positions were answered by proctors or advocates. In theory, the parties ought to have answered them personally.[34] And certainly the defendant's personal responses could be required if the plaintiff expressly requested them.[35] The defendant could be summoned 'tanquam legalior persona'. At Canterbury in the later fifteenth century, plaintiffs very frequently made this demand. But even here, the proctor or advocate doubtless had a hand in framing the answers. Certainly the formal, non-committal replies found on most surviving documents bear the impress of a legally trained hand.

Not every remaining record at York contains positions. Nor were they actually used in every case. Durantis noted that, 'in many places positions are not used'.[36] There was nothing improper about it. We find evidence of the same absence in surviving records from other dioceses, for example a case from Lichfield, where, 'the plaintiff repeats the libel divided into its parts with the force of positions'.[37] Or a London action of 1496: 'The libel [was] repeated by Keys and admitted by the lord [official] in place of positions.'[38] The issues in many marriage cases were clear-cut. The libel set them out sufficiently, and the formal and negative answers which were normally made to positions meant that nothing was gained by artificially separating the action into positions. No hope of piecemeal admission was possible. In such cases, the practice of repeating the libel to replace the positions was adequate and convenient.

---

[33] See Canterbury Sede Vacante S.B. III, no. 17 (1271); York C.P. E 18 (1326–7); C.P. E 108 (1370). An apparent exception is the practice before the Consistory Court of London, in which the positions were more fully answered. At least this is true if the *Liber Examinationum*, MS. 9065, is a fair sample.

[34] *Gl. ord.* ad Sext 2.9.1 s.v. *positiones*.

[35] The procedure for making this demand is set out in Oughton, *Ordo Judiciorum* I, 104–6, 109–10. Or see Hereford I/3, 8 (1499): 'Procurator partis actricis peciit partem ream principalem fore citandam ad personaliter respondendum dictis positionibus pro eo quod credit se relevari per responsionem eiusdem.'

[36] *Spec. Iud.* II, tit. *de positionibus*, no. 5:1: 'in plerisque locis non fiunt positiones'.

[37] B/C/1/2, f. 50r (1472): 'pars actrix repeciit libellum articulatum in vim positionum'.

[38] Greater London Council Record Office, DL/C/1, f. 4r (1496): 'Repetitoque libello per Keys et admisso per dominum loco positionum'. Other examples: Canterbury Y.1.6, f. 150r (1466); Y.1.12, f. 140r (1476); Hereford 0/3, 78 (1446).

(iii) *The articles*

The testimony of witnesses in canon law trials was taken out of court, either by the judge or by a court-appointed examiner. It was done privately and individually. Neither party was represented at the time. This examination was made according to a series of statements submitted by the plaintiff. These statements were the articles. They are recognizable by the initial phrase, 'Intendit probare quod . . .', followed by the point the plaintiff hoped the testimony of the witness would establish.[39] The theory was that the examiner would question each witness in turn on each article. The depositions show that this procedure was followed in most cases, although it may sometimes have been the practice for the examiner to read all the articles to the witness before asking him to testify.[40]

By the fifteenth century in York, the articles were almost always combined with the positions. The document then begins, 'Item ponit et probare intendit . . .'. There were good practical reasons for making this combination since, as has already been said, the narrowing of issues which the use of positions was supposed to accomplish did not usually work. No progress was made by the separation of articles and positions. It is probable that the combination of the two in the fifteenth century was a recognition of this practical failure.

In some cases, however, articles were neither combined with the positions, nor introduced at all. Durantis recognizes the possibility of their complete omission: 'If, however, articles are not given, . . . , I do not believe it is a sin, for procedure and judgment are to be made in accordance with the custom of the place.'[41] Total disuse of articles is not found in the records of any English Church court. But all appear to have omitted them in some cases. In these, the witnesses were examined on the basis of the libel, or sometimes the plaintiff's

---

[39] On articles, see Hostiensis, *Summa Aurea* II, tit. *de testibus*, no. 6. In the diocesan court at Paris, the articles were apparently referred to simply as the plaintiff's 'intendit'. See *Registre des causes civiles de l'officialité épiscopale de Paris, 1384–87*, ed. Joseph Petit (Paris, 1919), col. 65.

[40] See for example York C.P. F 175 (1432), where the witness is said to be 'super primo, ii°, iii°, iiii^to, v^to, vi^to, vii°, viii°, ix°, x°, xi° articulis divisim sibi expositis examinata'.

[41] *Spec. Iud.* I, tit. *de test.*, § *de articulis*, no. 3: 'Si tamen non dentur articuli, . . . , non credo esse peccatum, nam secundum loci consuetudinem iudicandum et procedendum est'.

positions.[42] The judge or his examiner, however, always retained freedom to go beyond the formal articles in the questioning, so that the use of other documents instead of actual articles probably made little difference.

(iv) *The interrogatories*

Like the articles, interrogatories were meant to be used by the judge or examiner in the examination of the plaintiff's witnesses. But they were introduced by the opposing party, and were designed to undercut the plaintiff's case. They were prepared by the defendant after he had seen the articles, and were in fact framed specifically to meet them.[43] That is, one interrogatory might instruct the judge: 'If a witness says that a marriage took place in a house, ask him in what part of the house, who was present, did the house have a second storey, what time was it, were the parties seated or standing, what was the weather at the time.' Others would be directed at other of the plaintiff's articles.

There were two basic kinds of interrogatories. The first aimed at destroying the credibility of the witness. Questions about his opportunity to see the events described, his family ties with the parties, his receipt of presents from them, are typical examples. The second sought to adduce positive evidence for the defendant's contentions. Thus, where coercion was set up as a defense to a claim that a valid marriage existed, the interrogatories typically asked the witnesses to comment on the use of threats, the availability of weapons, and so forth, at the time the contract was made.[44] It is worth noting that, unlike the documents mentioned so far, copies of the interrogatories were not given to the opposing party at the same time the original was submitted to the court. The danger was that the plaintiff might

---

[42] E.g. Canterbury X.10.1, f. 24v (1413): 'Interrogatus super prima parte libelli.' Other instances: Lichfield, B/C/1/1, f. 244v (1468); Rochester DRb Pa 1, f. 18v (1437); Hereford, I/3, 52 (1500).

[43] *Gl. ord.* ad Sext 2.10.2 s.v. *interrogatoria*: 'Interrogatoria sunt quae facit pars testibus productis contra se, et dantur super articulis de quibus praemissum est, ... unde datis articulis petit pars terminum ad danda interrogatoria.' And see Ely EDR/2/1, f. 7v (1374): 'Pars appellata petit articulos super quibus testes debent examinari, et quod non examinentur quousque ministraverit interrogatoria.'

[44] Durantis, *Spec. Iud.* I, tit. *de teste*, § *de interrogatoriis*, no. 7: 'In summa, nota quod duo sunt genera questionum: primum quod sit ad destruendum dictum testis; puta cum queritur de causis et circunstantiis, ..., secundum, quod sit ad fundandam intentionem producentis vel exceptionem eius contra quem producitur.'

instruct his witness.[45] They might agree on a set story, so that the effect of the interrogatories would be destroyed.

Surviving depositions show that interrogatories were not submitted in all cases. Sometimes we find the witnesses being examined on the basis of hostile questions. Sometimes we do not. Parties had their choice of whether or not they wished to submit interrogatories. And sometimes Act books record that a special term had to be set for their introduction.[46] But this was not the invariable practice.

A party was not necessarily prejudiced by failing to introduce interrogatories. In theory, all judges could supplement the lack by framing questions of their own.[47] But, if the depositions tell a reliable story, they rarely did so. If the defendant decided against the use of interrogatories, no hostile questions were asked. Here, as we shall find elsewhere, the initiative in marriage litigation lay with the parties themselves. It did sometimes happen that when the original depositions were incomplete or unsatisfactory, the judge decided to recall the witnesses for further interrogation. There are several examples of this exercise of judicial power.[48] But these occurred when the judge had found the original examination wanting. Judges did not intervene regularly in this aspect of the litigation.

(v) *The depositions*

The records of the examination of witnesses were called depositions or attestations.[49] Under either name, they are the most informative and interesting documents which have come down to us from marriage causes. Without the final sentence, they provide stories of marriage negotiations, market-place haggling, domestic squabbles, tavern quarrels, illustrations of the many sorts of disagreements which led to litigation in the Church courts. With the final sentences, they give the essential elements of a law suit: that is, the facts and the decision. They allow the historian to see how the law of marriage was enforced.

The testimony recorded on the deposition was taken outside of the

---

[45] *Gl. ord.* ad Sext 2.10.2 s.v. interrogatoria: 'Et haec interrogatoria de consuetudine et de jure non dantur parti adversae, ne posset super his instruere testes suos.'

[46] E.g. Canterbury Y.1.16, f. 150r (1494).

[47] *Gl. ord.* ad X 2.19.11 s.v. *interrogationes*: 'Vel ponuntur propriae interrogationes quae fiunt a iudice ex officio, quia quoties aequitas ipsum movet potest interrogare partes.'

[48] E.g. York C.P. E 85 (1362-3); Lichfield B/C/1/1, f. 99v (1466).

[49] See X 2.19.11 and Sext 2.10.1.

court; the witnesses were questioned individually and secretly. The depositions were drawn up by the scribe who was present at the examination. They were probably written afterwards, on the basis of notes made at the time of examination. At least, the regularity and order of the surviving documents suggest that they were the products of later organization and distillation.

In the court term set for publication of the testimony, the depositions were read aloud in open court. Each party also received a copy, the original remaining with the court records.[50] In some places the depositions were collected into books, which were kept alongside the Act books as part of the official records. Examples of these deposition books have come down from London and Canterbury.[51] Theoretically at least, the official publication of the depositions was the first the parties heard of the testimony. Normally, the substance of the testimony also determined the case. When the evidence was, for the first time, fully before the judge and the parties, it must often have been obvious what the sentence would be. It is, therefore, no surprise to find that many suits were completed very quickly after the reading of the depositions. No doubt, this is why cases in the later Act books so frequently were recorded only up to publication. The merits were clear, and no further action except a decision was taken.

(vi) *The sentence*

Of all the documents here described, the definitive sentence must be the most disappointing to the modern researcher. He can learn what the decision was, that is true. But the formalism and the apparently empty verbiage of the document tell him little besides. Sentences begin: 'In Dei nomine amen. Auditis et intellectis meritis cause matrimonialis . . . ', and then wind through a series of pious and conventional phrases to arrive, finally, at the actual decision.[52] But they give little real information. Particularly unfortunate is the fact that the sentence did not normally contain the judge's reasons for

---

[50] Durantis, *Spec. Iud.* I, tit. *de teste*, § *de attestationum publicatione*, no. 1; X 2.19.11. See also Oughton *Ordo Judiciorum* I, 130–54, although it is perhaps dangerous to use his descriptions from the eighteenth century, and apparently drawn mainly from the Court of Arches, for medieval practice except where confirmed by the actual records.

[51] Canterbury X.10.1; London, Greater London Council Record Office, DL/C/205 (1467–76). I have not been able to see the second of these. And London MS. 9065, though not properly speaking a deposition book, because it also includes litigants' personal answers to positions, is nevertheless a full source of depositions.

[52] See Appendix, p. 201 for a full transcription of a typical sentence.

reaching his decision. Canonists wrote that a judge might set out his reasoning. But he was not obliged to.[53] And the remaining documents show that judges rarely recorded either their decisions on legal points or their findings of fact except in the most general terms. Thus, in cases where the defendant both denied the plaintiff's contentions and set up an affirmative defense, a sentence for the defendant will often fail to declare whether it was the defense or the denial which was decisive. In many cases, the depositions will make it obvious. But we cannot be absolutely sure, and there are other cases where one cannot tell at all.

The elaborate language of the formal sentence is, to modern tastes, perhaps the strangest feature of the definitive sentence. The long-winded recital of each of the formal steps followed in the case, and the ritualistic assertion of the spirituality and impartiality of the court add little to the substance of the decision. Why were they included? In my view, there were two good reasons. First, the repetition of the formulae was meant to be a guarantee that proper procedure had been used. Canon law sentences were not infrequently challenged on the basis of an alleged procedural error. To have the sentence spell out, however formally, the legitimate steps the court had taken constituted at least a *prima facie* assurance of legality.

Second, the writing of the canonists shows the widespread belief that a degree of solemnity should surround the handing down of a sentence. A quick statement, rendered without ceremony, seemed inappropriate. Thus the law required that the sentence be rendered publicly, in court session. It could not be made 'in occulto'.[54] Moreover, it had to be read aloud. If a copy alone was handed over, the sentence was invalid.[55] And except for two minor exceptions, the judge himself had to do the reading.[56] He could not substitute another. He had also to be seated at the time.[57]

There can be little doubt that these rules were meant to encourage obedience to the sentences. Compliance with judicial decrees was not

---

[53] *Gl. ord.* ad X 2.27.16 s.v. *exprimantur*: 'Iudex potest apponere causam quae ipsum movet; si tamen non apponitur bene tenet sententia.' There is a good discussion of this subject for a later period in G.I.O. Duncan, *The High Court of Delegates* (Cambridge, 1971), 173–4.

[54] Durantis, *Spec. Iud.* II, tit. *de sententia*, § *de diversis sententiis*, no. 19.

[55] Ibid., § *sententia qualiter sit ferenda*, no. 5.

[56] *Gl. ord.* ad Sext 2.14.5 s.v. *et si sententia*.

[57] Ibid.; Raymond de Pennaforte, *Summa* III, tit. *de sententiis*, no. 6. See also Sayers, *Papal Judges Delegate*, 93.

automatic in the Middle Ages. To insist on a formal reading of solemn, deliberate language was to impress on the parties that something special and important was being decided. Legal practice of our own day shows the worth of a certain solemnity in the court room. Informal conduct by lawyers and judges discourages respect for the law and provokes contempt for its edicts. In medieval times, when problems of law enforcement were even more serious than they are today, there was much to be said for making the definitive sentence a formal and elaborate document.

FORMULARIES, BISHOPS' REGISTERS, AND OTHER SOURCES

Formularies have, of late, come to be regarded as valuable sources of information about medieval legal practice.[58] They are collections of documents, arranged in some order, originally assembled for use by the court scribe or by lawyers in the preparation of actual cases. The forms were models for lawyers and scribes to follow. They seem particularly close to actual practice because the formularies very often used documents taken from real cases.[59] The names of the original parties still appear in some documents. It has, therefore, been concluded that formula books have a great deal to tell us about the way in which the courts worked. I have come to the conclusion that for ordinary marriage litigation, this view is mistaken. Formularies are of little use in understanding actual practice. Indeed, they can be positively misleading. I reached this negative opinion reluctantly, after having transcribed parts of several of them. But the contrast between what the Act books tell us and the impression which emerges from any formulary is too great to allow for anything but a negative conclusion. Not that there is *no* valuable information to be found in formularies. There is some. But the documents must be used individually, and generalizations based on them drawn sparingly.

The difficulty, of course, lies not with the formularies themselves, but rather with the way we look at them. They were not designed to *describe* litigation. They were meant to give samples of correct formal documents, very much as a modern form book does. But we should not

---

[58] G. Barraclough, *Papal Notaries and the Papal Curia* (London, 1934), 3: 'Where the law is concerned, the purpose of the formulae is to illustrate the course of legal procedure.' See also Churchill, *Canterbury Administration* I, 458–60; C. R. Cheney, *English Bishops' Chanceries, 1100–1250* (Manchester, 1950), 122–30.

[59] See the remarks in F. D. Logan, 'An early thirteenth-century Papal judge-delegate formulary of English origin', *Studia Gratiana*, 14 (1967), 76.

expect to draw far-reaching conclusions about actual practice from a modern legal book of forms, and neither should we from a medieval formulary. Their purpose was to provide proper documents, *if needed*; not to be informative about what went on in court.

An illustration of the danger may be taken from Miss Churchill's use of the Rochester Precedent Book (originally from the Court of Arches) in her fundamental work on the administration of the province of Canterbury. She looked at the various documents containing preliminary objections. She remarked that 'the opportunities for delay appear endless to the modern reader'.[60] That is quite right. They were almost endless. But Miss Churchill was correctly careful in speaking only of *opportunities*, for it does not follow that because the possibilities for delay had few limits, the delays themselves were endless. As will be seen in the chapter on procedure, the exact opposite is true in marriage litigation. The delays were not long at all. The formulary gives a false impression. Or rather, over-confident use of the formulary could give that impression.

To take another example, formularies generally had sections devoted to triplications and quadruplications. These were part of the preliminary pleadings. Specifically, they were the plaintiff's reply to a defendant's exceptions and the defendant's own reply to that. It is not impossible to find triplications and quadruplications in records from marriage litigation.[61] But it is not easy. Only very rarely were they used. To assume on the basis of a formulary that these steps of canonical procedure were in regular use in marriage cases would be a mistake. The documents had to be included in the formulary. Every good form book must contain seldom used forms. But, for matrimonial litigation at least, it is an unwarranted leap to move confidently from formulary to conclusion about legal practice. Individual documents – for example a schedule of court fees – may profitably be used, but only for what they are.[62] That is, individual documents drawn from one (perhaps unusual) case.

Rather like formularies in the evaluation of marriage litigation are episcopal registers. England, it has often been remarked, is lucky in the wholesale survival of bishops' registers from the medieval period.

---

[60] *Canterbury Administration* I, 465, n. 2.

[61] E.g. York C.P. F 54–5 (1411): C.P. F 250 (1471); Canterbury Y.1.15, f. 16or (1489).

[62] See, for example, Miss Churchill's use of such a schedule, *Canterbury Administration* II, 202–5.

These do provide some good information about marriage cases. There are complete and interesting individual cases to be found scattered among them. Most give valuable information about the appointment and authority of court officers. And they contain almost all the references we have to the subject of dispensation for marriage within the prohibited degrees of affinity and consanguinity. But, for sustained descriptions of court practice, episcopal registers are of little value.[63] The occasional interesting case and the administrative details are all we can expect from them.

Other sources likewise provide momentary glimpses of marriage law in practice. There are some royal court actions, principally claims for dower, which tell incidentally of marriage cases in the canon law courts. The plea rolls of the secular courts have several interesting stories to tell. Literary sources sometimes describe the workings of the Church courts, although almost always for ends which are satirical or didactic. There are chronicles and letter collections which yield some information. For the early thirteenth century and before, we must rely entirely on them. For the later period they may be used, although they normally tell only of the lives of the great. We shall see that it is dangerous to generalize about ordinary matrimonial litigation on the basis of the practice of the nobility. The basic sources for the history of legal practice in this area must remain (along with the commentaries of the canonists) the Act books and Cause papers discussed briefly above. How fortunate we are that they have survived in sufficient quantities to tell a coherent story.

---

[63] An exception is the record of the *acta* of the Consistory court of Rochester for 1347–8, inserted in the middle of the register of John of Sheppey, now printed in the *Registrum Hamonis Hethe*, Canterbury and York Soc., 48 (1948), 911–1043.

II

SUITS TO ENFORCE MARRIAGE CONTRACTS

By far the most common matrimonial cause in the medieval Church courts was the suit brought to enforce a marriage contract. The preponderance of this type of suit is found for every year, in every court, and from every diocese for which records remain. It was not the petition for nullity which made up the bulk of marriage litigation. It was the petition which asserted the existence of a marriage contract and asked the court to enforce it by a declaration of validity and by an order, in most dioceses, that it be solemnized *in facie ecclesie*.[1]

A few figures may make this dominance concrete. Between November 1372 and May 1375 ninety-eight cases related to marriage were introduced into the Consistory Court at Canterbury. Seventy-eight were petitions to establish and enforce a marriage contract; ten were miscellaneous; only ten were cases involving divorce *a vinculo*.[2] At Lichfield between 1465 and 1468, suits brought to establish the existence of valid marriages outnumbered suits for divorce by a margin of thirty to fifteen.[3] The Consistory Court at Rochester from April 1437 through April 1440 heard a total of twenty-three matrimonial cases; fourteen were suits to enforce marriage contracts; four were miscellaneous; only five were petitions for annulment.[4] The exact proportion varied, but the same preponderance is found in whatever set of court records the searcher examines.

---

[1] Such an order was not a normal part of a sentence in the court at Canterbury, as it was at York. But probably it was understood; see, for example, Y.1.1, f. 11v (1373), where the parties are specifically recorded as promising to have their marriage solemnized under pain of excommunication.

[2] This may be thought actually to overstate the number of divorce cases, since four of them were begun *ex officio*.

[3] There were in addition twelve cases of restitution of conjugal rights, and there were three miscellaneous suits.

[4] Of the divorce actions one was *ex officio* and one was a combined divorce *a vinculo* and divorce *a mensa et thoro*.

This numerical superiority is a striking and a surprising fact. It is anachronistic to read back into the Middle Ages the conditions of a later day, when the petition for nullity was the normal action. Matrimonial litigation in medieval England was dominated throughout by the suit brought to establish and to enforce a marriage contract. To understand the nature of these cases, it may be well to begin with a word about the formal law of marriage, and about the way that law had been formed.

CANONICAL MARRIAGE

The classical law of the Church on the definition of a valid marriage was, in fact, fixed only in the course of the twelfth century.[5] One theory, the older and that supported by the great canonist Gratian and the Bolognese school, held that a marriage was initiated by the consent of the parties. But it was only rendered indissoluble by subsequent sexual union. Marriage is begun by the *desponsatio*; it is perfected by the *commixtio sexuum*.[6] Under this view, if a man contracted one marriage but left it unconsummated, then proceeded to contract a second and consummated it, the second marriage, rather than the first, was the valid one.

Against this formulation was the view held by Peter Lombard and the Masters of Paris. It distinguished between two types of *desponsatio*, one by words of present consent (*verba de presenti*), the other by words of future consent (*verba de futuro*). Drawing its inspiration, or at least its most important example, from the marriage between Joseph and the Virgin Mary, this theory held that present consent alone created a perfect marriage and an indissoluble bond. Consent, not coitus, makes a marriage valid.[7] Future consent, on the other hand, created an indissoluble union only when followed by sexual relations. Thus in the example of successive marriages, the prior unconsummated union would prevail over the second consummated match if the first had been contracted by *verba de presenti*; it would not prevail if contracted only by *verba de futuro*.

---

[5] For a more detailed treatment of the subject of the formulation of the Church's law, see Esmein I, 95–137; J. Jackson, *The Formation and Annulment of Marriage*, 2nd edn (London, 1969), 10–20; Pollock and Maitland, *HEL* II, 368–74.

[6] *Dictum* ad C. 27 q. 2 c. 34: 'Sciendum est quod conjugium desponsatione initiatur, commixtione perficitur.'

[7] X 4.1.25; the Roman law formula is 'Nuptias non concubitus, sed consensus facit.' Dig. 50.17.30. See the discussion, with references, in *Dalrymple* v. *Dalrymple* 2 Hag. Con. 54, 62 (1811); also Holt, C.J. in *Collins* v. *Jessot* 6 Mod. 155 (1705).

It was this second formulation which triumphed. After some hesitation, Pope Alexander III (1159–81) adopted the substance of Peter Lombard's position. It meant that a contract by words of present consent constituted, without more, the marriage bond itself. In theory, there was no difference between a contract of marriage and the act by which a complete marriage was initiated. The words of the contract by *verba de presenti* were, in J. L. Austin's terminology, performative words, themselves creating the bond of marriage.[8] Deciding whether that bond had been created by the contractual words spoken by men and women was to be the principal task of the Church courts in marriage litigation.

It is particularly notable that no public ceremony was required to make a marriage valid and indissoluble. Such a ceremony, preceded by publication of banns, was necessary to render a marriage fully licit. The parties sinned by marrying without publication of banns and blessing by a priest.[9] They rendered themselves liable to the spiritual penalties of penance. And the court records produce cases where men and women were punished for failing to secure solemnization, or at least ordered to do so under threat of ecclesiastical censure.[10] But this failure did not affect the question of the validity of the marriage. Only the contract itself did.[11] Although the principle was compromised in practice, in theory a man and woman joined by a contract of present consent, but without ceremony, had no choice about whether or not to solemnize and consummate their union. They were already married. Likewise, consent of parents or kinsmen, endowment of the woman, the *deductio in domum*, were all secondary. They were perhaps desirable. But they were not necessary to create the theoretically indissoluble bond of marriage. Only the exchange of present words of consent was necessary to create a valid union.

Had the habits of the populace conformed to the strict injunctions of the canon law with regard to publication of banns and celebration *in facie ecclesie*, few problems would have arisen. Marriages contracted

---

[8] *How To Do Things with Words* (Oxford, 1962), *passim*.

[9] X 4.3.3; In England, Archbishop Stratford's Provincial Constitution *Humana Concupiscencia* was the law used to enforce the Church's rules against clandestine marriages. See the text and commentary in Lyndwood, *Provinciale*, 274–7.

[10] Examples are York Cons. A B 2, f. 89r (1427); Hereford 0/10, 78 (1473); Rochester DRb Pa 4, f. 269v (1495); London MS. 9064/1, f. 24r (1470).

[11] E.g. Lyndwood, *Provinciale*, 276 s.v. *clandestina*: 'Scias tamen quod in quolibet casuum predictorum tenet matrimonium contractum quoad deum nisi aliud perpetuum impedimentum obstet.'

in the parish church with due solemnity would seldom have given rise to suits to secure their enforcement. But such was not the fact. The court records show that marriages were very often contracted privately, at home, before a few or even before no witnesses. For example, of the forty-one marriages contracted by words of present consent and found in the Canterbury deposition book of 1411–20, fully thirty-eight took place at home or in some other private place. Only three were made in church.[12] This is a slightly high figure, perhaps, but not greatly so. Father Sheehan has found that something over seventy per cent of the cases heard in Ely between March 1374 and March 1382 also involved private marriages, contracted away from the parish church.[13] These were, it should be stressed, not mere betrothals by *verba de futuro*. They were binding marriages by words of present consent.[14] Here is an example from the diocese of York in 1372 which is by no means unusual:

[The witness says that] one year ago on the feast day of the apostles Philip and James just past, he was present in the house of William Burton, tanner of York, about the third hour past the ninth, when and where John Beke, saddler, sitting down on a bench of that house, called in English 'le Sidebynke', called the said Marjory to him and said to her, 'Sit with me'. Acquiescing in this, she sat down. John said to her, 'Marjory, do you wish to be my wife?' And she replied, 'I will if you wish'. And taking at once the said Marjory's right hand, John said, 'Marjory, here I take you as my wife, for better or worse, to have and to hold until the end of my life; and of this I give you my faith.' The said Marjory replied to him, 'Here I take you John

---

[12] X.10.1; there are, however, two cases also recorded in which the woman refused to enter a contract before coming to church: e.g., f. 45v (1418), in which Joan More said she 'vovit quod non affidaret aliquem virum antequam veniret ad ostium ecclesie'. In Rochester DRb Pa 2, f. 24v (1445), a man, faced with the demand that he marry a woman, 'dixit quod noluit facere contractum, tamen dixit quod voluit desponsare eam et consenciit quod banna essent edita inter eos'. In York C.P. F 311 (c. 1500), a woman said to a suitor who was trying to persuade her to contract marriage with him, 'Non est consuetudo in partibus meis inter honestas personas quod fieret affidacio antequam veniret ad ecclesiam.'

[13] Eighty-nine of a total of 122 cases involving the existence or creation of the marriage bond dealt with clandestine marriages. See 'The Formation and Stability of Marriage', 249–50.

[14] The same thing has been found for marriages contracted in France at Toulouse in the fourteenth and fifteenth centuries. The contract was customarily made before a notary, outside of Church. And in 541 out of 551 cases, the contract was made by *verba de presenti*. See G. Laribière, 'Le mariage à Toulouse aux XIVe–XVe siècles', *Annales du Midi*, 79 (1967), 344.

as my husband, to have and to hold until the end of my life, and of this I give you my faith.' And then the said John kissed the said Marjory through a wreath of flowers, in English 'Garland.'[15]

What the witness describes here is essentially a private contract. It was made clandestinely, without 'benefit of clergy', and with no apparent thought of resorting to the parish church. Elsewhere we hear of marriages contracted under an ash tree,[16] in a bed,[17] in a garden,[18] in a small storehouse,[19] in a field.[20] There were marriages contracted in a blacksmith's shop,[21] near a hedge,[22] in a kitchen,[23] by an oak tree,[24] at a tavern.[25] Even the King's Highway was the scene of one alleged marriage.[26]

It should not, I think, be lightly presumed that the Church's laws against clandestine marriages were as little regarded as this evidence from the court records alone indicates. It is likely that most of the people who entered into these private agreements meant to have their

---

[15] York C.P. E 121: 'Die festi apostolorum Philippi et Jacobi ultimo preteriti fuit annus elapsus, fuit iste iuratus presens in domo Willelmi de Burton' alutarii Ebor, hora post nonam dicti diei quasi tertia, ubi et quando Johannes Beke sadeler sedens super scannum, anglice "Le Sidebynke" dicte domus, vocavit ad se dictam Marioram de qua agitur et dixit sibi, "Sede mecum". Que dictis verbis acquiescens sedit; cui dictus Johannes dixit, "Marioria, vis tu esse uxor mea?" Ac illa respondit, "Volo si vos velitis". Et accipiens incontinenti dictus Johannes dexteram manum dicte Mariore dixit, "Marioria, hic accipio te in uxorem meam pro meliori et deteriori habendam et tenendam usque ad finem vite mee; te ad hoc do tibi fidem meam." Cui dicta Marioria respondit, "Hic accipio vos Johannem in virum meum habendum et tenendum usque ad finem vite mee, et ad hoc do vobis fixem meam." Et subsequenter dictus Johannes osculabatur dictam Marioriam per medium unius serti, anglice, garland.' The picturesque kiss through the garland was not, however, normal. Usually, it is also stated that they drank together after the contract.

[16] York C.P. F 252 (1472).

[17] York M 2(1) f, f. 17r (1382).

[18] Canterbury X.10.1, f. 54r (1414); ibid., f. 121v (1420).

[19] York C.P. F 181 (1439).

[20] Canterbury Sede Vacante S.B. III, no. 35 (1293): 'in quodam campo... sub quadam arbore que vocatur haghelthorn'. See also the marriage contracted in a barn, recorded in F. J. Furnivall, Child-Marriages, Divorces, and Ratifications etc. in the Diocese of Chester, A.D. 1561–6, Early English Text Soc., Original Ser. 108 (1897), li.

[21] Canterbury Ecc. Suit, no. 300 (1292).

[22] London MS. 9065, f. 51v (1489).

[23] Canterbury X.10.1, f. 15r (1412).

[24] York C.P. F 172 (1427). In Hokerigge v. Lucas, Canterbury X.10.1, fols. 95r–95v (1417), the parties went 'ad quandam parvam silvam vocatam a grove' for the contract.

[25] York C.P. F 252 (1472).

[26] Canterbury Y.1.1, f. 103r (1375): '... et fatetur se contraxisse matrimonium per verba de presenti cum Elizabeth Sontwyk de eadem et huiusmodi contractus fiebat in regia strata.'

unions blessed by a priest at some later time. At least they probably intended to have the prescribed banns read. This was the conclusion of George Homans, and there is evidence in our records to support it.[27] For one thing, in the surviving cases the interval between the alleged contract and the start of the suit to enforce it was usually fairly short, seldom longer than two years. This suggests that long-standing marriage contracts were not commonly left unsolemnized. Also the record sometimes specifically states that the publication of banns followed the clandestine contract.[28] Occasionally we hear of a couple going directly from their marriage at home to the parish church for the solemnities.[29] On the other hand, there are cases in which it is pretty clear that no solemnization was ever intended, cases in which several years and the birth of children have passed since the making of the contract. Lapses of seventeen and thirteen years can be singled out.[30]

It is impossible, in my view, to be sure how often the marriage contract at home was the sole constitutive act of marriage, and how often it was followed by endowment at the church door and proper religious solemnities. But for the purpose of understanding matrimonial litigation, the question is beside the point. The essential thing is that the contract which created the marriage bond remained, as it had been in the early Middle Ages, a private act. It was done outside the glare of village publicity and quite apart from the direction of the Church. It was this sort of private marriage which was most likely to end in a court test. The Church was right in condemning these clan-

---

[27] *English Villagers of the Thirteenth Century* (Cambridge, Mass., 1942), 169. Laribière, *supra* n. 14, also believes that only a few days normally elapsed between the contract and the solemnization in Toulouse.

[28] In *Teneatre* v. *Chapman*, Canterbury X.10.1, f. 31v (1413), for example, the banns were read the Sunday following the marriage *in signum consensus*. In a case recorded in London MS. 9065, f. 196v (1494) a marriage had previously been contracted; the man 'tradidit huic iurato ii d. ut daret aquebaiulo sancte Katerine Colman pro bannis edendis'. Similar cases are found in Rochester DRb Pa 1, f. 356r (1443); Canterbury Y.1.5, f. 169v (1456).

[29] York C.P. E 186 (1392) tells of a contract, then 'traxerunt manus et osculati sunt; quo facto dicti contrahentes transierunt ad capellam de Quarlton' ad missam audiendam'. And see the remarks in Sheehan, 'Formation and Stability of Marriage', 239.

[30] London MS. 9065, fols 48r–48v (1489); York C.P. F 133 (1422). See also Canterbury Y.1.1, f. 9r (1372), in which the parties 'fatentur se matrimonium adinvicem contraxisse septennio elapso, carnali copula sepius subsecuta, prole etiam suscitata'; and York C.P. E 198 (1393), in which six years and children had intervened between the contract and the bringing of action. In Canterbury Ecc. Suit, no. 293 (1293) it was again six years.

destine unions, perhaps even in punishing them. They were the source of dispute, uncertainty, wrangling, and fraud. They lay open to difficulties of proof and of interpretation not found in marriages duly contracted and celebrated in the parish church. This is one reason that, as long as the private contract of marriage was a normal part of English life, the suit to establish the existence of a marriage, rather than the petition for divorce, would be the most frequent matrimonial cause in the ecclesiastical courts.

ENFORCEMENT OF SIMPLE CONTRACTS

In this litigation, the courts were presented with two basic problems. The first was the enforcement of the Church's rule about the nature of a valid marriage and its claims to exclusive competence over all marriage disputes. The second was the difficulty of interpreting the words of marriage contracts themselves. Marriage in the late Empire and early Middle Ages, we may recall, was not subject in practice to strict control by the Church. Practice offered considerable freedom of action to the parties, freedom not always compatible with ecclesiastical standards. That older view of marriage was a long time dying. Historians have sometimes thought that with the definitive formulation of the canon law in the later twelfth and thirteenth centuries, lay habits, or at least lay beliefs, fell quickly into line. But it is not so. The court records show the tenacity of the belief that people could regulate their own matrimonial affairs, without the assistance or the interference of the Church.

The large number of clandestine marriages is one expression of the continuance of older traditions. But even apart from the habit of contracting marriages privately, this point is also evident because most of the contracts brought into court were clearly by *verba de presenti*. Both parties had said 'I here take thee as my legitimate spouse'. The marriage was unquestionably valid at law. But one party refused, for some reason, to solemnize the union and to cohabit with the other. This refusal we meet again and again in the records. And the root cause is this: whereas the canon law regarded the contract by *verba de presenti* as a complete marriage, many laymen continued to regard it simply as a contract to marry. There was a clear difference between the formal law and the popular attitude on this score. Many people had simply not accepted the Church's definition of what constituted a complete and indissoluble marriage.

The law and the canonists themselves give a sign of the difficulty. Contracts made by words of present consent were considered by most men as a form of espousals, as *sponsalia de presenti*. The canonists pointed out the inconsistency. They wrote that such a contract was actually a marriage, not mere espousals.[31] But men did not therefore change their opinion. The older expression continued to be used. And in the depositions of witnesses, couples who had entered such a marriage were always spoken of as affianced (*affidati*), whereas they were, in canonical theory, already married.[32] What counted in the mind of many people was the formal solemnization and the consummation of the union.

A concrete case may well illustrate this important point. It is the story of a private marriage between John Astlott and Agnes Louth, which came before the court at York in 1422. Agnes and John had, witnesses said, been in love for two years. John was a merchant, and a fairly successful one; at least he was prosperous enough to have found a richer girl than Agnes. But they were in love and they meant to get married. Just before John was to leave on a business trip overseas, Agnes came to him. She begged him not to leave without marrying her. She was, she said, constantly being annoyed and troubled about the matter by her father. John agreed, marrying her by words of present consent before several witnesses at his own house. Then he went off on his trip. All would no doubt have worked out as planned. No court action would have arisen. But John lost a considerable part of his fortune on the trip. He came home, if not penniless, at least a much poorer man. He also found that Agnes had decided to break off their match. She felt she could do this, for they were, in ordinary eyes, only engaged. Their contract was only one of *sponsalia de presenti*.

---

[31] Raymond de Pennaforte, *Summa* IV, tit. *de spons.*, no. 1: 'Ista et talia dicuntur sponsalia de praesenti, sed improprie, quia vere est matrimonium'. Geoffrey of Trani, *Summa* IV, tit. *de spons.*, no. 3: 'Sponsalia de praesenti sunt idem quod matrimonium non consummatum. Inter matrimonium consummatum et non consummatum quo ad essentiam matrimonii nihil interest'. Panormitanus, *Concilia* (1425), f. 1r: 'Et vulgariter dicuntur sponsalia per verba de presenti, et sic solent nuncupari a multis nondum ad domum abducta viri'. See also the remarks in G. Fransen, 'La formation du lien matrimonial au moyen-âge', *Le lien matrimonial* (Strasbourg, 1970), 124.

[32] Canterbury X.10.1, f. 53r (1415); York C.P. E 102 (1365); F 74 (1417); For the similar French attitude, see G. Le Bras, 'Naissance et croissance du droit privé de l'église', *Études d'histoire du droit privé offertes à Pierre Petot* (Paris, 1959), 338–9.

Thus, John Astlott had to sue Agnes in the court at York to enforce their contract of marriage.[33]

The story of John and Agnes is not, we find, a very unusual one, although the depositions in the case give more detail about the parties' motives than is normal. Changed circumstances, outside pressure, or simple fickleness combined in other cases to create a desire to withdraw from a contract which was, in the eyes of the law, a true marriage, but which was not, in the opinion of most men, more than an agreement to marry. Certainly it was an important, even a solemn agreement. It was one which gave rise to an action in the bishop's court. But it was not an irretrievable marriage. The private nature of the contract, and the weakness of the Church's hold on popular attitudes towards marriage meant that such a contract was still open to dispute. Where one of the parties chose to insist on his rights, the result was the suit to enforce the marriage contract. Such suits came before the courts in considerable numbers.

* * *

Cases where *verba de presenti* had unquestionably been used were largely disciplinary in character. What legal difficulties they raised were caused by problems of proof. Those problems were sometimes considerable. However, other suits were brought which were more difficult legally. They point to the second reason for the predominance of the suit to enforce marriage contracts in the medieval courts: the problems encountered in interpreting the words used to contract

---

[33] The story comes from York C.P. F 46 (1422): 'Citra tamen huiusmodi contractum idem Johannes super mare ac citra et ultra mare perdidit plura bona per casum et fortunam, qua de causa iam ipsa Agnes ac parentes sui nollent quod ipse Johannes eandem Agnetem in uxorem suam haberet.' Unfortunately no sentence survives from this case. Another illustrative case is: London MS. 9065, fols. 2v–3r (1491), in which a party was said to have remarked after having contracted marriage: 'Sumus quoad hoc concordati, sed amici et domestici mei sunt ad hoc omnino contrarii, et ideo credo quod contractus habitus inter me et eam non sortietur effectum.' In Ely EDR D/2/1, f. 59r (1377) the parties were asked if they knew any reason which the court should not hold for marriage between them. They replied 'se nescire quicquam proponere nisi duntaxat quod iam mutarunt suam voluntatem quia credunt se invicem non diligunt propter resistenciam per dictam Johannam factam.' The court disregarded this appealingly frank explanation. See also Furnivall, *Child-Marriages, Divorces, and Ratifications*, 59, for a similar instance showing a man's belief that he could be released from such a marriage contract.

marriage. In many cases it was often uncertain whether or not a valid marriage had been contracted. The problem was to determine whether or not an enforceable contract existed.

Had the law specified exactly which words constituted *verba de presenti*, which *verba de futuro*, and which mere negotiation about marriage, the task of the courts would have been relatively simple. Even though made privately, the marriages could have been evaluated easily and enforced as a disciplinary matter, as in the cases just discussed. But, as in modern contract law, no precise formulae for making a valid contract were laid down. And, as Swinburne later remarked, 'so very little (very often) is the odds betwixt the form of words of these two Contracts, that the best Learned are at great variance, whether such Words make Spousals *de futuro* or *de praesenti*'. And again, 'some words are so untoward, that it is a question whether they make any kind of Spousals at all; and contrariwise, some words so flexible that they may easily be stretched to make either the one or the other'.[34]

Some words were necessary, most canonists held, as long as the parties could talk at all. The deaf and dumb might contract by signs. Ordinary men must use some form of words. Likewise, long-time co-habitation did not make a man and woman husband and wife. This was as compatible with concubinage as with marriage. What created the indissoluble bond was the exchange of words of present consent. And in the records of canonical practice, no problem is harder, more recurrent, and more annoying than this seemingly simple one: what words make a marriage? The Church prescribed none as necessary for validity, and there was considerable variation in practice.

Two doctrines of the law made the problem slightly easier for the courts. First, sexual relations subsequent to a contract by *verba de futuro* automatically converted it into one of present consent. By operation of law, the parties were held to have transformed their

---

[34] *On Spousals*, 11–12; Antonius de Butrio, *Commentaria* ad X 4.1.7, no. 9: 'Dic quod dubietas erga verba ad matrimonium potest occurrere multipliciter.' In Canterbury Ecc. Suit, no. 47 (1287) the defendant's lawyer objected to a general allegation of a contract by *verba de presenti*, which he alleged to 'continere in se obscuritatem in ea parte ubi dicit per verba mutuum consensum de presenti exprimencia, ..., qua variis et diversis verbis possit matrimonium contrahi et consensus exprimi ex quibus varie defensiones possint sibi competere.' For later years, however, I have found no such objections made.

future agreement into a present, indissoluble contract.[35] When this happened there was no need for the court to decide on the precise nature of the contract. And it is noteworthy that in practice, libels alleged *carnali copula subsecuta* wherever possible, even where they also alleged a contract by *verba de presenti*.[36] The subsequent sexual relations, if admitted or proved, would render the marriage indissoluble even if the court found the actual words were only words of future consent.

Second, contract by words of future consent were specifically enforceable in the Church courts. Even where the espousals were entered into without the force of an oath, where the contract was a *nudum pactum*, the canon law granted an action to secure its enforcement.[37] Such a contract by *verba de futuro* was dissoluble by an extensive number of circumstances, such as mutual desire of the parties, subsequent serious infirmity by one party, or long lapse of time. But where the contract was clearly by words of future consent, where no such supervening circumstances existed, and where it had not been followed by a contract with another by words of present consent, the Church courts would order the defaulting party to fulfill his contract.[38] In practice, this happened less frequently than might

---

[35] X 4.1.30. The law held also that the presumption was irrebutable, viz., 'contra praesumptionem tamen huiusmodi non est probatio admittenda.' For a fuller discussion of the doctrine of *matrimonium presumptum*, see Esmein I, 142–9. The absolute nature of the presumption is illustrated by a case recorded in Ely EDR D/2/1, f. 136r (1380), where the man alleged that 'antequam ipsam carnaliter cognovit protestabatur se nolle ipsam habere in uxorem'. This was disregarded by the court, which held in favor of marriage. But the case was appealed.

[36] At Canterbury, at least, the frequency of the allegation of sexual relations after a private contract is greater in the thirteenth century than in the fifteenth, perhaps suggesting that the requirement of solemnization before cohabitation was respected to a greater extent.

[37] Hostiensis, *Summa Aurea* IV, tit. *de spons.*, no. 9: 'Verius videtur secundum canones quod etiam ubi sponsalia nuda sunt, habet locum coertio nam ex nudo pacto actionem damus.' The two decretals on the subject of the specific enforcement of sworn espousals were contradictory, but canonists generally said that X 4.1.17, which held that the defendant 'moneri potius debet, quam compelli, ut contrahat', was not to prevail in the face of X 4.1.10, which called for compulsion. This rule, however, was limited by the doctrine that if the person persisted in his refusal to obey the sentence, he might finally be absolved. See, for example, the opinion apparently endorsed by Joannes Andreae, *Commentaria* ad X 4.1.10, no. 12: '. . . unde dicebat Hug [uccio] quod ecclesia compellet per excommunicationem, sed si videbit se non proficere, absolvet.' See also Antonius de Butrio, *Commentaria* ad X 4.1.10, no. 12: 'Nota ergo, quod etiam non penitens absolvi potest a vinculo excommunicationis, quando excommunicatio non proficit.'

[38] E.g. Canterbury Ecc. Suit, no. 36 (1271–72); Ely EDR D/2/1, fols. 25v, 28r (1375).

be thought, principally because a man or woman who repented of having made such a contract usually moved quickly to contract a second marriage by *verba de presenti*. But there is no doubt that the availability of specific performance simplified the tasks of the courts in interpreting some actual contracts.

Even with these rules of law, however, real problems of interpreting the words of marriage contracts remained. It is easy to give examples from the records of common and ambiguous phrases which were raised in court practice. For instance, what effect do mutual promises under some form of the word *volo* have? Is this a contract of present consent, or one of future consent? Or is it a mere expression of an unexecuted desire? As a French lawyer of the early fourteenth century noted, this was a 'bona questio et frequens'.[39] It was not an imaginary problem. The English court records show that marriages were often contracted using some form of the verb 'to will' or 'to wish'.

The great sixteenth-century Spanish canon lawyer, Thomas Sanchez, was able to elaborate four different opinions held by his predecessors on the subject of what sort of bond was created by the word *volo*.[40] The dominant medieval opinion seems, however, to have drawn a distinction based on the nature of the verb which followed *volo*. Where that verb denoted the *execution* of a marriage, the contract was by *verba de presenti*. Where it denoted merely the initiation, the words constituted *verba de futuro*.[41] 'I will take you as my wife' therefore constituted only *verba de futuro*, because the verb 'to take' refers to the start of a marriage relationship. But 'I will have you as my wife' was a present contract since the act of *having* a woman as a wife denoted the desire to participate in an already existing union. To desire the results of marriage was, according to this view, quite different from desiring the beginning of marriage. He who wills the consequence (having) must already have willed the antecedent (taking). Thus, when the couple exchanged mutual promises using the phrase *volo habere te*, they were indissolubly bound, for no man

---

[39] *Liber Practicus de Consuetudine Remensi*, ed. P. Varin, Archives legislatives de la ville de Reims (Paris, 1840), I, no. 260. And see Sheehan, 'Formation and Stability of Marriage', 244–6.

[40] See *De Matrimonio*, Lib. I, d. 18, nos. 22–9, in which the Spanish jurist has collected the opinions of preceding canonists.

[41] See, for example, the discussion in Panormitanus, *Commentaria* ad X 4.1.7, no. 5.

can wish to *hold* a woman as his wife unless he has already *taken* her for his wife, at least tacitly.[42]

Some canonists, however, rejected this dominant view. Their argument was that it is one thing to wish to accomplish an act, another actually to accomplish it. To wish to sell something, the common example went, is not equivalent to actually selling it. Under this view, *volo habere te in uxorem* would not constitute *verba de presenti*, but rather *verba de futuro*.[43] This seems, however, to have been distinctly the minority view. Most canonists raised it only to dispute it and to dismiss it. Guillelmus Durantis, Antonius de Butrio, Joannes Andreae, and Panormitanus all apparently held to the first opinion.[44] Swinburne also endorsed it as the sounder view, lamenting that some recent commentators had moved away from it.[45]

It is certainly possible to criticize the canonists' treatment of this problem. The distinction between words denoting the execution and the inception of a contract is a real one. But it does not necessarily follow that the expression of a desire for the execution of a contract means that the parties have already made the contract itself. More importantly, ordinary people are simply not as careful with their words as the distinction requires.[46] The line savours of the school-room, not of the language of everyday life. On the other hand, it can also be said that the canonists were not dogmatic. They left room for judges to hold that the words *volo te habere* did not constitute a present

---

[42] *Idem, Commentaria* ad X 4.1.9, no. 3: 'Per verba futuri temporis contrahitur quandoque matrimonium de presenti, quando scilicet verba denotant executionem matrimonii, non autem principium contractus, nam qui vult consequens tacite videtur velle et antecedens.' And *idem*, ad X 4.1.7, no. 7: 'Non potest haberi pro legitima coniuge nisi precedat matrimonium. Hec enim verba et similia denotant executionem matrimonii.'

[43] See Swinburne, *On Spousals*, 59, and the discussion in Henricus Bohic, *Distinctiones in V Libros Decretalium* ad X 4.1.9.

[44] Antonius de Butrio, *Commentaria in Quinque Libros Decretalium* ad X 4.1.9, no. 10: '. . . et hoc quia hoc consecutivum tractare vel habere vel habiturum non potest esse sine dispositione matrimonii precedentis, volens ergo hoc tempore hoc consecutivum necessario vult antecedens dispositivum'; Panormitanus, see above, n. 42; Durantis, *Spec. Iud.* IV, tit. *de spons. et matri.*, no. 6; Jo. And., *Novella Commentaria* ad X 4.1.7, no. 6.

[45] *On Spousals*, 75–6. Swinburne notes, *ibid.*, 88, what seems to be a general movement of the canonists' interpretations: 'That where the words of the Contract are indifferent or equally flexible to the signification of Spousals *de futuro* or matrimony; in this case the law presumed the matrimony to be contracted, except in certain cases elsewhere specified.' Hostiensis, *Lectura* ad X 4.1.9, no. 4, remarks after giving several doubtful cases that 'in talibus et similibus dubiis est semper pro matrimonio iudicandum'.

[46] Swinburne, *ibid*, 62–5, deals with the problem. He seems to appreciate its force, but maintains in the end that the canonists' distinctions are 'like Bloodhounds' and necessary in determining men's true meaning.

contract in any particular case. Where other language used by the parties, where other circumstances, or where the common custom of speech in a region showed that no present contract was intended, the canonists indicated that the phrase would not bind the couple in an indissoluble union.[47]

The position taken by most canonists was, in any event, that generally adopted by the English courts. Though the evidence is neither as thick nor as free from ambiguity as one would like, it appears that the English courts normally construed the phrase 'volo habere te in uxorem' as a contract of present consent, creating an indissoluble marriage. A case from York from the 1430s[48] and two from Canterbury, one from 1292 and one from 1397,[49] held that such marriages prevailed over other, second unions. And a fifteenth-century case from Canterbury held that a marriage contracted by the words, 'Ego volo habere vos pro uxore mea quamdiu vita mea durare poterit', prevailed over a prior, conditional marriage, a construction that the words amounted to a contract by present consent.[50]

A York suit from 1411–12 drew a clear distinction between the language 'to wish to have' and 'to wish to espouse' in evaluating a marriage contract. At issue was the translation and the interpretation of the word *desponsare*, used after the *volo* in the alleged marriage contract between Agnes Ketchyn and William Robinson and recorded on the deposition submitted to the court. The judge had apparently translated this as 'to have' in holding for the marriage's validity. This

---

[47] *Gl. ord.* ad X 4.1.7 s.v. *proposuit*: 'ad communem verbi intelligentiam recurratur'. Or, for example, Jo. And., *Commentaria* ad X 4.1.7, no. 6: 'Placet mihi desponsare, vel contrahere, videtur verum quod dixit Petrus, sicut de verbis volo eligere, . . . , nisi communiter in loco illa verba aliam interpretationem reciperent.' There is a long discussion of the problem in Antonius de Butrio, *Commentaria* ad X 4.1.7, nos. 1–12. See also Hostiensis, *Summa Aurea* IV, tit. *de matri.*, nos. 13–15: Innocent IV, *Apparatus* ad X.4.1.7; Sanchez, *De Matrimonio* Lib. I, d. 18, no. 26.

[48] C.P. F 201. This case certainly could have been decided the other way; it was in fact appealed. The first contract had been made twenty-one years previously under the form: 'Ego volo habere et conducere te in uxorem meam et ad hoc do tibi fidem meam.' This prevailed over a second solemnized marriage of nineteen years, contracted under the form: 'Hic accipio te . . . in coniugatem uxorem meam pro pulcriori, deformiori, pro meliori et peiori donec mors nos separet.' Two other York cases in which *volo habere te* was held to create a binding marriage, but in which the testimony about the second marriage is not entirely clear are C.P. F 28 (1406–7) and C.P. F 176 (1421–3).

[49] Sede Vacante S.B. III, no. 42; Y.1.2, f. 84.

[50] This case must be traced both in the Deposition Book, X.10.1, fols. 105r–105v, where the evidence is given, and in the Act book, Y.1.3, fols. 20r, 39r (1416), where the *acta* and notation of sentence are found.

translation was challenged on appeal. The appellant argued that 'the said term *desponsare* neither by law nor by common parlance nor in any other way can rightly receive this interpretation; nor does it in any way include the word *habere* within itself'.[51] The clear assumption is that, had the verb 'to have' been used, the ground for appeal would have collapsed; an indissoluble contract by *verba de presenti* would have been contracted.

Confirmation that the words *volo habere te* normally was thought to create a present contract comes from a case heard in the diocese of Ely in 1379. The petition expressly calls them *verba de presenti*.[52] Also in two other cases, expressions which are equivalent to *volo* were treated as forming valid contracts. 'It pleases me (*placet michi*) to have' made an enforceable marriage in a York cause of 1386.[53] And 'Ego sum in voluntate habendi te in uxorem', alleged as a prior contract in a Canterbury case from 1422, was enough to allow the suit to continue as against a subsequent marriage.[54] We cannot be sure of the judge's decision in the second case, but had that expression been thought of as only a future contract, the suit would probably have been dismissed at once, since the second contract would necessarily have prevailed under ordinary rules of the law.

There is, however, some evidence which points the other way. A York suit of 1442 held that affirmative answers to the question, 'Will you have me as your husband or wife?' did not create an enforceable

---

[51] C.P. F 43: '. . . cum rei veritate dictus terminus desponsare nec iure nec communi sermone nec quavis alia via recta huiusmodi interpretacionem recipiat nec dictum verbum habere sub se aliqualiter includat, et sic indebitam repeticionem fecisti . . . interpretacionem sive intellectualem exposicionem in premissis ut prefertur nequiter iudicialiter admisisti.'

[52] EDR D/2/1, f. 119v (1379): 'Dictus Philipus proposuit oretenus quod ipse et prefata Johanna matrimonium adinvicem contraxerunt per verba de presenti mutuum consensum eorum exprimencia, videlicet per ista verba, Ego volo habere te in uxorem et super hoc posuit fidem suam in manibus cuiusdam Johannis filii Thome de March, et ego volo habere te in virum.' The court held in favor of the marriage, but the decision was at once appealed.

[53] E 131 (1373). The case was actually slightly more complicated, since the man's answer was not exactly equivalent to the woman's vow. He said, 'Plus placet michi te habere in uxorem meam quam aliquam aliam mulierem viventem.' But the court held the marriage valid nevertheless. No subsequent sexual relations were alleged. Cases found in York M 2(1) c, f. 22v (1374) and Canterbury X.10.1, f. 94r (1416) also involved the same phrase *placet michi* used in the contract, but no result can be found for them. Hostiensis and Panormitanus seem to equate the two, since they treat the phrase *placet michi* together with *volo*. See *Summa Aurea* IV, tit. *de spons. et matri.*, no. 6, and *Commentaria* ad X 4.1.7, no. 5.

[54] Y.1.4, f. 65v. It may also be significant that the proctor representing the party to the second contract dismissed the case *tanquam causam desperatam* at f. 78v.

marriage, where a second marriage had later been contracted.[55] And
in a case from Rochester, the judge, confronted with the same case,
seemed uncertain of what to do. He deferred sentence, and the case
finally went off on another ground.[56] It seems fair to say that what
evidence there is suggests that the canonists' common opinion was
usually followed by the English courts. Not in every case. Certainly
there was considerable room for argument even within the norms of
the formal law itself. It is no wonder that suits involving the words
volo te habere were brought before the courts. The outcome could not
be predicted with absolute certainty. But the evidence suggests that
these words normally were considered *verba de presenti* and normally
created an indissoluble marriage.

*   *   *

A great many of the difficult cases which came before the Church
courts did involve a variant of the *volo* marriage. But by no means all
of the troublesome litigation did. The variety of words used in claimed
marriage contracts was very great. It may be worthwhile to examine
one difficult case at some length. *Roll* v. *Bullock*, heard in the diocesan
courts of York, presents a good example of one of the hard cases which
came into the English tribunals, and the canonical resources available
to the judges in deciding them.[57] The case is particularly worth
analysis because the two judges who dealt with it came to different
decisions. It was brought by Isabelle Roll, seeking to have John
Bullock adjudged her husband. He resisted the claim, and had actually
married another woman by *verba de presenti* before the litigation
began. The question was whether Isabelle could prove that the words
he had spoken to her constituted enough of a contract to upset this
second marriage.

Isabelle produced three witnesses. The first of these remembered

---

[55] C.P. F 262. The parties had said *volo* to the question. See also Canterbury, Sede
Vacante S.B. III, no. 49 (1293), in which it was held that no marriage had been contracted
by these words: 'Ego hic affido te de te habenda et tenenda pro uxore mea, muliere respondente, ego sum bene contenta de hoc.'

[56] DRb Pa 1, f. 324v (1443). The defendant later pleaded pre-contract with another
man. Perhaps this raising of another defense indicates that the judge would have held
the marriage valid, especially as the witnesses indicated that the parties were 'handfasting' at the time and twice kissed after the exchange of words, both normal signs of an
intent to contract marriage.

[57] C.P. E 71 (1351–4). This was, perhaps not accidentally, one of the longest running
cases I found in the surviving records.

that John had said to Isabelle either that he intended to do what was right (*quod decet*) by her, or that he intended to take or to have her as his wife.[58] The witness could not recall exactly which expression had been used, but said that the words 'sounded to be of that effect'. However, only this one witness could testify to these words, and since the law required two witnesses to prove a contract, Isabelle's case would have collapsed had it not been for a second exchange of words. All three witnesses testified that John had said to her, 'If I take any woman as my wife, I will take you.'[59] She had signified her assent to this, although the depositions do not make clear precisely what words she had used. All witnesses also testified that the two had frequent sexual relations afterwards. This part of the case was apparently undisputed.

The question, then, was whether these words were enough to make a binding contract. For an answer we look again to the formal law and to the work of the medieval canonists. They open up three arguments, at least, for Isabelle. The first is to treat John's promise as equivalent to saying, 'I will not take anyone except you as my wife.' Some canonists held that these words contained an implied affirmative expression: that is, 'I will take you, and not anyone else'.[60] If a man said, for example, 'I do not wish to give you any of my books except my copy of the Decretals', this could fairly be treated as a gift of his edition of the Decretals. So, they held, it was with a negative promise not to marry anyone else. The phrase, in the actual case, was a future promise, but since subsequent sexual relations had taken place, under ordinary principles of the law, the first union would prevail over the second marriage, allowing a judgment for Isabelle.

---

[58] Ibid., 'Et non recte recolit an dixit illud idem verbum "quod decet" vel dixit, "Intendo eam ducere seu habere in uxorem," sed firmiter credit quod verba sua sonabant in talem effectum.'

[59] 'Si aliquam mulierem ducerem, te ducerem.' This is taken from the testimony of John Manfeld, clerk; it records words admitted by John Bullock in the parish church of Langton.

[60] See Durantis, *Spec. Iud.* IV, tit. *de spons. et matri.*, no. 5: 'Si diceret nolo nisi te in meam uxorem; hec enim verba sic debent intelligi, id est, volo te et non aliam in uxorem meam.' Panormitanus, *Commentaria* ad X 4.1.7, no. 8: 'Et per hoc potest decidi questio satis dubia, quidam dixit mulieri, promitto quod non habebo aliam mulierem in uxorem nisi te, numquid per hec verba sit contractum cum illa matrimonium. Et [the opinion of Durantis and Joannes Andreae] que sentit matrimonium esse contractum quia dictio nisi cum sequitur negativam facit positivam, ..., Anonio [de Butrio] videtur hic sentire oppositum, ..., sed per predicta videtur mihi concludendum pro prima parte, nam si dixisset promitto quod te habebo in uxorem statim esset contractum matrimonium, ut supra dixi, ergo idem si dico quod non habebo aliam nisi te, nam videtur velle quod istam habebit in uxorem.'

The court at York was free not to accept this interpretation of the law, of course. It was a disputed opinion among the canonists themselves. Antonius de Butrio, for example, held to the contrary.[61] For a man to say, 'I do not wish to go anywhere except to Paris today', does not necessarily oblige him to go to Paris. And so for a negative promise of marriage. But at least the first argument made a plausible case for Isabelle; it provided a way the court could hold in her favor. And there were the obvious reasons for doing so. She had been wronged by John. He had led her to think he would marry her, and apparently given others the same impression. He had enjoyed sexual intercourse with her over a considerable period of time. It can also be said that one other English case where such negative words were directly used, one from Canterbury in 1424, apparently treated the phrase as creating a valid contract.[62]

The serious difficulty, however, is that the negative words were *not* directly used. This is not exactly what John had said. It is certainly close, perhaps equivalent in the minds of the hearers. But he had left open the possibility of not marrying at all. 'Si aliquam mulierem ducerem', he had said. And the canonists seem to have recognized that, where a man made clear that he was undecided about marrying at all, such words as those John spoke made neither espousals nor marriage.[63] John had, in the event, actually married another woman, so that it could be argued for Isabelle that he had never intended to remain single. But on the other hand he could certainly have changed his mind after deserting her. If the change in his resolve had come later, the second marriage would clearly prevail, for no sexual relations between John and Isabelle had occurred after the change of mind had given any possible legal force to his future promise. Isabelle's argument under this head probably falls for that reason.

A second argument for Isabelle can be based on a decretal of Pope Innocent III. It deals with a man who contracted marriage under a fictitious name in order to extort sexual intercourse from a girl. Innocent held that the marriage would not be valid if it could be

---

[61] *Commentaria* ad X 4.1.9, no. 10. He interprets the words as leaving open the possibility of no marriage at all.

[62] Y.1.4, f. 159v; issue was joined on whether or not each party had said that 'nollet habere aliquem in uxorem (virum) nisi . . . '

[63] Durantis, *Spec. Iud.* IV, tit. *de spons. et matri.*, no. 3: 'Possibile enim est quod hoc proferrendo intendit nunquam cum ea vel alia aliqua contrahere.' See also Swinburne, *On Spousals*, 99.

shown that the man had never truly consented.[64] But as developed in canonical thought, this decretal was taken to refer only to the internal forum of the consciences of the parties. In the external forum of the Church courts, there was a marriage enforceable by ordinary procedure. The summary noted that if anyone had used 'dubious words', with the intent of deceiving a woman, and afterwards knew her carnally, the case should be decided in favor of marriage in the judicial forum.[65]

Such a formulation *seems* to fit Isabelle's case. John very likely made his promise by ambiguous words in order to keep Isabelle as his mistress. She was deceived by him. This her witnesses said clearly. But, as with the first argument, this one comes up against two objections. First, not all canonists supported the necessary interpretation of the decretal – St Raymond of Pennaforte, the compiler of the Gregorian Decretals, for example.[66] Second, and more seriously, this case does not exactly fit the facts of the decretal. The canonists who supported the distinction assumed that the words of contract used would make a good marriage. In *Roll* v. *Bullock* it was the uncertainty of the words themselves which presented the problem. The reasoning of the canonists in interpreting Innocent III's decretal as they did – to uphold the enforcement of objectively valid contracts despite mental reservations – does not fit Isabelle's case.[67] They showed no inclination to extend the law to punish men who used other sorts of 'dubious words' besides false names.[68] Their expressed concern was to preserve the notion that the courts should pass on the external validity of marriage contracts. The contract in the case of false names was

---

[64] X 4.1.26; Innocent made it clear that there was a strong presumption of consent: 'Videtur forte pro coniugio praessumendum, nisi tu nobis expresse scripsisses quod ille non proposuit nec consensit illam ducere in uxorem, quod qualiter tibi constiterit non videmus.'

[65] X 4.1.26; and see Innocent IV, *Apparatus* ad id.

[66] *Summa* IV, tit. *de matri.*, no. 4; he notes, however, that 'in hoc casu diversi diversa sentiunt'.

[67] This is a principle often stated by the canonists; e.g. *gl. ord.* ad X 4.1.7 s.v. *ex litteris*: 'Uterque compellatur verba prolata in eo sensu retinere quem solent recte intelligentibus generare.' See also the comment in Antonius de Butrio, *Commentaria* ad X 4.1.26, no. 7: 'Nota, sexto, quod ubi verba sunt apta ad concludendum matrimonium, matrimonium est, licet non credant contrahentes ex verbis matrimonium contrahere.'

[68] The closest common example I have seen is given by Hostiensis, *Summa Aurea* IV, tit. *de matri.*, no. 17: 'Quid si dicat, tenebo te in uxorem quousque ponatur mihi terra supra oculos causa decipiendi ipsam? Dicunt quidam quod valet matrimonium indistincte, . . . , sed certe si apparet de dissensu et dolo, non est matrimonium, nisi forte carnalis copula subsequatur.'

made by words of present consent, binding by any objective test. This was not necessarily the situation in *Roll* v. *Bullock*. Therefore, it seems unlikely that this argument for Isabelle could have succeeded under existing canonical interpretations.

A third possible argument is that this was really a conditional contract. The words used were certainly couched in conditional form. John said, 'On the condition that I marry anyone, it will be you Isabelle'. Under this theory it is unnecessary to consider the effect of the second marriage, because the sexual intercourse between Isabelle and John transformed their conditional contract into an unconditional one. The law held that the parties had tacitly withdrawn the condition.[69] This was perhaps Isabelle's strongest argument. The problem is that it is uncertain whether this is the sort of condition the canon law recognized. The conditions the canonists dealt with as suspending matrimonial consent were events separable from the act of marriage itself: 'If you give me a sum of money', or 'if my parents agree', or 'if you become a Christian'.[70] No treatment of conditions in marriage contracts I have seen deals with words like John's. The canonists' discussion of the subject always speaks of decisions or events which existed apart from the act of contracting itself. And John's words amount to no more than saying, 'I agree to marry you, if I marry you'. The words can have no other meaning, since a marriage by John to another woman (the decision to marry *someone*) would render the first, conditional marriage void under ordinary canonical rules. By law, a second, unconditional contract prevailed over the prior conditional contract.[71] A marriage to Isabelle by *verba de presenti* would constitute a subsequent, separable contract of marriage. Therefore, the act of fulfilling the condition would either be marrying Isabelle without any condition at all, or nullifying the words spoken to her by marrying someone else. Thus, it appears that this is not a real condition at all. It may not be the sort of condition to which the canon law gave force. And if not, Isabelle's argument under this head necessarily collapses.

In sum, it is hard to know how the case should have been decided.

---

[69] X 4.5.6. As in the case of a contract by *verba de presenti* followed by relations, even a protest by the man that he intended specifically not to ratify the contract was of no effect, according to the common opinion. See *gl. ord.* ad X 4.5.6 s.v. *praesumendum*.

[70] A modern summary is given by S. Fraghi, *De Conditionibus matrimonio appositis* (Rome, 1941), 26: 'Conditio est circumstantia ipsi negotio extrinseca quaeque a voluntate partium apponitur; si ipsi negotio insit non est vera condicio et appellatur condictio iuris.'

[71] *Gl. ord.* ad X 4.5.5 s.v. *alieno arbitrio*.

And, of course, we do not know which, if any, of the preceding arguments were made before the court at York. But, there was clearly some disagreement among lawyers about the merits of the case. In the actual litigation, Isabelle was successful at first, before the official of the archdeacon of Richmond, Master Adam of York. But his verdict was overturned on appeal before the Commissary General of the Provincial court at York, in a judgment given on 17 March 1354. Isabelle in turn appealed this decision to the Official. But we know nothing of what he eventually decided. It is likely that the case was not appealed to the Roman court, since no record of further action survives along with the existing Cause papers. My own view is that the Commissary General correctly decided the case, that there was no binding marriage. But, it is worth noting that a similar case was heard in Canterbury some twenty years later. The man had said, 'If I will have any woman as my wife, I will have you', and this was followed by sexual relations. The court held summarily in favor of the marriage.[72]

* * *

Like this case of *Roll* v. *Bullock*, suits which came before the courts could raise complex problems of interpretation. It was sometimes impossible to tell whether the couple were canonically married or not. But this should be said before leaving the subject: all the cases required an actual exchange of promises and words which clearly related to marriage. The contract might be difficult to evaluate, but an actual contract there had to be. Where a man and woman 'clasped hands in the manner of contracting marriage, but no words were spoken', the court held that no marriage had been contracted.[73] Where, in a harder case, the woman's words were: 'Here I hold you as my lord under God', the Commissary General at Canterbury found this not enough to create a marriage.[74] A verbal undertaking to 'do

---

[72] Y.1.1, fols. 64r, 66r (1374); the man, in court 'negat omnem huiusmodi promissionem, dicit tamen quod dixit dicte mulieri, "Ego habebo tecum carnalem copulam", muliere respondente, "Non habebis mecum factum nisi velles habere in uxorem", ipso respondente, "Si aliquam mulierem volo habere in uxorem, volo habere te in uxorem". Et in nocte sequente iacuit cum eadem et eam carnaliter cognovit.'

[73] Canterbury Y.1.1, fols. 28r, 31r (1373).

[74] Canterbury Sede Vacante S.B. III, no. 51 (1293): 'Ego teneo te hic pro domino meo sub Domino. Et tenebo te pro domino meo sanum et infirmum.' Note, however, that there was a second marriage contracted by words of unquestionably present consent.

honor' to a woman and her relatives within a year, even when followed
by sexual relations, made no marriage.[75] Nor did a promise to 'make
her as good a woman as he was a man', although this probably was
meant to refer only to sexual relations.[76] The canon law, we saw in
the case of *volo* contracts, treated many close cases as *verba de presenti*
rather than as *verba de futuro*. But unless the words definitely referred
to marriage, the law was in practice unwilling to count them as creating any bond at all.

The canon law also refused to admit the existence of a valid marriage from conduct alone. Unlike Roman Law, it required considerably
more, enough to show definitely that mere concubinage could not be
intended.[77] A decretal of Alexander III instructed the archbishop
of Genoa to enforce as a valid marriage a union of ten years' standing
in which the parties had treated each other, in various ways, as
husband and wife, and in which public fame held that they were
married.[78] But the wording of the decretal was vague. It did not spell
out exactly what the requirements were. And the canonists gave it a
restrictive reading. There had to be the conjunction of three things
to make an enforceable marriage: (1) long cohabitation; (2) *fama
viciniae* that an actual marriage existed, and (3) other supporting
evidence. How long the cohabitation had to be, and what sort of
supporting evidence was necessary, the canonists did not define,
though they sometimes gave examples. Calling each other 'husband'
and 'wife' in ordinary conversation was one piece of evidence, but it
was not conclusive. Similarly treated was the gift of a ring to the

---

[75] York C.P. F 129 (1421): 'Lapso anno proximo iam venturo faciam ... amicis suis
complacenciam et sibi honorem.' See also Rochester DRb Pa 1, f. 15r (1437): 'Promisit
eundem honorare et ditare bonis suis,' but no result can be found. Some courts made efforts
to get men who had used similar language to contract and solemnize a marriage with
a girl they had consorted with. For example in Canterbury Y.1.1, f. 35v (1373), 'Vir dicit
quod promisit eidem mulieri quod vellet iuvare dictam mulierem,' but denied making a
valid contract because he 'habuit ius ad aliam'. He could not prove this, and the record
notes that the marriage was solemnized; but no actual sentence for the case was recorded.

[76] York M 2(1) b, f. 9v (1371). That something more than sexual relations was meant,
however, is indicated by the fact that the words were said in the presence of her parents,
and that 'mater dicte Beatricis voluit quod habuisset eam in uxorem suam'. The case
was also complicated by the fact that the man later admitted that he wanted to have her
as his wife at the time the words were spoken. Beatrice admitted the words, but said that she
had not wished to have him as her husband.

[77] Dig. 23.2.24; *gl. ord.* ad C. 30 q. 5 c. 1 s.v. *contubernia*; Hostiensis, *Summa Aurea* II,
tit. *de praesump.*, no. 3: 'Nam in liberae mulieris coniunctione et cohabitatione, lex praesumit
matrimonium, . . . , canon vero praesumit stuprum seu contubernium, nisi probetur
matrimonium.'

[78] X 2.23.11.

woman. The standards of required evidence were high.[79]

The English cases are entirely consistent with the canonists. In a York case from 1398, for example, three years' cohabitation, birth of children, and public repute that a couple were husband and wife, did not create an enforceable marriage. No actual contract was shown.[80] Likewise, marriage negotiations, followed by sexual relations between the parties, but not by an actual exchange of promises, did not make an enforceable marriage.[81] What did was the contract itself.

CONDITIONAL MARRIAGES

One of the possible interpretations of the words in *Roll* v. *Bullock*, discussed at length above, was to consider them a conditional contract. The canon law allowed certain sorts of conditions to be attached not only to future promises to marry, but also to marriages by *verba de presenti*.[82] 'I take you as my spouse if my father consents', is the example frequently given by the medieval canonists, and it, or a slight variation, is the most frequent condition found in the medieval court records.[83] The result of adding these words was to suspend the present consent until the condition was fulfilled. When the father did give his consent to the match, the marriage became unconditional at once. The conditional marriage required no renewal of vows. An exchange of promises of present consent or sexual relations between the parties before the condition was complete also rendered the marriage indissoluble.[84] But, like a contract by *verba de futuro*, if one

---

[79] The best discussion of the problem I have seen is given by Panormitanus, *Commentaria* ad X 2.23.11, nos. 3, 8.

[80] York C.P. E 236. Similar cases are York C.P. F 191 (1453); C.P. F 16 (1405–6).

[81] Canterbury, Y.1.4, fols. 55r–55v (1421). York C.P. F 129 (1421).

[82] On the subject of conditional marriages, I have consulted in addition to the general works on the canon law of marriage: R. Weigand, *Die bedingte Eheschliessung im kanonischen Recht* (Munich, 1963); S. Fraghi, *De Conditionibus matrimonio appositis* (Rome, 1941); M. Ferraboschi, *Il Matrimonio sotto condizione* (Padua, 1937); B. T. Timlin, *Conditional Matrimonial Consent* (Washington, 1934).

[83] Contracts were frequently made conditional on the consent of the *amici* of one of the parties. Exactly what persons were included? In a Rochester case, DRb Pa 1, f. 75r (1438), the party was apparently asked at the time of trial, and 'declaravit amicos illos esse patrem et avunculos'. In a case recorded in DRb Pa 1, f. 269r (1442), Benedicta Eldherst was asked the same question, and 'dicit quod Willelmum atte Hale et tres fratres suos'. In Canterbury X.1.1, f. 144r (1457), an uncle was mentioned as being included in the *amici* whose consent to a marriage contract was required.

[84] A note of some importance in practice is that, according to the *communis opinio*, even if the man expressly stated that he had no intention of withdrawing the condition before the sexual relations, he was held by the law to have done so. See *gl. ord.* ad X 4.5.6 s.v. *praesumendum*.

of the parties married someone else before fulfillment of the condition, this second marriage, not the prior conditional marriage, prevailed in any court test.

Conditional contracts came before the Church courts with some frequency. It is not surprising that this should have been so. The informality with which many marriages were made, before a few interested witnesses and without any writing, often led to honest disagreements between the parties about when a condition had actually been added to the contract. It was not always easy to know whether an effective limitation had been placed on the consent. The best example of this is the secret marriage, in which the man or woman asks all those present to swear not to make the contract public for a time. In an early Canterbury case, for instance, the girl 'made all the women who were present swear that they would reveal [it] to no one in that year'.[85] The line between a delay to break the news gently to one's father and a marriage conditioned upon his consent was a fine one. Especially when the father in fact indignantly objected, question and disagreement easily arose. The girl in the Canterbury case later claimed that she had made only a conditional contract. The court disagreed. The condition had not been made an actual part of the contract.

It was also difficult to draw a firm line between cases where there was an agreement to give the couple land or chattels *at the time* of the marriage and cases where the marriage was expressly made conditional on the receipt of such gifts. It was perfectly permissible under canon law to insert such a condition in a marriage contract. If left unfulfilled, the marriage was not binding. The law was, however, that the gift must have been made as a condition of the marriage's existence. The only case I have found for which a judgment remains indicates that the court followed that rule. The agreement by both

---

[85] Ecc. Suit, no. 10 (1269): 'Requisita si aliqua condicio fuit adiecta, dicit quod nulla nisi quod ipsa Cecilia fecit omnes mulieres affidare que interfuerunt quod in illo anno nulli demonstrarent, et hoc fecit post contractum.' Another instance is found in London MS. 9065, f. 52r (1489): 'Dixit dicta Johanna eidem Roberto, "I made you promise, but on my fader's good will", dicto Roberto contrarium asserente.' In a case from Canterbury X.10.1, fols. 95r–95v (1417), the contracting parties agreed 'quod omnia premissa, scilicet conventio inter eos facta et cetera dicta recitata inter eosdem, custodirentur in secretis per unum quarterium anni sequentis, ut possit idem Thomas tractare cum Brinchesle magistro dicte Godleve ad habendum bonum amorem suum.' In York C.P. E 103 (1367–9) one witness testified to the words, 'Ego volo ducere te in uxorem meam quam citius ego potero propter matrem meam.' Subsequent sexual relations were admitted, however, and the court held for marriage, so that it is impossible to tell whether this would have been treated as a good condition.

parents to give a couple two animals of equal value did not invalidate a marriage because one set of parents refused to make the gift. The contract itself had been simple. The gift had not been made as an express condition of the marriage itself.[86]

Even if the condition expressly referred to the marriage, by law it had also to be made at the time of the contract. A later condition counted for nothing. There were no canon law texts devoted expressly to this point. But here, as elsewhere, Roman law filled the gap. The rule from the civil law on gifts was applied. Once a gift was complete (*donatio perfecta*) no conditions could be added.[87] The gift stood. As applied to marriage by the canonists, this meant that the condition had to be made 'immediately' or 'in the very act of contracting'.[88]

There had to be some slight leeway, of course. The girl who says, 'I contract, if my father consents', cannot be treated differently from the girl who says, 'If my father consents, I contract'. Even if there is a pause, the two cases should be treated alike. But how long can the pause be? The problem is well illustrated by the attempt to enforce a marriage contract between John Sharp and Joan Broke, a case decided in the court at Rochester in 1442. The couple entered into a contract by *verba de presenti* 'in a certain field near a ruined tower'. The man and his friends were walking away, when Joan called after them, 'Listen, if my master and friends are willing to agree, I will assent to that contract.' The men called back, 'You are too late in saying such things. You should have said that sooner.'[89] Joan then refused to

---

[86] York C.P. F 168 (1427). A Canterbury case, for which no result survives, is recorded in X.10.1, f. 40r (1413); the agreement was to grant the woman a house worth ten pounds.

[87] Cod. 8.55.4: 'Perfecta donatio conditiones postea non capit.'

[88] *Gl. ord.* ad X 4.5.3 s.v. *huiusmodi verbis*: 'Statim conditione adiecta; alias ex intervallo admitti non debet.' Hostiensis, *Lectura* ad X 4.5.3, no. 1: 'in ipso contractu vel statim sine intervallo'. See also Sanchez, *De Matrimonio*, Lib. V, d. 6, no. 3: 'si conditio adjiciatur in ipso actu contrahendi matrimonii, secus si ex intervallo'. Antonius de Butrio, *Commentaria* ad X 4.5.3, no. 5, distinguished between future and present contracts, allowing later conditions in the former.

[89] DRb Pa 1, fols. 190r, 200r–200v. The full description of what happened after the contract is this: 'Et incontinenti dictus Johannes et iste deponens ac quidam Johannes Pery qui interfuit recesserunt ab illo loco. Et post modicum intervallum et spacium modicum dicta Johanna vocavit post eos et dixit, "Audiatis, si magister meus et amici velint consentire ego consentiam contractui premisso." Et responderunt Johannes Sharp et Johannes Pery ac iste deponens quod "Tarde venisti ad dicendum talia. Tu dixisses hoc citius." Et sic recesserunt.' The defendant in this case could have produced at least two Roman law texts in support of the proposition that 'immediately' meant only within three days, i.e. Cod. 3.1.18: 'ilico autem, id est intra triduum proximum', and Cod. 2.9.3: 'ex continenti, id est triduo proximo'. But, here again, we know nothing of what legal arguments were actually produced in court, if indeed any were.

solemnize the marriage, and John sued her in the Consistory court. The question was whether the condition was effective. This was certainly an arguable case. But in the event, the court held that the girl's condition was good. She had acted in time. The pause had not been too long.

The danger, of course, in allowing more than a momentary interval was that a man might enter unconditionally into marriage, later repent his act, and then add a condition to avoid the contract entirely. In a Canterbury suit of 1417, for example, the girl waited more than a month after contracting unconditionally. Then, questioned about it, she said the words she had uttered were only meant 'to find out the reaction' of a witness, and that she 'was not consenting to have [the man] as her husband unless her friends wished to consent to it'.[90] Here the court enforced the marriage. The girl had not simply forgotten to speak the condition for a moment. Whatever her actual state of mind at the time of making the contract, the external evidence indicated that she was trying to back out of a completed contract.

⋆　　⋆　　⋆

Apart from problems of determining whether a condition had been inserted in the marriage contract, the courts had often to evaluate the nature of the condition itself. Not all conditions inserted in marriage contracts were regarded alike. Not all were admissible. The canon law's treatment of the various kinds of conditions was highly schematic. Here is a list of the different sorts of future conditions discussed by the canonists, with the results which followed from each.[91]

	Type of Condition	*Example*	*Effect*
(1)	honest, possible	if father consents	condition effective
(2)	honest, impossible	if you touch sky with finger	condition disregarded
(3a)	dishonest, possible (against substance of marriage)	if you avoid offspring	marriage invalid

---

[90] This case can be reconstructed from the depositions in X.10.1, fols. 95r–95v and the *acta* in Y.1.3, fols. 8v–9r: 'Illa verba que vobis retuli pro tunc referebam vobis ad sciendam voluntatem vestram, quia non consentiebam ad habendum eum in maritum nisi amici mei vellent ad illud consentire.'

[91] The matter is clearly set out in Hostiensis, *Summa Aurea* IV, tit. *de cond. appos.*, no. 12.

(3b)	dishonest, possible (not against substance of marriage	if you kill someone	condition disregarded
(4)	dishonest, impossible	if woman celebrates Mass	condition disregarded

Two things, at least, are worthy of note in this classification system. First, the range of allowable conditions was restricted; in a great many cases a condition might be simply disregarded and the marriage held to have been unconditional. Second, every possible condition had to be fitted within the above scheme. And neither the classifications nor the standard examples solve all the problems which were raised in litigation.

The problems which arose in applying the canon law's classification scheme can be readily illustrated by cases which involved conditions relating to sexual relations between the parties. For instance, there is the situation of a man who wants to sleep with a woman, but is unwilling to marry her unless she conceives a child as a result; the woman will only consent if he makes an explicit promise to that effect. Such a case was that of John Wyk and Margaret Bele, heard at York in 1418. John said, 'If I conceive a child by you this night, Margaret, I will have you as my wife.' She replied similarly. They had sexual relations that evening, but no child resulted.[92]

Under canon law, this was a relatively easy case because of the doctrine that subsequent carnal relations meant that the parties had tacitly dropped the condition. The marriage became unconditional. The difficult part normally lay in proving the existence of the contract. Words like John's are not normally spoken before witnesses. But where proof was available or the language was admitted, this sort of condition did not have to be evaluated substantively. It was binding because of the sexual relations even without the birth of children. That was the result reached in *Bele* v. *Wyk*. It is perhaps an indication of the tenacity of many people's belief in the freedom to regulate their own matrimonial arrangements that such conditions continued to be made.

A different, harder case is presented by the conditional contract: 'I take you as my wife, if you permit me to know you carnally.' Suppose no sexual relations do follow. Is that a valid contract? The case arose in

---

[92] Cons. A B 1, f. 86v: However, the liaison was continued and two children were eventually born from it. Another such case is York C.P. E 79 (1359), in which the court held against the marriage because of lack of proof. For similar German examples, see R. Weigand, 'Die Rechtsprechung des Regensburger Gerichts in Ehesachen', 417, 446–8.

York in 1379.[93] The answer depends, of course, on what sort of condition this is. Certainly it is possible. Certainly it is not against the substance of marriage, in the sense used by the medieval canonists. But is it an honest or a dishonest condition? If the former, the condition takes effect and the marriage is not binding. If the latter, the condition is to be disregarded and the marriage held valid.

In dealing with the situation, medieval canonists drew a distinction according to the meaning of the parties in setting the condition. The copulation, according to the *glossa ordinaria*, may be meant as illicit, done for purposes of fornication. If so, the condition is dishonest, and to be disregarded.[94] An indissoluble marriage results. Or it may be that licit or 'matrimonial' copulation is intended. Here, if sexual relations follow, a valid marriage clearly results, since that was the desire of the parties in the first place.[95] But the gloss leaves open the case where no copulation occurs. And later medieval canonists distinguished further between contracts by *verba de presenti* and those by *verba de futuro*.[96] If the former, the conditional language is to be read merely as a cause, i.e. I contract *because* you permit me to know you carnally. But if the latter, and if the parties meant honest copulation, the condition would be valid, and the effect of the contract would be suspended until sexual relations occurred.

Perhaps the most that can today be said in favor of this distinction is that it offered an attractive result for a hard case. Otherwise, the canonists' treatment of the above condition seems over-subtle, to say the least. But for the defendant in the York case, it made available a possible argument, a way of escaping from a marriage one cannot help feeling he should not have been forced to complete. However, the difficulty was that the York contract had clearly been made by *verba de presenti*. The man had said, 'Accipio te in uxorem si etc.' Hence, following the canonists, the York court had no choice but to hold that the contract was binding. And this was the result reached in the case.

---

[93] C.P. E 116: 'Fatebatur quod contraxit matrimonium cum dicta Alicia per verba, "Hic accipio te Aliciam in uxorem meam si permiseris me carnaliter te cognoscere antequam te ducam in uxorem," set eam carnaliter nunquam cognovit.'

[94] *Gl. ord.* ad X 4.4.1 s.v. *si permiserit*: 'Si de fornicario coitu intelligas, conditio turpis est et ideo pro non adiecta debet haberi.'

[95] *Ibid.*, 'Si de legitimo intelligas, multo fortius tenet matrimonium si coitus subsequatur, potius enim videtur hortatio, id est quod permittat ei rem secum habere.'

[96] I have here relied on the summary of opinions given in Swinburne, *On Spousals*, 148–9. See also, Weigand, 'Die Rechtsprechung des Regensburger Gerichts in Ehesachen', 415–16.

The court ordered him to have the marriage solemnized *in facie ecclesie*. He appealed, but no subsequent decision can be found.

A last example of sexual conditions comes from a Rochester suit of 1443. The legal problem it raised is both more frivolous and more difficult than the first two. John Forster sued to established his right to Alice Burden, alleging a contract by words of present consent. Her answer was this:

She confesses that she contracted marriage with him about four years previously, under this condition however, that he should be able to act with her as a man ought to with a woman. And afterwards within a fortnight, she tried him, and because he could not she dismissed him and contracted with Thomas Ricard.[97]

This raises two possible problems of interpretation. One, was the condition specific enough to be considered by the court? Two, was it an honest or a dishonest condition? Suppose we assume the answer to the first. There was probably no real question that the words were meant (and understood) to refer to his ability to consummate the marriage. What sort of condition, then, was this one under the canonical categories?

I have seen no treatment of such language by medieval canonists. I can here only advance possible arguments. If the condition was equivalent to Alice's saying, 'I contract if you know me carnally', then we are in the same situation as in the last example. The condition would probably be dishonest and therefore be disregarded. But this is not exactly what Alice said. It was 'I contract if you *can* know me carnally.' Canon law allowed, as we shall note in the next chapter, divorce for impotence. It would therefore seem an even easier case to allow a marriage not yet begun to be conditioned on a man's potency. If a marriage could be *undone* for impotence, surely it should not be dishonest to avoid *initiating* one for the same reason. And since, under this argument, Alice had married another man, that second bond would prevail under the canon law rule that a present contract prevailed over a conditional one.

However, this line of argument could well be turned against Alice. She cannot be said to have given him a fair test in their one encounter,

---

[97] DRb Pa 1, f. 373v: 'Fatebatur se matrimonium contraxisse cum eodem, sub ista tamen conditione, si posset cum ea agere sicut vir deberet cum uxore. Et quod postea infra quindenam post contractum probavit eum, et quia non potuit dimisit eum et contraxit cum Thoma Ricard . . . '

and there was no evidence to show that he was permanently impotent. In fact, he had subsequently married another woman, suggesting that he was not. Perhaps, then, he fulfilled the condition before Alice contracted the second marriage. Also, since a marriage could be invalidated for impotence, John might claim that this was a condition which inheres by implication in every contract of marriage. It was to be understood, and the contract would be unconditional even if it were explicitly added. 'If I shall live' is an example of an implicit condition. All contracts were necessarily subject to it, and its inclusion in a contract did not necessarily change a simple contract into a conditional one.[98]

Forster v. *Burdon* was, in sum, a difficult case to decide. The arguments just advanced, let me note again, are only points which *could have* been made. There is no sign that they were raised, and I have found no medieval canonist who wrote on this sort of condition. The official at Rochester must have felt something of the same difficulty. Having heard the allegations and admissions, he 'said that he wished to deliberate'. He continued the case, and left the subsequent marriages of both parties intact 'until he ordered otherwise or they were summoned again'.[99] It seems likely that he then dropped the case entirely. No further recorded hearing appears in the Act book. If so, I find it difficult to attach any blame to his reluctance to decide the case. It is hard to know whether John and Alice were legitimately married or not. And since both had married again, there were good reasons for leaving them alone.

To these problems relating to sexual conditions should be added a few words on the minor and miscellaneous conditions which were sometimes inserted in marriage agreements. What the sixteenth-century canonist Sanchez described as 'impertinent conditions' raised several problems in medieval litigation. In a 1381 Ely case, for example, a man said to a woman, 'I will take you as my wife if you conduct yourself well (*si bene facias*).'[100] What exactly did those words mean? Had anything binding been contracted? And if so, what effect did the condition have?

---

[98] Swinburne, *On Spousals*, 116, 127.

[99] DRb Pa I, f. 373v: 'Unde dominus officialis dixit se velle super premissis deliberare, et causam in statu quo est continuavit quousque eis aliter duxerit intimandum.' The woman's second marriage had been solemnized and two children had been born of the union with Thomas Ricard, to whom she 'adheret et sic deberet et vult omnino, ut dicit, et non dicto Johanni Forster'.

[100] EDR D/2/1, f. 154v: 'Dictus vero Johannes fatetur quod promisit ipsam ducere in uxorem sub hiis verbis, "Volo te ducere in uxorem si bene facias."'

From one point of view, no binding agreement at all had been made. These words may be interpreted as a resolutive condition, that is one which will have the effect of nullifying an act which is valid *unless* or *until* the stated conditional event occurs.[101] The language of the Ely case can certainly bear this meaning: 'I will take you *unless* you act badly.' The man bound himself to marry her until some future act occurred. Resolutive conditions were suspect at canon law because one of three goods of marriage was indissolubility.[102] The very nature of a Christian marriage is that it is contracted for life. And if, as Panormitanus wrote, one contracted under specific condition, 'If you do not commit adultery', no binding marriage of any kind would result.[103] Or if, to take another example, a man contracted a marriage to last only for three years, the contract itself would be invalid.[104] The language used in both cases itself excludes indissolubility. In this sense, all resolutive conditions rendered marriages invalid, because they left open the possibility of ending the union *if* a specified event occurred. As Swinburne later put it, such a condition might 'be neither unhonest or unreasonable; yet fighting with the Substance of the Act, it doth mortally wound the Contract without hope of recovery'.[105] Under this argument, the judge at Ely should have held that no valid marriage contract existed.

It may be said, on the other hand, that the principal part of the contract at issue in the Ely case constituted only *verba de futuro*. And since, as noted already, future contracts could be avoided for a number of reasons (fornication, long absence, serious disease) this condition did not contradict the nature of a future promise in the same way it would have contradicted that of a contract by *verba de presenti*. That is not, of course, the end of the matter, even if that argument is accepted. When (as happened in the Ely case) there was following sexual intercourse, what was the result? Was there a valid

---

[101] See Esmein I, 176; Weigand, 'Die Rechtesprechung des Regensburger Gerichts in Ehesachen', 424–5.

[102] See *gl. ord.* ad X 4.5.7 s.v. *contra substantiam conjugii*: 'Et sic videtur quod omnis conditio quae est contra naturam contractus, ipsum impediat si apponatur', and *idem* s.v. *donec inveniam aliam*: 'Haec conditio est contra sacramentum, quod debet esse individuum'. For a later example, see J. T. Noonan, Jr, *Power to Dissolve; Lawyers and Marriages in the Courts of the Roman Curia* (Cambridge, Mass., 1972), 273.

[103] *Commentaria* ad X 4.5.7, no. 2: 'Quidam habens suspicionem de incontinentia future mulieris contraxit secum sub conditione quod si committeret adulterium liceret sibi recedere a matrimonio et aliam ducere. Certe non est matrimonium.'

[104] *Gl. ord.* ad. C. 32 q. 2 c. 6 s.v. *nolint*: 'Si enim apponitur inhonesta conditio quae est contra naturam matrimonii, matrimonium non tenet, ut si hoc modo dicitur, contraho tecum usque ad tres annos.'

[105] *On Spousals*, 141.

marriage at once? Or were the *verba de futuro* merely made unconditional? If so, sexual relations on two occasions had to be proved for a valid marriage to be established. On this point, there was apparently some disagreement among canonists.[106]

Alternatively, it could be argued that a vague condition like *si bene facias* was too insubstantial to be regarded by the law. Under one view, some trivial conditions, 'If you are beautiful' for example, were not admitted in the ecclesiastical forum. They were 'impertinent', that is they had no relation to the nature of marriage itself, and they were impossible to verify. Therefore, according to this theory, they were to be ignored.[107] On the other hand, there is support for the proposition that 'any condition not reproved by the canons can be used in [contracting] marriage'.[108] No text specifically condemns a condition because of vagueness or triviality. Therefore, the conditional language used in the Ely case must be effective.

Here again, the formal law gives no very definite answer. It is not clear where the condition *si bene facias* fits into the law's classification scheme. The evidence from other cases is, unfortunately, equally ambiguous. The records produce one case from Canterbury in which the condition was that the woman be a 'good materfamilias' and skilled in 'brewing, baking and weaving'.[109] But no result survives. There are three cases falling roughly under the heading of the Ely suit. In a York case, in which sexual relations followed a marriage contracted allegedly only under the condition of the woman's good conduct, the court held for a valid marriage, thus either disregarding the condition or finding that it had been 'purified' by the subsequent intercourse.[110]

---

[106] *Ibid.*, 148–9. And see the discussion in Antonius de Butrio, *Commentaria* ad X 4.5.6, no. 6: 'Dic quod secus est, si dicat, Contraham tecum si ᵕcoieris mecum; quia tunc per primum coitum fiunt sponsalia pura, per secundum matrimonium.'

[107] See Sanchez, *De Matrimonio*, Lib. V, d. 18, no. 2.

[108] Hostiensis, *Lectura* ad X 4.5.5, no. 4: 'Nota omnen conditionem posse apponi in matrimonio quae non siᵕ a canonibus improbata.'

[109] Canterbury X.10.1, f. 49r (1420): 'Apponit conditionem in contractu, . . . , videlicet quod si dicta Agnes esset bona materfamilias et sciret preparare illa que pertinet ad pandoxacionem pistrinam texturam lini et lanei.'

[110] In C.P. E 102 (1365) the defendant admitted only 'quod dixit eidem Mariorie antea talia verba vel consimilia, videlicet quod sic poterat facere quod forte eam duceret in uxorem sub bono gestu suo'. A complicating factor in the case is that the man may also have told her that if she desisted from the suit she had earlier brought against him, he would marry her 'as soon as he could after Easter'. Two other cases in which similar language was used, but for which no sentence has survived are York Cons. A B 1, fols. 98v–99r (1419): 'Si vellet ipsam bene et honeste tractare et gubernare'; and Canterbury Ecc. Suit, no. 49 (1288): 'Si se bene haberet in futurum'.

But the diocesan court at Lichfield in 1471 treated such a condition as legitimately suspending the parties' present consent, when no *carnalis copula* was alleged.[111] And in another case in which no sexual relations followed a contract made 'according to your good conduct' the court at Norwich at once declared the marriage valid and unconditional.[112] It must be confessed that no very definite rules emerge from these cases. The result of the Ely case, where the marriage was contracted *si bene facias*, is also hard to evaluate. The Act book records that the defendant agreed to marry the woman 'absque aliqua compulsione' while the case was still being heard. Perhaps this suggests that the court inclined towards upholding the marriage's validity, but was reluctant to do so without the man's acquiescence. In this area, where the law itself was not clear, it is easy to see why a judge would choose this course. Certainly we should not be surprised that contracts like this one ended up as the subject of litigation. Conditional contracts often caused real difficulties of legal interpretation. The uncertainty of the law itself inevitably resulted in court tests.

MULTI-PARTY LITIGATION

We have noted in dealing with the interpretation of marriage contracts that some of the cases were brought where two men or women alleged a valid contract with the same person. The question was, which contract had been made both unconditionally and by *verba de presenti*? And if both were, which was prior in time? Medieval canon law held that a prior marriage always prevailed over a later one, even if the first was a simple contract and the second had been solemnized and followed by cohabitation of many years. A plaintiff could wait fifty years before enforcing a claim under a contract of present consent, if he could find witnesses to prove it.

Where multiple contracts were alleged before the English courts, the records normally gave the case a particular name: the *causa*

---

[111] Lichfield, B/C/1/2, f. 18v (1471). The man confessed 'se matrimonium contraxisse per verba de presenti sic dicendo, "Ego accipio te in uxorem meam et ad hoc do tibi fidem meam sub ista conditione quod si ipsa conservaret eam bone fame et opinionis illese per spacium trium annorum," et mulier respondit eidem sub eodem modo.' He was ordered to solemnize the marriage at the end of the third year, but, at f. 51r, he came into court after having married Elena Ryse unconditionally before the end of the term. This second marriage was declared valid.

[112] Acta et Comperta 1a, s.d. Saturday after the feast of St Faith (1417). The actual words were 'Ego sum bone voluntatis habere te in uxorem meam secundum tuam bonam gestionem.' The court of the Prior and Chapter, before which the case had come, was however inhibited by the bishop from taking further action.

matrimonialis et divorcii. The contending plaintiffs were styled *competitores*. Sometimes one of the competitors had already entered a permanent union with the defendant and they were living together. Here the object of the other plaintiff was to break up the existing marriage and to enforce his own marital rights. Sometimes each plaintiff could allege only a bare marriage contract. The normal suit in practice was a three-cornered affair, with two plaintiffs and one defendant. But in a few cases there were as many as three[113] or even four[114] of these competitors, all claiming a valid contract of marriage with the same person.

The number of these multi-party suits brought before the English courts was substantial. At Canterbury between November 1372 and 1375, thirty-five of these cases were introduced into the Consistory court, only eight fewer than the total number of marriage cases between two parties. In the Consistory court at Rochester between April 1437 and April 1440, the numbers were identical: seven cases of each. Multi-party cases also usually outnumbered suits for divorce *a vinculo*. In the fourteenth-century Cause papers at York, there are fourteen marriage and divorce cases; for the same period there are only ten petitions seeking annulment of a marriage.[115] In the years 1416 and 1417 in Canterbury, fully thirteen of the thirty-five suits to establish a marriage were multi-party lawsuits; there were only four petitions for divorce *a vinculo*.

Together with all suits to enforce marriage contracts, the total of multi-party cases had declined in the second half of the fifteenth century. At Lichfield, for instance, between 1465 and the end of 1468 there were only eight three-sided marriage suits, while there were fifteen suits brought for divorce. At York between 1450 and 1500, we find only six multi-party cases out of the total of twenty-seven suits

---

[113] EDR D/2/1, fols. 43v, 44r, 70v, 71r. In Canterbury Y.1.2, f. 113r (1398), this untidy set of actions was brought: Joan Gybbe sued Simon Saundre; Simon Saundre sued Christina Meller; and Christina Meller was also sued by Thomas Faws, all being suits to establish marriage. In Canterbury Ecc. Suit, no. 189 (1294), the woman 'fatebatur ad oppositionem dicti officialis in iudicio se cum dictis W., W., et J. diversis temporibus matrimonium de facto contraxisse.'

[114] C.P. F 123 (1438). This was a complicated case appealed from the official of the archdeacon of Nottingham. John Gregory was the man, and contracts were alleged with Alice Strelley, Margaret Passingchambe, Margaret Capton, and Alice Shildewonman'. One of the women, however, was not present in court.

[115] It should be said that some of the files related to marriage have not been counted, since not enough process remains to discover the exact nature of the suit, e.g. where the only process is against witnesses for perjury.

to enforce a marriage contract.[116] Against this there were seven suits for divorce. Marriage questions were, in other words, coming up more frequently in suits for nullity, less often in multi-party litigation, than had been the case a hundred years before.

The legal difficulties involved in this litigation were normally no greater than those raised by simple suits to enforce marriage contracts. The only additional question lay in determining the priority in time of two contracts. But multi-party litigation is worth examining separately, because it provides clear evidence of the realities of matrimonial life in the later Middle Ages. Most strikingly, of course, these cases show something we examined above. Men or women who had entered into a contract by *verba de presenti*, but who had not solemnized or consummated the union, felt some freedom to withdraw their consent. The contract was widely considered a form of espousals, not a completed, indissoluble marriage. When a man or woman withdrew, and married someone else, the result was often the *causa matrimonialis et divorcii*. At least it was when both possible plaintiffs decided to press their claims in a court of law.

This multi-party litigation also shows in a particularly clear way the freedom people felt to regulate their marital affairs without direct intervention by the Church courts. The cases provide instance after instance of what might be called 'self-divorce'. When a man has been married to a woman for some time, then leaves her and takes another woman as his wife, he has in effect divorced himself. This is commonly called repudiation. But, for the Middle Ages, the other term is probably more accurate. Rarely did men claim the right to repudiate their wives without an excuse which was at least vaguely canonical. Almost always they had a reason for the invalidity of their first marriage. But it was the man himself who worked the divorce. The distinction is important. No one would claim that freedom of divorce, as we know it today, was accepted in the fourteenth century. But a degree of lay control over marriage, control which allowed spouses to act without express sanction of the Church, and control which permitted the bending and sometimes the breaking of canon law rules, did persist well into the later Middle Ages.

---

[116] For York 1400–50, there are eighteen multi-party suits, but only five petitions for nullity. Of course, all these figures from York, unlike those of other dioceses, depend on the chance of perhaps random survival. Act books are more dependable in giving a complete list of cases brought during a specific period, but, as noted in the first chapter, even these may not be entirely reliable.

An illustrative case, in which a witness told a relatively full story of the motives of the parties, comes from the records of the diocese of London. John Paynaminuta had married a girl named Katherine *in facie ecclesie*, believing that his first wife Conesyn was dead. John had not seen Conesyn for eleven years. He had had no notice of her, and they had no children. He was living happily with Katherine. But one day a man came to him who had seen Conesyn living in the city of Bayeux. The record states that the witness told John, 'that the said Conesyn was alive. John then told the witness that he was sad [to hear] of the life of the same Conesyn. And he said that, nevertheless, it was necessary to be divorced from Katherine his wife.'[117] In the story told by the record John said nothing about securing a divorce from the London Consistory court. He spoke only of 'being divorced'. And in fact, he divorced himself. The case came before the court later when Katherine sued to be restored to full rights of cohabitation with John. Had she not brought that suit, no doubt John would have been left alone, freed (in this case unhappily) from the bonds of the second marriage as effectively as if he had procured a canonically complete divorce.

Where a man or woman, for a reason like John Paynaminuta's, deserted one spouse and adhered to another, the result, where the two spouses were determined to assert their rights, was the multi-party suit. A woman at Canterbury had been married, as she claimed, while she was below the age of consent. She left her husband and married another. The result was a three-cornered action involving the two men as competitors.[118] In another case a man learned that his wife had pre-contracted with another man. He therefore felt that he could marry someone else. He did, and the two women ended in a court test over him.[119] A man at York believed his union was invalid because of force and fear. He married again, and the consequence was a multi-party suit.[120] News came to a woman at Rochester which led her to believe that her marriage was barred by consanguinity. She passed to new vows. The question of consanguinity arose only when the first husband sued to enforce the first contract.[121]

---

[117] MS. 9065, fols. 2114–222v: 'retulit eidem Johanni quod dicta Conesyn fuit superstites. Qui quidem Johannes retulit huic iurato quod tristis erat de vita eiusdem Conysen; et dixit quod tamen oportet divorciari a Katerina uxore mea.'

[118] Canterbury Sede Vacante S.B. I, p. 103 (1293).

[119] Canterbury X.10.1, f. 23v (1412); Y.1.4, 115r (1423).

[120] York C.P. E 62 (1348). See also *Das Imbreviaturbuch . . . Hubaldus aus Pisa*, 132–3.

[121] Rochester DRb Pa I, f. 27v (1437); York M 2(1) c, fols. 5v–6r (1372).

Sometimes we shall not think much of the excuse. A man alleged he had married a woman 'ignoranter'.[122] A woman claimed that 'the things she said with her mouth were not in her heart'.[123] A man felt himself free to marry again because his first 'was compelled by ecclesiastical censures'.[124] Or we find this revealing story told incidentally in an action for dower in the royal courts from 1280:

And the jurors chosen by consent of the parties say on their oath that the aforesaid William, formerly the husband of the same Denise, during the life of the father of the same William, espoused Denise by words of present consent and had issue by her, namely a son and a daughter. And after the death of his father, when his inheritance had devolved upon him, alleging that he was improperly (*incompetenter*) married, he repudiated the aforesaid Denise and contracted with a certain other Denise, whom he espoused *in facie ecclesie* and kept as his wife for some time.[125]

What legal theory lay behind William's claim that he had first married *incompetenter* we cannot say for sure. What we do know is that he did have an excuse, and that he did use it to justify repudiation of his wife.

There are many cases in which the reason for a party's decision to leave his spouse cannot be determined. Where the excuse was as weak as a few of those found in the Act books, no doubt it was only a pretext for escaping from an unhappy marriage. But the powers of human rationalization are great. What may seem to the disinterested observer only an excuse for giving free rein to passion or greed may seem valid and worthy to the man or woman involved. How easy it must have been for many men to convince themselves that there was defect enough in their first marriage to allow them to pass to new, and

---

[122] Hereford 0/3, 60 (1445). The court at Hereford allowed this plea, perhaps because the man and woman denied any sexual relations. He was allowed to purge himself *proprio iuramento*, she *cum secunda manu*.

[123] Canterbury Y.1.1, f. 9r (1373); in some circumstances this might have been made into a creditable plea, but the girl here made it after she had actually given birth to a child by the plaintiff. She was given a day 'ad proponendam causam rationabilem', and she subsequently pleaded pre-contract. See also Rochester DRb Pa 1, f. 189r (1446), where the man claimed that he had only entered into the contract 'ex nuga iocosa'.

[124] York M 2(1) c, f. 23r (1374).

[125] P.R.O. K.B. 27/64, m. 24: 'Et iurati consensu partium electi dicunt super sacramentum suum quod predictus Willelmus quondam vir ipsius Dyonisie, vivente patre ipsius Willelmi, affidavit ipsam Dyonisiam per verba de presenti, et procreavit ex ea prolem scilicet filium et filiam. Et post mortem patris sui, quando hereditas sibi devoluta fuerat, asserens se imcompetenter (sic) fuisse maritatum, sprevit ipsam predictam Dyonisiam et contraxit cum quadam alia Dyonisia quam desponsavit in facie ecclesie et per aliquod tempus eam tenuit tanquam uxorem suam.'

happier, vows. In a society where 'self-divorce' was not infrequent, and where the impediments to a marriage were many and uncertain of proof, how welcome must have been the suggestion, how sincere the acceptance, of the existence of a canonically valid reason for repudiating one's spouse. The result, where the deserted partner objected, was the multi-party suit. As long as a sentence of divorce was not first sought from the consistory court, it would be this type of action, not the suit for nullity, in which battles over impediments and consent were most commonly fought.

The canon law itself was partly responsible for this situation. Modern commentators have frequently pointed out that although canon law made contracting marriages easy, it also made proving them difficult.[126] The same applies to divorce. A man had to be able to *prove* consanguinity, lack of consent, pre-contract, or any other of the impediments, before he could secure a divorce from a competent tribunal. Lacey, in his work on *Marriage in Church and State*, contended that divorces were granted on the basis of 'evidence that was seldom sufficiently verified'.[127] If what Lacey meant was that witnesses perjured themselves, he may be right. It is impossible to tell except in rare instances. But if he meant that the courts granted divorces without demanding evidence which was *prima facie* good and first-hand, his statement is quite wrong. High standards of proof were required. It could easily happen that a man with a legitimate cause for divorce would be unable to prove it.

The situation of John Paynaminuta, the man at London whose first wife was found living in Bayeux, is a good example. How would he prove that she was alive, so that he could secure a divorce? Apparently only one man had seen her there. And in canon law the testimony of one witness was insufficient evidence of any fact. A court would have found against John under ordinary canonical rules of evidence. 'Self-divorce' may have been, in fact, the only realistic alternative for him. A somewhat more common case was this. A man had married two women by present words of consent, but either there were no witnesses at the first contract or none of those present would testify. Only

---

[126] See Pollock and Maitland, *HEL* II, 385–6, and Esmein I, 189–91 on the problems of proving a marriage.

[127] *Marriage in Church and State* (London, 1912), 159; Lacey maintained that 'almost any inconvenient husband or wife could be repudiated', given the 'chicanery' available under canon law. We shall see, in the following chapter, that such careless statements cannot be supported by the actual evidence of the court records. It is noteworthy that Mortimer modified this passage in his reissue of Lacey's work. See rev. 1947 ed., 138.

the second marriage could be proved in court. In any actual suit, the man would be held the husband of the second woman. What should he have done? No doubt he should not have married the second time. But perhaps he had to reckon with parental pressure or vastly changed circumstances. It happened often enough. If such a man was scrupulous, or if his conscience was stirred by discord with the second woman, he knew that before God he was married to the first. But he knew also that whatever court he resorted to would condemn him to live in adultery with the second.

Canonists dealt with this dilemma. One answer was that the man must live as a brother with the second woman. But that is a foolish answer. Generally, the canonists said that the man must desert the second and patiently suffer excommunication by an earthly court, knowing that he would be absolved before the final Judge.[128] Hostiensis wrote that although a man would be excommunicated, he should tolerate the excommunication, since no one should act against conscience.[129] William Hay, a late fifteenth-century Scottish canonist, suggested that the man should accept the excommunication and go with his true wife to some place where he was unknown.[130] Surely this was a realistic solution. The cases show that it was very often the alternative taken. How many men lived out their lives in a different village, having abandoned one wife for another, and how many did so out of scruples of conscience in cases where the external forum of the Church courts would have condemned them to perpetual adultery, are not, of course, questions the remaining records allow us to answer with certainty.[131] We see the cases only when two or three of the people determined to bring the matter into the Church courts, or when public rumor plus ecclesiastical vigor combined to catch the couple in an *ex officio* prosecution. But the multi-party actions which

---

[128] E.g. *gl. ord.* ad X 2.13.13 s.v. *tolerare*: ' . . . ubi mulier certa est, potius debet Deo obedire quam iudici'. See also the remarks in Pollock and Maitland, *HEL* II, 385.

[129] *Summa Aurea* IV, tit. *de cland. despon.*, no. 3: 'In iudicio animae consuletur eis, ut non reddant debitum contra conscientiam, in foro autem iudiciali excommunicabuntur nisi reddant; tolerant ergo excommunicationem, . . . , nemo enim contra conscientiam venire debet.'

[130] *William Hay's Lectures on Marriage*, ed. J. C. Barry, Stair Soc. 24 (1967), 24: 'Ipse tamen non debet obedire sed sufferre pacienter excommunicationem et se cum sua coniuge transferre ad locum in quo ipse est ignotus . . . '

[131] In Canterbury Y.1.5, f. 69v (1455), we find an exceptional statement of conscience. A woman said that she had left her husband 'non spoliando eum a iure suo, sed propter conscienciam volens redire ad proprium maritum'. She had married the second believing (mistakenly) that the first was dead.

resulted from such situations always represented a significant part of matrimonial litigation. Self-divorce was by no means rare. Multi-party litigation was the inevitable result.

Men's scruples sometimes led them into this sort of litigation. But there is another side. The *causa matrimonialis et divorcii* could be used as a weapon of fraud, as a tool for dissolving long-standing marriages unjustly. There was no preference in the canon law for the settled marriage as against a mere contract by words of present consent. Nor was there a statute of limitations. This meant that established marriages could be upset by the stalest of contracts.[132] Against this aspect of the canon law one of the Reformation statutes rightly objected. 'Not onely muche discorde between laufull maried personnes hath contrarie to Godde's ordenance arisen, muche debate and sute at the lawe . . . and many juste mariages brought in doubte and daunger of undoing and also many times undoone.'[133] The allegation of a pre-existing clandestine marriage in the *causa matrimonialis et divorcii* was the most frequent way existing marriages were dissolved in the medieval courts.[134]

A good example of such a case is a suit brought before the court at York in 1430. The contracts involved are best set out in chronological order:

(1) In 1409 Robert Esyngwald contracted marriage with Joan Ingoly in a garden before witnesses. For whatever reason, nothing more was done.

(2) In 1411 Robert married Elena Wright at the church door and with a nuptial mass. Thereafter they lived together.

(3) In 1418 Joan Ingoly married John Midelton at her parish church. They also lived together.

(4) Finally in 1430, Joan decided to vindicate her right to Robert Esyngwald under the 1409 contract. This she accomplished before

---

[132] Some examples of stale claims drawn from the cases: York C.P. F 101 (1431), thirty-six years; C.P. F 133 (1422), thirteen years; C.P. F 158 (1425), sixteen years; C.P. F 201 (1430), twenty-one years; Ely EDR D/2/1, f. 153v (1381), thirty years; London MS. 9065, fols. 48r–48v (1489), seventeen years; Canterbury Sede Vacante S.B. III, no. 35 (1293), fifteen years; Y.I.3, f. 107v (1419), nineteen years; Rochester DRb Pa 3, f. 514r (1465), sixteen years. There is a case involving a twenty-year delay in Furnivall, *Child-Marriages, Divorces and Ratifications*, 198–200.

[133] 32 Hen. VIII c. 38.

[134] The Henrician statute enacted that when a marriage had been solemnized and consummated, it could not later be challenged by a suit based simply on a contract by words of present consent. But it was repealed in 1548 (2 & 3 Edw. VI c. 23), and it was not until the passage of Lord Hardwicke's Marriage Act in 1753 (26 Geo. II c. 33) that suits for simple contract were made unenforceable at law.

the diocesan court at York, the result being that two unions, one of nineteen years' standing and one of twelve years', were dissolved. Joan had witnesses to the first marriage, and the court was satisfied with their excuses for not having reclaimed during the publication of banns between Joan and John Midelton. They had not thought it would do any good, and they felt she had a right to marry because Robert had himself taken a wife several years before.[135]

Whether this case was a collusive action, based on perjured testimony, or whether an aging Joan Ingoly was at last moved by her conscience to end the silent adultery in which she had lived for so many years, we cannot be sure. On a rare occasion fraud was actually confessed. One example comes from the York records. Geoffrey Brown and Alice Palmer were lawfully married. But Alice was unhappy with the marriage. 'Great dissension' had arisen between them, according to one witness. And she gave Ralph Fouler five shillings to allege that he had pre-contracted with her in a suit brought in the court of the archdeacon of the East Riding. Ralph began a *causa matrimonialis et divorcii* there. The official of the archdeacon held in his favor, and the marriage between Alice and Geoffrey was dissolved. The fraud was not confessed until some years later, for when it appears in the surviving records, it was before the court at York. Alice petitioned that court to annul the earlier judgment, on the grounds that she had herself procured it by fraud. She sued to regain Geoffrey as her legitimate spouse and to invalidate the marriage he had later contracted with another. Alice introduced evidence of the bribe she had herself given.[136] The canon law rule was that a sentence dissolving a

---

[135] York C.P. F 201; Robert Dalton, asked why he did not reclaim, told the examiner, 'quia credidit pro firmo quod si aliquam reclamationem contra huiusmodi solempnizationem fecisset nullum cepisset effectum eo quod matrimonium inter dictum Robertum et Elenam per plures annos tunc elapsos fuit solempnizatum.'

[136] York. C.P. E 25 (1332). In Canterbury Ecc. Suit, no. 33 (1271), we find this story: Isabella Kynebanten sued William Beresham to establish marriage, alleging *matrimonium carnali copula subsecuta*. William admitted this, but Matilda Wenebe also intervened to claim him, setting up a contract made eight years before. On one of the days set for production of witnesses, however, 'dicta M. in iudicio confitebatur se non habere testes, dicens se nunquam contraxisse cum eodem matrimonium, sed inducta per ipsum W. falso eundem petiit in virum.' In Canterbury, Reg. Islep, f. 107b (1355), a man 'de veritate dicenda super premissis ad sanctam Dei evangeliam iurato, se ad dictum Margeriam nullum ius habere confitente, set ipsum ad molestandam eam ut libellatur solicitum fuisse et inductum.' In London MS. 9065, f. 64v (1489), it was said that a man with a possible claim to marriage 'recepit x s. a dicto Salmon de pacto quod non vexaret dictum Thomam nec istam iuratam pretextu sue vigore alicuius contractus matrimonialis.' See also DRb Pa 4, f. 272v (1495). The whole matter is usefully discussed with examples in M. Aston, *Thomas Arundel* (Oxford, 1967), 99–109, esp. 106.

marriage did not prevent a subsequent raising of the question, even by the party who had procured the earlier judgment. The law and the canonists considered the danger to the souls of the parties. They concluded that there could be no *res judicata* where divorce was concerned.[137] To allow a litigant to base an action on his own wrongdoing shows how far the Church courts were prepared to go in the application of that rule.

Perhaps now enough has been said about the uncertainties, the collusion and the unseemliness of clandestine marriages, and the resulting multi-party litigation. Much of it has been said before, and in harsher tones.[138] On the other side, it can also be said that in practice the courts sometimes decided in favor of the established marriage, in the face of evidence which pointed to a verdict for the uncelebrated, unconsummated marriage. In some cases they dismissed the stale claim, allowing the accepted marriage to stand, though the strict logic of the *verba de presenti* doctrine directed otherwise.[139] It is difficult to be certain about this, of course. We can only infer the conclusion from conflicting testimony left in the depositions and from the judge's decision in favor of the apparently second, but settled, marriage. And there are certainly many such cases where the prior contract prevailed. We can say only that some judges appear in some cases to have bent the law to fit their normal, and sensible, prejudices.

---

[137] E.g. Hostiensis, *Summa Aurea* II, tit. *de sent.*, no. 8: 'Hic tamen notandum est quod tria sunt genera casuum. Unum quod nunquam transit in rem iudicatum, quando scilicet ea servata anima periclitaretur, sicut in causa matrimoniali.'

[138] See the remarks and opinions quoted in Esmein II, 127–30; Jackson, *Formation and Annulment of Marriage*, 17; Howard, *History of Matrimonial Institutions* I, 340–50; Pollock & Maitland, *HEL* II, 368–9.

[139] For example, in *Merssh & Rye* v. *Leeman*. Canterbury X.10.1, fols. 98v–99r, Y.1.3, f. 52r (1417), one petitioner could show only a causal contract, entered into because the owner of the house where she and the defendant wanted to spend the night refused to admit them unless they were married. The other petitioner proved a contract entered into before family and other witnesses. The banns were duly read. This was clearly the 'official' marriage. The first was prior in time, but the court held in favor of the validity of the second. However, the ruling was appealed to the Court of Arches. Other cases in which the court (apparently) held in favor of the preferred union, as against the prior contract, are: Rochester DRb Pa 1, f. 373v (1443); York C.P. E 79 (1359); F 262 (1442); M 2(1) c, s.d. 18 March 1377; Canterbury Sede Vacante S.B. III, no. 35 (1293); no. 49 (1293); Y.1.1, fols. 13r, 23v (1373); Y.1.5, fols. 48r, 104v, 182v–183v (1455). For French practice, see J. M. Turlan, 'Recherches sur le mariage dans la pratique coutumière (XIIe–XVIe siècles)', *Revue hist. de froit fr. et étr.*, ser. 4, 35 (1957), 510–45, esp. 511, n. 100. For German examples, see R. Weigand, 'Die Rechtsprechung des Regensburger Gerichts in Ehesachen', 412.

RESTITUTION OF CONJUGAL RIGHTS

Canon law, like Roman law and English Common law, distinguished between possessory and proprietory or petitory actions. The distinction was carried into marriage law in the form of the suit known as restitution of conjugal rights.[140] If a plaintiff could show only a contract by *verba de presenti*, he must use the petitory action we have been discussing. But if he could show the fact of marital possession, he could take advantage of this special remedy. He had to be able to allege a presumptively valid contract and consummation of the union. And he had also to show, at least by the fifteenth century, solemnization of the marriage *in facie ecclesie*.[141] The man or woman deserted by his partner of some years, in other words, rather than the person with a mere right to enforce a contract of marriage, was the normal plaintiff in restitution suits.

The result of successful prosecution of a suit for restitution was basically the same as that in a petitory action: that is, an order that the defendant accept the plaintiff as his legitimate spouse and treat her with marital affection. The only difference was that no order to solemnize was issued in possessory cases. But the advantages of using the possessory remedy were substantial.

First, a defendant could not in theory raise the question of the validity of the marriage.[142] If he wished to assert that the marriage was invalid by reason of pre-contract, for example, he must accept the woman back in the meantime, and bring a separate suit for divorce. In the second suit the burden of proof would be on him to prove the invalidity. In a petitory action the burden of proof was on the person who sought enforcement of the marriage contract. Second, the plaintiff in a possessory cause could claim alimony, or subsistence payments during the hearing of the case. And third, a plaintiff could

---

[140] Hostiensis, *Summa Aurea* IV, tit. *si mulier pet. in virum aliquem*, nos. 2–3: 'Item quia aliud est si mulier agat petitorio, . . . , aliud est si mulier agat possessorio.'

[141] Esmein II, 16; Pollock and Maitland, *HEL* II, 381. The fnatter is not, however, so clear for the earlier period. Esmein's evidence appears to come only from Panormitanus, and Maitland used Esmein's work as his authority. The *glossa ordinaria* ad X 2.13.8 s.v. *et ab eo cognita*, states: 'Et sic patet quod duo debet probare qui petit restitutionem, videlicet legitimam desponsationem, vere vel presumtive, et carnalem copulam.' This says nothing of solemnization. Innocent IV, *Apparatus* ad X 2.13.8: 'Not fit restitutio nisi probetur legitime desponsata, id est per verba de presenti et insuper cognita.' See also Jo. And., *Commentaria* ad X 2.13.14 no. 7. But cf. John of Acton, *Constitutiones*, 38 s.v. *clandestine*: 'Scias quod petens restitutionem non auditur de jure, ubi matrimonium est contractum clandestine, scilicet bannis non editis.'

[142] X 2.13.10; and see Hostiensis, *Summa Aurea* II, tit. *de rest. spol.*, no. 5.

demand payment of the expenses of bringing the action as a preliminary to a restitution case. Demands for expenses and alimony were regularly made in English court practice. And they were regularly granted.[143]

Given these advantages, it is surprising to find how infrequently suits for restitution appear in the remaining Act books. Relatively few possessory actions were brought, compared with the total number of petitory suits to enforce marriage contracts. For example, forty-two marriage cases involving the enforcement of marriage rights remain in the fourteenth-century Cause papers at York. But there are only three actions for restitution of conjugal rights. From April 1437 through April 1440, a total of fourteen marriage cases were brought in the Consistory court of the diocese of Rochester, but only one possessory suit. The highest percentage I have found comes from Lichfield, where from 1465 through 1468 fifteen restitution cases were heard, as against thirty-three petitory suits. Given the frequency of desertion in the Middle Ages, it is remarkable that so few of them were brought. Restitution of conjugal rights would seem, under the law, to have been the ideal way to seek redress.

What explanations for this small percentage are there? Several are likely. First, the major difficulties and disputes in marriage litigation were caused by the lack of any definite marriage formula, and by the habit of contracting marriages privately. Where no solemnization or cohabitation could be alleged, and where interpretation of an informal contract was at issue, the petitory, not the possessory, action was appropriate. Second, we saw above how frequent it was for a man or woman who had deserted his or her partner to marry again without securing a divorce from an ecclesiastical tribunal. It does not appear to have been possible for the deserted spouse to use the possessory action in the resulting multi-party litigation. The *causa matrimonialis et divorcii* was the appropriate remedy. This at least was what happened in practice, although I have found nothing in the canonists which would absolutely have forbidden the bringing of a possessory suit in such a situation.[144]

---

[143] E.g., Canterbury Y.1.3, f. 111r (1419): 'In cause restitutionis obsequiorum coniugalium inter Willelmum Bergh de Rodmersham et Johannam uxorem suam . . . monitus est dictus Willelmus ad ministrandum uxori sue pro alimentis xii d. pro qualibet septimana quousque posset invenire sufficientem securitatem de honesto modo tractando eandem.'

[144] Oughton, in the eighteenth century, called these actions *causae divortii a vinculo matrimonii et restitutionis obsequiorum conjugalium*. See *Ordo Judiciorum* I. 283. But the medieval practice was otherwise.

A third reason for the restricted use of restitution of conjugal rights is suggested by the blurring, in practice, of the distinction between petitory and possessory causes. Like the English possessory assizes, which came in time to try title to land almost as conclusively as writs of right, a suit for restitution of conjugal rights could be used to try the validity of a marriage as well as the fact of matrimonial possession. In theory, it was noted above, no exceptions raising the question of validity could be made. But the canonists themselves made an inroad on this principle. The existence of an indispensable grade of consanguinity could be raised in defense, because of the peril to the couple's souls which an order of immediate restitution would entail.[145]

In practice, this exception became the rule. Defenses going to the question of validity were often raised and tried before restitution was ordered. The claim that the words used did not make a valid contract could be raised despite subsequent matrimonial possession.[146] So could an exception of pre-contract.[147] The diocesan court at York allowed the defense of *infra annos nubiles* to be brought forward in a restitution suit,[148] and in an Ely case the defense of impotence was apparently tried.[149] Two cases have survived in which the question of invalidity because of coercion against the defendant was heard and determined in a possessory suit.[150] In this instance practice allowed what the formal law denied. The procedural advantages of quickness and restitution pending outcome of the dispute over validity were lost in the actual trial of restitution of conjugal rights. Perhaps this, with the other two factors mentioned, discouraged wider use of the possessory remedy in marriage cases. The cases provide no answer which would explain why the advantage of alimony and expenses, available in restitution but not in marriage causes, was not inducement enough for greater use of this remedy.

---

[145] Hostiensis, *Summa Aurea* II, tit. *de rest. spol.*, no. 5.

[146] York C.P. F 44 (1394); wrongly filed with fifteenth-century cases.

[147] Canterbury Y.1.4, f. 102 (1422), in which William Baker, the defendant, answered 'quod diu ante quemcumque contractum inter ipsum et uxorem suam precontraxerat dicta Alicia cum quodam Johanne Exetr', quare non tenetur impedire sibi obsequia conuigalia. Igitur commissarius assignat sibi ad proponenda premissa in debita forma iuris.' Other examples are: Rochester DRb Pa 3, fols. 313v–314r (1456); London MS. 9065, fols. 221r–222v (1494); Canterbury Y.1.5, f. 69v (1455).

[148] York C.P. E 89 (1365–7). And see Lichfield B/C/1/1, fols, 203r, 209r (1468) where actions of divorce *a vinculo* and for restitution were kept formally separate in the Act book though they involved the same parties. They were tried in the same sequence, so that the procedure was identical in substance to the other cases cited.

[149] Ely EDR D/2/1, fols. 91r, 92r, 102v.

[150] Canterbury Y.1.5, f. 141r (1456); York C.P. F 97, 98, 105 (1429–32).

EX OFFICIO PROSECUTIONS

The litigation covered so far has been instance litigation, begun at the suit of private parties. But the Church also exercised an extensive *ex officio* jurisdiction. And from it questions involving the validity of marriage could and frequently did arise. *Ex officio* actions were either begun by the court itself or 'promoted' by a person not connected with the court. In either case, their professed aim was disciplinary, to correct the wrongdoing of the parties, as for adultery, fornication, or any other sin. Enforcement of the Church's standards for marriage was often undertaken by these office prosecutions, though private quarrels must have lain behind many of them.

The way in which questions of marriage arose from these prosecutions can be seen easily. A common example is that of a man cited by a judge for having expelled his wife from his house. Such a man might claim, as in a Rochester case of 1457, that he had previously contracted marriage with a third woman, by way of justification for the expulsion. This claim, contested by the ejected spouse, raised an ordinary question of the validity of each marriage contract;[151] and so with prosecution of a man and woman for having contracted marriage in defiance of the law's prohibitions against marriage within the fourth degree of consanguinity;[152] or for having two, or even three, living wives;[153] or for having contracted clandestinely;[154] or (as in one Hereford case) for living with a woman when 'it is not known whether she was his wife or not'.[155] In all these, the question the courts had in the end to answer came to this: is a claimed marriage valid? What had begun as a disciplinary hearing easily became a hearing on the validity of marriage.

The Church courts would not, on the other hand, undertake an *ex officio* prosecution against a man for using coercion to force a woman to marry him, for non-consummation because of impotence, or for marrying below the age of puberty. It was possible to secure an annulment on these grounds, as we shall see in the next chapter, but

---

[151] Rochester DRb Pa 3, fols. 313v–314r (1457); Ely EDR D/2/1, f. 153 v (1381).

[152] Canterbury, Ecc. Suit, no. 118 (1293); Rochester DRb Pa 1, f. 32r (1437); Ely EDR D/2/1, f. 143r (1380); and see Chapter 3, n. 24.

[153] Hereford 0/2, 74 (1442); Rochester DRb Pa 2, f. 79r (1447); DRb Pa 4, f. 38v (1472). On multiple marriages see Lyndwood, *Provinciale*, 266 s.v. *urgente necessitate*.

[154] Ely EDR D/2/1, f. 35r (1376); York M 2(1) f, f. 28v (1397).

[155] Hereford 0/3, 50 (1446). Here the man alleged due solemnization at St Albans.

they did not seem such violations of the nature of marriage as to warrant public prosecution without the initiative of either party. According to canon law, no one but the parties themselves could question the validity of marriage on these grounds.[156] This rule apparently bound the judges. At least, I have found no trace of any cases raising these impediments in the surviving records.

Once the parties appeared in court, *ex officio* prosecutions closely paralleled ordinary instance litigation. Take the case of a man and woman cited for an alleged clandestine contract. If both of them denied the contract under oath, the judge dropped the case. The parties were 'dismissed to their good consciences'.[157] If one party denied, while the other affirmed, that there was a true contract, the affirming party was given a term to prove his case. Thereafter the case was treated just like an ordinary piece of instance litigation. One party became the plaintiff, the other the defendant.

The courts, in other words, merely brought the question of marriage out into the open, and required the parties to tell the truth under oath. The judge conducted no investigation of his own. A regime which at first sight appears inquisitorial, leaving tremendous opportunity for abuse by court officials, was actually less harsh because of the way the procedure was organized. On occasion, a man might have to produce compurgators to verify his oath.[158] This was often done where the charge was adultery, almost never where there was simply public fame of a clandestine marriage. But in no case did the court undertake to search out the facts for itself, and attempt to impose the law on the parties after having found them.

There is one exception to this, and an interesting one. It is the marriage allegedly barred by consanguinity. Here, when parties were cited for having married within the prohibited degrees, courts often called witnesses *ex officio*.[159] If their evidence proved the consanguinity, whatever the affirmations or the desires of the man and

---

[156] On this see Esmein I, 406.

[157] E.g., Ely EDR D/2/1, f. 136v (1380); York Cons. A B 2, f. 89r (1427).

[158] E.g., Rochester DRb Pa 4, f. 29v (1472).

[159] *Supra*, n. 145. However, some distinctions must be made between different sorts of kinship disqualification. In Canterbury Y.1.11, f. 348r (1474), where a man was cited for marrying his *soror spiritualis*, he was allowed to purge himself *proprio iuramento* when he denied the relationship. At f. 308r (1473), the same single-handed purgation was apparently used where the man denied the 'spiritual' relationship caused by marrying a widow whose child he had sponsored in baptism. This is, I think, a sign that the courts considered these impediments as less dangerous than actual consanguinity.

woman involved, their union was dissolved.[160] It is, I think, a
measure of the seriousness with which the kinship disqualifications
were taken, that these inquisitions were undertaken. In other cases,
the courts left the prosecution of cases, once begun, to the parties
themselves. *Ex officio* actions devolved easily into instance litigation.
In the context of this study, they must be considered mainly as
another way in which questions of marriage were raised. They cannot be placed in an entirely separate category, even where (as was
often the case) office and instance cases were recorded in separate
Act books.

SUMMARY

Matrimonial litigation in later medieval England was, above all else,
litigation over the interpretation and enforcement of marriage contracts. The principal business of the Church courts was not determining whether an existing marriage could be dissolved: their main
task was the settling of disputes about the initiation of the marriage
relationship. The large number of petitory marriage suits and the
only slightly smaller number of multi-party cases are the expression
of this fact. The records suggest that the cause of this characteristic
lies in the conjunction of two things. First was the lack of a required
formula by which marriage had to be contracted and the legal difficulties of interpreting the words used in practice. Second was the
continued vitality of an older view of marriage as a private contract. What the law regarded as a complete and indissoluble marriage,
many men regarded as a contract to marry. Their attitude normally
regarded, but it did not slavishly adhere to, the law found in the
official texts. The first of these two was perhaps the more important
at the time. But the second is the more interesting for an historian.
We must see the process by which the Church vindicated its control
over marriage as a longer and more gradual process than has hitherto
been thought. It did not come with the definitive formulation of the
classical canon law in the twelfth century. Rather it was the product
of slow growth and acceptance, which was almost imperceptible to
contemporaries but is apparent in the records of the Church courts.
The Council of Trent's decree *Tametsi*, requiring the presence of the

---

[160] That the divorce was contrary to the parties' desire is sometimes expressly stated:
e.g. Ely EDR D/2/1, f. 143r (1380): 'Licet dicta Alicia nollet a dicto Thoma Biley separari
sed summe affectat ipsum habere in virum, ac per famam vicine et aliis legitimis probationibus
coram nobis ministratis luculenter constat,...' the court going on to annul the marriage.

parish priest for a valid marriage, in a sense was made possible by this slow acceptance over the course of the thirteenth through the sixteenth centuries. We shall take a closer look at this process in Chapter 6. Here we have had to deal with the consequences of the persistence of the attitude towards marriage inherited from the early Middle Ages. For the Church courts, the principal consequence of that attitude was the large place suits to enforce private marriage contracts had in canonical litigation.

III

SUITS FOR DIVORCE AND
INCIDENTAL MARRIAGE CAUSES

Divorce in the modern sense of the word did not exist in medieval England. Marriages validly entered into were theoretically indissoluble for any cause which arose after they had been contracted. But the term 'divorce' is used throughout the medieval records. It normally meant what we call an annulment, a declaration that a marriage had been invalid *ab initio*.[1] The term was also used to refer to a judicial separation. But when mere separation was meant the records usually called the case specifically divorce *a mensa et thoro*. This allowed the man and wife to live apart, but did not break the bond between them. They could not remarry. I have followed the medieval practice in describing the following litigation. The miscellaneous marriage causes, discussed at the end of this chapter, are likewise classed according to the names given them in the Act books.

DIVORCE A VINCULO

The most striking fact about divorce litigation in medieval England is how little of it there was. Excluding the multi-party suits, in which each petitioner's primary aim was to establish his own claim of marriage, the total number of divorce cases, both in percentage and absolute terms, was quite small. Of twenty-three marriage cases heard from April 1437 through April 1440 in the Rochester Consistory court, only five were for divorce. There are eighty-eight cases involving marriage in the York Cause papers of the fifteenth century; only twelve of them are divorce suits. A scant ten of the ninety-eight matrimonial cases heard in Canterbury between November 1372 and May 1375 were actions between a man and woman to dissolve their marriage. In the Registrum Primum for the Consistory

---

[1] The records occasionally refer to them as *cause divorcii seu nullitatis matrimonii*, to distinguish them from suits for divorce *a mensa et thoro*; e.g. Hereford o/3, 78 (1446); Rochester DRb Pa 1, f. 3r (1437). On the use of terminology, see generally Howard, *History of Matrimonial Institutions* II, 51–3.

court at Ely there are sixty marriage cases recorded; only twelve of these are suits for divorce.[2]

These figures are surprising at first sight; particularly so because historians have told us that marriages were easily and frequently dissolved in the Middle Ages. It is said that because of the multiple and artificial impediments of the canon law, divorce was readily available to the unhappily married man or woman. Maitland, for instance, thought that 'spouses who had quarrelled began to investigate their pedigrees and were unlucky if they could discover no *impedimentum dirimens*';[3] others have reiterated the conclusion.[4] The most recent report on Marriage and Divorce for the Church of England takes it as established fact that those who needed or wished to dissolve a marriage 'could probably discover a ground for its nullity'.[5] But this judgment, however often repeated, is not supported by the evidence of the court records. Suits for divorce were not numerous; they were far outnumbered by cases involving the enforcement of marriage contracts. And by no means every suit to secure dissolution was successful. Divorces were not freely granted by the English courts.

This fact requires explanation. Why were there so few divorce cases? One reason for this has already been given and investigated. Men and women invalidly married simply divorced themselves. Since the direction of matrimonial litigation lay largely with the parties themselves, we see these 'divorces' only in multi-party litigation. The extent of this litigation, at least before the late fifteenth century, was usually greater than that of simple divorce cases. But this is only a partial explanation. Examination of the surviving records, considered under the separate grounds available for divorce in Canon law provides some instructive answers. Not every possible cause for divorce produced enough litigation to warrant discussion. But enough

---

[2] See Sheehan, 'Formation and Stability of Marriage', 257; the other figures given in this paragraph are taken directly from the records.

[3] Pollock & Maitland, *HEL* II, 393.

[4] R. Haw, *The State of Matrimony* (London, 1952), 39: 'It was as simple as it must have been lucrative for the ecclesiastical lawyers to discover a reason for the nullifying of a vast proportion of apparently sound marriages at the behest of those eager to pave the way to a more delectable union.' Remarks less emphatic in tone but identical in conclusion can be found in Jackson, *Formation and Annulment of Marriage*, 20; Lacey, *Marriage in Church and State* (1947), 138; Bryce, *Studies in History and Jurisprudence* (London, 1901) II, 434; J. F. Worsley-Boden, *Mischiefs of the Marriage Law* (London, 1932), 87.

[5] *Marriage, Divorce and the Church* (London, 1972), 9.

cases of divorce based on most existing impediments have survived to tell us a good deal about the nature of divorce litigation, and to suggest some reasons why there was not more of it.

(i) Pre-contract

The reason that there were not more suits to dissolve a marriage for a pre-existing contract is clear. Most cases involving pre-contract were brought in the form of the multi-party *causa matrimonialis et divorcii*. The way in which a marriage could be dissolved because of the existence of a prior contract by *verba de presenti* was discussed at length in the previous chapter. Two competitors sought the enforcement of separate marriages with the same defendant. No more of substance needs to be said about these cases. If they are counted as suits for divorce, of course, it is wrong to say that divorce played a minor role in actual litigation. But the primary aim of these suits was not simply to dissolve a marriage between two parties. It was to establish that a prior marriage was valid and to secure its enforcement. To a large extent this is only a question of terminology. The relatively large number of these cases is the important thing. But, because of the distinction in primary aim and because the Act books give these suits a special name, the *causa matrimonialis et divorcii*, it seems proper not to class these as cases of divorce *a vinculo*.

It was not strictly necessary, however, to have the party to the pre-contract present in court to dissolve an existing union. If a man, for example, could prove that he had contracted with another woman before contracting marriage a second time he could divorce the woman he had married second. Such a suit was brought by John Elme against his wife Mariona at York in 1389. He alleged his own pre-contract with Isabelle Brigham.[6] Normally, of course, the first partner was joined in a *causa matrimonialis et divorcii*.[7] This, perhaps

---

[6] York C. P. E 153. The bringing of such suits was limited by the rule that where the first wife was dead, and the second had not known of the existence of the first marriage, only the wife could challenge the validity of the second marriage on the grounds of pre-contract. The man who had fraudulently married twice could not bring a suit for divorce. See X 4.7.1: 'Quia tamen prefata mulier erat inscia quod ille aliam haberet uxorem viventem, nec dignum est, ut praedictus vir, qui scienter contra canones venerat, lucrum de suo dolo reportet.'

[7] I am not sure that this was legally required. The canon law was that where the partner under the first contract was alive, either party might accuse the marriage of invalidity even if his own turpitude were involved. See for example, Panormitanus, *Commentaria* ad X 2.27.7 no. 6: 'Audiatur allegans turpitudinem propriam ut evitetur periculum animae.' Sometimes, however, the joinder was probably *pro forma* only. This is likely where, as sometimes happened, one of the competitors was not represented in court. See, for example, York C. P. F 248 (1459), where one of the parties was in the diocese of Norwich.

more than anything else, must explain why so few straight divorce cases on this ground appear in the remaining records.

In practice, it was more common for the plaintiff in a simple divorce case to set up the defendant's pre-contract with a third person than it was for him to allege his own prior contract. For example, all three of the cases of divorce for pre-contract which were heard in Canterbury between 1416 and 1418 were brought this way.[8] The plaintiff alleged his partner's pre-existing marriage, usually adding that notice of it had only recently come to his attention. If he could find reliable witnesses to that first marriage, he could secure a divorce. Edmund Dronefeld of York, for instance, divorced his wife Margaret Donebarre in 1364 on the grounds that she had married another man eighteen years previously. The first husband was at the time a captive in Scotland.[9] It is obvious, however, that problems of proving such a pre-existing contract would normally have been great, especially if the defendant were unwilling to cooperate. Perhaps this goes part of the way towards explaining the paucity of such suits in the remaining records. But certainly there were not many.

(ii) *Consanguinity and affinity*

It is the impediment arising from blood, marriage and 'spiritual' ties which has provoked the greatest criticism of medieval marriage law. These impediments seem to have offered a ready escape from the marriage bond. The rules on consanguinity and affinity moved Maitland to strong language, which is worth quoting. 'Behind these intricate rules', he wrote, 'there is no deep policy, there is no deep religious feeling; they are the idle ingenuities of men who are amusing themselves by inventing a game of skill which is to be played with neatly drawn tables of affinity and doggeral hexameters.' He spoke of the 'incalculable harm' caused by the rules.[10] Surely, it is hard to

---

[8] E.g. Y.1.3, f. 19r (1416): 'Petit dictus Robertus se divorciari a thoro et consortio dicte Johanne pro eo et ex eo quod dicta Johanna habet maritum superstitem nomine Ricardum Basset in diocesi Wintoniensi. Cui petitioni dicta Johanna respondet affirmative.' It is not entirely clear that Robert was asking for a divorce *a vinculo* here. But certainly his allegation, if proved, would have that result. The two other cases are *Cokke* v. *Walter*, found in the session of 24 Sept. 1417, and *Crostman* v. *Crostman*, found in that of 4 July 1418. There were, during the same period, thirteen cases of multi-party litigation.

[9] York C.P. E 87. Other examples: Canterbury Y.1.1, f. 28v (1373); York C.P. F 3 (1401), F 236 (1448), F 248 (1459).

[10] Pollock and Maitland, *HEL* II, 389. There was some contemporary support for this position among theologians. See J. W. Baldwin, 'Critics of the Legal Professions: Peter the Chanter and his Circle', *Proceedings of the Second International Congress of Medieval Canon Law*, eds. S. Kuttner and J. Ryan (Vatican City, 1965), 249–59.

believe that he was wrong. The number of marriages disqualified or subject to dissolution under them was very great.

In 1215, the Fourth Lateran Council had reduced the probibited degrees of consanguinity and affinity from seven to four.[11] But the remaining prohibitions still covered a very broad range of possible marriages. It meant, for example, that everyone descended from the same great-great-grandfather was barred from marrying anyone similarly descended. The method was to count down each line of descent from the common ancestor. If this took four steps or fewer to reach the man or woman on each side, the relationship was consanguineous.[12] Any marriage between the descendants was invalid. Affinity was the tie between a man (or woman) and the blood kin of the person with whom he had become 'one flesh'. Normally, this impediment was a result of marriage. But it was also the product of any sexual intercourse. If a man once had sexual relations with a girl, he could not thereafter marry her sister. They were barred by the first degree of affinity: and so with the first, the second, or the third cousins of any woman with whom he had carnal dealings.[13] In addition, there was the impediment of 'public honesty'. This barred marriages between the relations of a man and woman who had exchanged *verba de futuro*, but had not ultimately married.[14] And last, there were the purely 'spiritual' ties, contracted with the immediate kin of a person's sponsors in baptism or confirmation. Under this impediment, for instance, a man might not marry the widow who had previously stood godmother to a child by his first wife.[15]

From this it is obvious that a great many marriages were barred

---

[11] X 4.14.8. The entire subject of these impediments is treated historically and exhaustively in Freisen, *Geschichte des kanonischen Eherechts*, 371–561. See also Esmein I, 335–84; Joyce, *Christian Marriage*, 507–69.

[12] Thus a couple might be related in the third and fourth degrees of consanguinity where it took a different number of steps to reach the common ancestor on each side. The two degrees are often given in the records; e.g. Ely EDR D/2/1, f. 108r (1379). Sometimes the party's documents speak of consanguinity more generally; e.g. York C.P. E 33 (1337): 'in tercio gradu et infra quartum gradum consanguinitatis attingente'.

[13] See the capsule summary of the difference between affinity and consanguinity in John of Acton, *Constitutiones*, 154 s.v. *consanguinitate*: '[Consanguinitas] est vinculum diversarum personarum ab eodem stipite descendentium carnali propagatione contractum; sed affinitas est proximitas diversarum personarum ex carnali coitu proveniens, omni carens parentala.' Examples can be found in Canterbury Sede Vacante S.B. III, no. 319 (1277); Ecc. Suit, no. 292 (1294); Ch. Ant. A 36 IV, f. 54 r (1341); Y.I.1, f. 5v (1373); Ely EDR D/2/1, f. 108r (1379); f. 143r (1380); York C.P. E 33 (1337); E 212 (1394).

[14] I have, however, found no divorce granted on this ground in the remaining English records.

[15] E.g. York M 2(1) c, f. 21r (1374), Durham *Reg. Langley* II, no. 325 (1414).

by the impediments of affinity and consanguinity. A little genea-
logical research, as Maitland suggested, would appear capable of
turning up an impediment to most medieval marriages. The tempta-
tion for the unhappily married man or woman would be very great
to undertake such a search, and to dissolve his or her marriage as a
consequence. It is but an easy step to conclude that this was done in
fact. It is all but irresistible to conclude that divorces were often
procured under the system of kinship disqualification.

The Church court records, however, do not support that conclusion. The hard fact is that there were few divorces on these
grounds. And lest we think that there were many divorces which we
simply do not see coming into the Church courts, we ought to recall
that most suits to enforce contracts of marriage were vigorously contested. If consanguinity or affinity could always have been found, we
should find it frequently raised by way of defense in those suits. But
we do not. How can the relative absence of cases raising these impediments be explained?

One reason for the absence is that men seldom married women if
they were aware that the marriage was open to objection on grounds
of consanguinity. It is dangerous to read our own belief in the artificiality of these rules back into the Middle Ages. When a man believes
that it is wrong to marry a kinswoman, when he considers these impediments something more than a fanciful limitation invented by a
celibate and irresponsible priesthood, he does not violate the rules.
To argue the contrary assumes that medieval men cynically broke the
rules to get married, then just as cynically broke them again to secure
a divorce. That is not consistent with human nature. And it is not
consistent with the testimony of the Church court records. We find,
most commonly, cases in which the reason people refused to marry,
in fact hotly resisted all proposals of marriage, was their belief that
consanguinity or affinity stood in the way.[16] There is one particularly

---

[16] In York C.P. E 210 (1384), a witness said that 'audivit Willelmum Botry de Ryvaux
dicentem quod ipse libentius duceret Anabillam predictam in uxorem quam aliquam aliam
viventem si non obsistaret gradus consanguinitatis'. In York C.P. F 257 (1476), a woman urged
to contract a marriage thought to be consanguineous, replied 'Trewly to dy prefere, I will never
consent to you for we er over mere sybbe.' In Hereford, 0/4, 119 (1447), a man said 'quod
vellet facere matrimonium solempnizari cum muliere si hoc posset fieri, dubitat tamen quia
audivit quod unus sibi attingens in quarto gradu consanguinitatis predictam Margaretam prius
carnaliter cognovisset.' In York M 2(1), e, s.d. 9 April 1377, the chaplain first asked to
solemnize the marriage refused, saying 'In feith sir, I will not do it, for it is agayns the law
for ye er within the gree of marriage.' Other examples can be found in Rochester DRb Pa 1,
fols, 27v, 32r, 35v (1437); DRb Pa 3, f. 456r (1462); Hereford 0/10, 94 (1474); York C.P.
E 108 (1370); F 126 (1415); Canterbury X.10.1, f. 113r (1418); Y.1.5, f. 127v (1456).

revealing death-bed monition by the father of a man who had married a girl he had made pregnant:

> I warn and charge you that when an opportune time shall come, as you are willing to answer for both of us on the day of judgment, that you do not delay in revealing and making known the consanguinity between my son Robert and Isabel Yonge his wife; for I know in my conscience that they will never flourish or live together in good fortune because of the consanguinity between them.[17]

That is not the statement of a man who thought that the rules about consanguinity were trifles. He believed that a marriage contracted without regard for them could not stand or prosper.

Confirmation of the reluctance to marry within prohibited degrees can also be found in the extent to which people married outside their own communities. It is easy to imagine that there was very little 'social mobility' in medieval times, at least among ordinary folk. But not everyone married a girl from his own village. The parishes of parties to marriage actions are often given in the court records. The figures which emerge from counting them are interesting. In the fifteenth-century Cause papers at York, there are forty cases where the parties to marriage contracts can be identified as coming from different parishes. There are thirty-eight, or two fewer, in which they came from the same parish. In the 1411–20 Deposition book from Canterbury, I found equal numbers of each – twenty-one cases of both identical and different parishes. The Act book from November 1372 through 1375 produces a seventy-three to forty-five preponderance in favor of cases in which the parties' parishes were identical. But in Lichfield from 1465 through 1467, the preponderance was in favor of cases involving different parishes – twenty to thirteen.[18]

In themselves these figures do not prove a great deal about population mobility. They may be unrepresentative of marriage in general,

---

[17] York C.P. F 202 (1462); 'Ego requiro te et moneo te quod cum tempus oportunum tibi evenerit, prout vis pro me et te in die Iudicii respondere, quod tu consanguinitatem inter Robertum filium meum et Isabellam Yonge uxorem suam publicare et promulgare non deferas quia ego scio in consciencia mea quod nunquam vigebunt nec simul fortunaliter stabunt propter consanguinitatem inter eos.' It ought to be noted, however, that the couple had been married for eighteen years. They were allegedly related in the fourth degree of consanguinity.

[18] From February 1455 to December 1458 the Canterbury Act book Y.1.5 produces eleven identifiable cases of different parishes, ten in which the couple came from the same parish. See also the conclusions of P. D. A. Harvey, *A Medieval Oxfordshire Village: Cuxham, 1240 to 1400* (Oxford, 1965), 128.

and I have not been able to calculate the average distance between parishes. But they do at least suggest that marriage partners were commonly found outside the immediate circles of each community. St Augustine had written that one of the aims of kinship disqualification was the increase of charity. People already tied by family should move outside, including others in the bonds of friendship.[19] Perhaps the figures from the medieval Act books show Augustine's injunction taking effect. They do certainly indicate one reason that there were not more claims of consanguinity and affinity in the Church courts.

Part of the explanation for the scarcity of divorce actions on kinship grounds thus lies in the attitudes and habits of the people. There is also an important requirement of the law which itself discouraged the bringing of such suits. That is the need to *prove* consanguinity. Parties could not simply swear that they were related. Reliable witnesses who had first-hand knowledge had to be produced. In 1215 the Fourth Lateran Council had tightened up the requirements for proving consanguinity and affinity. The trustworthiness of the witnesses must be above suspicion. And witnesses who had no first hand knowledge of the claimed relationship, who were only *testes de auditu*, were excluded except in special circumstances.[20] The aim was to ensure that no sentences of divorce were to be based on mere rumour. What had been allowed before, because of the impossibility of proving consanguinity to the seventh degree, was to be permitted no longer, now that the prohibited degrees had been reduced to four. Singled out for especial care was the case where knowledge of consanguinity had sprung from only one man.[21] This was not enough to

---

[19] C. 35 q. 1 c. un.: 'Habita enim est ratio certissima karitatis, ut homines, quibus esset atque honestissima concordia, diversarum necessitudinum vinculis necterentur.' But cf. the explanation in *gl. ord.* ad X 2.13.13 s.v. *divina lege*: 'Sub gratia vero, scilicet tempore Christi plurimae personae excluduntur ut locum haberet continentia.'

[20] X 2.20.47; on previous practice, see *gl. ord.* ad C. 35 q. 6 c. 5 s.v. *audisti*: 'Hic admittitur testimonium de auditu, quia difficulis est quod aliquis sciat quousque consanguinitas protenditur.' Note also Panormitanus, *Commentaria* ad X 2.20.47, no. 3: 'Item nota quod ubi admittitur testimonium de auditu non sufficit quod quis audiverit post motam litem.'

[21] *Gl. ord.* ad X 2.20.47 s.v. *ab uno*: 'Item et si plures essent testes et quilibet eorum audivisset ab alio quam alter non valebit testimonium nisi quilibet illorum audivisset a pluribus.' See also Innocent IV, *Apparatus* ad X 2.20.47: 'Non est necesse quod quilibet audiverit, sed necesse est quod plures sint principium huius auditonis.' The case of *Tangerton* v. *Smelt*, Canterbury Ecc. Suit, no. 188 (1294), is a good example. A witness, asked where his information about consanguinity came from, answered, 'a Johanne le Wlf conteste suo preexaminato, qui quidem Johannes isti testi et aliis contestibus suis subsequentibus hac instanti die inquisitionis sive examinationis in ecclesia Christi Cant' dictos gradus exposuit.' No divorce was therefore celebrated. A similar case is recorded in Canterbury X.10.1; fols. 14r-14v (1412). One witness said, 'quod nescit quicquid deponere nisi ex relatu Agnetis Markyn contestis sue.' No sentence from this case survives, however.

warrant a divorce, no matter how many witnesses he convinced that he knew the truth of the matter. First-hand knowledge of more than one man was required.

Behind this rule lay the belief that it was better to risk allowing consanguineous unions than to risk separating couples God had legitimately joined together. We must not imagine that all marriages of kin were thought to be equally sinful. Except for the closest degrees, the prohibitions were the work of men, not of God.[22] Human law left room for manoeuvre. As the Lateran Council's Constitution said, 'It is more tolerable to leave couples joined together against the statutes of man than to separate, against the statutes of the Lord, those who are legitimately joined.'[23]

It was therefore no sure thing to seek a divorce for affinity or consanguinity. There was a presumption of sorts in favor of marriage in these cases. The burden of proof lay with the party claiming the impediment. And he had to meet high standards in his proof. English Church courts took, so far as we can tell, an uncompromising position in requiring the plaintiff to prove the prohibited relationship. Practice called, in many cases, for the summoning of a sworn inquisition *ex officio* on the question. In the thirteenth century, the inquisition was usually made up of twelve men, the number declining in the next century.[24] It is a measure of the seriousness with which the courts took divorce for consanguinity that this was done.

In evaluating the evidence before them, the courts took an apparently strict line. A good example, taken from the thirteenth-

---

[22] See, for example, Panormitanus, *Commentaria* ad X 2.20.47, no. 4: 'Nota quod fere omnes gradus sunt prohibiti lege humana et non divina; pauci enim sunt prohibiti lege divina.' And *ibid.*, 'Nota ultimo quod ubi agitur de impedimento a canonibus inducto iudicandum est in dubio semper pro matrimonio.'

[23] X 2.20.47: 'Tolerabulius est enim aliquos contra statuta hominum dimittere copulatos, quam coniunctos legitime contra statuta Domini separare.' The distinction between dispensable and non-dispensable grades also stems from this difference. See Pollock and Maitland, *HEL* II, 389.

[24] E.g. Canterbury Sede Vacante S.B. III, no. 124 (1294), in which an order issued to the rural dean of Charing: 'Mandamus quantinus peremptorie citetis vel citari faciatis duodecim vel circiter viros fidedignos . . . quod compareant coram nobis in ecclesia de Wytercheshame die mercurii proxima post octabas Sancte Trinitatis super consanguinitate que dicitur esse inter eosdem quicquid sciunt et intelligunt dicturos.' In Canterbury Sede Vacante S. B. III, no. 129 (1293), the inquisition was to be drawn from 'duodecim viros vel circiter proximiores consanguinitati eorum.' Otherwise, I have not been able to find any evidence on how the witnesses were chosen. Other instances where inquisitions were used: Sede Vacante S. B. II, p. 51 (c. 1200); Ch. Ant. A 36 IV, f. 35v (1340); Y.1.1, fols. 72r, 74r (1374); f. 106r (1375) Ely EDR D/2/1, f. 108 v (1379); Rochester *Reg. Hamonis Hethe*, 940 (1347); DRb Pa 1, f. 32r (1437), in which the procedure is said to be aimed 'ad evitandum fraudem et collusionem'.

century records at Canterbury, is the attempt to dissolve a marriage between Richard Broke and his wife Joan. A certain Peter Daneys claimed, first, that he was related to Richard in the second degree of consanguinity and, second, that he had carnally known Richard's wife Joan before the marriage. This, as we noted above, would warrant a divorce because of the rule that affinity arose not from marriage, but from *copula carnalis*. An inquisition was called. But its answers were vague. Elias Hegham, for example, asked about the consanguinity between Peter and Richard, said 'that there was a certain ancestor whose name he does not know, from whom sprang another he does not know, but he well knows that they (Peter and Richard) sprang from two sisters'. On the question of sexual relations Elias testified to public fame that Peter had had sexual relations with Joan. Elias was inclined to believe it – 'credit melius famam esse veram quam falsam' – but he could not say for sure. Neither could anyone else. Some did not believe it was true at all. No one, in fact, had *first-hand* knowledge of those relations, which is hardly surprising. They were not much more conclusive about the consanguinity. As a result, the court held that no cause for divorcing the couple had been made out.[25] The impediment had not been proved.

As in this case, practice shows that it was often very difficult to find witnesses with requisite first-hand knowledge of claimed consanguinity and affinity. Especially was this so where the higher degrees were claimed. And proof of sexual relations necessary in divorce for affinity was sometimes equally difficult to produce. In one case from York where a suit for consanguinity was in the end successful, there were five witnesses. One was in his sixties, two in their seventies, one in his eighties, and one (who testified *in lecto suo*) was said to be one hundred years old.[26] Such men were understandably hard to find. In a Canterbury case from the fourteenth century, both parties admitted to prohibited relationship. But the witnesses called apparently could not

---

[25] Canterbury Sede Vacante S.B. III, no. 58. A similar case is *Bruning* v. *Brūning*, Canterbury Sede Vacante S.B. III, no. 21 (1294), an attempt to dissolve a marriage for spiritual affinity, contracted by sponsorship in baptism. The question was whether the plaintiff's mother had 'raised from the sacred font' the woman whom the plaintiff had married sixteen years before. Several witnesses testified that she had, but none had actually been present at the baptism. There were, in other words, no eye-witnesses. And for that reason no divorce was celebrated. See also Canterbury Sede Vacante S.B. III, no. 27 (1294) where the reason given is that after marriage and consummation 'famam subsequenter fuisse exortam videlicet quod dictus Thomas congnovit carnaliter consanguineam dicte Mabel'. Similar cases are Canterbury Ecc. Suit, no. 310 (1269); York C.P.E 181 (1389–90); F 189 (1454).

[26] York C.P.F 202 (1362); the fourth degree of consanguinity was involved.

verify the facts as stated by the parties. The court therefore left their marriage intact.[27] The records show that unless there were unimpeachable witnesses who could testify with certainty that the impediment of consanguinity or affinity existed, the courts would not dissolve a marriage.

The records also make clear one reason that proof of kinship was not more readily available. People forgot, or never knew, exactly how others were related. There is good evidence of this in the Act books. Witnesses were often uncertain of what degree of consanguinity or affinity, if any, existed. In a Canterbury case of 1293 for instance, some witnesses claimed the parties were related in the fourth and fifth degrees of consanguinity; others said it was the third and fourth degrees; some said they were not related at all.[28] The result is that no divorce was celebrated. We find the same unsureness in other cases. There is testimony that 'some say they are related by consanguinity; some that they are not'.[29] There is talk of consanguinity, but the witness thinks it is only because the couple 'have the same surname'.[30] A man is unwilling to object at the reading of the banns; 'he was uncertain of the computation of the direct line of consanguinity, therefore he was silent'.[31] That there should have been uncertainty and forgetfulness is hardly surprising. The memories of medieval men were no doubt more tenacious of genealogy than our own.[32] But they were not infallible.[33] And, except sometimes for the upper classes, there were few birth records or official documents to help them. Especially when men moved from one part of England to another, the

---

[27] Canterbury Ch. Ant. A 36 I, f. 11r (1326), an *ex officio* divorce for precarnal knowledge of a woman said to be related to the wife in the third and fourth degrees of consanguinity.

[28] Sede Vacante S.B. III, no. 39 (1293). 'Dicit se nichil scire de aliqua consanguinitate inter predictos H. et M. Dicit tamen quod quidam retulerunt sibi quod sunt in tercio et quarto, aliqui in quarto et quinto gradu consanguinitatis.'

[29] Ibid., no. 37 (1293): 'Quidam dicunt quod sunt consanguinei, et quidam quod non.' Lyndwood, *Provinciale*, 75 s.v. *justum errorem*, seems to envision the likelihood of mistake or uncertainty in these cases; also of fraud.

[30] York C.P. E 108 (1370).

[31] York C.P. F 202 (1462). Another reason for his silence was that the girl was pregnant. Other instances: Rochester *Reg. Hamonis Hethe*, 931–92; York C.P. E 140 (1371–72); Canterbury Sede Vacante S.B. III, no. 59 (1292); X.10.1, f. 87r (1415); Ely EDR D/2/1, f. 113v (1379), Lichfield B/C/1/1, f. 322r (1471).

[32] See H.M. Cam, 'Pedigrees of Villeins and Freemen in the Thirteenth Century', *Liberties and Communities in Medieval England* (London, 1963), 124–35.

[33] Ibid., 129–30, noting a case in which a dispensation for the fourth degree of consanguinity was sought even though no one was actually able to trace the relationship.

difficulty of finding men who could remember accurately the requisite pedigrees was considerable. The conjunction of this difficulty with the canon law's high requirements of proof was, I suggest, an effective bar to many claims of divorce for affinity and consanguinity. Even if an unhappily married man or woman were cynical enough to think of it as an escape, it would often have been a matter of extreme difficulty to find witnesses who could prove the relationship.

Whether or not this is sufficient explanation for the small number of these claims is not, perhaps, a matter which can be proved absolutely. One thing is certain, however. There is little evidence in the court records that Papal dispensations played a role in relieving the hardships of the system. Esmein was of the opinion that the rules of consanguinity and affinity could never have worked, had it not been for the availability of dispensations.[34] Certainly *a priori* one would have thought so. And we should have expected some at least to turn up in Act books. From an occasional mention we learn that process on dispensations from Rome naturally came before Church tribunals. The normal dispensation was not a blanket Papal approval of the legitimacy of a particular marriage. It was an authorization for the local bishop to permit the marriage if he found the facts to be as stated in the dispensation. Further proceedings by the bishop and his officials were called for, and proceedings of a judicial nature.[35] Only after a finding, for example, that the relationship was exactly as given in the Papal letter, that the parties were both willing for the matter to go forward, that the girl had not been abducted, and so forth, could the bishop allow the marriage to be celebrated.[36] In addition, we should expect to find dispensations pleaded defensively in divorce suits, and perhaps in *ex officio* prosecutions.

Whatever our expectations, however, the surviving court records yield almost no information. There was a dispensation from the impediment of affinity claimed in a 1373 Canterbury suit. But when

---

[34] Esmein, I, 90.

[35] A case recorded in Rochester DRb Pa 3, f. 424v (1461) is styled *negotio dispensationis*. There is also dispensation process recorded in a York Act book slightly after the period covered by this study: Cons. A B 5, fols. 6r–6v (1507).

[36] For example, the dispensation for John earl of Pembroke and Anna daughter of Walter de Manny in Canterbury Reg. Langham (Lambeth Palace Library), f. 68r (1368) is a letter to the archbishop first setting out exactly the grade of consanguinity covered, then continuing, 'Fraternitati tue de qua in his et aliis specialem in domino fiduciam obtenemus per apostolica scripta committimus et mandamus quatinus si est ita, dictaque Anna propter hoc rapta non fuit, ac parentum et maioris partis consanguineorum circa tercium gradum comitis et Anne predictorum ad id accedat assensus . . . auctoritate nostra despenses.'

time came for proof, the party could not produce it.[37] A dispensation was put in by way of defense in an Ely *ex officio* prosecution of 1381. The court held it insufficient.[38] There is a solitary case at Rochester. The Cause papers at York, which generally deal with litigants of higher social standing, provide three cases of disputed dispensations.[39] But that is all. Dispensations otherwise do not appear outside episcopal registers, in which there are normally only declarations noting a finding in favor of the grant. Probably, as historians have often said, dispensations were simply not available to ordinary people. The chaplain in one York case who had been sent to the Papal court to obtain a dispensation covering the third and fourth degrees of consanguinity came back without success. He said that 'even a hundred pounds would not have secured it'.[40] Perhaps this was just an excuse for his ineptitude, but it may also be that dispensations were simply not easy to obtain. In any event, we must look elsewhere than to Papal dispensations in explaining why divorces for affinity and consanguinity were so few.

Before leaving this subject, let me turn to an objection. A real difficulty is that the explanations given here do not square with what is usually said about the habits of the nobility and upper gentry. We know that these people secured dispensations to marry their kin. And we know that they did secure divorces on the grounds of consanguinity and affinity. The question has not, so far as I know, ever been statistic-

---

[37] Y.1.1, f. 8v (1373).

[38] Ely EDR D/2/1, fols. 108r, 151v, 153r (1381): 'Johannes Slay . . . exhibet quandam dispensacionem a cardinali Raven' sibi factam, sed quia dicta dispensacio non est sufficiens, ideo demandetur sentencia divorcii.'

[39] C.P. E 140 (1371–2); C.P. F 187 (1452); C.P. F 280 (1491). It is worthy of note that the first two of these cases held *against* the applicability of the dispensation, the grounds being that its terms did not specifically cover the situation. Whether any judicial process had been held when the letters of dispensation had first been issued by the collector does not appear. For example, in the 1452 case, Alice Houghton sought to divorce Robert Shirburn for kinship in the third and fourth degrees of consanguinity. He put in a dispensation, against which her lawyers argued: (1) the dispensation made no mention that Alice was kept by force until the marriage had been solemnized; (2) no cause was expressed in it; (3) the dispensation says that Alice sought relaxation of the law, while she was in fact ignorant of the whole matter; and (4) it mentions Alice's duty to have children for Robert, whereas in fact she was past child-bearing age. The dispensation had been issued by the Papal collector in England.

[40] C.P. E 109 (1370): 'Ipsemet accessit ad Romanam curiam in urbe et ibidem fecit et adhibuit omnem diligenciam quam potuit pro huiusmodi dispensacione optinenda et finaliter responsum fuit quod si potuisset dedisse centum libras pro huiusmodi dispensacione, eam non optinuisset. Et sic iste iuratus non expedito negocio ad patriam rediit.' Another witness recalled that the chaplain had multiplied the figure to one thousand pounds by the time he told the witness the same story.

ally studied.[41] Probably it can never be. We do well, therefore, to be cautious.[42] But there is real evidence that the upper classes did not treat these rules as absolute. This makes it especially hard to accept an explanation for the relative absence of such cases from the medieval Act books which is based, at least in part, on a general belief in the rightness of the Church's kinship regulation. Especially does the difficulty appear substantial when we see the upper classes marrying without having secured the necessary dispensations, but only, as the phrase went, *sub spe dispensationis*.[43] This argues for a kind of carelessness about consanguinity, for an attitude closer to our own impatience with such rules. Can the attitude of the common people have been different? I do not suppose that this difficulty can be entirely got over. But part of the answer lies in the widespread acceptance of the power of the Church. Holding that marriage with a kinswoman is normally wrong, but accepting that the power entrusted to the Church is sufficient to allow relaxation in any one case is perhaps not our own attitude. It is nonetheless a perfectly rational point of view. The lower classes, cut off from relief by Papal dispensation, simply accepted the kinship prohibitions. Perhaps the forgetfulness, the lack of records, the stiff requirements of proof, and the freedom to move about in search of marriage partners were enough to make the system, with all the artificiality so irritating to us, workable within medieval conditions. Whatever may be thought, however, historians do wrong to speak of the ease and the frequency of divorce for consanguinity and affinity in medieval England. It is not so.

(iii) Impotence

The canon law, we saw in the previous chapter, held that consent, not coitus, made a marriage valid. This principle was not, however, carried to the point of enforcing a marriage which either of the parties was incapable of consummating. It was possible to secure a divorce *a vinculo* because of the impediment of impotence. Canonists dis-

---

[41] See the remarks by C. N. L. Brooke, 'Problems of the Church Historian', *Studies in Church History*, 1 (London, 1964), 14–15.

[42] On the danger of generalizing from evidence about the upper classes, see Lawrence Stone, 'Marriage among the English Nobility in the 16th and 17th Centuries', *Comparative Studies in Society and History*, 3 (1961), 182.

[43] There is also another common phrase, e.g. Canterbury Reg. Islip (Lambeth Palace Library) f. 162v: '. . . ipsi scientes se quarto affinitatis gradu adinvicem esse coniunctos tanquam simplices et legis ignari et non in contemptu clavium matrimonium. . .'

tinguished several possible causes of the incapacity – lack of sexual organs, natural frigidity, 'quasi-natural' frigidity, and impotence caused by *maleficium* or *sortilegium*. Slightly different legal consequences followed from each. Esmein traces these in detail.[44] All but one of the cases I found, however, alleged the man's natural impotence.[45] The libels in these cases followed a fairly standard pattern, on the model of the language of the decretals. The woman alleged a legitimate marriage, subsequent cohabitation (usually for the canonically prescribed three year period), the woman's desire to be a mother, and the man's inability to satisfy that desire. She asserted that as a consequence the marriage could not stand, and asked to be divorced.[46]

The difficult problem in these cases was that of proof. The canonists were quick to point out the danger of collusion.[47] They suggested several ways of verifying the fact of impotence. One was a three-year trial period.[48] A second was seven-handed compurgation of the parties' oaths that no intercourse was possible.[49] A third was inspection of the woman's virginity by qualified matrons.[50] Hostiensis and Panormitanus allowed a fourth: inspection of the man by 'expert and honest men', on the theory that what was used for women should be applied equally to men.[51] There was some variety of opinion among the canonists as to what combinations of these methods should be

---

[44] Esmein, I, 241–50; the fullest discussion I have seen in the works of the canonists is Hostiensis, *Summa Aurea* IV, tit. *de frigid. et. malefic.*, nos. 1–9.

[45] York C.P. E 259 (1369) is a lone exception; the man was alleged to lack any sexual organs.

[46] E.g. Canterbury Sede Vacante S.B. III, no. 127 (1293); York C.P. E 105 (1370).

[47] E .g. *gl. ord.* ad X 4.15.7 s.v. *septima*: 'Omnis enim cautela quae adhiberi potest in talibus est adhibenda propter periculum animae.'

[48] X 4.15.5: 'Si frigiditas prius probari non posset, cohabitent per triennium: quo elapso, si nec cohabitare voluerint et iuxta decretum Gregorii, mulier per iustum iudicium de viro probare potuerit quod cum ea coire non possit, accipiat alium.' On proof in impotence cases, see Esmein I, 250–67.

[49] X. 4.15.5; 'Cum septima manu propinquorum vel vicinorum bonae famae, si propinqui defuerint, tactis sacrosanctis evangeliis uterque iureiurando dicat quod. . .'

[50] See X 4.15.7: '. . . a matronis bonae opinionis, fide dignis, ac expertis in opere nuptiali dictam fecistis inspici mulierem.'

[51] *Summa Aurea* IV, tit. *de frid. et male.*, no. 14: 'Dic virum inspiciendum [est] per homines expertos et honestos'; Panormitanus, *Commentaria* ad X 4.15.1, no. 5. The medieval English canonist William of Pagula probably meant the same thing. He wrote, 'membrum viri est inspiciendum', but did not specify who was to carry out the inspection. *Summa Summarum*, Huntington Library MS EL 9/H/3, f. 266v.

used.[52] But no canonist I have seen prepares us for the method used in English practice. What we find in the records from York and Canterbury is a group of 'honest women' deputized by the court to inspect not the woman, but the man. Together, the women attempted to incite, with appropriate action and exhortation, the man's sexual desires. The story of one such 'inspection' may be set out:

The same witness exposed her naked breasts, and with her hands warmed at the said fire, she held and rubbed the penis and testicles of the said John. And she embraced and frequently kissed the same John, and stirred him up in so far as she could to show his virility and potency, admonishing him that for shame he should then and there prove and render himself a man. And she says, examined and diligently questioned, that the whole time aforesaid, the said penis was scarcely three inches long, . . . remaining without any increase or decrease.[53]

That done, the women (there were the canonical seven present at the time) cursed the unfortunate man for his failure, and walked out.[54]

This crude method was not used in every case, even at Canterbury and York. In some actions the court was satisfied with the canonically appointed oath or proof *per aspectum corporis* of the woman.[55] There

---

[52] Innocent IV advises leaving the method of proof to the discretion of the judge. *Apparatus* ad X 4.15.1, no. 2: 'Sed discretus iudex providebit, et utrum unum solum vel duo vel omnia tria iuramenta faciat prestari. Et cum in sentencia separationis matrimonii periculum anime vertatur, melius est quod superabundent probationes quam deficiant.' But this sensible suggestion was not taken up by most other canonists. See Esmein I, 255–8.

[53] York C.P. F 111 (1433): 'Ipsa iurata ostendebat mammillas suas denudates ac manibus suis ad dictam ignem calefactis virgam et testiculos dicti Johannis palpavit et tenuit ac eundem Johannem amplexabatur ac sepius osculabatur ac eundem Johannem ad ostendum virilitatem et potentiam suam in quantum potuit excitavit, precipiendo sibi quod pro pudore tunc ibidem probaret et redderet se virum. Et dicit examinata et diligenter requisita quod toto tempore supradicto predicta virga vix fuit longitudinis trium pollicium . . . , absque incremento vel decremento aliquali permanens.'

[54] *Ibid.*, 'Mulieres, ut dicit, tunc una voce maledicebant eo quod ipse presumeret ducere in uxorem aliquam iuvenem mulierem ipsam defraudendo nisi potuisset eidem melius deservire et placere.' See also York C.P. E 105 (1370); Cons. A B 3, f. 56v (1430); Canterbury Sede Vacante S.B. III, no. 127 (1292). Ely EDR D/2/1, f. 140 v (1380) may refer to the same method: '. . . quia commissa est palpacione viri, certificatum est nobis de eius sufficienti potencia.' The only other case I found in which the man 'passed' such an exam was in York C.P. F 175 (1432); one of the women testified that, 'Virga predicti Willelmi fuit melioris quantitatis in longitudine et grossitudine quam virga ipsius mariti uncquam fuit.'

[55] Canterbury Y.1.1, f. 77r (1374): 'Producta vii manu propinquiorum qui iurabant se credere dictam mulierem verum iurasse.' See also Ely EDR D/2/1, f. 91r (1378), in which the woman 'se offert per corporis sui aspectum et alio modo legitimo probaturam'. In Canterbury Y.1.1, f. 70r (1373), a team of five men investigated a man's alleged impotence.

is also no evidence for its continued use after 1450. I can find no authorization for it in the writing of the canonists. Perhaps 'inspection' by a team of women was an aberration of two English dioceses, one which had disappeared by the middle of the fifteenth century. The method does, however, illustrate the length to which the English courts went to prevent the abuse of divorce for impotence. There were few such divorce actions brought.

(iv) Force and fear

The present age must find the impediment of force and fear among the most interesting aspects of the medieval canon law. It is an index to the mentality of the times. And it held within it the seeds of later expansion. A marriage contracted under duress could be subsequently dissolved. The claim is found in the records both in divorce cases and as a defense in suits to enforce marriage contracts. We also find evidence of the use of threats to induce unwilling sons and daughters, or sometimes prospective spouses, to agree to a match. There are a few scenes in the records reminiscent of the 'marriage by capture' celebrated by anthropologists. But there is no reason to think that these were common.[56] The more usual case is that of the father who told his daughter that he would 'break her neck' unless she agreed to the young man he favored.[57] Or the man who, meeting resistance from his desired bride, knotted a towel around her neck and said, 'I shall throttle you with this towel', in order to win her agreement, or at least her acquiescence.[58]

Given the violence of medieval life, we should expect to find many cases like the above. But there were obstacles. One was that action subsequent to the marriage could easily prevent the claim from being

---

[56] The abduction of Esota Donwell by William Oddy and others is described in York C.P. F 253 (1472). The men arrived at her house, finding her upstairs, 'quam vocavit iste iuratus, ut dicit, dicens "Decende, Esota, quia certe nobiscum ibis." Ipsa Esota decendit ante adventum dicti Radulphi (her brother) sola camisa induta et assumpsit sibi vestes et induit se et exivit cum eis. Et famule ... isti iurato dixerunt adtunc sub hac forma: 'Allas, John, what mene ye that ye er of consell to take away our deme.' Quibus ipse, 'I lat you with that it is for her wele.' Et dictam Esotam, ut dicit, abinde usque domum habitationis cuiusdam Ricardi Redehed de parochia de Ripon contestis sui eadem nocte cariarunt.' The marriage was also subsequently solemnized *in facie ecclesie*. In York C.P. E 248 (1346), there is this description: 'Robertus de Gayrgrave ... et Simon de Monkton de quo agitur manus violentas in maiori ecclesia beati Petri Ebor' in Agnetem de qua agitur iniecerunt et ipsam invitam et reclamantem ac entus clamantem portarunt extra ecclesiam predictam, videlicet dictus Simon per capud et Robertus predictus per pedes.'

[57] York C.P. E 62 (1348).

[58] York C.P. F 257 (1477).

made. Later consent, sexual relations (except where themselves extorted by violence), or cohabitation for a sufficient time meant that there could be no divorce. These acts were held by the law to purge the effect of force and fear, and to ratify the previously voidable marriage.[59] A union entered into under duress became indissoluble. How many such cases were there which never came before a court? We can scarcely hazard an intelligent guess.

A second obstacle lay in the considerable degree of force necessary to warrant a successful claim for divorce. Not every argument, every strong inducement, or every threat was enough. This was a period, the canonists tell us, when it seemed right and natural for children to follow their family's wishes. The headstrong girl marrying for love alone, against the desires of her family, did not win the approval of the canonists for upholding the ideal of free consent in marriage. She was within her rights, and she should incur no penalty or punishment, but she was acting against a legitimate authority.[60] To allow divorce for every subtle pressure seemed both unnecessary and wrong. The standard adopted by the canon law was this: if the threat of force were such as to have moved a 'constant man' or a 'constant woman' the marriage could be invalidated. If it were less, no divorce was available. Now, such a standard was necessarily flexible. Apart from community standards, perhaps it had no meaning at all. It laid down no binding test. Neither can the cases give us an absolute rule. They can only provide some instances of the way the 'constant man' test was applied in the later Middle Ages.

Here are some examples drawn from the records. In one case the threat of death to a girl and her father was enough to warrant a

---

[59] *Gl. ord.* ad C. 1 q. 1 c. 111 s.v. *post mensem*: 'Argumentum quod si aliqua alicui invita tradita fuerit et aliquanto tempore cum eo in domo manserit et cum potuerit non effugerit, si postea virum dimiserit, poterit revocari ab eo quia ex tanto tempore consensu ratum fuit matrimonium.' The usual length of time was given as a year and a half by canonists, on which see X 4.1.21. See also Panormitanus, *Commentaria* ad X 4.1.28, no. 6: 'Carnalis copula subsequens pargat metum praecedentem et convalidat matrimonium, saltem ex nunc.' See also X 4.1.28; 4.18.4; 5.17.7; this last decretal uses the revealing phrase, 'si prior dissensio transeat postmodum in consensum, et quod ante displicuit tandum incipiat complacere'. A case where later sexual relations were admitted but claimed to be the result of force is found in Canterbury Y.1.2, f. 122r (1398).

[60] E.g. Hostiensis, *Summa Aurea* IV, tit. *de matr.*, no. 27: 'Quicquid leges dicant, incurrit tamen filia vitium ingratitudinis nisi voluntati patris consentiat.' Guido de Baysio, *Rosarium* ad C. 31 q. 2 s.v. *si verum*: 'Non ideo dicit quod sine patris et matris et consanguineorum non sit matrimonium firmum, sed debet ibi esse ut honestius non ut necessarius vel efficiens.' *Gl. ord.* ad C. 22 q. 4 c. 22 s.v. *matrimonium*: 'Vel loquitur quando levis fuit coactio, illa enim non impedit matrimonium.'

divorce, although it does not appear that the actual weapon to be used in the murder was brought out.[61] So was the threat of imprisonment where the place 'ad modum carceris' was ready and probably shown to the girl.[62] But the threat to a young girl that she would be taken by her ears and thrown into a pool unless she contracted marriage was not enough, at least where others were present who would probably have prevented it.[63] In one case a brother caught a young man in a suspicious place waiting for his sister and prevented his departure with unsheathed swords. This was sufficient force to invalidate the marriage contracted there, though no open threat of using the swords was made.[64] But for a woman to surprise a young man in bed with his girl and oblige them to repeat present words of consent by harsh tones, added to the natural awkwardness of their situation, was insufficient.[65] For a father to say to his daughter, 'thou shall never have penyworth of goodes of myne and thou shall have goddis malisoun and mynn', unless she agreed to the desired match did warrant a divorce, where the girl had first indicated her dislike of the arrangement.[66] But the mere loss of a 'certain portion of land' to the family did not raise enough force and fear to sway a constant woman.[67] Where the

---

[61] Lichfield Reg. Le Scrope, fols. 86r–91v. This came to be recorded as part of an *ex officio* action against the woman, Elizabeth, daughter of Robert Lumpley, for living in alleged adultery with the husband she had taken after the original divorce. She was absolved, at f. 91v (1393).

[62] York C.P. E 259 (1368). Impotence was also alleged in this case, however. In *Barker* v. *Waryngton*, York C.P. F 127 (1417), the threat by a master to turn his servant over to a local court for punishment because of repeated acts of fornication was also held enough to warrant a divorce. It is significant that the servant sought for some time to persuade his master not to force the marriage, making it clear that he would not have married the girl except for the threat of the court action. See Cons. A B 1, fols. 36v, 38r for the outcome.

[63] York C. P. E 85 (1362–3).

[64] York C. P. E 26 (1334). For a French case also involving unsheathed swords, see *Registre des causes civiles de l'officialité épiscopale de Paris, 1384–87*, ed. J. Petit (Paris, 1919), col. 50 (1385).

[65] York M 2 (1) f, fols. 17r–17v (1382). This case very closely resembles one recorded in X 4.1.15.

[66] York C. P. F 268 (1485). In *Harvngton* v. *Savvell*, York C.P. F 263 (1443), the brother's threat to deprive a widow of her property rights was likewise held enough to invalidate the marriage. Witnesses said that he could have carried out the threat, and the woman was crying at the time of the marriage. In Canterbury Y.1.1, fols. 93r, 110r (1375) a divorce was granted where the parents confessed to using 'verbera et minas' to secure their daughter's consent. Unfortunately, the record is not complete enough to say what the actual threats were.

[67] York C.P. F 97, 98. 105 (1429–32). A divorce had been granted in the first instance, before the official of the archdeacon of York. This was reversed on appeal. This was in turn appealed to the Roman court. Much of the argument on appeal, however, relates to the veracity of the witnesses.

girl was fiercely beaten with staves prior to the marriage to induce her consent, divorce was allowed.[68] But where the girl's family brought staves to the marriage contract only (they said) for use in getting over ditches on the way, no divorce was granted.[69]

Whether any consistent principles emerge from these cases is hard to say. It is important to remember that other factors than the nature and quantity of the threatened force could be equally important in a decision. What were the ages and reputations of the people present at the time? How had the girl acted before and after the marriage? How often had she expressed her dislike of the whole idea? Medieval canonists always suggested the importance of the surrounding circumstances in the application of the 'constant man' test.[70] And, if the record of the matters introduced into evidence give a reliable picture, judges took that suggestion seriously. It was relevant, for instance, that the woman had been unable to hold a cup of beer without spilling it on the day of her marriage.[71] So was it that one witness had never seen the couple 'speaking amicably or favorably as husband and wife' since the time of the contract.[72] That a girl had been thinking seriously of going 'to other unknown and remote parts' in preference to marriage was recorded in one deposition.[73] Sometimes the witnesses were asked to give their own estimates of whether the threats had been enough to sway a constant man or woman.[74] Properly speaking a legal rather than a factual question, the estimate of the

---

[68] York C.P. F 223 (1442).

[69] Canterbury Y.1.1, fols. 17v, 21r (1373): 'Item an compellerunt dictum Alanum per verbera ad contrahendum matrimonium cum ea, dicit quod non. Item an dicti testes venerunt ad eam de nocte cum baculis, dicit quod venerunt cum baculis ad saltandum ultra fossas patrie sicut oportuit quia de longe venerunt, et non ad malignandum.'

[70] Innocent IV, *Apparatus* ad X 1.40.6, no. 1: 'et si negetur iustus metus, arbitrio iudicis relinquitur'; Raymond of Pennaforte, *Summa* Iv, tit. *de impedimento violentiae*, no. 3: 'Et sic iudex, secundum diversitatem personarum et locorum iudicabit qualis sit metus, et iudicabit matrimonium aliquod, aut nullum.' Hostiensis, *Summa Aurea* IV, tit. *de matr.*, no. 27: 'Breviter, bonus iudex examinabit, et determinabit, inspecta qualitate personarum inferentium vim, et patientium, et violentiae seu coactionis loci et temporis, et assiduitatis minarum ratificationis expresse vel tacite vel continuationis dissensus.'

[71] See York C.P. F 37, 54, (1410).

[72] York C.P. F 268 (1486): 'Nunquam vidit ipsos favorabiliter aut amicabiliter ut virum et uxorem colloquentes citra tempus matrimonii inter ipsos contracti.'

[73] York C.P. F 223 (1442). The girl also said to a witness that, '... se málle presenciam parentum suorum relinquere et eorum paternitatem et maternitatem amittere quam consentire ad habendum predictum Thomam in maritum suum.'

[74] E.g. York C.P. E 26 (1334). One witness answered candidly, 'Sed an idem metus potuisset in constantem virum cadere, qui ut dicitur eidem Johanni fuerat per eundem Ricardum illatus, nescit.'

witness was evidently helpful to the judge in reaching a fair judgment.

Cases arising under the impediment of coercion, in other words, necessarily left a good deal of discretion in the judge. We cannot formulate an exact rule, from canonists or from practice, as to exactly how much force was necessary to meet the canonical test. All we can say is that the menace of loss of a person's inheritance or the threat of serious physical harm, backed with the sight of the instruments by which it was to be inflicted, appears to have weighed heavily with the judges. There had to be proof of the real possibility of the use of force or of the imminent loss of one's expected inheritance. The light fear, the 'reverential' fear which has been more largely developed in Catholic canonical practice of our own day played no part in marriage litigation of the later Middle Ages. The force and fear which moved a constant man had to be more than the insubstantial threat, the minor inconvenience, or the parent's urgent entreaty. We should not wonder at the paucity of divorce actions under this heading.

(v) The impediment of crime

The Church seems long to have felt a special repugnance towards the man who has lived in adultery with a woman, then gone on to marry her after the death of his first wife. It had once been a rule of canon law that no man might marry a woman he had 'polluted' by adultery. It may even have been true that an adulteress disqualified herself entirely from subsequent marriage.[75] But these were harsh rules, and no doubt impossible to enforce in a society where marriage customs were unstable and adultery not uncommon. By the time, therefore, that the classical law of the Church had been fully developed in the thirteenth century the impediment of crime had been considerably restricted. It required the conjunction of three things: the adultery, knowledge of the existing marriage by both offenders, and either 'machination' in the death of the first spouse or a sworn promise of marriage during her life. Only if all three elements were present were the two adulterers disqualified from contracting after her death. But this was a perpetual impediment. A divorce could be secured after any such second marriage had occurred. The adulterers were permanently disqualified from marrying.

The records produce only a few cases in which this impediment was raised. And these cases do not provide a clear or a consistent

---

[75] Esmein I, 384–93; J. F. Donohue, *The Impediment of Crime* (Washington, 1931).

picture of the way the prohibition was enforced. Alone of the canonical impediments treated here, there is a real possibility that this one was actually disregarded in practice. It seems best, therefore, to set out what evidence there is. An apparently clear instance of attempted enforcement of the prohibition is an *ex officio* prosecution heard in the Consistory court at Rochester. William Wrigt was cited for 'espousing a certain Edith Watt of the parish of St Mary, Hoo whom he had previously polluted by adultery'. William denied the charge *in toto*, and was assigned a day to undergo canonical purgation four-handed in support of his oath. But the Act book records no more of the case, so that it is impossible to tell what the outcome was.[76] Two cases, one from Ely the other from Hereford, raised the question of the impediment arising from adultery plus 'machination' in the death of the first spouse. In the Ely case, however, three causes for the second marriage's invalidity were in fact alleged, the second being affinity and the third the woman's pre-contract with another man. And since the court had reached no decision by the term covered by the last page of the Act book, it is impossible to know what disposition was made.[77] The Hereford case is also inconclusive, although for a different reason. In it a man was cited *ex officio* for having contracted marriage with two different women. He alleged, by way of defense, that he had previously secured a divorce from the first woman, the grounds being this perpetual impediment. That is, he alleged that a canonical divorce had been granted to him because he had married a woman he had previously 'polluted' by adultery. He was assigned a term to produce evidence of that sentence of divorce. But the Act book shows no sign that he did so.[78] In short, these three cases suggest the possibility of annulling a marriage for the impediment of crime. But they do not

---

[76] DRb Pa 4, f. 29v (1472): 'Willelmus Wrigt de Halgsto notatur quod desponsavit quandam Editham Watt de parochia Sancte Marie in Hoo quam prius polluit per adulterium, prout publice est detectus super eodem apud Eltham xxii[do] Junii. Comparet et negat articulum et habet ad purgandum se apud Roffam cum iiii[ta] manu vicinorum etc.' See also Canterbury Y.1.11, f. 341v (1474), in which Henry Lucas was cited *ex officio* because 'uxore sua scienter vivente duxit Isabellam Skypton in uxorem'. He submitted to the court and was ordered 'quod non veniat in consortio dicte Isabelle quousque docuerit quomodo disoneratur a prima muliere.' It is not entirely clear, however, that the first wife was dead at the time of this prosecution.

[77] EDR D/2/1, f. 149v (1381); the possible existence of the impediments was raised during the reading of the banns: '... et pro causis reclamationis proponunt quod dictus Nicholaus vivente uxore sua ipsam Margeriam in adulterio polluit quodque ipsi Nicholaus et Margeria in mortem dicte uxoris sue fuerant ymaginati; proponunt insuper quod quidem Walterus Grym ipsum Nicholaum in gradu consanguinitatis prohibito attingens eandem Margeriam carnaliter precognovit et cum ea matrimonium precontraxit.'

[78] O/10, 96 (1474); the defendant alleged that the 'divorcium per ipsum prius allegatum fuit celebratum, etiam dicit quia Isabella quam primitus desponsavit machinavit mortem ipsius.'

provide even one instance in which a court can be shown to have done so.

There is also evidence which points to non-enforcement. In 1342 Alice the wife of Sir Thomas Longley sought to divorce him in the court of York, alleging that during her marriage with Walter Kyrkebride she had lived in adultery with Thomas and contracted to marry him after his death. She produced several witnesses who so testified. The court held against her, refusing to grant the divorce. It may be, however, that the court simply did not believe her witnesses. Sir Thomas's proctor in fact objected to them as habitual liars.[79] The result may thus stem from simple failure of proof. In another case, heard thirty years later, witnesses testified to frequent adultery between a man and woman in the house of the man and his first wife. They testified that they had heard the man say, 'I give you my faith that I will espouse you after the death of my wife if you are then living'.[80] The court at York later held in favor of enforcing a marriage between the two adulterers after the death of the first wife, and against the man's exception of the existence of the impediment of crime. However, the difficulty is that the woman had not answered the above promise of marriage with a sworn pledge of her own. She had merely said, 'I hold thar to'.[81] It is possible, therefore, to explain the result of this case by assuming that the court did not find the requisite *mutual* promise of future marriage during the life of the first spouse.

The other cases raising the impediment are all susceptible of such interpretation. In one case, the testimony showing that the first spouse was alive at the time of the promise may not have been proved.[82] In another, both parties admitted all the requisite elements of the impediment, but were apparently unable to find witnesses to prove them.[83] And confession of the parties alone did not suffice to secure dissolution of the marriage. In a third case, the record is now too damaged to be sure that the three elements were proved.[84]

---

[79] York C.P. E 46: '. . . persone suspecte, leves et faciles ad deierandum.'

[80] York C.P. E 111 (1372): 'Do tibi fidem meam quod te sponsabo post mortem uxoris mee si tunc vivas.' The man himself only admitted to having said, 'Ita bene deligo te quod vellem ducere te in uxorem si uxor mea esset mortua.' The witnesses testified to the first language.

[81] Ibid.; the Latin given in the deposition is 'Sto ad illud', but the translation given in my text is also provided in this instance in the record of the deposition itself.

[82] York C.P. E 198 (1393).

[83] Rochester DRb Pa 1, f. 37r (1437). On this, see Jo. And., *Commentaria* ad X 4.7.8, no. 7: 'In foro iudiciali non crederetur coniugibus etiam ambobus si dicerent inter eos adulterium et fidem praecessisse.'

[84] York C.P. E 153 (1389).

One other case should be mentioned, since it appears to be an actual sentence of nullity granted for the impediment of crime. It was a suit for divorce between Peter Southchurch and Eva Lovecot. Peter had originally been married to Matilda Peyfrere. Five years later, 'led by fear of his parents and the loss of his inheritance', he repudiated her and married Eva. They lived together for several years, producing several children. But then Peter's father died. Peter took possession of his inheritance and left Eva. Matilda, his first wife, also died. Then – how much later is not clear – he brought an action of divorce against Eva before the official of London, alleging the existence of this perpetual impediment. On the facts given, he had a good case under the law. The judge at London did grant the divorce, after normal proof. But the sentence specifically stated as one of the grounds for the decision: 'Nor does any consent newly given appear proved between the aforesaid Peter and Eva.'[85] No fresh agreement of marriage had been given after the death of Matilda, the first wife. This assumes that, had there been new consent, the case would have come out differently. Eva and Peter could have validly contracted marriage again. So the case actually suggests the non-observance of the rule under discussion.

This is what evidence there is. It is difficult to interpret. We shall probably do wrong to base a firm conclusion on the one or two cases where the result seems clearest. But at least, we can say with some assurance that the impediment of crime was very hard to prove. None of the cases gives a clear instance of a divorce granted on this ground. That much cannot be said of any of the other impediments treated here. Possibly, the very frequency of the fact situation discouraged strict enforcement of the rule. We saw, under the heading of multi-party actions, how often it happened that a man married two women. Under the law and assuming consummation in both cases, the second wife could never lawfully marry the man if she had been aware of the first marriage. Even after the first wife's death, she was disqualified. Had the law been strictly enforced, therefore, substantial numbers of marriages would have been open to attack. The rule was, in addition, one of positive law only. Canonists wrote that it did not stem

---

[85] Canterbury Ecc. Suit, no. 220: 'cum nec aliquis consensus inter predictos Petrum et Evam de novo probatus appareat.' The sentence of divorce also adds, 'salva eidem de novo consensus si quam de iure habeat questionem'. An apparently similar case, in which no divorce was granted because new consent had been given, but in which also the couple claimed that they had abstained from sexual relations after notice of the first marriage came to the woman, can be found in Lichfield, Reg. Boulers, fols. 52v–53r (1454).

from divine law.[86] In consanguinity and affinity cases, the Church courts adopted a policy which discouraged divorces for the purely positive rules of kinship disqualification. Doubtful cases were decided in favor of marriage where the claimed degree was prohibited simply by human law. It may be that the same attitude towards a strictly positive rule of law was adopted here, particularly since it would have meant the upsetting of some long-established unions. But I confess that this can be no more than a suggestion.

(vi) Infra annos nubiles

Canon law held that a marriage contracted by a child below the age of seven was void. A marriage contracted between seven and puberty was not invalid. It had rather a suspended quality.[87] The child had the choice of ratifying the contract or of reclaiming against it on reaching the age of puberty. Subject to two rather difficult exceptions, the age of puberty was fixed at fourteen for boys and twelve for girls.[88] In the normal course of affairs, approval was shown by cohabitation and consummation of the union. Dissent had to be made publicly, and it was in theory to be made before the bishop or his court.[89]

It is often said, and with some reason, that marriages were often contracted by, or for, children in the Middle Ages.[90] It is therefore somewhat surprising how few cases appear in the Act books involving reclamation against such marriages. Perhaps almost all children ultimately agreed with their parents' choice. No court proceedings were then necessary. It is also possible, however, that many public disavowals were made, but that no court action was brought. Although properly made before a court, reclamation did not have to be made there. It was valid without a formal court action. Hostiensis noted

---

[86] Panormitanus, *Commentaria* ad X 4.7.3, no. 4: 'Cum illud sit impedimentum juris positivi, non debet ita taxari ut restringatur facultas contrahendi matrimonium contra dispositionem juris divini.' Sanchez wrote, *De Matrimonio* Lib. 7, d. 79, no. 24: 'Postremum observendum est, hoc impedimentum esse solo jure ecclesiastico inductum, atque ita non habere locum inter infideles nisi speciali lege sit apud eos inductum.'

[87] X 4.2.14: 'Si puella nubilis non erat aetatis, . . . , proculdubio inter eos non coniugium, sed sponsalia contracta fuerunt.' See Esmein I, 211–16.

[88] The boy might be old enough in years, but 'talis appareat quod nullo modo possit generare'; *gl. ord.* ad X 4.2.3 s.v. *tardissime*. The girl might be too young in years, but old enough in body so that 'malitia supplet aetatem'; *gl. ord.* ad X 4.2.3 s.v. *generare*. There is a long discussion of the problem in Lyndwood, *Provinciale*, 272 s.v. *non pervenerit*.

[89] *Gl. ord.* ad X 4.2.7 s.v. *iudicio ecclesiae*: 'Et ita patet quod sponsalia dissolvi debent iudicio ecclesiae tantum.'

[90] E.g. Pollock and Maitland, *HEL* II, 390–2.

that, if necessary, reclamation could be made simply before witnesses.[91] Proceeding in the Church courts entailed some expense, and
when there was no debate about the legal merits, the only concrete
result was publicity. Sometimes publicity was worth having.[92] But
usually a legal action was superfluous; the parties made their own
arrangements. Only when the parties themselves disagreed and when
each felt that he could present a valid argument, was there need for
the divorce suit which appears in the remaining Act books.

Most suits which do remain turned on the question of proof of age.
It was not always easy to determine exactly how old children were in
the Middle Ages. On the question of whether children had in fact
reached the ages of twelve and fourteen, we meet real uncertainty and
disagreement. There were, of course, no records of birth or baptism
to settle the question. Witnesses were thrown back on *aide-mémoires*
like the coincidence of the birth of their own children, their arrival
in a village, and so forth.[93] It is also worth noting that a number of
suits for divorce by reason of non-age added a claim that the marriage
was invalid because of force and fear.[94] The two go naturally together,
of course. Children are more likely to be coerced than adults. And
particularly when proof of age was not certain, it must have seemed
appropriate to add a second allegation that the child had been forced
into the marriage. If one failed, the other might not.

[91] *Summa Aurea* IV, tit. *de desp. impub.*, no. 14: 'Dic quod tunc sufficit quod fiat coram
presbytero proprio et in eius defectum coram vicinis.' He added, however, that the party
should appear before the bishop as soon as possible.

[92] An example of ratification is found in York M 2 (1) c, fols. 10v-11r (1372), in which
the couple, married ten years before and now fifteen and twenty-five years old, were asked by the
judge if they were 'constanter perseverans in spontanea voluntate habendi' each other. They
said yes. The object was, obviously, to prevent any question thereafter being raised. Much
curious and interesting material on this subject, although from a later period, is collected in
Furnivall, *Child-Marriages, Divorces and Ratifications*. Suits to ratify or dissolve under-age
marriages seem to have been rather more common after the Reformation, but the author rightly
insists, at p. xxv, that they were legally unnecessary: 'But tho the first marriage was void, it was
of course sensible of persons of position and property, to prevent any future question arising, to
have this void wedding declared null by the Bishop's Court.' See also Oughton, *Ordo Judiciorum* I,
284: 'Solent tamen personae (in hoc casu) ante has secundas nuptias, agere [contra personam
illam cum qua de facto matrimonium fuit solemnizatum].'

[93] E.g. York C. P. F 89 (1425), in which the witness said she remembered the birth
because on that day 'ipsa iurata et maritus suus egerunt publicam penitentiam'; Canterbury
Ecc. Suit, no. 10 (1269), in which one witness recalled the date because 'frater suus venit
tunc de Ybernia'.

[94] E.g. Canterbury Ecc. Suit, no. 10 (1269–71); York C.P. E 89 (1365–7); E 97 (1368);
F 97 (1422).

(vii) Other grounds for invalidity

The preceding six impediments to the contracting of a valid marriage are those raised in the surviving records. The list does not exhaust the impediments that existed in medieval canon law. Error of person, error of condition, solemn religious vows, disparity of cult, and major holy orders all subjected a marriage to dissolution by divorce.[95] Of these, the second gave rise to a small amount of litigation. If a free man married a person of servile status, without knowledge of that status, he could secure a divorce after learning of the true condition, unless he subsequently ratified the marriage by fresh consent or sexual relations.[96] Three surviving suits raised this impediment. In one a divorce was granted.[97] In one it was denied on the grounds that the servile condition was known by both parties at the time of the contract.[98] And in one, the fact of servile status was denied, but no sentence has survived.[99]

My research has turned up no examples of the other impediments. I am far, however, from claiming that there were no cases raising them in actual practice. The surviving records are incomplete, and many Act books give the subject of each case only in general terms. But with these reservations, the negative evidence seems worth stating. If the other impediments were raised in actual practice, I have not found them.

DIVORCE A MENSA ET THORO

A divorce *a mensa et thoro* was a judicial separation, a declaration by an ecclesiastical court permitting a man and wife to live apart, but without granting them the right to remarry. The marriage bond remained intact. There were three causes for which a divorce *a mensa et thoro* could be secured under canon law: adultery, 'spiritual' fornication (heresy or apostasy), and cruelty (*saevitia*).[100] Reconciliation subsequent to the act of cruelty or adultery, or a plaintiff's own adultery, barred the separation. But subject to these qualifications, the canon

---

[95] A succinct exposition of these can be found in Hostiensis, *Summa Aurea* IV, tit. *de matri.*, nos. 26 & 27; see also Esmein I, 211–402.

[96] See C. 29 q. 2; X 4.9.2.

[97] York C. P. F 59 (1410).

[98] Ely EDR D/2/1, fols. 55(B)v, 58v–59r (1376).

[99] York C. P. E 237 (1397).

[100] X 4.19.5; X 4.19.7; Esmein II, 89–95; the last of these, divorce for *saevitia* was not found directly in the canonical texts, but was developed by the canonists themselves.

law would not force a man and woman to live together if one partner threatened the principles of true religion, the rule of marital fidelity, or the physical well-being of his spouse.

These suits do not occur frequently in surviving court records. Perhaps many separations were arranged privately. We can say nothing of them. But the suit for divorce *a mensa et thoro*, despite its scarcity, deserves examination and discussion. It illustrates, perhaps better than any other type of litigation, the flexibility of the ecclesiastical tribunals. In most marriage cases, the judge determined the legal merits of cases presented by rival litigants. The outcome depended on application of the law to the evidence presented. In separation cases, the judges acted as arbiters of points of law if the parties demanded a legal decision. But preferably they took the role of mediators. The cases show that their paramount goal was to bring quarrelling couples to concord and agreement. If we think of the ecclesiastical judge as a rather heavy-handed marriage counsellor, we come nearer the truth than if we see him as a man who limited himself to the determination of points of law.

This characteristic is explained, in part, by the fact that almost all the separation cases were brought for cruelty, rather than for adultery or heresy. And cruelty depends largely on the attitude of the parties themselves. How do they regard each other? Do they understand fully the duties involved in marriage? What does it seem likely they will do in the future? In cases of *saevitia*, the courts apparently sought to change the attitudes of the parties, to end the discord which lay behind the acts of cruelty. Robert Handenby, to take a specific instance, was sued before the Capitulary court at York in 1390 by his wife Margaret. She asked for a sentence of separation. 'Discord has recently arisen', she explained. But there was no trial. After discussion it was agreed that they should live together as man and wife; 'and in the event', the court held, 'that the aforesaid Robert shall in the future treat the same Margaret badly, and this can be proved by two legitimate witnesses, then the aforesaid Margaret may effectively secure a divorce with respect to bed and mutual servitude between herself and the same Robert.'[101] This has all the marks of a compromise, of an amicable settlement. It has none of the marks of a formal trial. The

---

[101] York M 2 (1) f, f. 20v: 'Et in eventu quod de cetero prefatus Robertus ipsam Margaretam male pertractaverit et hoc per duos testes legitimos poterit probari, quod ex tunc licebit prefate Margarete divorcium quod ad thorum et mutuam servitutem inter ipsos Robertum et Margaretam prosequi cum effectu.'

same movement to concord appears in other cases; for example, this one from Canterbury:

Thomas Waralynton appeared and was sworn to treat Matilda Trippes his wife with marital affection with respect to bed and table, and to furnish her with those things which are necessary in food and other materials according to his ability. And the woman was sworn to obey him as her husband etc.[102]

The authority of the court, or the persuasion of the judge, was enough to enforce a return to their marital duties on a quarrelling man and wife.

One means at the command of the judges was the power to impose a guarantee (*cautio*) on the husband to treat his wife fairly and honestly. According to the canonists, this might take several forms: by sureties, men willing to stand behind his good behavior; by the pledge of goods or money; or in a suitable case by the man's oath alone.[103] To whom a money pledge was given is not specified in the records. But in any event, considerable use of the *cautio* was made in practice. Men were commonly obliged to find the sureties imposed by the court. Once they had done so, their wives had to return to their conjugal duties.[104]

Sometimes the marital discord had progressed to a point where no agreement to live together was possible, even with a *cautio*. Perhaps the couple were irrevocably set on a separation. The Church court

---

[102] Canterbury Y.1.1, f. 28v (1373); 'Comparuit Thomas Waralynton et iuratus est tractare Matildam Trippes uxorem suam maritali affectione tam in mensa quam in lecto et ministrare sibi necessaria in victualibus et aliis materiis iuxta posse suum. Et mulier iurata est obedire sibi ut marito suo etc.' In Canterbury U.41, f. 58r (1394), this settlement is recorded: 'Dictusque Ricardus Merwyn in iudicio coram prefato domino commissario personaliter comparens fatetur et dicit se velle ministrare prefate Johanne alimenta necessaria si voluerit secum commorari.' Something like the opposite situation apparently occurred in London MS. 9065, f. 56v (1489), where the husband admitted having said, 'quod si ipsa Anna rediret ad eius consortium ipse peius eam verberaret quam prius fecit casu quod non mutaret eius conditionem.' No result survives, however.

[103] *Gl. ord.* ad C. 32 q. 1 c. 5 s.v. *sub cautela*: 'Si mulier nihil allegat de suspicione viri, dic sufficere nudam promissionem; si autem dicit eum esse suspectum oportet ut idonea cautio ei prestatur, scilicet fideiussores vel pignora vel etiam iuramentum si forte illud magis timet vir.' For an example see Lichfield B/C/1/1, f. 244v (1469), where the man was assigned a term 'ad producendum duos fideiussores pro securitate pacis'.

[104] E.g. Hereford o/3, 78 (1446): 'Dicta mulier proposuit quod non audebat commorari cum viro suo propter eius seviciam, quare commissarius decrevit ipsam fore committendam custodie patris et amicorum suorum quousque vir securitatem sufficientem invenerit de dampno corporali eidem mulieri per ipsum non inferendo.' This would seem to have left the husband some choice, and some room for bargaining between the couple.

then normally served to sanction the arrangement. Doubtless some efforts at reconciliation were made. But if in the end a man and wife persisted, they were not compelled to share the same table and bed. A case of 1454 from Canterbury is particularly revealing of what went on in such cases. John Colwell and his wife Margaret asked the court for a divorce *a mensa et thoro*. The judge then sought, by words both smooth and harsh (*per blanda et aspera*) to persuade them to change their minds. But they said they would prefer death in prison to living together. They claimed they were living in daily fear of their lives as it was. Finally, they both said they wished to live apart chastely. The court granted them license to do so without calling any witnesses.[105] In a York case of 1420 Richard Wilkynson and Margaret his wife appeared in court. The record states that they had 'unanimously consented to live separately and apart, and for that reason to divide, separate and distribute equitably between themselves all their common goods and belongings'.[106] This was allowed, and four arbiters, two nominated by each party, were chosen to carry out the division.

Whether or not these apparently arranged separations were legal under formal canon law is open to argument. At first sight, they seem clearly contrary to the law. The Church strongly reproved the institution of the 'pact of mutual separation', the private arrangement by which two parties swore never to sue each other for restitution of conjugal rights. Such pacts had the effect of a divorce *a mensa et thoro*. The law held them to be null and of no effect.[107] Also, there was sufficient reiteration in the texts that husband and wife were bound to live together. Unless there was a specific and sufficient cause for divorce they both must fulfill their marital duties.[108]

---

[105] Canterbury Y.1.5, f. 37v: 'Tandem concorditer dixerunt quod vellent continenter vivere. Et quilibet eorum petiit licenciam ab altero ad continenter vivendum et optinuit. Et interrogavit iudex de etate ipsorum; vir dixit se liiii annorum et mulier xlviii. Et iudex consuluit eisdem quod super hoc bene deberent deliberare et ante perfectionem voti licenciam ordinarii haberent et cogitarent bene ...' In Hereford o/2, 86 (1442): 'Ex consensu partium iudex prebuit consensum quantum in ipso fuerat quod separater maneant dumtamen caste vivant et non aliter.' No adultery or cruelty is recorded in the Act book as having been alleged or proved.

[106] York Cons. A B 1, fols. 177r–177v; another York case, M 2 (1) c, f. 22v (1374), contains this solution: 'Et dictus Ricardus et Alicia unanimiter consenserunt seorsum et separatim commorandi et hoc a domino officiali instanter petierunt. Set dictus dominus officialis dixit expresse quod noluit eis licenciam concedere seorsum commorandi, set bene permitteret ad tempus quousque pax et concordia inter eos melius fuerit reformata.'

[107] On this see Dauvillier, *Marriage*, 354–6.

[108] *Ibid.*, 350–2.

Is it fair, however, to say that the law meant to exclude these judicial separations entirely? The ruling against private pacts of separation does not *necessarily* cover this situation, for those pacts were simple private acts, not judicial sentences. What parties acting on their own could not lawfully do, perhaps an ecclesiastical court could. This might seem particularly appropriate where there was no question of breaking the marriage bond, but only of allowing a separation which could itself be undone by subsequent concord of the parties. A second argument for their legality is that, according to Panormitanus, where separation was sought because of adultery, the confession of the parties alone sufficed.[109] Unlike cases of divorce *a vinculo*, no independent proof was necessary. Could not the same be applied to cruelty cases?[110] If the parties confess that they cannot cohabit without savage fighting, could not the court sanction a result in accord with their confession, even if it is also in accord with their desires? A certain flexibility was called for in any case, because this ground for separation came not from the requirements of the canonical texts themselves: it came from the development by the canonists, reflecting the needs of the legal system in daily practice. If the canonists might permissibly go this far, might not the courts take the next step for the same practical reasons? To encourage quarrelling couples to come before the Church courts was certainly a worthwhile goal. There, effective efforts at reconciliation could be and apparently were made. It would have been scant encouragement had a man and wife known that, unless they had witnesses to prove cruelty, a court would be bound to pronounce a sentence against their desire to live apart.

The bulk of the separation cases in the remaining records were handled by monition and concord. The judge sought to bring the parties to agreement. But not every case could be settled amicably. Not every man and woman had agreed beforehand on a result. Not every one could be brought to compromise. When the parties insisted on a strictly legal hearing, the courts heard their cause accordingly. On the basis of admittedly meagre evidence (there are many more cases of agreement), two things about these cases are worthy of note.

---

[109] *Commentaria* ad X 4.19.3, no. 2: 'Ubi agitur de adulterio ad separationem tori valet confessio solius conjugis; nam ad solam confessionem mulieris fuit hic separatum matrimonium quod torum. Secus est ubi agitur de substantia vinculi.'

[110] One case in which this was expressly stated is Lichfield B/C/1/2, f. 25v (1471): 'Dictus David confessus est ceviciam suam et dicta Agnes iuravit ad sancta dei evangelia per ipsam corporaliter tacta quod timet cevisiam mariti sui, et statim post lata est sentencia divorcii a mensa et thoro.'

First, physical force or injury was necessary to warrant a divorce *a mensa et thoro*.[111] Probably a good deal more was necessary than was required to invalidate a marriage initially contracted under threat of violence. All the cases examined involved the actual infliction of physical harm. Margaret Neffeld of York, in a contested action of 1395–6, produced witnesses to show that her husband had once attacked her with a knife, forcing her to flee into the street 'wailing and in tears'. Another time he had set upon her with a dagger, wounding her in the arm and breaking one of her bones 'vulgariter nuncupatum le Spelbon'. Margaret's husband disputed the petition. Whatever he had done, he claimed, was reasonable, honest, for a licit cause, and solely for the purpose of 'reducing her from errors'. The court held that no cause for divorce had been made out. Subject to a reasonable *cautio* to guarantee fair treatment, the couple were compelled to live together.[112]

What is interesting about this case is not so much what it says about the amount of violence required to constitute actionable *saevitia*. That could vary from case to case. Perhaps the judge here felt that the woman had provoked her husband. Its interest lies rather in the variety of treatment between those cases where the parties could reach agreement and those in which they were real contestants. Where they insisted on their rights under the law, the results were quite different from where they did not.

The second fact of note about contested cases is that, besides showing actual violence, they normally contained allegations and charges of more general character. These seem to have been designed to convince the judge of the innocence and good faith of the one party and of the unworthiness and deceit of the other. Usually they were little more than recorded shouting matches. In *Wyvell* v. *Venabils*, for instance, the petitioner described her husband as 'vir valde et multum ferox, astutus et terribilis'. He, on the other hand, described himself as 'honestus, mansuetus, sobrius, pius, affabilis, quietus, pacificus, humilis, ac aliis virtutibus multipliciter insignatus'. The wife thought

---

[111] On this subject, see J. M. Biggs, *The Concept of Matrimonial Cruelty* (London, 1962) which covers the post-Reformation period and incorporates cases from the Court of Arches.

[112] York C.P. E 221 (1395–6); it is worth noting that, despite the degree of violence necessary to warrant separation, the allegations in this case speak of the same 'constant man' standard as applicable: 'propter iustum metum dicti Thome . . . qui potuit et debuit in constantem mulierem cum dicto Thomas in thoro et mensa aut eidem ut viro suo legitimo adherere non audet nec audebit aliqualiter in futurum.' However, in York M 2(1) c, f. 15v (1374), trying to kill one's wife by throwing a knife at her was enough to warrant a divorce *a mensa et thoro*. In Cons. A B 1, f. 16or (1420), a separation was allowed where the man had broken the wife's arm.

she could fairly be called 'mulier honesta, humilis, benigna et suavis'. Her husband saw her as 'inobediens, crudelis, horribilis, terribilis, abhominabilis, inquieta, vociferox, et clamosa, et quasi virago'. What weight such extravagant allegations had with the judge can only be conjectured. In this case they were coupled with a claim of an armed attack by the husband, during which he cut his wife so badly that her eye fell out of its socket onto her cheek. It would have been lost for good had not the woman's mother replaced it 'gently and subtly'.[113] Properly speaking, the general and conclusory allegations had no legal force. One had to prove cruelty by concrete acts, not by mere name-calling. But in this area, where the courts looked to the harmony of the couple as often as to the legal merits, we cannot be sure that the sharpness of the descriptions was irrelevant to the judge's decision.

Before leaving this subject, there is one minor point to be discussed. It is a question raised, but not settled, by Esmein. Did a divorce *a mensa et thoro* leave the obligation to support one's wife intact?[114] The English cases, unfortunately, do not furnish a clear answer, although they do provide evidence. Most of the cases noted above do not, even where the sentence has survived, mention any continuing alimony payments. But there are a few cases where it was made part of the decree. In *Dencourt* v. *Mervyn* we find:

And it was agreed then and there between them that the aforesaid Richard should pay or cause to be paid to the aforesaid Joan Dencourt his wife every year to the end of her life the sum of five marks sterling.[115]

One other instance in which payments were specified in the decree comes from Canterbury.[116] The question cannot be dealt with conclusively. Perhaps as suggested by the language of the quoted case, the matter was one for bargaining in each individual suit. Such an answer has the merit of consistency with the judicial attitude towards

---

[113] York C. P. F 56 (1410). The court held for divorce, but adultery was also alleged. The man's principal defense was remission by the wife: 'ex sua certa sciencia ac hillari et iocundo vultu eidem Henrico amicabiliter et graciose remisit.'

[114] Esmein II, 95–6; he found one canonist who supported the continuance of the obligation, but also one case from 1371 which pointed the other way.

[115] Canterbury U. 41, fols. 70r–70v (1394): 'Et concordatum est tunc ibidem inter eosdem quod prefatus Ricardus solvet aut solvi faceret prefate Johanne Dencourt uxori sue singulis annis ad terminum vite sue ... quinque marchas sterlingorum.'

[116] Y.1.4, f. 79r (1422): 'Insuper fatetur dictus Robertus quod prefatus magister Philippus Morgon assignavit dicte Matilde vi s. viii d. de bonis dicti Roberti solvend' annuatim tempore vite sue. Et huiusmodi summam fatetur se solvisse.'

divorce *a mensa et thoro*. They were the object of negotiation and concord wherever possible.

MISCELLANEOUS CAUSES

(i) *Reclamatio bannorum*

The *causa reclamationis bannorum* deserves mention both because cases appear in the Act books specifically so styled, and because its existence illustrates the importance of the publication of marriage banns in medieval society.[117] That publication was not the quaint but pointless formality it has become today in English churches. For the young man or woman with a past of careless words or actions, the reading of the banns must have been a moment of real anxiety. The vicar's question, 'If any of you know just cause why they may not be lawfully joined', was not infrequently answered. John Fisher, to take an interesting example, stood up during the reading of the banns between John Frost and Amy Brid and said, 'Mirabile est quod mulieres ita variant. Si fuisset fidelis, fuisset uxor mea.'[118] The ordinary procedure was then to suspend solemnization of the match (the contract by *verba de presenti* may have taken place already) and to cite all parties concerned before the appropriate court. On occasion, however, the incumbent went ahead with solemnization, or the matter was settled locally.

As suggested by the instance of John Fisher, most cases of reclamation during banns occurred when the person objecting had a claim to be married to one of the parties. These cases usually resolved themselves into the three-party suits described in the preceding chapter.[119] Most of the surviving cases seem to have been based on *bona fide* claims of marriage contracts. A few, however, were plainly

---

[117] See the discussion in Lyndwood, *Provinciale*, 273 s.v. *solemnem editionem*; Esmein I, 422–7.

[118] Ely EDR D/2/1, f. 85r (1377).

[119] Rochester DRb Pa 1, f. 65v (1438) is a good example: 'Johannes a Hale de Estpecham citatus est per vicarium de Eldyng super reclamatione in bannorum editione in ecclesia predicta inter Johannem Simond iuniorem et. Johannam Rugmer alias Harblott filiam Willelmi Rugmer de Eldynge. Compareant partes personaliter et iurati de veritate dicenda, dicit pars reclamans, impetitus de causa reclamationis sue, quod precontraxit cum eadem muliere sub ista forma videlicet quod dixit eidem, "Ego veni causa habendi te in uxorem meam," et illa respondebat, ... "In me non invenietis defectum si amici mei ad hoc consentiant." Et dicta mulier dixit quod nunquam matrimonium contraxit cum eodem. Super quo idem reclamans produxit Thomam Forde, dicendo se plures testes non habere.' This witness was examined and found to know nothing of the alleged contract. 'Et dominus officialis direxit literam vicario de Ealdyng' ad solempnizandum matrimonium inter dictos Johannem Simond et Johannam Rugmer ... reclamatione predicta non obstante.'

vexatious. In hopes of securing a bribe, or without any possible way of proving a claim, a man or woman objected to a proposed marriage.[120] One reason this could happen is that anyone was allowed to object to a marriage at the time of the reading of the banns for whatever reason. No prior claim or family tie with the couple was required.[121] A person was by law obliged to reclaim if they wished to be heard against the marriage at a future date, unless they could present a legitimate excuse for not having done so.[122] The prohibition against later accusation by those who had stayed silent during the banns was, however, one of the rules of canon law most laxly enforced. Witnesses were allowed to testify when their only reason for failure to reclaim was that they had not believed it would do any good. Or they were not absolutely positive about the impediment.[123] Arriving at the truth about the matter was more important than the enforcement of an essentially procedural rule.

(ii) *Alimentatio prolis*

Panormitanus wrote that a parent's duty to care for his child was part of the natural law. Given the necessity, it could not be disregarded.[124] That duty found concrete expression in the action for support of a child, often brought by the mother of a child born out of wedlock against the father. How frequent the arrangement was and how careful the Church courts were to secure the rights of such children cannot be determined. Most of the agreements or settlements were probably made informally, or at least not recorded in the court

---

[120] In Canterbury Reg. Islep, f. 107b (1355), a man later confessed, '. . . se ad dictam Margeriam nullum ius habere confitente, set ipsum ad molestandum eam ut libellatur solicitum fuisse et inductum.' In Hereford I/3, 46 (1500), the reclaimer did not even appear at the court hearing. It is possible, of course, that he had been induced not to press a legitimate claim in the meantime.

[121] Reclamation must be distinguished from the *accusatio* against an existing marriage; in the latter a number of rules restricted the number of people who could question the marriage's validity. See Hostiensis, *Summa Aurea* IV, tit. *qui admittitur ad accus. matr.*, no. 1; Esmein I, 422. An example of the reclamation made by an apparently disinterested party is found in Rochester DRb Pa 1, f. 356r (1443), in which the reclaimer said that the woman had earlier told him that she had only contracted conditionally. In Canterbury Y.1.7, f. 18v (1459) a man reclaimed because he had heard that the woman had made a prior contract of marriage with another man; he had no apparent interest himself.

[122] X 4.18.6.

[123] E.g. York C. P. F 201 (1430). Canterbury Ecc. Suit, no. 49 (1288); no. 181 (1294).

[124] *Concilia* (Lyons, 1555), f. 76v: '. . . sed ipsum ius alimentandi data necessitate tolli non potest cum sit de iure naturali.' See also Antonius de Butrio, *Commentaria* ad X 4.7.5, no. 11: 'Nam educatio filiorum est de iure naturali, et ius naturale ex instinctu naturae procedit.'

records. The records contain, by and large, only actions to enforce arrears of payments. We see the case only when the father had first defaulted.

There is, therefore, little to be said about this aspect of practice beyond the fact of its existence. The amount of support (where there is evidence) varied between one penny and three pence per week for each child.[125] In one York case the man paid five shillings to cover the following half year.[126] Very likely, as with alimony payments in divorce suits, the amount depended on the resources of the father. In one case, the father alleged poverty (*insufficientia bonorum*) after he had been ordered to pay two pence weekly. The court allowed this. The action ended with the man swearing an oath to satisfy mother and child 'according to the effect of that decree when he shall come to more abundant fortune'.[127] This suggests that, in practice, the duty was not so absolute as Panormitanus suggested.

(iii) *Subtractio uxoris*

The modern legal action called 'alienation of affections' has an ancestor of sorts in medieval canonical practice. It was possible to sue someone who had participated in the 'diversion' of one's spouse. For example, Thomas Holmaston sued Thomas Frogenhall in 1422, charging that Frogenhall 'subtraxit [eam] de marito suo ac consensum et favorem sibi prebuit ad subtrahendum se de marito suo'.[128] It is likely, however, that most such claims were made in the royal courts. Professor Milsom has recently shown the availability of the writ of trespass to cover abduction of one's spouse.[129] And Statutes of 1275, 1285 and 1382 expressly granted a right of action for the abduction of a wife.[130] Money damages were available in the royal courts, whereas the ecclesiastical courts offered only restitution of the abducted spouse ar 1 penance imposed on the offenders. Most litigants seem to have been satisfied with the secular remedy. The scarcity of these cases in

---

[125] 2d. in York Cons. A B 2, f. 65r (1425); 3 d. in Canterbury Y.1.2, f. 103v (1398); 3 d. in York M 2(1) f, f. 22v (1388); 1 d. in *Reg. Hamonis Hethe*, 951 (1347); 2 d. in Canterbury Y. 1.1, f. 83r (1374); 3d. in Canterbury Y.1.3, f. 185v (1421).

[126] York M 2(1) b, f. 9r (1371); he also paid 4s. 3d. in arrears.

[127] Y.1.1, f. 83r (1374).

[128] Canterbury Y.1.4, f. 78r. Frogenhall denied the claim, however. The suit called *causa impedimenti restitutionis obsequiorum coniugalium*, occasionally found in the records, almost certainly amounted to the same thing. See Canterbury Y.1.8, f. 299r (1472), in which such a suit was brought together with an ordinary restitution action against the woman.

[129] 'Trespass from Henry III to Edward III'. *L.Q.R.*, 74 (1958), 210–11.

[130] 3 Edw. I (West. I), c. 13; 13 Edw. I (West. II), c. 36; 6 Ric. II, st. 1, c. 6.

the surviving Act books appears to support that conclusion. There are, in any event, not enough of these suits to allow for extended treatment. We can say only that the Church courts would entertain them, noting their existence as an interesting instance of duplication in jurisdiction between royal and ecclesiastical courts.

(iv) *Enforcement of gifts in consideration of marriage*

Of somewhat similar nature is the suit to enforce a promise made in consideration of marriage, typically the *maritagium*. A man promises to a couple twenty-five shillings when they marry, and then refuses to pay. The couple may sue to get the money. Or the money is given in advance and then the marriage is dissolved or does not occur. The man may sue in the ecclesiastical court to get his gift back. This type of suit could not have been prohibited by the royal courts, according to Bracton, if the gift consisted of money rather than land.[131] An aggrieved party had his choice between an action in the royal courts and one in the Church's tribunals. A sample verdict from the Church court records, one settled on appearance and confession of the defendant, is taken from the diocese of Bath and Wells: 'He confesses that he owes 100 s. to John Sweting and his wife Sourmilde from his promise in consideration of their marriage, for which sum the said official adjudges him liable.'[132]

This suit, accessory to matrimonial cases properly speaking, was not frequently brought in the Church courts. It deserves our attention principally as showing the wide net cast by the Church's jurisdiction, and the flexibility and utility of the courts in dealing with problems related to marriage. It ought also to be noted that I have found but three cases heard in the Church courts for the recovery of dower.[133] This was doubtless an area which, whether through force of prohibitions, acquiescence of Church officials, or choice of litigants, was normally left to the royal courts.

---

[131] Bracton, f. 407b; Glanvill, *Tractatus de legibus et consuetudinibus regni Anglie*, vii, 18, ed. G.D.G. Hall (London, 1965), 93: 'Spectat enim ad iudicem ecclesiasticum placitum de maritagio tractare si pars petentis hoc elegerit.'

[132] D/D/C A1, 48; 'Fatetur se debere Johanni Swetyng et Sourmilde uxori sue ex promisso suo ad maritagium eorundem C s., in qua summa dictus officialis condempnavit eundem.' In York C.P. E 12/1 (1323) action was brought both to recover 180 marks and to enforce a promise of enfeoffment of land worth 20 marks.

[133] York Cons. A B 1, f. 135v (1419): 'Tradita per dictum M. J. Willyng quadam proposicione in scriptis petendo dotem et res parafornales dicte Emlay.' Two other examples: Rochester DRb Pa 1, f. 224v (1440); Canterbury Y.1.4, fols. 5v, 13v (1419).

SUMMARY

Suits to annul marriages made up a secondary part of marriage litigation in the Church courts throughout the medieval period. They were
always outnumbered by cases involving the enforcement of clandestine
marriage contracts. The small number of divorce cases cannot be
accounted for by any one or two factors. Each impediment must be
examined separately. For some, like consanguinity and affinity, the
explanation lies in the combination of the people's serious attitude
towards the impediment and the law's stiff evidentiary requirements.
For others, like the annulment of marriages contracted before the
age of puberty, the correct explanation probably lies in the fact that no
legal consequences hinged on the bringing of such a suit. For some,
like the impediment of crime, it is impossible to do much more than
suggest possible reasons for the scarcity of cases. The records do not
tell us more. However, they do show one thing beyond doubt. The
Church courts were not divorce mills. Whether they 'failed miserably
as guardian of the holy estate' of matrimony, as Lacey thought, is
perhaps a separable question.[134] But it cannot be said that the ecclesiastical courts of England did a thriving business dissolving marriages
on the basis of flimsy, artificial, and inadequately proved impediments.

In divorce cases, as in suits to enforce marriage contracts, it can be
objected that the courts looked at the marriage bond in a 'com-
mercialized' way. They treated the litigation as a branch (though a
rather special branch) of the law of contracts. But in handling cases of
judicial separation, and in hearing the miscellaneous causes discussed
above, no such reproach can be made. Here the courts showed real
flexibility. The judges attempted to restore marital harmony if that
was possible, to make the best settlement if it was not. The wide
range of remedial actions available for the care of children and for
the relief of deserted spouses shows the same usefulness of the canon
law in meeting men's needs. We shall find something of the same
practicality and flexibility in passing to the subject of the next chapter,
the procedure used in the Church courts.

---

[134] *Marriage in Church and State* (1912), 159.

IV

PROCEDURE IN MARRIAGE CASES

The importance to our topic of the examination of procedural practice should not be underrated. Few things are more valuable in understanding the law of marriage. The study of procedure reveals much about who controlled the progress of each case. It shows how far many parts of the law were put into effective practice. It allows for some conclusions about the canonical system in general. It even answers questions about the nature of marriage in the later medieval period. This chapter seeks to explore the salient features of procedure as they affected practice in marriage cases. It does not attempt an outline of formal libellary procedure. As we shall see, that would be misleading. Instead the chapter begins with an evaluation of the effectiveness of the courts in handling litigation. It then moves to a more detailed look at the important aspects of the procedural steps taken in most marriage cases.

It is best, however, to begin with a word of caution. There was scarcely a rule of procedure which did not, in practice, admit of exception. If we say that witnesses were examined secretly and outside of court, that would be true. But it is easy to produce specific cases in which the witnesses were examined openly before the parties, and during the regular session of a court.[1] If we note that the defendant answered the plaintiff's positions as the first step after the libel, before any witnesses had appeared, that too would be correct. Yet we find cases in which the positions were only answered after the examination of witnesses had taken place.[2] Or if we say that the courts depended

---

[1] E.g. Rochester DRb Pa 1, f. 65v (1438): 'Idem reclamans produxit Thomam Forde, . . . , et dictus officialis statim examinavit eundem et summarie in ista causa de consensu partium tunc ibidem.' Canterbury Y.1.3, f 122r (1419): '. . . deinde productis pro parte Simonis antedicti Johanne Hoth de Bredman et Johanne Bekell de parochia Dunstani, quibus et admissis ac examinatis apud acta et clare deponentibus per verba de presenti.'

[2] E.g. Canterbury Ch. Ant. A 36 IV, f. 18r (1340), where a term was set 'ad videndum terciam productionem et respondendum positionibus'; Lichfield B/C/1/1, 242r, 244v (1468), where a term was given 'ad publicandum dicta testium, reservato termino ad respondendum positionibus et articulis.'

almost entirely on the evidence produced by the parties themselves, that is a true and a significant fact. But practice shows at least one case in which the judge produced two witnesses of his own 'to supplement the failure and the contumacy' of the plaintiff.[3] The historian should, therefore, be guarded in making generalizations about procedure in the Church courts. Particularly should he avoid the assumption that what he reads in formularies or *ordines judiciarii* accurately describes what went on in court. There were too many exceptions. The interests and the desires of individual parties, lawyers, and judges too often combined to muddle any clear picture which the historian might be tempted to draw.

The variation in procedural practice is obviously significant in itself. It focuses attention on a simple but absolutely fundamental characteristic of matrimonial litigation in our period. Its object was to settle actual disputes between people who disagreed. If we regard marriage practice principally as the enforcement of principles of indissolubility or of kinship disqualification on the laity, we misjudge the matter. Such enforcement was sometimes undertaken, as in *ex officio* actions, though even here initiative lay finally with the parties themselves. But mainly, the Church courts were concerned with settling disputed claims of marriage. Thus, it is no surprise to find the parties and their lawyers agreeing to abide by procedure other than that found in formularies. What mattered to them was reaching an acceptable result, not following a fixed procedural pattern. Their freedom to vary the course of a lawsuit was not unrestricted, of course. The interests of opposing proctors and supervision by the judges were a check. The relationship between lawyers, court officials and litigants is a complicated matter. We shall find no precise formula to characterize it. But it is important to remember this: all of them had, first of all, an actual disagreement to be settled; that task took precedence. Procedure was a tool to be used in the task, not a model into which the disagreements were squeezed.

SPEED AND EFFECTIVENESS

Canonical procedure has commonly been criticized on two counts: first, for its long delays; second, for the inability to compel obedience

---

[3] Ely EDR D/2/1, f. 76v (1377): 'Ad supplendum defectum et contumaciam ipsius partis actricis.'

to its decrees.[4] Lengthy process, freely available dilatory tactics, and frivolous appeals meant that litigation in the Church courts could not be settled without inordinate trouble, time, and expense. And with only the sanction of excommunication, a weapon which had lost its terror through over-use and application to trivial and unworthy goals, the Church courts were unable to enforce either their sentences or their summonses. The records show that neither of these criticisms is warranted for marriage litigation. Whatever may have been true in actions over tithes or prebends, marriage cases were settled quickly and without serious difficulty from contumacy. There were, inevitably, some exceptions. A suit begun at York in December of 1386 was still going in October of 1389.[5] In a 1419 case at Canterbury, a defendant refused to appear in response to a final sentence of excommunication. The court had to threaten to write to the king, requesting the defendant's caption in accordance with the English practice of invoking the secular authority to enforce ecclesiastical discipline.[6] But these were unusual. The exceptional case should not be generalized into a rule.

Figures illustrate the relative effectiveness of the Church courts' handling of marriage cases better than descriptions of individual cases. Large numbers of them are unfortunately not forthcoming, because of the deterioration of recording standards in the Act books of the fifteenth century. Often the scribes did not set out all the procedure, so that we cannot expect to extract reliable figures from them. But there are enough complete records left to yield some useful information.

The records show, first, that the length of time taken to settle most marriage cases was fairly short. Many lasted only one hearing. Sometimes the plaintiff had no witnesses and his suit was summarily dismissed. Sometimes the defendant admitted the validity of the case against him, and the couple were declared married *per decretum*.

---

[4] E.g., A. Engelmann, *A History of Continental Civil Procedure*, trans. R. W. Millar (Boston, 1927), 453: '... circuitous methods and numerous adjournments'. And see D. M. Stenton, *The English Woman in History* (New York, 1957), 49; R. Hill, 'The Theory and Practice of Excommunication in Medieval England', *History*, 42 (1957), 10–11; W. W. Capes, *A History of the English Church in the Fourteenth and Fifteenth Centuries* (London, 1903), 239.

[5] York C.P. E 138.

[6] Y.1.3, fols. 98r, 101r, in which however the contumacious party subsequently appeared as a result of the threat. In Lichfield B/C/1/1, fols. 87r, 96r (1466), the only marriage case I found for the ten-year period 1465–74 in which signification was threatened, the contumacious party also appeared before it had to be put into execution. In Y.1.1, fols. 3v, 5r (1372), there was a threat of signification in a *causa alimentationis prolis*, but the defendant appeared in the next session so that the threat was not carried out.

Occasionally proof was immediately available and the case could be settled at once. But suppose we disregard all the cases settled in one or two hearings and take as a sample the first Canterbury Act book, running from November 1372 through May 1375. There are thirty-eight cases for which introduction and sentence can be traced.[7] The average time taken for their hearing was only five months and slightly less than seven and a half days. This seems rather quick for contested lawsuits. The Cause papers from York provide a second sample. There are sixty-one marriage cases from the fourteenth and fifteenth centuries in which dates for the introduction of the libel and final sentence are available. We should expect these cases to have taken longer. The parties were often of a higher social status and many of the cases were brought on appeal, so that harder legal issues were involved. Even so, the average time for completion of a case was only seven months and a little more than sixteen days.

At Rochester between 1437 and 1440 we have a much smaller sample. There are nine cases in which we can trace the opening and the definitive sentence. But here the average time was four months and about ten days. For cases introduced at Canterbury in 1416 and 1417 in which the start and finish can be seen – only eight if we again exclude cases heard in one session – the average comes out at a similar figure of four months and thirteen days. At Lichfield, in suits where the Act books record the introduction and sentence, the average time taken for hearing marriage cases in the ten-year period 1465–74 was six months and twenty-three days. All of these figures suggest, I think, that the delays in contested litigation were not great. Most cases were settled within a reasonable time.

Disobedience in the face of judicial orders also seems to have caused little serious difficulty in marriage cases. Most Act books contain many instances of minor contumacy. Parties sometimes failed to appear at the start of litigation in answer to a citation. The penalty for this sort of contumacy to answer a summons was usually suspension *ab ingressu ecclesie*. But this sanction was normally effective to bring the parties, or their representatives, before the court in an immediately following session. No recourse to excommunication and application for caption by the king had to be made. And on the more serious point of continued refusal to submit to ecclesiastical jurisdiction in marriage

---

[7] This involves omitting those cases which had been introduced before the start of the Act book and those uncompleted at the end. Some distortion of the average figure may therefore be involved, but since no cases overlapped at both ends, that distortion is slight.

cases, the Act books give evidence of no widespread disobedience.[8] The first Canterbury Act book is again the fullest record we have. Ninety-eight actions relating to marriage were heard in all; eight of these were still being heard at the end. But of all the rest, only two were not concluded by some sort of decision of the court. In only two cases, that is, does the entry 'pendet' indicate that the unwillingness of the parties to appear prevented a case from being closed. Figures drawn from the Ely Registrum Primum are only slightly less impressive. Between March 1374 and March 1378, eight of a total of fifty-five cases ended in a reading of 'pendet'. This does not seem excessive, particularly since most of the eight were apparently left pending because the plaintiff did not wish to prosecute.

The number of appeals taken after definitive sentences in marriage cases was not negligible. But the figures are not so great as to suggest that the right to appeal was frequently and deliberately misused. There are, of course, a great many appeals recorded in the York Cause papers. But that is one reason why they were preserved. And, on the other hand, some of the Act books produce no appeals at all. For example, none of the marriage actions heard at Rochester between 1437 and 1440 was noted as having been appealed. There are only two cases from the first Canterbury Act book in which an appeal was recorded. It may be that these are exceptional, or that the scribe simply did not record the fact of an appeal. In a Canterbury Act book of slightly later date, covering 1393 through part of 1395, we can be more certain. In it the scribe specifically recorded whether or not a sentence had been appealed. Here, of forty-one sentences seven were appealed to a higher court.[9] Later, in the years 1416 through 1418, we find sixteen sentences rendered in Canterbury marriage cases; of these three were appealed. In Ely, between March 1374 and March 1378, eleven appeals were taken out of a total of fifty-five cases. I cannot think that any of these figures justifies a conclusion that appeals were consistently misused. When one considers how uncertain the law was about what words make a valid marriage, how very large an area there was for legitimate doubt and disagreement in marriage cases, even the higher figures do not appear excessive.

---

[8] The incidence of deliberate and continued contumacy was, however, greater in *ex officio* prosecutions, as in disciplinary actions for fornication. It is probably dangerous to speak of a general attitude towards the Church courts without differentiating between different sorts of litigation.

[9] U. 41; the terminal date of this volume is not clear. It was not organized along the same strictly chronological order that most Canterbury Act books were.

It is regrettable that similar figures cannot be given for all dioceses. The unevenness of Act book recording makes it impossible. But certainly the figures given above are not misleading. It was a rare case which went on for more than a few months.[10] When one did, the explanation almost always was that the plaintiff had failed to prosecute it. Rarely were long delays due to the dilatory tactics or contumacy of the defendant. I do not contend that this necessarily holds true for other than marriage litigation. The exact opposite may be true elsewhere, although probably in no instance were the ecclesiastical courts as ineffective as the English royal courts at Westminster. Anyone who reads through an appreciable number of fourteenth-century plea rolls from the King's Bench or Common Pleas must be struck by the overwhelming number of cases in which nothing was done.[11] By contrast, the Church courts seem speedy and effective. Certainly they were in marriage litigation.

*   *   *

What explanations are there for the apparent effectiveness of the Church courts in settling marriage cases? Discussion of this question may be useful before passing to a more detailed look at the normal steps of litigation. One reason, perhaps the most important, is that marriage cases involved disputes over personal status. There is naturally greater urgency about settling the question of whether one is free to marry than there is about determining a question of land title or debt. Both plaintiff and defendant need to have their personal status clarified. And there is usually not, as a motive for delay, the hope of arriving at a compromise settlement, where each party gets part satisfaction, in suits to enforce marriage contracts or to annul existing unions.

Litigants also accepted that the Church courts were the proper place for determination of questions of marital status. There was no competing secular jurisdiction in England.[12] The older tradition of lay

---

[10] See also the remarks of E. F. Jacob, 'The Archbishop's Testamentary Jurisdiction', *Mediaeval Records of the Archbishops of Canterbury* (London, 1963), 49; M. Bowker, 'The Commons Supplication Against the Ordinaries', *T.R.H.S.*, 21 (1971), 67.

[11] See N. Neilson, 'The Court of Common Pleas', *The English Government at Work, 1327–1336* (3 vols, Cambridge, Mass., 1950) III, 265–6; M. Hastings, *The Court of Common Pleas in Fifteenth Century England* (Ithaca, 1947, repr. 1971), 168, 175–6.

[12] Questions concerning marriage could, of course, arise incidentally in the royal courts. And they were sometimes dealt with there. See Pollock and Maitland, *HEL* II, 380–4. For French practice, see Esmein I, 31–46.

control over marriage questions, we have already seen, was very much alive during this period. But the continuance of older ideas does not mean that people regarded the ecclesiastical tribunals as illegitimate or oppressive. It does not imply a resistance on principle to the summons or the sentences of the Church courts. Rather those courts were normal and accepted parts of life. If a man were involved in a marriage dispute, he might settle it privately, but he would not be surprised or outraged if the matter ended in the courts. We do, of course, find some objections. A man in London claimed he would 'break the head' of Richard the apparitor, 'or any other apparitor coming to cite him'.[13] A defendant in Rochester said angrily that 'whether the judge cursed or blessed [him], he would not obey the court's orders'.[14] There were 'murmurings' against the court at York in 1353.[15] But these are the complaints of angry and disappointed litigants. Evidence of widespread discontent with the Church's jurisdiction over marriage does not appear.

Court systems must generally depend on the acceptance of the people themselves. A system which relies on threats of punishment alone works with difficulty, if at all. Some men will always be unhappy with particular judgments, no doubt. But a broad base of agreement among those subject to a court's jurisdiction is a normal, perhaps even a necessary, condition if the system is to function. This was particularly true in medieval times when the courts did not have the powerful machinery of enforcement of our own day. And, to judge from our court records, the legitimacy of the canonical system of marriage law was accepted and approved. The survival of the system intact after the Reformation is a measure of how general that acceptance was. People expected to be cited before a Church tribunal in marriage disputes. And they normally were anxious to end the disputes. This expectation itself explains part of the apparent efficiency of the Church courts.

Second, the procedure and organization of the courts themselves

---

[13]   MS. 9064/1, f. 7v (1470): 'Dixit quod voluit frangere caput eius vel caput alicuius alterius apparitoris venientis illuc ad citandum eum.'

[14]   Rochester DRb Pa 2, f. 70v (1447). The man was summarily excommunicated, but appeared during the next session and submitted to the court.

[15]   Reg. Thorsby, f. 14r (1353); the Archbishop wrote to the official: 'Sicut accepimus quidam contra vos murmurare videntur, pretendentes quod curia nostra Ebor' minus bene regitur.' In Canterbury Y.1.11, f. 342v (1474), a man was cited for allegedly having said 'coram multitudo (sic) populi quod curia consistor' est falsa et omnes occupantes in eadem sunt falsi'. He denied the charge, however.

suggest several reasons for the effective way most marriage cases were handled. It is extremely difficult to picture what actually happened within a typical session of any court. But probably we should not imagine it as a very formal affair. If the records tell the truth, the courts were often crowded with litigants, witnesses, and their friends. They were said to be present 'in multitudine copiosa'.[16] It is no surprise, therefore, to have the scribe speak of 'magnitudo clamoris et diffamationis' in the court at Canterbury.[17] The language spoken was not rigidly controlled, for we read of Latin, French, and English all being used in the courts.[18] Sometimes the parties, even in the presence of their proctors, broke out in open protests against an action taken by the judge.[19] On a rare occasion, we can actually see the proctors bargaining informally with the judge. In one case from Durham, the official refused to accede to a proctor's request to go outside the court to interview a client. But he sought to persuade the proctor to continue with the case anyway. The proctor remained silent, until one of the apparitors present remarked sarcastically, 'Obmutescit et ludit mutum deum', whereupon the official concluded the case. The proctor immediately took an appeal *a gravamine*.[20]

There is little room for dogmatism here, but it is likely that informal discussion and bargaining between the interested parties went on all the time. That sort of informality provided an atmosphere in which cases could be moved relatively quickly to settlement. For instance, the judge at Canterbury in 1459 rejected one proctor's arguments. The proctor threatened to appeal, and the judge agreed to rehear what

---

[16] E.g. Ely EDR D/2/1, f. 28v (1375): York C.P. E 15 (1324); Durham *Reg. Langley* II, no. 325 (1414).

[17] Sede Vacante S. B. III, no. 464 (1269–72). In London MS. 9065, f. 155r (1493), it is recorded that William Billoke 'expulsus fuit a curia domini ibidem propter ebrietatem suam'.

[18] Canterbury Ecc. Suit, no. 380 (1270): '. . .a qua tanquam ab iniqua sedem Cant' primo sine scriptis gallice incontinenti. . .appellavit;' Canterbury Ecc. Suit, no. 34 (n.d.): '. . .sine scriptis vocetenus verbis anglicis dicta Alicia personaliter ob causam supradictam appellavit.' York C. P. F 132 (1421): 'Dictus officialis et procuratores aliquando in verbis latinis et aliquando in anglicis loquebatur.' Hereford I/1, 344 (1499): 'Dicta pars rea in anglicis asseruit "I appele and y aske wrytyng."' Canterbury Sede Vacante S.B. III, no. 7 (1271): 'Dicit etiam quod etiam in scriptis latine et vocetenus gallice et anglice sic fuit appellatum.' And in Canterbury Y.1.1, f. 85v (1374) there is express mention of a petition being read out 'in vulgari' to a defendant.

[19] York C.P. F 178 (1421), in which the defendant, duly represented by proctor, still objected when particular witnesses were introduced for the plaintiff: 'Eadem Agnes viva voce et vulgari lingua publice protestabatur.' A literary allusion to such an outburst is contained in the poem called 'A Satyre on the Consistory Court', *The Political Songs of England*, ed. T. Wright, Camden Soc., 6 (1839), 158.

[20] York C.P. F 132 (1421).

the witnesses had to say if he would withdraw the appeal.[21] In a suit before the official of the archdeacon of Nottingham begun in 1421, the defendant refused to agree to the sentence when it was read. The court agreed to hear the whole case over from the start, on the condition that the defendant would accept the new verdict 'absque diffugio appellationis cuiuscumque'.[22]

One reason such informality was possible is that the number of proctors practising in any court was seldom very large. The same men appeared over and over. Doubtless, they all got to know each other very well. Before the Commissary General of Hereford, for example, from 1497 through 1499 only four proctors appeared in marriage cases.[23] At Rochester, between 1437 and 1440, there were again only four men serving as proctors in marriage cases.[24] Even at the more important court of York, there were only seven proctors representing parties to marriage actions heard in 1417.[25] The matter cannot be absolutely proved, but it seems reasonable to suggest that the familiarity which must have grown up between these lawyers and the judges worked for speed and fairness in the handling of marriage litigation. Men who worked together constantly and who were not tied to rigid rules of procedure (as we shall see they were not) could the more easily move cases through the courts.

A third factor which made for quick handling of marriage litigation was the existence and the use made of summary procedure. Process 'simpliciter, de plano ac sine strepitu et figura iudicii' had been authorized by Pope Clement V in 1306.[26] His intent was to encourage the faster hearing of marriage disputes. The constitution *Saepe* authorized the judge to cut down the delays available, to omit the *litis contestatio*, to repel frustratory appeals, to restrain the number of witnesses.[27]

---

[21] Canterbury Y.I.7, f. 22v (1459): 'Tunc iudex reiecit materiam alias per Blundell propositam; et Blundell protestabur de appellando, et iudex propter informationem sue consciencie repetiit testes primitus in forma iuris iuratos etc.' A similar instance is recorded in York Cons. A B 1, f. 130r (1419).

[22] C.P. F 176 (1421–3). The defendant did not, however, accept the sentence. She appealed to the court at York.

[23] 1/2: Richard Wolfe, Hugh Grene, John Hide, and Hugh Jonys. There were also four proctors serving at Canterbury between 1416 and 1418. See Woodcock, 121.

[24] DRb Pa 1: William Swan, Henry Wilkhous, John Hisham, Richard Letot.

[25] Cons. A B 1: John Willingham, William Driffeld, John Ragenhill, Robert Esyngwald, Thomas Appelby, John Stanton, and John Sturneton.

[26] Clem. 5.11.2. The abbreviated process was probably in use before this date, however. See M. B. Hackett, *The Original Statutes of Cambridge University* (Cambridge, 1970), 29.

[27] See also Clem. 2.1.2 (*Dispendiosam*) (1311), which elaborates on the use to be made of summary procedure.

It did not define, however, exactly what procedure was to be used. We are left with the question, how did summary procedure work in fact? What difference did Clement V's constitutions make?

A post-Reformation canon lawyer defined the abbreviated process in these words: 'Now the Summary proceeding is said to be that in which no reason of order is kept, but rather all order is deserted, the Truth of the Fact only being inspected.'[28] This does not say much. Medieval canonists do not give much more exact definitions.[29] But they do say something instructive about canonical procedure in general. On the question of whether a written libel had to be introduced, for example, the Gloss on *Saepe* says, 'The libel should be introduced if it is demanded by a party, but if not demanded it is sufficient that it be recorded in the *acta*'.[30] Whether or not there had to be a libel depended on the wishes of the parties. This is just what we find in practice. Actions were often begun orally. If the defendant objected, the plaintiff reduced his petition to writing in a formal libel.[31] If he did not, if he answered the oral petition, the case went on without any libel.[32]

Under a system where the choice of procedure so often lay with the parties, it is impossible to define summary procedure exactly. Nor is

---

[28] Conset, *Practice*, 178. Oughton, however, suggests a number of more precise differences. For example, in plenary hearings exceptions were to be made in the term *ad proponendum omnia*, in summary cases in the term *ad audiendum sentenciam*. See *Ordo Judiciorum* I, 186. But I have not discovered that the medieval procedure was so precise, if indeed post-medieval practice was.

[29] E.g. Panormitanus, *Commentaria* ad X 2.5.1, no. 12: 'Nota quod potest iudici dari potestas per partes inquirendi et arbitandi non servato ordine iudiciario.' Lyndwood, *Provinciale*, 302 s.v. *summarie*: 'Breviter: ita tamen quod totam substantiam comprehendat, nihil omittendo de substantialibus.' For a fairly detailed discussion written before the formal adoption of summary procedure for canon law see Durantis, *Spec. Iud.* I, tit. *de off. omnium iudicum*, § *de summaria cognitione*. On summary process, see generally H. K. Briegleb, *Einleitung in die Theorie der summarischen Processe* (Leipzig, 1859, repr. 1969); Engelmann, *History of Continental Civil Procedure*, 492–504.

[30] *Gl. ord.* ad Clem. 5.11.2 s.v. *necessario*.

[31] E.g. York Cons. A B 2, f. 62v (1425): 'Magister Willelmus Driffeld peciit oretenus nomine dicte domine sue, ut asseruit, predictum Johannem Kyrkeby eidem domine sue in virum et maritum suum legitimum adiudicari, ... predictusque Johannes Kyrkeby peciit huiusmodi petitionem sibi dari in scriptis. Tandem datur dies crastinus eisdem partibus ad dandum et recipiendum huiusmodi libellum.'

[32] E.g. Canterbury Y.1.4, f. 99r (1423), where the plaintiff 'viva voce loco libelli peciit dictam Margaretam sibi adiudicari in uxorem.' Margaret answered negatively, and the action proceeded at once to proof. An interesting, rather similar record is found in Ely EDR D/2/1, f. 51r (1376), a suit on a marriage contract brought on appeal against Margery Smyth: 'Dicta Margaria consentit expresse quod procedatur in causa principali omisso articulo appellationis, eo quod dicta causa principalis est causa matrimonialis et accelerationem desiderat.' The express desire for 'acceleration' of marriage cases is also recorded in Rochester DRb Pa 1, fols. 248r–248v (1442); Canterbury Y.1.7, f. 84r (1461).

it always easy to differentiate between those cases heard summarily and those given fuller treatment. Clement V's constitutions served rather as a license for litigants and lawyers to speed up the hearing of a case according to their own interests and desires than it did as an exact model of the procedure to be followed. There are cases in which a hearing 'de plano ac sine strepitu et figura iudicii' was specifically asked for. But these cases sometimes used full documentation and dragged through multiple terms.[33] Equally, there are cases in which summary procedure was not requested which were handled with all the abbreviated steps we should expect from summary handling. It is probably fair to say that a plaintiff's request for summary process usually made some difference. But the wishes of the parties, together with the judgment of lawyers and judges, were, in my view, the more important factors. Their interests determined the form which, in actual practice, summary procedure took.

The records show several ways in which the process was commonly shortened. Acceleration was not normally accomplished by utter disregard for form. Most contested actions did follow an ordered pattern, albeit not a rigid one. There were, for instance, usually three terms for the production of witnesses. There was a term for speaking against the witnesses, one 'ad proponenda omnia in facto consistencia', one for concluding, and one for hearing sentence. English Church courts met (roughly) once a month or once every three weeks, exclusive of the harvest vacation. Had a separate term been used for each step, marriage actions would necessarily have lasted a long time. Therefore, the terms were often consolidated or compressed. Several steps were done at the same time. A day was often given, for example, 'ad ponendum, articulandum, et primo producendum'.[34] A term was sometimes set 'ad proponenda omnia in facto, et nichil proposito ad audiendam sentenciam'.[35] That is, more than one step took place during the same session of the court.

Moreover, several separate hearings were frequently held within the same monthly term. Witnesses, for example, were produced in

---

[33] E.g. York C.P. E 36 (1338), in which the petitioner asked for summary process, but still submitted a formal libel and positions divided into twenty-nine different points. In York C.P. E 87 (1364), the plaintiff asked for summary process, but produced twenty-two witnesses to prove his case.

[34] Bath and Wells D/D/C A1, 232 (1464).

[35] Canterbury Y.1.1, f. 67v (1374). Or see, for example, Canterbury Y.1.2, f. 84v (1397), where a term is simply assigned 'ad faciendum in dicta causa quod est iustum'.

the morning, and then a term was assigned 'ad publicandum hora tercia post nonam eiusdem diei'.[36] Or the libel and answer were made on one day, and 'iudex assignavit Hoog' ad ponendum et articulandum in crastino eodem loco'.[37] Or, in the term for publication of the depositions, the parties, 'hincinde exhibuerunt omnia acta etc. et hincinde concludebant'. The judge was able to set the time for giving sentence on the following morning.[38] It was common for two, three, even four or five steps to be handled within the same term.

Finally, the terms could be, and often were, renounced outright. Suppose, for instance, that a party produced all the witnesses he had during the first of the three terms available for the production of witnesses. Of what use were the normal subsequent terms? None at all. They could be, and often were, eliminated.[39] So could almost any of the other terms be dropped if the parties, or their lawyers, agreed. It is therefore natural to find that formal sentences often specifically make note of the renunciation of terms: 'ceterisque iuris solempniis in hac parte de iure requisitis in omnibus observatis seu saltem renunciatis'.[40] Renunciation of terms, along with the compression of several steps into one hearing and the multiplication of hearings within one term, were normal parts of canonical practice. Whether actually called summary process or not, they allowed for faster and more efficient hearing of marriage cases.

STEPS IN LITIGATION

It is impossible, therefore, to be dogmatic about the steps followed in marriage cases. There was too much variation in practice. We must be content with the observation that the nature of the litigation, the availability of summary procedure, the desires of parties and lawyers, and a certain informality in organization combined to move most cases easily through the courts. But there is good reason to examine a few characteristic aspects of the different parts of the cases. Such an examination opens several doors to understanding marriage practice in general.

---

[36] Hereford I/2, 121 (1499).

[37] Canterbury Y.1.7, f. 42v (1460).

[38] Canterbury Y.1.17, f. 111r (1498).

[39] E.g. Canterbury Y.1.3, f. 34r (1417): 'ex consensu partium renunciatis ulterioribus productionibus.' See also York C.P. E 23 (1332); Lichfield B/C/1/1, f. 269r (1469).

[40] Canterbury Y.1.5, f. 47r (1455).

(i) Opening hearings

It was usual, during the opening stages of an action, for both parties to be personally present in court. In law, representation of the defendant was not theoretically required.[41] As long as a legitimate citation had been made, a marriage cause could proceed against a contumacious defendant. The citation need not even have been made personally; if that was impossible, it was enough that it have been read in the defendant's parish church, near his house, or at other appropriate places. There is an occasional example of this, called citation *viis et modis*.[42] But usually both parties appeared, and generally in person at the start of the action. Afterwards they were normally represented by proctors. The courts, in fact, took some trouble to assure the first personal appearance. Even when legitimately represented by proctors, parties were often cited to appear personally. In the phrase most commonly used, a litigant was the 'legalior persona, et melius sciat veritatem'.[43]

The usefulness of such an initial appearance is obvious. It provided a chance for the court to hear the story of each litigant from his own lips. It allowed many actions of marriage to be settled at once, on confession of the parties. It is difficult to penetrate beyond the formal *acta* in most cases. But occasionally we catch a glimpse of this stage of a case. Alice Sagon, party to an action of marriage and divorce and *uxor de facto* of Robert Ederich, appeared before the court in Rochester in 1439. She told the judge that, 'as long as he satisfied her in her dower rights, it pleased her that there should be a divorce between them'.[44] Whether this blunt declaration had any weight with the judge we cannot tell. In the actual case, Alice and Robert were in fact divorced. Another striking instance of the importance of these initial hearings comes from a Canterbury case of 1455. John Water, appearing by proctor, asked to have Joan Chaundler adjudged his legitimate wife. His petition alleged mutual promises of marriage under the form,

---

[41] X 2.6.5 §Porro; *gl. ord.* ad X 2.6.1 s.v. *servetur*: 'Ubi agitur de foedere matrimoniali potest agi contra contumacem lite non contestata ad diffinitivam sententiam.'

[42] X 2.14.10. E.g. Rochester DRb Pa 1, f. 97r (1439): 'Et non potest eam personaliter apprehendere quia abscondit se et latitat, unde dominus officialis decrevit eam publice et per edictum in ecclesia de Hadlo et domo habitationis peremptorie fore citandam.' Ely EDR D/2/1, f. 8or (1377): '... viis et modis quibus poterit coram notis et amicis suis per quos huiusmodi citatio ad ipsius noticiam verisimiliter poterit pervenire, et ad domum suam ubi morari consuevit, et nichilominus in ecclesiis parochialibus ubi divina audire solebat.'

[43] Ely EDR D/2/1, f. 2or (1375); London DL/C/1, f. 2v (1496).

[44] Rochester DRb Pa 1, f. 109v: 'Dumtamen eidem ... de dote sua satisficiet placet sibi quod fiat divorcium inter eosdem.'

'accipio te in uxorem (virum) meam'. Subsequently cited to appear in person, John said that the actual contract had been by the words, 'I will take thee to my wyfe'. This put the case on a rather different footing. It may be that the second made a valid contract. The word 'volo' in marriage contracts was a troublesome one.[45] But it is certain that 'I will take' was not an exact translation of 'accipio'. The first hearing and personal appearance, in this case, considerably changed the issue.[46]

This initial appearance was enforced by the appropriate canonical sanctions, suspension from entry into the parish church, then excommunication, then (although very infrequently) by invocation of the 'secular arm', by requesting the royal government to order the sheriff to imprison the offender. The first of these was almost always enough. After the opening of a case, it was usual for any punitive action to be taken against an unrepresented or absent party. The penalty for contumacy, after the beginning stages of a lawsuit, was normally only the loss of a term. In the term set for speaking against witnesses, for example, if nothing could be done because of one party's contumacy, it was usual for the court to take this action: 'in penam contumacie, cedat terminus, datusque est dies in proximo ... ad audiendam sentenciam'.[47] Or in another case, the plaintiff failed to appear in the term set for 'ponendum, articulandum, et producendum'. The judge pronounced him contumacious, and in punishment for his contumacy decreed that he should be summoned for the next Friday 'ad secundo ponendum, articulandum et testes producendum'.[48] In other words, unless the other party demanded it, no ecclesiastical censure was imposed on the absent party.[49] The action went along as if he had been present and done nothing. The absent party merely forfeited one term.

At the end of each case, when it came time for sentencing, an

[45] According to the common opinion of most canonists, however, the words would constitute only *verba de futuro* since the verb 'to take' denotes initiation rather than execution of the marriage relationship. See Chapter 2, n. 42.

[46] Y.1.5, f. 155r; unfortunately no result survives for this case.

[47] Ely EDR D/2/1, f. 50v (1376).

[48] Canterbury U. 41, f. 68v (1394). This was perfectly lawful; no specific penalty for contumacy was prescribed by canon law, and as William of Drogheda noted, *Summa Aurea*, ed. L. Wahrmund, *Quellen zur Geschichte des römisch-kanonischen Processes im Mittelalter* (Innsbruck, 1914), II:2, 36: 'Ubi autem non fuerit certa poena a lege imposita, ibi iudex ex officio suo potest unam vel aliam imponere.'

[49] See P. Floyer, *The Proctor's Practice in the Ecclesiastical Courts* (London, 1744), 64–5: 'A Person cited, and not appearing, is not contumacious, unless the adverse proctor has expressly accused his Contumacy.'

effort was also made to secure the representation of both parties. But even here, their presence was not absolutely required. By the fiction that the absence of the defendant was 'filled by the presence of God', the court could proceed to give final sentence.[50] It is, of course, another matter whether the party so represented would obey the court's decision. No doubt this practical problem explains why the attempt was made to make sure both parties were present at the sentence, and why very often the only serious delays in litigation were at the end of a case. The definitive sentence was sometimes repeatedly delayed to allow time for the reluctant party to be brought, hopefully to agreement, at least to acquiescence. But, in any event, contumacy was seldom a serious problem. Once the parties had made their initial appearance, litigation proceeded at the pace the plaintiff pushed it, whether the defendant came or not. If the plaintiff were the contumacious party, the penalty was simply that he lost one term. Certainly, this practice was one reason that marriage litigation was settled relatively quickly. Contumacy which is ignored, or disregarded, and which does not impede the progress of an action, cannot frustrate the effectiveness of the court system.

There is one more fact worthy of note about the beginning of marriage cases. That is the use made of alternative or contradictory pleading by defendants. The Church courts would not force litigants to choose one of several possible issues, and to abide by his ability to prove the one he had selected. For example, the defendant could claim that he had not given free consent to a contract and also that he had pre-contracted with a third party.[51] Some of the defenses used in litigation were in fact mutually exclusive. All could not have been true, but any one of them would defeat the plaintiff's claim. For example, one York defendant claimed that no contract could possibly have been made because he was in another village on the day in question, but that, assuming he had been present, he had only made the agreement 'iocandi animo et non aliter'.[52]

Most cases, of course, turned on only one issue. But the possibility of raising multiple and contradictory issues is important because it shows with particular force the attitude which the courts took towards

---

[50] E.g. Canterbury Y.1.5, f. 51r (1454), where the defendant was 'citatum ad hunc actum et per contumaciam absentem, cuius presenciam dei presencia reputamus esse repletam, ...' See also *gl. ord.* ad X 2.14.3 s.v. *causam quae*, 'Si actor est contumax, reo instante, diffinitiva sententia ferri potest.'

[51] Canterbury Y.1.1, fols. 9r, 18r (1373).

[52] York C.P. E 121 (1372). Other examples: Canterbury Ecc. suit, no. 10 (1269); York C.P. E 189(1391).

marriage cases. First, the procedure provided enough flexibility so that a litigant was not obliged to hazard the outcome of a suit on his ability to prove one of several possible defenses. If he had several reasons for disputing a contract's validity, he could state them all separately. Second, the courts were not inquisitorial tribunals, intent on penetrating all the thoughts and actions of the parties. Had they been, they would not have allowed possibly contradictory defenses. In the York case mentioned above, for example, the court would have taken the defendant and asked, were you really present at the time of the contract or not? And if so, exactly what did you say? But, in fact, defendants could raise multiple and contradictory issues. What they had to do was to disprove the plaintiff's claim. The courts judged the legal issues raised by the parties in almost all instance litigation. The judges might, as we shall note, recall witnesses or litigants to clarify issues. But which issues were raised was up to the parties. The court's essential duty was to settle a dispute between two parties, a dispute that happened to concern marriage.

(ii) *Taking of evidence*

The function of the opening stages of a lawsuit was to determine what issues had to be proved. The initial hearing, the submission of positions, articles, and interrogatories were designed to frame the issues. In English practice, actual proof in marriage cases was almost always by witnesses. Documents were rarely introduced.[53] Except for some divorce cases, the witnesses were named and produced by the parties themselves, rather than cited *ex officio* or assembled by an official of the court, as a sheriff assembled an English jury. Here again, initiative lay largely with the parties. Three terms for production of witnesses were usually given, although they were often combined with other steps and sometimes renounced. After examination, there was a day for publication of the depositions and usually a day set for the opposing party to speak against the witnesses. If necessary, the defendant could produce witnesses of his own to impugn the testimony or the character of the plaintiff's witnesses. In that case, the plaintiff was also given a chance to challenge those witnesses.

Only a few (two to five) witnesses were produced for either side in

[53] An interesting exception is found in Lichfield B/C/1/2, f. 246v (1469) where the woman in a matrimonial case exhibited the gifts she had received as part of the marriage agreement and apparently left them with the court registrar. For a detailed study of the work of the system, apparently largely much the same for the post-Reformation period in the Court of Delegates, see Duncan, *High Court of Delegates*, 114–55.

most marriage cases. Canonists insisted that one of the judge's func-
tions was to restrain the use of multitudes of witnesses.[54] In practice
the parties to marriage actions seem to have done so themselves. They
normally paid each witness's expenses; in fact a man could refuse to
testify until his expenses had been met by the party producing him.[55]
The cost of production, coupled with the uselessness of the multiplication of identical testimony, was probably the most effective restrain-
ing force. If a witness named by a party were unwilling to appear, the
party could apply to the court for application of canonical sanctions
to enforce his appearance. This was by no means infrequently done.
Almost always it was successful.[56] In the three year period, 1493–5,
for example, the Commissary court at Canterbury heard eighteen
marriage cases which went to the point of hearing testimony. Forty-
nine witnesses were produced. Of these, four at first refused to come
and had to be summoned by compulsory process. All of them appeared.

The examination itself was carried out away from the court session
by an examiner who might be, but was not necessarily, also the
judge.[57] Each witness was interviewed separately and secretly. To the
modern lawyer, this part of canonical litigation must appear among
its strangest, and its weakest features. It had the advantage of assur-
ing privacy for the examination, and it provided some possible protec-
tion against the intimidation of witnesses. But it had this weakness.
The opposing party had no chance to examine the witnesses; he was
limited to submitting written interrogatories in advance. Worse, the

---

[54] See Durantis, *Spec. Iud.* I, tit. *de teste*, § *de numero testitum*, no. 13.

[55] Ely EDR D/2/1, f. 21v (1375): 'Testes compulsi nondum sunt examinati eo quod nolunt
deponere prius quam habeant expensas; allegatoque per procuratorem dicti Willelmi Anegold
quod optulit cuilibet eorum xii d.'

[56] The normal manner of making the demand is shown in this extract from Canterbury
U.41, f. 3v (1395): 'Dicit insuper quod requisivit Grenhill ad perhibendum testimonium veritati
in causa predicta, in virtute iuramenti sui superius prestiti, et obtulit sibi viaticia etc, et
petens ad hoc prefatum testem compellendum fore ad perhibendum testimonium.' It was
apparently necessary to offer to pay the expenses of every witness before a demand for compulsion
could be made. See Oughton, *Ordo Judiciorum* I, 122.

[57] Joannes Bononiensis wrote that the judge ought to examine all witnesses by himself;
'consuetudo tamen tenet quod testes quasi semper per notorium examinentur'. *Summa Notarie
de his que in foro ecclesiastico*, L. Rockinger, *Briefsteller und formelbucher des eilften bis vierzehnten
Jahrhunderts* (2 vols, Munich, 1863, repr. 1961), 670. And see John of Acton, *Constitutiones*,
59 s.v. *procurent*: 'Non ergo est necesse per seipsos examinare.' The court at York had an officer
called the examiner general, see R. Brentano, *York Metropolitan Jurisdiction and Papal Judges
Delegate, 1279–96* (Berkeley and Los Angeles, 1959), 76–7. For the same office in the Court
of Arches, see Churchill, *Canterbury Administration* I, 446–50. See also Oughton, *Ordo
Judiciorum* I, 132.

judge often never heard any of the testimony on which his decision was based. The examiner simply submitted to him written depositions recording what each witness had said. The judge proceeded on the basis of what he read in them. It is thus almost literally true that the medieval judge knew no more about the evidence of a case than the historian who picks up the depositions six hundred years later. The disadvantages of such a system are evident. The judge could not see the demeanor of the witnesses. There was little opportunity to clear up difficult or confusing points of evidence. Everything depended on the skill and the conscientiousness of the examiner.

There were some mitigating factors. First, the witnesses were first produced in open court to be sworn. It may be that there was some discussion at that time of the merits of the case. In one suit from York, for example, there must have been; a witness later admitted that everything he knew about the case he had heard during his own production before the court.[58] The judge had at least this one chance to gauge the reliability of the witnesses for himself. Second, if the judge found the information given by the depositions incomplete or unsatisfactory, he could recall the witnesses and cause them to be re-examined. He could, and sometimes did, frame interrogatories of his own 'pro informatione consciencie sue'.[59] When, for example, the judge of the Commissary court at Canterbury found a deposition with a suspicious erasure in the testimony of the second witness, he had him recalled to clear up the matter.[60] The judges were not required to do this, however. In an action from Ely of 1374, the deposition left out the words 'in virum' and 'in uxorem' in recording a marriage contract. Here the judge held that there was merely scribal error. He

---

[58] C.P. E 102 (1368 or 1369). In *Tangerton* v. *Smelt*, Canterbury Ecc. Suit, no. 188 (1294), one witness deposed that what he and the other witnesses knew about claimed consanguinity they had learned 'hac instanti die inquisitionis sive examinationis in ecclesia Christi Cant'.

[59] E.g. Canterbury Y.1.1. f. 26v (1373): 'repetitis duobus testibus ... alias productis pro parte partis ree pro informatione consciencie iudicis.' Other examples: Rochester DRb Pa 1, f. 15r (1437); Lichfield B/C/1/1, f. 99v (1466). See also Durantis, *Spec. Iud.* II, tit. *de interrogationibus*, rubr., 'Sciendum est igitur, quod generaliter iudex potest semper interrogare ante litis contestationem et post et ubicumque ipsum aequitas movet, etiam postquam fuerit in causa conclusum.' The judge could also interrogate one or both of the parties for the same reason; e.g., Rochester DRb Pa 1, f. 15r (1437): 'pro informacione consciencie sue secrete examinavit dictum Henricum fide sue media an unquam contraxit matrimonium cum dicta Agnete per aliqua verba.'

[60] Ecc. Suit, no. 12 (1469–71): 'Propter suspicionem quam conceperat iudex super rasura huiusmodi ... decrevit iudex testem super eodem articulo fore repetendum.'

gave judgment as if the absent words had in fact been said.[61] Third,
the examiner sometimes noted his own opinion of the trustworthiness
of each witness on the deposition itself. This included the simple
emphasis of essential facts; the scribe might write 'nota hic bene'
beside a key point, or 'nota variationem temporis' where two witnesses
had testified inconsistently about the weather at the time of the
contract.[62] It could also include more personal judgments on the
witness. The examiner in a 1291 action from Canterbury added to
one deposition the note: 'This [witness] deposed in vacillating
fashion, and also gave the cause of his knowledge as if he were
suborned'.[63] In a case from York in 1364, to one deposition has been
added this interesting comment:

This witness often changed his manner of speaking during his deposition,
sometimes pretending to be a southern Englishman, sometimes a pure north-
erner, sometimes a Scot in the manner of Scotsmen speaking the English
language. And therefore it seems to the examiner that less faith should be
placed in him.[64]

Why the witness should have thought it worthwhile to vary his accent
in this way does not appear from the record.

Even with these safeguards, there remained a real and unfortunate
separation between the investigation of facts and the decision of the
case in marriage litigation. There were barriers between evidence and
decision in medieval English law as well, so that it would certainly be
wrong to pretend that the canonical procedure was 'inferior' to the
Common Law on this point.[65] But the difficulties caused by the

---

[61] EDR D/1/1, f. 13r: 'Pro eo quod primus et secundus minus plene fuerant examinati eo
quod non dicunt in virum et uxorem in ea parte attestationum ubi dicunt et deponunt ad
habendum te etc. prout in eisdem attestationibus plenius continetur, et quia constat nobis ut
iudici quod licet minus sit scriptum satis fuerant in ea parte per nos examinati, . . . , ideo
illa verba prefatis verbis ad habendum te decernimus fore adicienda et cum effectu adicimus,
factaque statim adiectione dictorum verborum tam in registro nostro quam in copiis attestationum
predictis Willelmo et Margarete traditis.'
[62] York C.P. F 253 (1472).
[63] Canterbury Ch. Ant. M 365: 'Vacillanter deposuit iste et etiam reddit causam sciencie
tanquam esset subornatus'. In Canterbury Ecc. Suit, no. 205 (c. 1300) this comment was made
about the deposition of Robert Parage, 'Requisitus, . . . , per que verba solet contrahi matrimonium, dicit se non bene scire licet ipse hoc anno uxorem duxerit.'
[64] C.P. E 87: 'Iste testis in depositione sua sepius mutavit modum loquendi, fingendo se
aliquando anglicanum australem, aliquando borialem mere, et aliquando scottum per modum
scottorum sonando ydeoma anglicana. Et ideo videtur examinatori quod minor fides est sibi
adhibenda.'
[65] See S. F. C. Milsom, 'Law and Fact in Legal Development', U. of Toronto L.J., 17 (1967),
10ff.

separation may nevertheless well be pointed out. And particularly was the separation damaging in marriage litigation, where so much depended on precisely what words had been used in the contract. Those words were spoken in the vulgar tongue. Most witnesses must also have been examined in English or French. But, until the end of our period, the depositions were normally recorded in Latin. This set up a level of distortion between the judge and the facts of each case. There were already barriers enough.

Of rules of evidence in the modern sense, we can hardly speak. The canonists gave extensive treatment to problems of evidence. But it was essentially advice for the judge in weighing the probative value of different kinds of testimony. The witnesses were allowed to range widely, to insert information which was irrelevant or even highly prejudicial. Indeed they could sometimes not be stopped from doing so. The apparently exasperated examiner in a Canterbury case noted of one witness: 'Est sexaginta annorum et constanter loquitur.'[66] The parties submitted articles and interrogatories, specific questions to be put to the witnesses. But the testimony could range beyond them. Apparently the examiner might even ignore the written questions, as in one suit where he complained that the interrogatories were 'valde prolixa'.[67] He could simply ask the witnesses to tell him what they knew about the case. At the end of the formal questions, it was common for him to ask the witnesses if they knew any more about the matter.[68] This opened the way for a broad scope of testimony.

It is not surprising, then, that the depositions contain a good deal of material to which a modern English lawyer would take exception. This complaint to a girl by a man languishing near death for love of her was received in evidence: 'I have a cause to curse you while I lyve, for the thengs I have take for you is al the cause of my sekenes.' The girl answered, 'I am come now to make amendes.'[69] Such a sad

---

[66] Sede Vacante S.B. III, no 57 (1292).

[67] Canterbury Ecc. Suit, no 329 (1293), on dorse. Sometimes the parties themselves asked for the examiner to go outside their own articles and interrogatories; e.g. York C.P. E 245 (1391), where beside the party's questions is written, 'Cetera suppleat discretio examinantis'; or Canterbury Ecc. Suit, no. 239 (1294), where we find, 'Fiant predicta interogatoria et alia si placet ex ingenio vestro.'

[68] E.g. Canterbury X.10.1, f. 12r (1412), in which the witnesses were finally asked, 'an scit aliquid aliud deponere quantum ad contractum'. Joannes Bononiensis wrote that this should have been done before examination by articles, Summa, 673: 'Et lectis articulis, faciat testem dicere super dicto negocio quicquid novit, antequam ipsum interrogaret de aliquo.'

[69] London MS. 9065, f. 34r (1487); an interesting instance of a death-bed curse introduced into evidence comes from York C.P. E 108 (1370): 'Johannes respondit elevatis manibus de lecto et dixit, "Si aliqui de filiis meis faciant tibi iniuriam ego do eis ita plene maledictionem meam sicut eos generavi."'

story might be prejudicial to the woman's case. It had no apparent relevance to the issue. Somewhat more material perhaps, but no less prejudicial, was the evidence that a woman had for some time been keeping the defendant's cattle in a York case of 1361. It was the source of public opinion that the couple were married.[70] Hearsay evidence was commonly introduced. What, for instance, a servant of one party in a York marriage case had said about his master's plans was given in evidence.[71] In an even more striking instance, testimony by John North that William Gore had told him of seeing a marriage contracted between Alice Sanders and John Resoun was received as evidence of the marriage in one Rochester suit.[72] Out of court admissions made by either party were also a standard part of the evidence recorded in marriage litigation.[73]

Evidence of the birth of children was often introduced in marriage cases. Strictly speaking, this was irrelevant to the merits of the case except as evidence of sexual intercourse between the parties. Beyond that, what sentimental force it had on the judge is hard to say. Certainly less than it would today. The validity of a marriage depended on the existence of a marriage contract, not on the birth of children. That was equally compatible with the assumption of concubinage. An admission by the defendant that he had fathered a woman's children was by no means enough of itself to turn vague words into a valid marriage.[74] But it is difficult to believe it had no influence at all.

One striking sort of evidence commonly recorded relates to the status and the wealth of the parties. This might be material. It was unlikely that a very rich man would have married a very poor girl. And such evidence was not at all excluded by the canon law.[75] In a more socially stratified society than our own there was perhaps reason for using wealth and position as one criterion in judging the parties'

---

[70] C.P. E 84: 'Custodiebat pecora sua.' The court did hold in favor of the woman in the case.
[71] C.P. F 189 (1454).
[72] DRb Pa 1, f. 316r (1443).
[73] E.g. Canterbury X.10.1, f. 17v (1412): 'Dicit iste iuratus quod nichil scit deponere super dicto contracto matrimoniali nisi quod sepius audivit prefatum Thomam dicentum in presencia eiusdem mulieris quod contraxit cum dicta Agnete.' The probative force of such out of court statements, a problem which arose frequently, is one of the questions about canonical procedure I have not been able to answer. On the general problem, see T. O. Martin, 'Hearsay at Common Law and at Canon Law', The Jurist, 11 (1951), 58–76.
[74] E.g. York C.P. E 236 (1398), where the court held against marriage despite the admission of children.
[75] E.g. Jo. And., Commentaria ad X 4.1.8, no. 3 states that one of the criteria for determining the probability of a marriage should stem 'ex qualitate contrahentium personarum'.

intentions and actions. Such facts, in any case, were often introduced into evidence. When, for instance, Isabella Foxholes sued John Littyst in 1419 to establish a contract of marriage, John introduced witnesses to show that he stood far above her 'divitiis, potencia, nobilitate vel honore'. She was, his witnesses alleged, 'pauper vilis et abiecta persona'. We do not know what effect this testimony had. But in the event, Isabella lost her case.[76]

It is pleasant to be able to produce a striking case in which the court heard such evidence, but disregarded it. The facts of the case, heard at York in 1407, seem to have been these. Agnes Nakerer met and fell in love with a travelling minstrel named John Kent. He married her clandestinely, apparently without her parents' knowledge and certainly without their consent. When they learned of their daughter's adventure, they quickly caused her to contract marriage with John Thorpe. The resulting dispute came before the court as a multi-party suit. Kent and Thorpe were *competitores*. In the litigation, Thorpe's attack on Kent and his witnesses was particularly strong. Kent was described as lacking in the most basic rudiments of honesty, and derided as a 'public minstrel and juggler, frequently, dishonestly and shamefully engaged in sport and displays of his body for the sake of profit'. Kent's witnesses, who were his fellow minstrels, were attacked as 'infamous (*infames*) in law and fact'. But against all this, the York court held in favor of the minstrel and against the marriage with Thorpe which the family obviously preferred.[77] Prejudicial evidence was not necessarily conclusive evidence.

In sum, court practice was to allow almost any sort of evidence to be put before the judge, but to rely on his discretion to sift the relevant from the irrelevant. It seemed most important to have as much testimony as possible before the court, particularly since the judge often had not himself examined the witnesses. This is well illustrated by a case from Ely. Excommunicated persons were, by law, excluded from testifying. But in the case an admittedly excommunicated witness was absolved *ad cautelam* by the court so that he could give evidence, 'ne veritatis probatio, presertim in tam ardua causa, subtrahatur'.[78] The judge could decide for himself what effect the man's status should

---

[76] York C.P. F 81, 88 (1419). Similar cases are: York C.P. E 93 (1365); E 103 (1369); E 179 (1390); Canterbury Sede Vacante S.B. III, no. 43 (n.d.); X.10.1, f. 49v (1420); X.1.1, f. 131r (1456).

[77] C.P. F 33.

[78] EDR D/2/1, fols. 133r–133v (1380). The record states, however, that this was done 'de consensu partium'.

have on the reliability of his testimony. As the judge was trained in the law, the burden of assessing the evidence rightly lay with him. There was, in other words, good reason for this practice.

(iii) *Final steps*

There remains one part of procedure in marriage cases which should be discussed. That is the conclusion. One feature has already been mentioned. Sentence could be given even in the absence of a contumacious party. But, partly because controversy could later arise over whether a party had in fact been contumacious, and partly because the courts sought to secure the agreement of both sides to the fairness of any sentence, an effort was made to secure representation of both parties. Delays were allowed and special orders issued to call both litigants before the court for the giving of definitive sentence.[79]

However, before the actual sentence, there was normally a term set 'ad proponenda omnia in facto consistencia'. This being accomplished, either the case was immediately concluded and a term set for definitive sentence, or a separate term was inserted 'ad concludendum'. In these terms whatever legal argument there was must have taken place. The term, of which the post-Reformation canonist Oughton speaks, *ad audiendum informationes* on points of law from the advocates, does not appear in the medieval Act books.[80] Only occasionally and by chance do the records reveal any trace of specifically legal argument. There was no reason to set it down in the Act books.[81] It was not a part of the Cause papers kept by the court. Two legal memoranda have survived from Canterbury. From them we learn that arguments based on the *glossa ordinaria*, Geoffrey of Trani, Hostiensis, and the Digest were introduced.[82] But this is not much. How frequent, how lengthy,

---

[79] E.g. Canterbury Y.1.16, f. 33v (1492): 'Et iudex decrevit mulierem fore vocandam ad interessendum tempore prolacionis sentencie in proximo;' Y.1.1, f. 82v (1374): 'In termino ad audiendam sentenciam, decretum est quod partes vocentur.'

[80] *Ordo Judiciorum* I, 192. But cf. York Cons. A B 1, f. 89v (1418), where there is a term set 'ad informandum iudicem'.

[81] The closest the Act books come to recording legal argument is an entry like this one from York C.P. E 1 (1303): 'Habitaque altercatione magna super rationibus et exceptionibus in ultimo capitulo propositis et responsionibus factis ad easdem, quia non est sufficienter deliberatum super eisdem intendimus deliberare usque in proximo et facere super eis quod justicia suadebit.'

[82] Sede Vacante S.B. III, no. 91 (n.d.); no. 131 (1292) which begins 'Ad informationem domini iudicis ad sentenciandum in causa matrimoniali.' Examples of model oral argument can be found in H. Silvestre, 'Dix plaidoiries inédites au XIIe siècle', *Traditio*, 10 (1954), 373–97, esp. 384–8.

and how sophisticated were the legal arguments in marriage cases must remain obscure. Few things are more to be regretted by the historian of law than the lack of some canonical equivalent to the English Year Books.

Most cases ended in definitive sentences or, where the hearing had been short or the proof incomplete, by an order of the court generally styled *decretum*, occasionally *pronunciatio*.[83] But there were also some cases which ended without a final order by the judge. They raise a question of real interest. Could a marriage case be compromised? Could the parties bargain and agree on a result without final recourse to the decision of a court? The canon law is clear. They could not. In the words of the gloss: 'Thus it is evident that in marriage, agreement or composition has no place, lest anything be determined against marriage.'[84] This makes perfect sense. If two people have contracted marriage by words of present consent, they are married. They cannot agree to pretend that they are not. The danger of derogating from what might be a legitimate marriage meant that no compromise could be allowed. Likewise, canon law held that it was unlawful to submit a marriage case to arbiters.[85] They had to be handled by competent and regular ecclesiastical courts.

Practice tells a different story. Matrimonial cases were, in fact, sometimes compromised. The easiest way of doing this was for the plaintiff to decline to prosecute an action he had begun. When this happened the court scribe sometimes continued to record the case through successive terms in which neither party appeared and no action was taken. The Registrum Primum from Ely contains several such cases. In them the scribe, after many sessions, finally wrote: 'Neutra pars comparet; ideo pendeat causa quousque pars actrix prosequatur.'[86] Usually, however, the action was quietly dropped from the records. This is certainly the explanation for the disappearance of many cases from the fifteenth-century Act books. Besides these cases, we also find actions in which the claimant, having begun an action and prosecuted it for a time, came into court and said that he wished to withdraw his suit. There is one case from Canterbury in which the

---

[83] Durantis, *Spec. Iud.* II, tit. *de primo decreto*, § *quot modis dicatur decretum*, no. 1, notes that, 'Dicitur ergo decretum sentencia diffinitiva quandoque.'

[84] *Gl. ord.* ad X 1.36.11 s.v. *sacramentum*. 'Sic patet quod in matrimonio non habet transactio sue compositio locum, ut contra matrimonium aliquid statuetur.'

[85] Panormitanus, *Commentaria* ad X 1.43.10, no. 1: 'In causa matrimoniali non possunt arbitri assumi, . . . , nec admittit aliquam compositionem.' See X 1.36.11.

[86] Ely EDR D/2/1, f. 50r (1376); there is a wholesale dropping of stale actions after f. 149.

court specifically and rightly refused to admit the request. The plaintiff's proctor first said:

The same Denise does not wish to pursue further her aforementioned cause, and the same Robert withdraws and will withdraw for the future, as far as he can, this cause or causes from the Canterbury consistory.[87]

The court refused to accept the dismissal. The judge went on to give sentence in favor of the marriage in question.

This, however, was unusual. Normally we find entries like this one: 'The man says he does not wish to proceed further, and the defendant asks to be dismissed; and the plaintiff not prosecuting, [the defendant] is dismissed.'[88] There were cases in which both parties appeared and specifically alleged a concord between them.[89] After that, their case appeared no more. In the Consistory court at Lichfield in 1474, a marriage suit was continued by the court itself *sub spe concordie*.[90] Sometimes we find the simple word 'pax' written beside a marriage case, indicating the same thing.[91] In one case from Bath and Wells, contrary to the canonical prohibition against the use of arbiters in marriage cases, we find:

The aforesaid principal parties personally appearing before the aforenamed vicar general, the same parties entirely compromise the aforesaid matrimonial

---

[87] U. 41, f. 30v (1394): 'Ipsa Dionisia non vult ulterius prosequi causam suam memoratam, sed ipse Robertus causam sive causas huiusmodi a consistorio Cantuarien' in quantum potest retrahit et retrahet in futurum secundum posse suum.'

[88] Rochester DRb Pa 2, f. 26r (1445): 'Et vir dixit se nolle ulterius prosequi, et pars rea petiit se dimitti; et actore non prosequente, dimissa est.' Similar instances: York Cons. A B 2, f. 90r (1427): 'Dimissus est ab instancia Katerine servientis Roberti Karlell non curantis prosequi ulterius contra eum;' Canterbury Y.1.18, f. 41r (1499): 'Dimissa de consensu partium;' Rochester DRb Pa 1, f. 114v (1439): 'In causa matrimoniali mota per Willelmum Clement contra Matildam Berwys, partes non comparent, ideo respic;' Canterbury Y.1.5, f. 132v (1456): 'Stet causa, partes sunt concordati.' Other examples: Hereford 0/2, f. 5r (1422); Rochester DRb Pa 1, f. 251r (1422); Canterbury Y.1.7, f. 112r (1462); Y.1.10, f. 35v (1469); Y.1.13, f. 83r (1480); Y.1.14, f. 69r (1485); Y.1.17 f. 13r (1496).

[89] E.g. Canterbury Y.1.3, f. 33r (1416): 'Nullus instat propter concordiam allegatam per magistrum Johannem Egerden;' Y.1.6, f. 149r (1465): 'Et allegavit compromissum inter partes.' Oughton also seems to envision the possibility of compromise; he says that even if the plaintiff does not *componere causam*, it can happen that his delay will have the same result. *Ordo Judiciorum* I, 302. For French examples, see *Registre des causes civiles de l'officialité épiscopale de Paris*, cols. 33, 39–40, 65, 95 (1385).

[90] Lichfield B/C/1/2, f. 158r. The parties to this action, however, were apparently unable to agree, since the hearing resumed, at f. 164v.

[91] Lichfield B/C/1/1, f. 46v (1465); B/C/1/2, f. 55v (1472); York Cons. A B 1, f. 58r (1418); Canterbury Y.1.1, f. 39v (1373); Hereford I/1, 163, 165 (1494).

cause in the venerable men Masters Thomas Overay and Thomas Mersh, residenciary canons of the cathedral church of Wells.[92]

In all these situations, the parties reached a settlement. The court scribe simply recorded that fact. Whether the settlement was in each case consistent with what the court would have decided, we cannot say. Any opinion would be no more than a guess. But it is certain that the canonical rule against compromises in marriage cases was not observed in practice.

The noncompliance with this rule is of real interest. It illustrates, first, that practice in marriage cases followed the normal pattern of medieval litigation. That is, a compromise arranged after a lawsuit has been brought. Most modern legal disputes are also settled without formal sentence by any court. But lawyers today almost always try to settle without going into court at all. Medieval litigants and their lawyers began lawsuits with less hesitation. They went to law more quickly. But they were no less ready to compromise in the end. Agreement of the parties was the most satisfactory way of ending a dispute.[93] Even in marriage litigation, which is usually unsuited for compromise, and in which private agreements were illegal, this pattern of initial suit and subsequent compromise is found.

Second, the availability of compromise in marriage cases shows how dependent the Church courts were on the initiative of the parties. The steps an English judge would take on his own in actions of marriage were few. But what should he have done? Suppose a plaintiff would not produce witnesses after starting a case. Should the judge have called witnesses on his own? Should he have put legal arguments into the plaintiff's mouth? Perhaps. It would have required energy and expense. It would probably have meant the appointment of a *defensor vinculi* to promote the case.[94] This was adopted during the eighteenth century in Catholic tribunals, but it is an institution better suited to litigation in which divorce, not the establishment of

---

[92] D/D/C A1, 305 (1461): 'Partibus antedictis principalibus coram prenominato vicario generali personaliter comparentibus, eedem partes causam matrimonialem antedictam compromiserunt totaliter in venerabiles viros M. Thomam Overay et Thomam Mersh canonicos residenciarios ecclesie cathedralis Wellen.' Another assignment of arbiters is found in York Cons. A B 1, f. 97v (1418); two of the men assigned were the proctors in the case.

[93] See, for example, the remarks and statistics in *Civil Pleas of the Wiltshire Eyre, 1249*, ed. M. T. Clanchy, Wiltshire Records Soc., 26 (1971), 21–9.

[94] On the development of this official, see Leo de Guise, *Le Promoteur de la justice dans les causes matrimoniales* (Ottawa, Canada, 1944); J. T. Noonan, Jr., *Power to Dissolve, Lawyers and Marriages in the Courts of the Roman Curia* (Cambridge, Mass., 1972), 126–9 and *passim*.

marriage, is the common goal of most law suits. The English Church courts did not undertake the task of promotion. What they did was to settle disputes involving marriage. Given the conditions of the later medieval period, this was perhaps task enough.

We see the effects of the almost total reliance on the initiative of the parties in the relative independence of each Church court. One of the weaknesses of the canon law system was that coordination between different dioceses was very difficult. In marriage cases, this problem was evident when parties appeared in court for a time and then disappeared. The scribe noted, 'recesserunt a diocesi', or 'dimittitur causa quia mulier cepit fugam'.[95] No apparent efforts were made to track these people down. Whether they were finally caught in the courts of the diocese to which they fled, we cannot learn. Perhaps they were later cited *ex officio* for immorality, or for having two wives. But in any event, the first court, baulked by a vanished plaintiff, normally took no steps by itself to bring the party back to the bar of justice. It is, I think, indicative of the seriousness with which most people accepted the jurisdiction of the Church courts in marriage cases that there are not more entries of 'recesserunt' left in the Act books than there are.

The previous two chapters dealt at some length with showing the continuing vitality of older Germanic and Roman notions of marriage. It was a private contract, subject to negotiation, bargaining, and settlement. Few thing show more openly the extent to which that attitude was shared by the men who staffed the Church courts than the allowance of compromise in marriage litigation. Canonically, it was prohibited. Logically, it was impossible. But the people did not always see it that way. And the Church courts did not force them to. Probably they could not have done so — at least without a drastic reorganization of canonical procedure. Either the canon lawyers thought it too ambitious a task, one better left for another day, or, and as I think more likely, they shared something of the prevalent attitude towards marriage.

SUMMARY

Most marriage cases passed through the courts to final sentence efficiently and quickly. In contested litigation the average time from start to finish ranged from four months to a little over seven months

---

[95] Rochester DRb Pa 1, f. 353v (1443); DRb Pa 4, f. 203v (1487).

in the five samples available. Appeals, while not negligible, were not consistently abused to prolong litigation and to delay enforcement of decrees. Nor did the contumacy of parties greatly hinder the Church courts in marriage actions. After the initial stages of a case, most parties were represented by proctors. If they were not and failed to appear, the courts in effect ignored their absence, by moving to the next step of litigation as if the party had been present but taken no action. When called for, the sanctions of suspension from entry into church and excommunication almost invariably were successful in bringing parties into court. Probably the general acceptance among the English people of ecclesiastical jurisdiction over marriage, together with the parties' shared interest in reaching a decision about their own future, were at least as important in this as was the threat of excommunication, although it must have been very hard to separate them at the time.

Procedure itself was flexible in the extreme. The lengthy and complicated libellary process was abbreviated, compressed, renounced, and stretched out of shape in actual practice. The litigants and their lawyers largely controlled the progress of each case. They determined the shape of actual procedure. But the availability of summary process, and the smallness and familiarity of the group of lawyers and judges who served in the Church courts also appear to have contributed to the relatively quick settlement of marriage actions.

No very exact summary of the actual steps of marriage litigation can therefore be given. Concentration has been centered on some aspects of procedure which are important in understanding the nature of marriage practice. The examination of witnesses out of court, by a special examiner, and submission of written depositions to the judge is the first such feature. The problems inherent in such a system were only partly compensated for by the initial production of each witness in court, by the judge's power to recall witnesses for personal examination, and by the examiner's freedom to note his own opinion of testimony on the deposition record itself. Second, it is noteworthy how broad was the range of testimony introduced in the courts for consideration by the judge. Canon law did not rely on rules of exclusion, but on the discretion of a learned judge to evaluate the importance and relevance of what witnesses had said. And third, we examined the use of compromise and composition in actions of marriage. These agreements, illegal under canon law, were not infrequently allowed in practice. They illustrate the extent to which initiative and enforcement in marriage litigation lay in the hands of the parties themselves. That control was not total, but it was very much greater than has often been thought. Compromise also suggests that the Church court officials shared at least something of the lay attitude towards marriage as an essentially private contract, one open to bargaining, at least before the establishment of a consummated and settled relationship. Even if that attitude was not shared, it was in this instance openly tolerated.

V

JUDGES, LAWYERS, WITNESSES AND LITIGANTS

A survey of even a restricted class of litigation requires some analysis of the people involved in the court system. Who were they? What training did they have? How well did they do their jobs? The information that can be discovered, it will be seen, is in no case complete. Nor is this the place for a full-scale study of the careers of court personnel, although such a study would be useful in its own right and would be, at least for some courts, entirely possible. Here we must be content with a discussion directed specifically at marriage litigation. It is artificial, of course, to separate marriage cases from other sorts of litigation in describing court personnel. But marriage law did have rules and problems of its own. Even though the conclusions must be tentative and incomplete, it would be wrong to omit any consideration of the people connected with this subject.

THE JUDGES

Correct decision of marriage cases required both training in the law and evident sound judgment in dealing with people. The variety of words used to contract marriage and the fine distinctions evolved by the canonists for evaluating them rendered the first of these necessary. The nature of the subject matter itself, which dealt with the difficult and personal problems of enforcing the bond of marriage, rendered the second equally imperative. The high requirements for judging marriage cases were, in fact, recognized by the canon law itself. The *ius commune* vested jurisdiction over them exclusively in the bishop of each diocese.[1] In effect, this meant the bishop's official, the man specially appointed by each bishop to carry out his judicial duties in a regularly scheduled court. The law recognized that the delicacy and closeness of the issues, together with the danger to men's souls which was involved, made the rule necessary. As Lyndwood wrote,

---

[1] *Gl. ord.* ad X 5.31.12 s.v. *dignitatis.* See also *Councils and Synods* I, 85, 147, 353, 377, 413, 718 for various diocesan statutes restricting the extent of non-episcopal jurisdiction in matrimonial causes.

'In matrimonial causes, discretion is necessary, and therefore it is dangerous for them to be judged by unqualified men (*a simplicibus*).'[2]

The limitations of the sources used in this study make it impossible to speak with great confidence about the extent of learning among the judges. They were not absolutely required to hold degrees in law.[3] But it does seem fairly clear that during the period for which the Act books have survived in substantial quantities, almost all the men who served as judges in the Consistory courts were university graduates with degrees in either canon or civil law, sometimes in both.[4] The Act books often specify the degrees held by the judge sitting. Thus, some samples can be given. Nine men judged marriage cases on a regular basis in the Provincial court at York from the 1370s through the 1420s. Four were graduates in canon law, three in civil law, and two in both laws. Five of them were graduates of Oxford, and two of Cambridge. For two the university connection has been impossible to trace.[5] At Canterbury, the office of Commissary General was held by thirteen men during the fifteenth century. Six held degrees in canon law alone, two in civil law alone, and five in both laws. For only one (who served however only briefly *sede vacante*), no university degree is given.[6] The same picture emerges from looking at the smaller courts. At Rochester there were seven Officials Principal from the time of the first surviving Act book (1436) through the end of the century. All were university graduates, although one (John Hornley) was exceptional in having taken a theological degree.[7] At

---

[2] *Provinciale*, 79, s.v. *et infra*. See also the discussion in Aston, *Thomas Arundel*, 99–109.

[3] John of Acton, *Constitutiones*, 59 s.v. *peritiam*: 'Non dicit doctoratum vei magistratum; quia non requiritur summa perfectio in artifice, . . . sed sufficit quod statuta canonum non ignorent.' See also, on the general requirements, Hostiensis, *Summa Aurea* I, tit. *de off. ord.*, no. 2.

[4] On the usefulness of training in Roman law, see John of Acton, *Constitutiones*, 58 s.v. *et scientia:* 'Et peritia juris civilis hoc casu prodesse possit.' See also Lyndwood, *Provinciale*, 76 s.v. *et civile*.

[5] Men who served as either official, commissary general and examiner general have been counted, the last because examiners general often served as judges by delegation. They are: Richard Arnall. B.C.L. and B.Cn.L (Oxon.); Richard Conyngton, LL.D. (Oxon.); William Cawod, Lic.C.L. (Oxon.); John Wodham, B.Cn.L. (Oxon.); Roger Esyngwald, LL.B.; John Schefford, B.Cn.L.; Richard Burgh, LL.B. (Cantab.); Robert Alne, B.Cn.L. (Cantab.); and Walter de Shirlawe, D.Cn.L. (Oxon.). This information has been taken from the Act books for the appropriate dates. University affiliation has been taken from E. B. Emden, *A Biographical Register of the University of Oxford to A.D. 1500* (3 vols, Oxford, 1957–9) and *A Biographical Register of the University of Cambridge to A.D. 1500* (Cambridge, 1963).

[6] See Woodcock, 115–17. Six were from Oxford, four from Cambridge; three cannot be definitely connected with either university.

[7] See A. L. Browne, 'The Medieval Officials Principal of Rochester', *Archaeologia Cantiana*, 43 (1941), 29–61. John Candour, D.Cn.L., is the only judge I have found whose degree has been traced to a continental university, Padua.

Lichfield, two men served as Official during the period covered by the two surviving Act books (1464–79).[8] Each held an Oxford degree in both civil and canon law.

It seems fair to say, then, that most judges had adequate legal training. They had also at least the possibility of using the books which are the foundation of real learning in the law, the legal treatises of the canonists and civilians. A few judges have left, through their wills, records of owning some of the basic texts.[9] William Cawode, Official at York in the early fifteenth century, had a personal library of at least thirteen law books.[10] The cathedral libraries, many of them at least, had quite good collections.[11] The judges would certainly have had access to these. What we do not know is how much use they made of that privilege. The records tell us next to nothing. But it is clear that adequate reference to law books and the commentators was available for the judges of the Consistory courts.

The evidence, though not conclusive, does suggest that the judges in the Consistory courts fulfilled the canon law's requirements of learning in the law. Rather less impressive, however, is the extent to which jurisdiction in marriage cases was in actual practice dispersed among inferior judges. By the *ius commune*, we have noted, jurisdiction belonged exclusively to the bishops and their courts. Ideally, marriage cases were to be handled by a small group of expert judges in the bishops' courts. Particularly important, it seemed, was the exclusion of rural deans from the exercise of matrimonial jurisdiction. They were, Lyndwood recorded, 'commonly inexperienced and ignorant of the law'.[12]

In actual practice, however, matrimonial jurisdiction was considerably more dispersed than the *ius commune* dictated. In the first place, subordinate officers might serve by special delegation of the bishop.

---

[8] John Fox, B.C.L. and D.Cn.L. and Thomas Reynold, B.C.L. and B.Cn.L.

[9] Robert Raulyn, Commissary General at Canterbury, bequeathed a copy of the Decretals and Joannes Andreae's *Addiciones*. See Woodcock, 116. See also *Reg. Chichele* II, 562 for the books left by William Lovelich, Registrar of the Commissary court.

[10] Emden, *Biographical Register . . . Oxford* III, 2160.

[11] See M. R. James, *The Ancient Libraries of Canterbury and Dover* (Cambridge, 1903), 150–1. For Durham and Hereford, see N. R. Ker, *Medieval Libraries of Great Britain*, 2nd edn (London, 1964), 61–76, 96–100. All the basic texts are represented: Decretum, Decretals, the Liber Sextus and Clementines, and the *Corpus Iuris Civilis*. The treatises of Hostiensis, Guillelmus Durantis, Innocent IV, Joannes Andreae, Guido de Baysio, and many others were in these libraries.

[12] Lyndwood, *Provinciale*, 79, s.v. *audire presumant*; on rural deans, see A. H. Thompson, 'Diocesan Organization in the Middle Ages: Archdeacons and Rural Deans', *Proceedings of the British Academy*, 39 (1943), 184–94; R. Dunning, 'Rural Deans in England in the Fifteenth Century', *Bulletin of the Institute of Historical Research*, 40 (1967), 207–13.

They often did. More importantly, competence in marriage cases might be acquired by others besides bishops by means of prescription. Custom could validly give jurisdiction.[13] The ideal of the *ius commune* was subject to variation in practice. And English records show that prescriptive jurisdiction had spread to many lesser ecclesiastics. They also suggest that the question was fluid in some places. Contention for jurisdiction between bishops and archdeacons was not everywhere settled. We find, from 1294, a case in which it was held by the Commissary court of Canterbury, *sede vacante*, that the archdeacon of Stafford was illegally usurping marriage jurisdiction which belonged to the bishop of Lichfield.[14] In that same year the bishop and the dean of the City of Norwich were at odds over the right to hear matrimonial and other kinds of litigation.[15] As late as 1438, the official of the archbishop of York was disputing with the archdeacon of Nottingham's official over competence in marriage cases.[16] And in 1446, the Consistory court of Rochester had to send an inhibition to the archdeacon's official, ordering him not to proceed in an action between Thomas Chaloner and Mariana Haliday, 'since he has no jurisdiction to take cognizance of marriage'.[17]

It is probable, although it cannot be absolutely proved, that the bishops' courts had some success in restricting marriage jurisdiction over the course of our period. In the 1290s, the Canterbury court complained that 'almost all rectors of exempt parishes in the diocese are usurping such cognizance for themselves'.[18] The unhappy and uncanonical result was that marriage cases were being heard 'by simple priests or clerics having little or no experience in law or fact'.[19] We do not find such complaints from later Canterbury records. And the archdeacon's court books, which are pre-

---

[13] *Gl. ord.* ad X 2.13.13 s.v. *in tua:* 'In his enim consuetudo servatur quae dat iurisdictionem.'

[14] Sede Vacante S.B. III, no. 360. See also the evidence from Ely and notice of the removal in 1401 of the archdeacon's marriage jurisdiction in M. Aston, *Thomas Arundel*, 109.

[15] Sede Vacante S.B. III, no. 372. On the office of dean of the city of Norwich, see W. Hudson, *Leet Jurisdiction in the City of Norwich*, Selden Soc., 5 (1891), xci.

[16] York C.P. F 123.

[17] Found in a seventeenth-century copy of court records from Rochester, British Museum, Add. MS. 11821, f. 14r: ' ... cum ad cognoscendum de matrimonio nullam habet iurisdictionem.'

[18] Sede Vacante S.B. III, no. 84: 'Quasi omnes rectores exempti in predicta dyocesi huiusmodi cognitionem sibi usurpant.' The destination of this document, which begins *Memorandum quod* and goes at once to recitation of this grievance, is unfortunately not clear to me.

[19] Ibid., ' ... per simplices sacerdotes seu clericos experienciam iuris vel facti modicam vel nullam habentes.'

served from the fifteenth century, show no sign of marriage litigation.[20]

These are examples of disputed questions of jurisdiction. There are also cases in which the matter was undisputed, in which the lower official heard marriage actions without challenge. It is, of course, only when the correctness of decisions was challenged on appeal that we find reference to these. No records of such subordinate jurisdictions have survived in regular series. But what does remain is worth noting. Many archdeacons, those of Derby and Richmond for example, lawfully entertained marriage actions by custom. The *custos spiritualitatis* of Selby Abbey heard and decided a marriage case in 1368.[21] There is mention of a marriage action being heard by the sacristan of Ely cathedral in 1374.[22] A prebendary of Lichfield cathedral, sometime just prior to 1472, celebrated a divorce between two litigants in the parish church of Prez, which belonged to his prebend.[23] The receiver of the archbishop of York's exchequer heard a matrimonial dispute in 1431.[24] The rule of the *ius commune* vesting exclusive matrimonial jurisdiction in the diocesan bishop was, in other words, not observed in fact. Unlike the case of academic learning, where the attainments of the judges generally exceeded the law's requirements, in this area the standards of practice were lower than the canon law's ideal.

It is worth noting, incidentally, that there was a quite natural reason within the law that marriage disputes were sometimes heard by subordinate officials, even where long usage did not give them jurisdiction. That is the wide extent to which corrective powers over sexual offenses were shared. Such authority was broadly held by archdeacons, rural deans, and cathedral clergy. Not infrequently, when a man and woman were cited by one of them for fornication, either the man or the woman would take the occasion to allege a contract of marriage. Legally, the judge should then have remitted the matter to the diocesan tribunal. This sometimes happened.[25]

---

[20] See Woodcock, 83.

[21] York C.P. E 97.

[22] EDR D/2/1, f. 26v.

[23] B/C/1/2, f. 90r. The divorce was said to have been done 'per viii annos elapsos et ultra.'

[24] C.P. F 200.

[25] Norwich, Acta et Comperta 1a, s.d. Friday after the feast of St Matthew, 1417, in which the court of the prior and chapter took this action: 'Et quia defuit ibidem copia iurisperitorum, dictas partes in statu quo tunc erant ab officio suo totaliter dimisit et eas quatenus de iure potuit ad audienciam domini officialis consistorii domini Nor' episcopi remisit.' Two other examples: Hereford O/3, 48 (1446); Canterbury Sede Vacante S.B. III, no. 115 (1293).

But it was by no means the rule. Often the man with corrective juris-diction went on to hear the evidence and give sentence himself. The whole matter was probably finished in one sitting. The line between office and instance jurisdiction was never kept as clear as theory dictated. Indeed, it would have wasted time, increased expense, and required an artificial separation of the facts in many cases to have maintained the division. The blurring of that line meant that the canonical rules about who should judge marriage cases were part-icularly difficult to enforce.

Given the extension of matrimonial jurisdiction beyond that specified by the *ius commune*, it is perhaps surprising to find that there were very few complaints about judicial misconduct or incompetence. So far as surviving records tell an accurate story, objections were rare. There are a few examples. Against the official of the archdeacon of Cleveland in 1391, it was objected that he was 'notorie coniugatus et sic communiter et notorie habitus et reputatus et ut merus laicus'.[26] The judge at Rochester was challenged in a suit in 1495. A litigant refused to appear before him, alleging that 'he was not a competent judge'.[27] There is one instance of recusation of a judge in a marriage case, that is an attempt to disqualify him for bias or interest in the outcome of the suit.[28] But in general, the court records produce few complaints against the competence or conduct of the judges in marri-age actions. Sentences were sometimes appealed, but the appeals rarely were based on an attack against the character of a particular judge.

More interestingly perhaps, the court records show few signs of venality among the Church court judges. One finds scarcely any ac-cusations of corruption or bribery. There are a very few. The official of the archdeacon of Stafford was challenged as 'muneribus cor-ruptus' in a 1294 marriage suit.[29] The official of the archdeacon of Northumbria was challenged in 1389 as a taker of bribes.[30] The records of the royal courts produce an occasional accusation. The sequestrator of the bishop of Lincoln, John Leek, was said to be wrongfully citing men and women before him, refusing to cease from

---

[26] York C.P. E 191.

[27] Rochester DRb Pa 4, f. 270r (1495): The man said, 'quod non compareat hic coram legitimo iudice quia dicit quod non erat competens iudex.'

[28] York C.P. F 176 (1421–3). Lichfield B/C/1/1, f. 323r (1471) may also refer to recusation. A general study of the law on this subject is L. Fowler, '*Recusatio iudicis* in Civilian and Canonist Thought', *Studia Gratiana*, 15 (1972), 717–85.

[29] Canterbury Sede Vacante S.B. III, no. 360.

[30] York C.P. E 137.

disturbing them until they had given him forty shillings.[31] But these were unusual. The competence and impartiality of the ecclesiastical judges did not often come under attack, either before or after their judgments.

Whether this lack of complaint is proof of the uprightness of the judges is unclear. Certainly there is no *prima facie* reason that challenges against judges should not have appeared in the records. Alleged defects in lower court judgments were frequently set out in appealed cases. Accusations against the integrity of witnesses were often made and recorded. Why do we not find similar charges against the lower court judges? The nature of the records themselves do not, in this case, provide an explanation. Of course, it was probably normal for the parties to give some small payment to the judge.[32] This was a fact of life in the Middle Ages, one accepted by litigants and canonists alike. But it is another thing to postulate widespread corruption. Some historians, moved perhaps by the satires of Chaucer or the strictures of *Piers Plowman*, have argued that venality and corruption were built into the canonical system. It must be admitted that there is some evidence to support that judgment.[33] Perhaps apparitors and minor clerks were routinely corrupt. But, to the balance should be added that the actual court records do not support any such harsh verdicts against the judges. In them, the judges appear either to have been generally competent and uncorrupted, or to have hidden their imperfections and misdeeds so effectively that no accusations could be made.

THE LAWYERS

Most parties in marriage cases were represented at some point in the litigation by a professional proctor, one of the lawyers attached to each Consistory court. Litigants were not required to hire a proctor, and some apparently did not choose to do so. But most did. It is at

---

[31] P.R.O. K.B. 27/365 Rex, m. 12 (1351).

[32] There is also one very interesting extra-judicial appeal to the judge in a marriage case, inserted by chance on a separate sheet of paper between pages 24 and 25 of Hereford I/2 (1497). It reads: 'Mayster Comissary y recommend me unto you with all my hert, certifying you that as for the contract that is in veryauncie in your quort before you betwex John Hyggyns and Jowan Warham, his fryndes and y been agreyde and they shal be maryede shortly with godis grace and y prey you lett your quort be drawon and y ame youris in that y can, knowithe god, who preserve you. Skribbilt with the hande of, Your Lover Richard Harley.' The hand of this note appears to me, however, to be slightly later than 1497, although it is difficult to be sure.

[33] A. H. Thompson has collected some of this material in *The English Clergy and their Organization in the Later Middle Ages* (Oxford, 1947), 60–3. And see John Yunck, *The Lineage of Lady Meed: The Development of Mediaeval Venality Satire* (Notre Dame, 1963), 143–70.

this stage of investigation impossible to say much about the training of most proctors. What evidence there is suggests that, unlike the judges, most proctors did not have degrees in law. The Black Book of the Court of Arches, the most important ecclesiastical court in England, specified only that proctors with the status of bachelor in canon or civil law were to be preferred to those without a degree.[34] There was no requirement. If this was true in the Court of Arches, it seems reasonable to assume that standards were at least no higher in lesser tribunals. This possibility is supported by two pieces of evidence from the records themselves. First, the degrees of the proctors were never recorded in the Act books, whereas those of the judges were. Second, it has proved impossible to find the names of more than a very few of the proctors in Emden's Biographical Registers of the graduates of Oxford and Cambridge. Of the eight men who served as proctors at Lichfield between 1466 and 1474, for example, only two can be traced as graduates in law, although one other may also have studied at Oxford without taking a degree.[35] Five men practised in the court at Canterbury between 1415 and 1425. Only one of them, James Burbaych, can be found in Emden's Registers.[36] Sometimes, in fact, none of the proctors practising in a court has any record of university affiliation. The five men who served at Rochester in 1496–7 provide one example of this, although one of them may possibly have taken an arts degree.[37] The list of nine proctors in the York Act book of 1417–20 fails to produce a single proctor who can be traced surely to either Oxford or Cambridge.[38]

---

[34] Wilkins, *Concilia* II, 690–1.

[35] Thomas Colt, B.C.L. (Oxon.) and John Croftes, B.Cn.L. (Cantab.); John Couper studied civil law at Oxford. The other proctors are John Paynell, William Hudson, William Calton, Thomas Pennesby, and Christopher Paynell.

[36] Woodcock, 121; it is surely significant that Burbaych was the only one of these men to become a judge, the official of the archdeacon of Canterbury. In 1455, there were six proctors who appeared in the court at Canterbury. One of them had a degree: John Quynton, B.C.L. (Oxon.) For the others, John Byllys, John Brede, Nicholas Lyde, Thomas Barton, and John Egerdon, I have not been able to trace any university connection.

[37] William Lancaster may be identified with the arts graduate listed in Emden, *Biographical Register . . . Oxford*. The other proctors are John Bere, Martin Bere, William Halsnoth, and John Major. Of the ten men who served as proctors at Hereford, 1491–9, only Thomas Merton, B.C.L. and B.Cn.L. (Oxon.) can be surely identified as a graduate. The others, Hugh Jones, Hugh Green, Richard Wolffe, David Jonys, William Gregge, Hugh Gyles, John Hughes, John Hyde, and Eliseus Ruthyn cannot, although the last two named might possibly be identical with Oxford graduates; see *Biographical Register . . . Oxford* II, 992 and III, 1613–14.

[38] Thomas Stanton may be the man referred to in Emden, *Biographical Register . . . Cambridge*, 551. The other proctors were Robert Esyngwald, John Willyngham, William Driffeld, John Ragenhill, Thomas de Alta Ripa, Thomas Appylby, John Sturneton, and ? Lepyngton.

One piece of evidence which seems to support a university connection for the proctors is that almost all of them are styled *magister* in the Act books. But since that term was often given by courtesy to notaries public, a position many of the proctors held, the use of the title does not prove conclusively that they were graduates.[39] This does not mean, of course, that they were ignorant of the law. A few may have studied abroad. Many may have been at a university but left without taking a degree. And much law could certainly be learned during an apprenticeship in any court.[40] The regularity of their appointment in marriage cases certainly suggests that parties considered their service worth having. But the evidence does suggest that most of them lacked the formal legal training which almost all the judges had.

The men just discussed, who served in all the Consistory courts, were proctors. In canon law there was also a second kind of professional lawyer, the advocate. His function, something like that of an English barrister, consisted in the formulation and argument of specifically legal points. He did not ordinarily introduce facts or organize evidence, as the proctor did. An advocate might frame the articles or interrogatories, but his principal duty came only after all proof had been introduced. It was then that he argued the legal merits of the case, seeking to persuade the judge of the strength of his client's legal position.[41] A proctor, on the other hand, was a straightforward representative for his client. By his appointment, he became (in the standard phrase) *dominus litis*, capable of acting as if he were the party himself.[42]

---

[39] See C. R. Cheney, *Notaries Public In England in the Thirteenth and Fourteenth Centuries* (Oxford, 1972), 89–90.

[40] There is some evidence that new proctors served a sort of apprenticeship; at least there was sometimes a considerable delay between their admission and first case. See, for example, K. Burns, Ecclesiastical Courts of the Diocese of York, unpublished study at Borthwick Inst., 148; 'Morland, admitted in December 1427, had to wait until June 1429 to secure his first client.' For the post-Reformation period, see R. A. Marchant, *The Church under the Law* (Cambridge, 1969), 55.

[41] See Lyndwood, *Provinciale*, 77 s. v. *advocatus*: 'Cuius officium non est sigillum apponere, sed suo clientulo in his, quae sunt juris, consulere, et eius desiderium in judicio proponere, et pro eo publice postulare.' The duties of an advocate are conveniently summed up by P. Gillet, in 'Avocat', *D.D.C.* I, 1524–35, and P. Fournier, *Les Officialités au moyen âge* (Paris, 1880), 33ff. Samples of advocates' work are contained in H. Silvestre, 'Dix plaidoiries inédites au XIIe siècle', *Traditio*, 10 (1954), 373–97.

[42] R. Naz, 'Procureur', *D.D.C.* VII, 324–39; and see Ely EDR D/2/1, f. 72v (1377): 'Et quia per litis contestacionem facti sunt domini litis et sic non possunt deferere causam, ... ideo cum eis duximus procedendum in causa.' Canterbury Y.1.6, f. 21r (1464): 'Duraunt exhibuit procuratorium apud acta et fecit se partem pro domino suo.'

Advocates were used in some English courts. The Court of Arches in London and the Provincial court at York had a not inconsiderable staff.[43] There is also mention of the presence of advocates in the courts at Ely and at Bath and Wells. But it seems fairly clear that some of the diocesan courts, particularly those in which few or no appeals were heard, did without the services of advocates altogether. The court records give no sign that they appeared in the Consistory courts at Rochester, Hereford, or Canterbury. Probably they did not appear at Lichfield either. There is one reference to action taken in the presence of an advocate, but it was a special case heard *in pleno consistorio episcopali*, so that perhaps an advocate was brought in for a particularly difficult case.[44] Elsewhere in the Lichfield records, the presence of proctors alone is mentioned.

The absence of advocates from many of the courts raises an interesting problem of the relation of canonical theory to practice. According to the law, any party had the right to demand that an advocate be assigned to him. He had the right to professional legal advice.[45] What was the situation in those courts in which advocates were not used? The most likely answer is that in these the proctors served a dual function, acting both as representative and as legal adviser. At Canterbury, in fact, the same men who appeared as proctors were in three cases actually styled *advocati*.[46] Two cases, one from Canterbury, the other from Hereford, also speak of the proctors giving *consilium* to litigants in a marriage case.[47] The proctors must have done both jobs there.

Perhaps this combination of roles explains, at least in part, the general disregard of the rule that proctors were to serve without fee.

---

[43] See Churchill, *Canterbury Administration* II, 450–1. Ten proctors and sixteen advocates were authorized to practise at one time in the Court of Arches. In York, twelve advocates and eight proctors were authorized to practise; See Wilkins, *Concilia* II, 409–13.

[44] B/C/1/2, f. 289r (1477–8); and note B/C/1/1, f. 219v (1468): 'dicta causa erat continuata coram domino episcopo pro advocato adquirendo.' See also *The Ecclesiastical Courts, Principles of Reconstruction* (London, 1954), 14.

[45] X 1.32.1; and see, for example, York M 2 (1) e, s.d. 10 February 1377: 'Idem Driffield petiit consilium advocatorum dicte curie dominis suis et sibi eorum nomine in presenti negocio assignari.' This was granted.

[46] U. 41, f. 30v (1394); f. 48r (1394); Y.1.3, f. 4v (1416), where John Egerden was the advocate-proctor in question. See Woodcock, 121. One entry from Canterbury Y.1.1, f. 46v (1373) is problematical: 'Et pars actrix iurata dicit quod liberavit huiusmodi interrogatorias tempore competenti advocato qui omisit liberare iudici huiusmodi interrogatorias tempore competenti. Et procurator partis ree fatetur omissionem huiusmodi.' It is not clear to me whether an actual advocate is meant, or whether this is simply another case of confusing the two offices.

[47] Y.1.7, f. 42r (1460); Hereford I/1, 28 (1492).

This rule found support among some canonists. And it was found in Roman law.[48] But, in fact, there are several cases in the Act books in which proctors brought suit against their former clients to enforce payment of their fees.[49] And, where costs were assessed against losing parties, the proctor's fee always figured as part of the legitimate expenses.[50] If, in practice, the proctors regularly performed duties which required legal expertise, as they must have when no advocates were available, it was logical and necessary that they should be paid for their services. Surely, the regular staffs of proctors attached to the Church courts would not have existed without routine provision for payment.

How competent and conscientious were the proctors who earned these fees? The question is at least worth asking, even though the answer cannot be clear. There are a few instances in which a proctor was disciplined or rebuked by a judge for inefficiency or misconduct. David Mareys, a proctor at Canterbury, was precluded from one term in a suit 'because of [his] laziness and negligence'.[51] William Leverton was excluded entirely from the Ely court for refusing to swear to observe its statutes and customs.[52] A proctor at Canterbury in 1460 failed to file the proper exceptions for his client, because, he claimed, 'he did not have sufficient time to write the exceptions'.[53] But there are not enough of such entries to warrant any firm conclusions. Nor is it here permissible to argue from silence, to suggest that the small number of complaints means that the lawyers normally did their jobs well. Unlike accusations against judges, objections against lawyers were unlikely to be the basis for an appeal. And we normally learn of faults in the system when a case was ap-

---

[48] Cod. 2.12.15; 'quod officium gratuitum esse debet'; Hostiensis, *Summa Aurea* I, tit. *de proc.*, no. 1: 'Is qui negotium domini gratuito administrat, . . . , gratuito autem, ideo dicitur in descriptione: quia si interveniat merces, locator dicitur operarum, non procurator.' Richardus Anglicus, *Summa de Ordine Iudiciarii*, ed. Wahrmund, *Quellen* II:I, 21. But cf. Durantis, *Spec. Iud.* I, tit. *de salariis*, § *de salariis procuratorum et tabellionum*. X 1.38.6 allows expenses to the proctor, but that is of course a different matter from a professional fee.

[49] E.g. Canterbury Y.1.1, f. 25v (1373), styled *causa salarii*; Hereford I/3, 43 (1500); Ely EDR D/2/1, f. 51r (1376); f. 79r (1377).

[50] See Churchill, *Canterbury Administration* II, 203; Woodcock, 135–7; York C.P. F 190 (1454), where an entire schedule of expenses is also preserved along with the other Cause papers.

[51] Y.1.4, f. 33v (1420): 'Precluserunt partem ab illo termino ad dicendum contra, propter desidiam et necligenciam procuratoris.'

[52] EDR D/2/1, f. 131v (1380).

[53] Y.1.7, f. 61r (1460) '. . . quia ut asseruit non habuit tempus sufficiens ad scribendum excepciones in causa.'

pealed. We cannot expect complaints against the competence of the lawyers to appear in the surviving records.

Something of the same difficulty exists in trying to form an accurate notion of how far the canon law's ethical standards were observed by the proctors. I have found only one explicit complaint against the character of a proctor. In a Canterbury case of 1294, one proctor was challenged as 'infamis et perjurius'.[54] But again, the absence of widespread complaint is not conclusive. Complaints against unethical conduct would not normally appear in the records. There is however, some positive evidence in this instance. It suggests, even if it does not prove, that proctors commonly respected the ideal that lawyers were to serve justice impartially.[55]

In theory, ecclesiastical lawyers were held to high standards. Besides the standards of Western church law, they were bound to the courts by a series of oaths which they took on admission to practice in a court, and which they renewed annually. They were sworn to deal honestly in all things with their clients, to take only moderate fees, to serve poor litigants without charge. They were to accept only cases they believed to be rightfully brought and, rather significantly, to give up participation in a case, even during its prosecution, if they discovered their client's position was groundless. The law and their oaths enjoined them not to suborn witnesses, not to propose unnecessary delays, not to launch frivolous appeals.[56] In short, the canonical ideal was that the practising lawyer should always act in the interests of justice, even if this were sometimes at the expense of his own client's.

Under an adversary system of justice, lawyers are normally expected to represent their clients to the limits of their competence, as long as they avoid outright unethical practice. There is an opposing notion, one perhaps increasingly heard today, that the lawyer is also an officer of the court. But I think it is fair to say that the modern trial lawyer is expected to give his client the best and most complete representation he can. We believe that the truth of a case will emerge from the confrontation of two skilled adversaries. Clearly, this was

---

[54] Sede Vacante S.B. III, no. 346.

[55] There is a fuller treatment of this subject, covering all types of litigation, in my 'Ethical Standards for Advocates and Proctors in Theory and Practice', *Proceedings of the Fourth International Congress of Medieval Canon Law* (Vatican City, 1975).

[56] See Wilkins, *Concilia* II, 27; Churchill, *Canterbury Administration* I, 450–51; EDR D/2/1, f. 62v, giving the text of the oath. For the diocese of Exeter, see *Councils and Synods* II, 1030–1.

not the assumption of the canon law. Each proctor and advocate was sworn to serve his client, of course, but only so far as he believed that client's cause was just. The difference is one of degree, perhaps. But it is a real difference. Ecclesiastical lawyers owed, by virtue of their oath, their first allegiance to the interests of impartial justice.

Of course, the existence of an oath is one thing. The execution of its provisions is another. Can we assume that the law's standards were obeyed? The Act books, while not conclusive, do contain real evidence of the continuing force of the oath each lawyer took. There are cases where the proctor's responsibility to the court and to the law's ethical standards was plainly stronger than his duty to a client. Some are of a negative sort. A proctor asked for a delay, but when required to swear he had a good reason for it, he did not conscientiously feel that he could do so. He refused, and the case proceeded to sentence.[57] Some examples are more positive. A proctor knew that the facts of the case had not been fully revealed. He believed that his client could make them known. Therefore, he asked the court to order the party, his client, to appear in person to clear the matter up.[58] In these cases, the duty to the interests of justice came ahead of the proctor's responsibility to his patron's wishes.

The most frequent entry of this sort was the abandonment by a proctor of a case he considered to have been shown as without foundation during the course of the trial. It was a *causa desperata*, one which he could no longer defend in good conscience. There are quite a few examples of this.[59] Admittedly, for a lawyer to give up in the middle of a case is not terribly attractive by modern standards. It left the litigant without representation. The effect on his chances in the suit may well be imagined. On the other hand, its relative frequency points to a positive feature of practice by the lawyers. They had sworn

---

[57] Ely D/2/1, f. 22v (1375): 'Et quia procurator dicti Nicholai dictam exceptionem proponens recusavit expresse iurare quod maliciose non proponit, ideo dictam exceptionem reicimus;' Canterbury Y.1.7, f. 42v (1460): 'Tunc iudex mandavit Griff' iurare quod hoc non petiit animo differendi litem, quod iuramentum recusavit prestare, ac iudex postea posuit eis silencium.' See also Rochester DRb Pa 1, f. 6r (1437).

[58] See 'Ethical Standards' (note 55), *passim*.

[59] E.g. Hereford I/2, 35 (1497): 'Et deinde procurator partis actricis dimisit causam desperatam. Et iudex decrevit dictam partem actricem principalem fore citandam . . . pro eo quod procurator suus de causa desperat.' Other instances of similar dismissals in marriage cases are found in Hereford I/1, 344 (1499); I/2, 88 (1499); 110 (1499); I/3, 46 (1500); Canterbury Y.1.1, f. 12r (1373); Y.1.3, f. 152r (1420); Y.1.4, f. 28r (1420), f. 28v (1420), f. 78v (1422); Rochester DRb Pa 1, f. 23v (1437); f. 318v (1443); DRb Pa 4, f. 195r (1486); Bath and Wells D/D/C Al, 157 (1481), 161 (1485); Lichfield B/C/1/1, f. 109r (1466); B/C/1/2, f. 125v (1473).

not to take up or to continue a case they believed to be unjust. They acted on that oath. If this meant sacrificing the temporary advantage of their client, that had to be accepted. And, in courts where spiritual values were not irrelevant, it could never have been in the real interest of any litigant to win a case on the basis of perjured evidence or an unjust claim.

It would be misleading to claim that examples of the effectiveness of the proctors' oaths appear on every page of the Act books. They do not. But we should also remember that the ordinary, day-to-day control of litigation by lawyers would necessarily have been done outside of court. It would never have been recorded. We can see only a small part. Doubtless there were unscrupulous lawyers and sharp practice in marriage litigation, but the evidence of the service of many proctors as real officers of the Church courts should, in my view, also be remembered. Certainly there is more of it in the surviving records than there is evidence of the chicanery we sometimes associate with the legal profession.

THE WITNESSES

Something has already been said under the heading of procedure about the role of witnesses in marriage litigation. Most cases did not involve great crowds of witnesses. From two to five were normal. In part, this is because the marriage contracts which were the subject of most suits were made at home. They were seldom witnessed by more than a few people. In part, it is because of the necessity of paying the expenses of each witness. The parties had normally to meet the out-of-pocket costs of each man or woman who came to give testimony for them. Since the litigants in most cases which have survived were neither rich nor powerful, this practical consideration limited the production of superfluous witnesses.

Canon law prohibited certain classes of people from giving testimony. For example, a perjurer was in theory absolutely incapable of giving testimony.[60] But procedure in the courts was so organized that the issue of a man's status as a common perjurer was usually raised only after he had already given his evidence and submitted it to the court. First came the introduction of a party's witnesses; next came the taking of depositions; and then the term for speaking against the

---

[60] Hostiensis, *Summa Aurea* II, tit. *de testibus*, no. 2: 'Qui non est integrae famae, non admittitur ad testimonium, nam si vita bona defuerit, fide carebit. . . . Infamis ergo de iure repellitur a testimonio.'

status or the character of the witnesses. Testimony and argument on
that issue followed that term. In other words, the testimony of a witness had normally already been put into evidence by the time he could
be challenged. According to the canonical rule, every witness was
presumed suitable until the contrary had been proved.[61] The combination of this rule with the delayed procedure of attacking witnesses
meant that the apparent rules of exclusion did not keep objectionable
testimony from coming to the attention of the judge.[62] It is tempting
to say that the rules of exclusion thus did not work at all. But we cannot look inside the minds of the judges. They may have been able to
disregard testimony of witnesses subsequently shown to be excluded
under the canon law.

In one, perhaps two, cases the rules did, however, apparently effectively exclude witnesses. Testimony by children below the age of
puberty was forbidden.[63] And the ages of the witnesses, when given in
the surviving depositions, was always sixteen or above.[64] Witnesses of
servile status were also excluded by law from giving evidence.[65] And
the records almost invariably style witnesses *libere conditionis*. However, there are a few cases in which the opposing party challenged the
status of a witness, and in which the testimony of villeins does appear
to have been admitted.[66] Even this rule was apparently not invariably
enforced.

The most significant question about the witnesses in marriage
litigation does not, however, revolve around their status or the procedure used in their production. It is this: were marriage suits commonly brought and won on perjured testimony? Evidence in virtually
all English marriage cases was exclusively by witnesses. In the nature
of the disputes, written evidence was not available. Any estimate of

---

[61] *Gl. ord.* ad X 2.20.1 s.v. *idonei.*

[62] In York C.P. E 103 (1367–9), for example, Richard Wydowson was challenged as an
unsuitable witness because he was allegedly a common perjurer, an excommunicate, and of
servile status. His deposition nevertheless appears along with the others submitted to the
court.

[63] Hostiensis, *Summa Aurea* II, tit. *de testibus*, no. 2: 'In causa civili impuberes repelluntur.'

[64] But in Ely EDR D/2/1, f. 159v (1381), witnesses were recalled because they had been
under age *tempore admissionis.*

[65] See Hostiensis, *Summa Aurea* II, tit. *de testibus*, no. 2, where this reason is given for
the prohibition: 'nam saepe servus metu dominantis supprimit veritatem.'

[66] E.g. York C.P. F 227 (1441), where it was objected that one witness had falsely claimed
to be of free status, whereas 'revera . . . est servilis conditionis et nativus nobilis domine
committisse Cantibr.' Canterbury Ecc. Suit, no. 12 (1269); York C.P. E 103 (1367–69); and C.P.
E 198 (1393) are other instances.

the effectiveness of the canon law of marriage must, therefore, take this problem into account. How reliable were the witnesses? How often did they give false or manufactured evidence? How successful were the courts in diagnosing fraud? Answers to these question are obviously exceedingly difficult; sweeping generalizations will not inspire confidence. But this much may be said with certainty: the evidence in the surviving records of the introduction of perjured testimony is a great deal stronger than the evidence of corruption among the lawyers and judges. Whatever court record one picks up, one will not go far before finding some evidence of the use of suspect witnesses and false testimony.

One such indication comes from simple attacks on the trustworthiness of witnesses. These were frequent. In *Pollyn* v. *Parker*, to take an example from the diocese of London, the primary witness for the plaintiff was challenged as 'commonly known as a man of slippery tongue and a liar'. The allegation noted that 'he was expelled from the said parish because of his evil tongue'.[67] A witness in a York case of 1355 was said to be 'pauper, humilis, vilis et abiecta persona levis opinionis et male fame'.[68] In a thirteenth-century case from Canterbury this exception was raised against a woman's claim of marriage: 'Mulier alias confitebatur se non habuisse testes, et modo producit ribaldas.'[69] Such allegations do not, of course, prove that the witnesses were liars and their testimony false. The allegations may themselves have been false. On the other hand, it is hard to believe that they would have been made as frequently as they were unless there was often some truth to the charges.

In another sort of case we may be more certain about the perjury. That is the case in which the plaintiff claimed a contract of marriage, and the defense was an alibi. The defendant said he had been in some other town or village at the time. Physically, he could not have been present. He himself produced witnesses to prove the alibi. In some

---

[67] MS. 9065, f. 24r (1488).

[68] C.P. E 70.

[69] Ecc. Suit, no. 239 (1293). Other examples: Canterbury Ecc. Suit, no. 16 (1270); Sede Vacante S.B. III, no. 57 (1292); X.10.1, f. 16r (1412); X.1.1, f. 133v (1456); Y.1.1, f. 24v (1373); London MS. 9065, fols. 178r–178v (1494), York C.P. F 169 (1427); C.P. F 176 (1421); C.P. F 182 (1438); C.P. F 123 (1434), in which the last witnesses were said to be 'nimis obscure deponentes, variantes et perjurii necnon veritatem occulantes'. In London MS. 9065 B, f. 15v (1488) there is this description of a witness as 'mulier lubrice lingue et multum mendax et quod solet sepe unum dicere et affirmare jurata et statim post illud quod prius affirmabat negare'. On the other hand, it is possible that at least some of the allegations were of a purely formal nature. See Oughton, *Ordo Judiciorum* I, 156–7.

cases there was room for honest misunderstanding by witnesses over exactly what words had been spoken. But here, particularly since more than one witness appeared for each side, one set of witnesses must have been lying. In a case from 1432, for example, Agnes Brignall set up a contract of marriage with John Smyth, purportedly made on the Wednesday before Palm Sunday in the city of York. Smyth, however, produced witnesses who swore that he was at Pontefract, eighteen miles from York, for most of that day. In the afternoon he had set out for Doncaster, where he spent the night. There was thus no way he could have been in York to contract marriage.[70] We cannot be sure in this instance which story was correct. But both could not have been.

Other examples of this sort may be taken from the York records of the first half of the fifteenth century. In all cases the plaintiff alleged a contract of marriage at a specific time. In one, the defendant produced evidence that he had been in London for a two-week period, including the time of the supposed contract.[71] In a second, the defendant tried to show that he had spent the entire day at his parents' house half a mile away.[72] In a third, he and his fellows said they had played football all that day.[73] In a fourth, a defendant's witnesses testified that he had been working in the fields at the time of the claimed marriage.[74] In all these cases, one party's arguments almost certainly rested on false testimony.

In these instances, we do not actually see the bribery or instruction of witnesses taking place. We must simply infer it from the results. Occasionally, there was direct evidence given, but this was usually by accident. A conversation was overheard, a chance remark was dropped, or the rumor spread that a man's new animal had come to him as a bribe. Chance brought the story to light. In an interesting case from Canterbury, Richard Wydott testified that he had seen the witnesses meeting together. He remembered that 'they had a piglet to eat in that place, where they spoke among themselves about this matter of marriage. And he said that they there agreed how they would

---

[70] C.P. F 104 (1432).
[71] C.P. F 113 (1433).
[72] C.P. F 79 (1418).
[73] C.P. F 137 (1423).
[74] C.P. F 186 (1450). Similar examples from the thirteenth century Canterbury records are: Ecc. Suit, no. 12 (1269–71); no. 36 (1271); no. 270 (1293); and no. 288 (1292–3).

testify in this marriage case'.[75] In another, a witness apparently confessed that she had been promised two bushels of wheat for giving testimony favorable to one party.[76] And in a third the party had used intimidation, threatening the witness with the loss of money if his testimony was unfavorable.[77] Usually, however, such evidence was not available. The agreement or bribery was made out of sight, and we can know nothing of it.

Bribery was also particularly difficult to prove because the line between paying a witness's expenses and buying his testimony was not firmly fixed. The first was, of course, perfectly legal. Indeed it could be required. The second was cause for rejecting the witness's testimony. But even in the rare instance in which exact evidence of the size of the payment was forthcoming, it was difficult to decide on which side of the line the payment fell. Perhaps a payment of six shillings and eightpence, from a York case of 1464, was clearly too much to be merely expenses.[78] Surely eightpence, paid in 1440 in a Rochester case, was all right.[79] What about two shillings and eightpence in a London case of 1494?[80] Does it make any difference to find expenses of twelvepence reduced to sixpence in the Ely court in 1375?[81] I do not suggest that any set figure should have been adopted. Legitimate expenses must vary according to the status of the witness, the distance he had to travel, and variations in cost of living. The line between bribery and expenses is a difficult one in any age. Nonetheless, the problem in marriage litigation was a real one. It added difficulties to the problems of proving bribery, and it offered temptations to build up a case with witnesses who had a monetary interest in the result.

---

[75] Y.1.1, f. 106v (1455): 'Habuerunt unum porcellum ibidem ad prandendum, ubi habuerunt inter se tractatum de ista materia matrimoniali. Et dicit quod ibi erant concordati qualiter deponerent de ista causa matrimoniali.' In an exceptional case from Canterbury, Sede Vacante S.B. III, no. 34 (1293), a witness candidly admitted that there had been prior agreement on what the testimony would be: 'Requisitus si concordavit cum aliis contestibus suis sic dicere, dicit quod sic.' The other two witnesses denied the prearrangement.

[76] Canterbury Ecc. Suit, no. 322 (1293): 'Dicit quod Beatricia est munere corrupta per Amiciam de Port que promisit sibi duos busellos bledi cuiusmodi ignorat et hoc se dicit scire per relatum dicte Beatricie que hoc isti testi ut dicit confitebatur.'

[77] Canterbury Sede Vacante S.B. III, no. 19 (n.d.): '... quod faceret eum amittere pecuniam suam si testificaretur contra eum.'

[78] C.P. F 204.

[79] DRb Pa 1, f. 144r. Note, however, that the witnesses in this case objected to the amount as too small. The proctor protested that his client was too poor to pay more, and the case went forward.

[80] MS. 9065, f. 167v.

[81] EDR D/2/1, f. 21v.

How successful were the Church courts in identifying perjury? There were devices used to catch it. The primary of these was challenge by the other party. This has just been discussed. Second, witnesses were often asked specific questions as a means of control. Typical questions were these. What was the weather like on the day of the contract? Who was present at the time? What were the parties wearing? In what part of the house were they standing? Were there candles burning? If different witnesses gave variant answers, their testimony was naturally suspect. Sometimes this device worked. A man at York, caught in such a contradiction with another witness, later came into court to try to change his story. He explained that when he had given evidence, 'he was so tormented by the sickness of fever that he did not realize what he was saying, but now he was better advised'.[82] In other cases, we find the examiner's scribe specifically marking places in the depositions where witnesses had answered differently.[83] But there is a real question whether it is reasonable to expect witnesses to remember details perfectly. Particularly so when the events at issue had occurred several years before, as was sometimes true in marriage actions. Perfect coincidence in detail may in fact be evidence of a prearranged story.

It is therefore impossible to give a final verdict on the effectiveness of the Church courts in dealing with perjured testimony. The extent of such false swearing is also hard to assess. It must be enough to note that the records contain several indications that false and untrustworthy evidence was commonly introduced. This is all the more striking for the lack of similar complaints against lawyers and judges. And we should also note that there were real problems involved in dealing with the situation. Lack of cross-examination by the judge and opposing party, the necessary looseness in defining bribery, and the relative weakness of methods for discovering and evaluating contradictions were among these. Though we cannot give an authoritative verdict, the evidence rather points to an unflattering judgment on this aspect of marriage litigation.

THE LITIGANTS

Study of procedure in marriage cases has shown the large extent to which the parties themselves directed the enforcement of the canon law. It is particularly important, therefore, to make some observations

---

[82] C.P. F 113 (1433): 'Taliter fuit vexatus infirmitate febris quod nescivit bene quid dixit sed iam melius deliberatus fuit.'

[83] E.g. York C.P. F 253 (1472): 'Nota variacionem loci a primo teste.'

and judgments about the litigants, as they appear in the surviving records. To begin, what was their economic and social status? So far as the remaining *acta* are representative, the parties in the Consistory courts were drawn from all stations save the very lowest and the highest. Participation in marriage litigation was by no means limited to the upper strata of medieval society. We find merchants, shop keepers, potters, tailors, and shoemakers.[84] Apothecaries, goldsmiths, cordwainers, and masons all appeared in litigation.[85] There are agricultural workers and peasants of no particular note or property.[86] We come across litigants described as 'servientes', or 'in statu simplicis valetti'.[87] On the other hand, men and women of servile status do not figure in the court records. They were excluded by law from giving testimony, and the records which survive do not show them as litigants. There is only one exception to this. By ancient law, it was possible for a free man to dissolve a marriage contracted with a slave if he was ignorant of the condition at the time of this marriage. This rule was applied to villeins in the Middle Ages. There is thus an occasional example of such a divorce for error of condition.[88] Here, by definition, the defendant was of servile condition. Otherwise, there is no evidence remaining that they resorted to the Church courts to settle their marriage disputes. Probably they settled them privately, as indeed people of higher standing sometimes did.

The absence of litigants of the upper classes is also worthy of note. It is fairly certain that the cases where the record gives no occupation for the parties did not involve people of high standing. We can infer this because when they did appear, their status was specifically identified. Their title was given, they were specifically styled *dominus*, or the fact of their lordship of a manor was recorded. Several examples appear in the Cause papers at York.[89] In fact, the York records and

---

[84] Canterbury X.10.1, f. 108v (1417); Ecc. Suit, No. 239 (1294); Ely EDR D/2/1, f. 51v (1376); York C.P. E 111 (1372); E 121 (1372); C.P. F 46 (1422); York M 2(1) f, f. 22r (1394).

[85] York C.P. E 245 (1391); E 248 (1346); E 138 (1389); M 2(1), f, f. 19r (1379).

[86] York C.P. F 186 (1450); Canterbury X.10.1, f. 54r (1414); Rochester DRb Pa 2, f. 102v (1448).

[87] York C.P. E 155 (1374); Cons. A B 2, f. 8v (1424); Canterbury X.10.1, f. 12r (1411); Y.1.1 f. 62r (1374); Hereford 0/2, 74 (1442); Ely EDR D/2/1, f. 90v (1378); Rochester DRb Pa 1, f. 352v (1443); London MS. 9065, f. 71v (1489).

[88] York C.P. E 237 (1397); C.P. F 16/3 (1405); C.P. F 59 (1410); Ely EDR D/2/1, f. 59r (1376).

[89] E.g. York Cons. A B 4, f. 88r (1486) is a suit between 'preclara ac nobilis domina domina Cecilia Plantagenet contra Radulphum Scrope de Upsall'. Other examples of upper class litigants: York C.P. E 12/1 (1323); C.P. E 46 (1340); C.P. E 179 (1390); C.P. E 259 (1368–9); Canterbury Ecc. Suit, no. 203 (1294); no. 219 (1301); no. 297 (1293).

the thirteenth-century Canterbury *sede vacante* material produce almost all the litigants of the upper classes that we have. In other dioceses, few or no persons of any rank appear.[90] This may seem strange. We usually think that it was the upper class which made most liberal use of marriage law, especially in suits for divorce. The most likely explanation for their absence from our records is that the gentry and nobility usually brought their disputes directly to the bishop, to be heard by him in person or in his court of audience. The case of Margery Paston, who made an undesirable marriage with her father's bailiff and had recourse to the Church in the ensuing dispute, is a concrete example. The matter was handled personally by the bishop. No action was ever taken in the Consistory court at Norwich.[91] Also there is reference to marriage cases involving upper class families in most episcopal registers. This again suggests that these people went directly to the bishop. Perhaps greater privacy was thus available.

Considering the expense of a court action, we may also wonder that so many people of humble status were able to bring matrimonial cases before the courts. Litigation was not cheap. An apparently ordinary suit over marriage heard in Lichfield in 1473 cost one party 26s. 8d.[92] A case of restitution of conjugal rights came to 33s. 4d.[93] An estimate made in 1367 of the cost of bringing a marriage suit with subsequent appeal to the archbishop's court in York amounted to the large sum of 55s.[94] Forty shillings were said to have been spent in a Canterbury case heard in 1456.[95] According to canon law, a form of pleading *in forma pauperum* was available.[96] Under this, the party paid nothing; the court and its officials bore the expenses of the action. It is not impossible to find examples of this.[97] But they were rare. Litigants had to find money for expenses themselves.

---

[90] An exception is Lichfield B/C/1/1, f. 270r (1469), where a litigant was styled *armiger*.

[91] *The Paston Letters, A.D. 1422–1509*, ed. James Gairdner (6 vols, London, 1904), no. 721. See also Canterbury Ch. Ant. A 36 II, 38 (1330), where 'dominus Willelmus Cheyne' appeared in the Archbishop's Court of Audience.

[92] B/C/1/2, f. 102r.

[93] *Ibid.*, f. 54v (1472).

[94] C.P. E 102 (1365); See Woodcock, 126, for a table of expenses in a testamentary case; Churchill, *Canterbury Administration* II, 202–5 for those of a tithe case.

[95] X.1.1, f. 131r.

[96] X 1.32.1; and Lyndwood, *Provinciale*, 68 s.v. *ad pauperes audiendos*; and for a modern commentary on the rights of poor litigants, see B. Tierney, *Medieval Poor Law* (Berkeley and Los Angeles, 1959), 15–19.

[97] E.g. Canterbury Y.1.7, f. 81r (1461); f. 122v (1462): 'Iudicialiter facta fide per mulierem, dominus Commissarius admisit eam in forma pauperum.' Other examples in marriage litigation: Rochester DRb Pa 1, f. 16v (1437); Canterbury Y.1.7, f. 81r (1461); Y.1.12, f. 145r (1476); Lichfield B/C/1/1, f. 4v (1464).

How ordinary men and women could afford such large sums is a little difficult to understand. It is not peculiar, of course, to marriage litigation. The quickness to go to law and the apparent willingness to spend amounts out of proportion to the visible profits is characteristic of the Middle Ages and long afterwards. Presumably, the stakes in making an advantageous marriage were also substantial. But the cost involved must have discouraged some litigation. At least it must have worked to bring the parties to agreement short of full proof.[98] Expense was not, however, enough to stop quite ordinary people from bringing marriage cases before the Church courts.

We turn now to consider the attitude of the parties towards the law of marriage and its enforcement in the courts. Here again, we must avoid facile judgments. But the question is of importance and should be raised. It is probably a safe generalization to say that in any sort of litigation where direction is left largely in the hands of the parties and in which the interests of those parties are not necessarily antagonistic, some collusion will result. The danger is particularly real in matrimonial suits. And that many people took advantage of the possibilities during the Middle Ages we have the testimony of the *glossa ordinaria*. Confessions against marriage were not to be accepted. The reason was the danger of collusion which, the gloss asserts, 'many practice'.[99] Without the element of control furnished by the Defender of the Bond in modern Catholic tribunals, the obstacles to collusion were not insurmountable.

An example may be drawn from the records at York. Alice Palmer had married Geoffrey Brown and lived with him for some four years. The union was not a happy one. The record states that 'the aforesaid Geoffrey injured the said Alice badly and treated her exceedingly ill'. As a result, Alice and her father found another young man, Ralph Fuler, and 'gave him gifts so that he would say that he had contracted marriage with the said Alice before any contract and solemnization of marriage between the aforesaid Geoffrey and Alice'. This strategem worked. Alice and Geoffrey were divorced. The whole matter came to light only some years later, after Geoffrey had in fact married another girl. Alice then sued to annul the previous judgment and get him back.[100]

---

[98] E.g. Canterbury Y.1.17, f. 144v (1498), in which the case was apparently ended by agreement after the handing in of the libel. The judge taxed the expenses at only 7d.

[99] *Gl. ord.* ad X 4.15.7 s.v. *in fraudem.*

[100] C.P. E 25 (1337).

No adequate machinery for stopping this sort of fraud existed in the medieval Church courts. The judges would not undertake an independent investigation into the lives of the parties. They left prosecution of causes largely to the parties themselves. As long as this was true, and no Defender of the Bond was appointed, the door was open to collusion. Some litigants, obviously, took advantage of the opportunities. How many did so we can only guess. It was only by chance that this sort of fraud was confessed. Had Alice not changed her mind about whom she wanted as her husband we should have known nothing about it.

This is one side of the picture. The other may be illustrated by another York case. William Gell married Joan Serle by words of present consent at home and in the presence of a few witnesses. Later, one witness related, William heard 'about certain evil and harmful conditions of the said Joan. [He] wished and aspired to be released from the same Joan.' Therefore, in a suit before the court at York, he swore that he had no witnesses to prove the contract. The case was therefore dismissed and he was declared free to marry whom he chose. William went home and told his father the whole story. But, instead of approving William's skill, the father reproved him, saying, 'Son, may it never happen that you so rashly damn your soul. It will be less bad for you to put up with vexation and loathing in your life than after your death to be damnably tortured by the pains of Hell.'[101] William was apparently frightened and convinced. He returned to the York court and confessed the fraud. He began the case again, although the record is unfortunately not complete enough for us to be certain of the final verdict.

This story well illustrates the countervailing force to the openings for collusion and fraud. The law could not be disregarded without danger to one's immortal soul. For many men, this was not a trifling matter. An interesting comment on the subject can be drawn from the Paston Letters. Sir John Paston had made an oblique reference to the possibility of using fraud to upset an undesirable marriage between his sister Margery and the bailiff Richard Calle. Margaret Paston picked up the suggestion, but wrote to him, 'As for the divorce that ye write to me of, I suppose that ye meant, but I charge you upon my blessing that ye do not, nor cause no other to do, that should offend

---

[101] C.P. F 168 (1427–8): 'Fili, absit quod ita temere dampnares animam tuam, . . . minus malum erit tibi hic in vita tua malestationes et tedia tolerare quam post mortem tuam penis infernalibus dampnaliter cruciari.'

God and your conscience, for if ye do, or cause for it to be done, God will take vengeance thereupon.'[102]

The strength of that belief can be found in the words and actions of litigants throughout the surviving court records. The formula which dismissed parties 'to their consciences' when there was no adequate proof of a marriage was not necessarily empty form.[103] The canonical system depended on men's consciences. The strength of that intangible but considerable force is found, for example, in cases where men at first denied contracting marriage, but then admitted they had done so when they were required to take the oath *de veritate dicenda*.[104] Of course we find the opposite as well: men whose disregard for the sanctity of an oath and the principle of indissolubility seems well-nigh complete. Not all men act or think alike in any age. Our picture of the litigants in marriage cases must contain, although it cannot resolve, both of these attitudes.

---

[102] *Paston Letters*, no. 721.

[103] E.g. Ely EDR D/2/1, f. 76r (1376): 'Sed quia dicta Matilda asserit iurata quod non habet testes ad probandum intencionem suam, ideo ipsum Johannem ab impeticione predicte Matilde sentencialiter et diffinitive absolvimus et dimittimus per decretum, eorum conscienciis penitus reliquendo.'

[104] Examples are: York M 2 (1) b, f. 10r (1371); C.P. E 153 (1389); C.P. E 102 (1367); Cons. A B 1, f. 86v (1418); Canterbury Y.1.1, f. 5v (1372); Ch. Ant., M 365 (1291); Ely EDR D/2/1, fols. 58v–59r (1376); Rochester DRb Pa 1, f. 15r (1437). And see Furnivall, *Child-Marriages, Divorces and Ratifications*, liii.

VI

CHANGES AND VARIATIONS IN PRACTICE

Historians normally treat the canon law of marriage in the later Middle Ages as a unit.[1] Applicable in every country of Western Europe and without appreciable substantive change from the thirteenth century to the sixteenth, the law of marriage appears as a unified and unifying system of social control. There is much to commend this view. The Liber Sextus, the Clementines, and the Extravagantes, which contained the law enacted after the publication of the Decretals in 1234, added virtually nothing to the law on marriage. Their sections on the subject are brief and devoid of innovation. And this law, with the additions and qualifications of the canonists, was in force in the Church courts of every country in Latin Christendom.

How far does this unitary picture correspond with reality? Is it fair to treat the entire period as one? Or were there developments and variations in practice which call for modification of the picture? Obviously, this question cannot be satisfactorily answered from the records of one country alone. We should need comparative studies of the courts of several different countries. The aim of this chapter must therefore be more modest. It is to describe some of the changes which took place in English marriage litigation during the late medieval period. And it is to examine a few differences in practice between the several Consistory courts. We should not expect, nor shall we find, great changes in the law. There is no doubt that the unitary view, for England at least, is justified in the main. The standard texts of the Decretum and the Decretals were the basis for decision of marriage cases throughout the period. They imposed control and stability. But examination of actual litigation does reveal some significant changes and variations. There was room for variety and growth within the canonical system.

*　　*　　*

[1] See, for example, Esmein I, 139–87; Maitland, *Roman Canon Law in the Church of England*, 38–40.

The most notable and significant change in marriage litigation over our period involved no variation in the law applied. It is the decline in the volume of marriage cases. Both absolutely and comparatively, matrimonial suits occupied a smaller place in the Church courts as time went on. There were fewer marriage causes, and there were more causes of other sorts. Regrettably, the records do not exist in sufficient quantities to allow for many comparative statistics. But what there is seems convincing.

At Canterbury, most of the litigation preserved in the thirteenth century *sede vacante* material concerns marriage. Brian Woodcock was able to identify sixty-two suits, constituting the 'great bulk' of what remains.[2] In 1373, the precentage was still substantial. Of 113 cases heard in the Consistory court, fully fifty-seven dealt with marriage.[3] By 1417, however, the percentage had dropped markedly. In all, 265 cases were heard; only fourteen of them related to marriage.[4] And by the end of the fifteenth century, in 1497, there were 393 suits heard, but only nine of them were matrimonial causes.[5] The drop, in other words, was from more than half to a small fraction of the Canterbury court's total business. And the numbers in absolute terms showed a similarly marked decline. The rise in the total number of cases is accounted for by a rising number of 'perjury' cases, that is suits in which a claim of debt was founded on the breach of a man's oath.

At Rochester, between April 1347 and April 1348 sixteen of thirty-four instance cases concerned marriage, only slightly less than half of the total.[6] In the next century, in 1438, the percentage had fallen to ten per cent. Ninety cases were heard by the court. Only nine of them were marriage actions. In the last decade of the century the total went even lower. In the three-year period from November 1493 to November 1496, nine marriage cases in all were heard, an average of only three per year. Unfortunately, it has not been possible to calculate the total number of cases of all sorts from this Rochester Act book, so that this example can show only the absolute decline in numbers.

---

[2] Woodcock, 83. This is also in accord with Miss Sayers' findings about the early thirteenth century. See *Papal Judges Delegate*, 205.

[3] Here and in the figures which follow, unless otherwise stated all cases have been counted in which at least one of the hearings occurred in the year(s) in question.

[4] I have taken the total in this instance from Woodcock, 89.

[5] In 1485, there were according to Woodcock (p. 84) about 800 cases in all heard at Canterbury. Of these, only twelve dealt with marriage questions.

[6] There were also thirteen debt recognizances which have not been included.

In other dioceses in which the Act books were arranged systematically enough to permit compilation of accurate statistics, the same
story emerges. At Lichfield, between 1465 and 1468, 338 suits were
heard. Of these sixty-seven, or between nineteen and twenty per
cent, dealt with marriage. This is not an inconsiderable segment of
the total, but it is far below the figures given above for the fourteenth
century. Before the official of Hereford, from Michaelmas of 1491
through the same term of 1493, 238 suits were begun. The insignificant number of four related to marriage. The bulk (161) was made
up of perjury actions.

There is no reason to think that the above examples are not representative. Indeed, other Act books support the conclusion they
suggest.[7] The number of marriage actions was declining. Where
matrimonial litigation represented a large percentage of the matters
heard in the thirteenth and fourteenth centuries, it was only a small
part in the fifteenth. As suggested in earlier chapters, the explanation
for this decline may well lie in the gradual adoption of more settled
attitudes and habits related to marriage. Most matrimonial litigation
was brought to enforce disputed claims of marriage. The habit of
contracting marriage at home, the ambiguity of the words used, and
the continuation of older notions regarding marriage as a private
contract made for large numbers of such claims. But with the gradual
assimilation of the Church's standards — exclusive competence over
marriage disputes and solemnization *in facie ecclesie* — the decline in
number of marriage cases followed as a matter of course. When there
was less uncertainty involved in the inception of marriages, there was
less need for marriage litigation to sort out the ensuing tangles. When
the constitutive act of marriage was more frequently the contract duly
solemnized in church, rather than the private agreement entered into
at home, there followed naturally a decline in the number of marriage
cases.

The rising proportion of divorce cases, as against multi-party
litigation, is another possible sign of the growth in matrimonial stability. Suits for divorce, we noted in examining multi-party suits,

[7] The Ely Registrum Primum, from the 1370s, contains a large percentage of marriage
actions. But an exact figure cannot be worked out, since some of the appeal cases were not
noted by subject, and because a great many of the entries covered office and miscellaneous
business. See the remarks in M. Aston, *Thomas Arundel*, 99 n. 2. Margaret Bowker has also
found that only 3.5% of the cases heard between 1514 and 1520 in the bishop of Lincoln's Court
of Audience involved matrimonial disputes. See 'The Commons Supplication against the
Ordinaries', *T.R.H.S.*, 21 (1971), 67.

played a larger role in marriage litigation in the fifteenth century than they had earlier.[8] This suggests that 'self-divorce', repudiation of a spouse without recourse to the Church, was becoming less acceptable in English society. More care was taken to secure a formal sentence of dissolution before passing to a new marriage. People were gradually absorbing the standards of the Church's marriage law. The process was not complete by 1500. And it may well be true that other factors reversed the process in the sixteenth century. But what evidence there is suggests some growth in stability of marriage customs by 1500.

★   ★   ★

The fall in numbers of marriage cases was something over which the courts had no direct control. It depended on factors quite apart from any changes in the law applied by the courts. But there was some development in legal practice as well. Of this there are no more significant or interesting examples than the rise of sequestration *pendente lite* and the decline of abjuration of sexual relations *sub pena nubendi*. Both are worth examining.

One of the real obstacles to the enforcement of the marriage canons was the freedom of action enjoyed by the parties during a lawsuit. We have seen that despite the law's prohibitions, parties could withdraw, compromise, or abandon marriage cases. Besides providing opportunities for evasion of the law, the ability to abandon a suit caused another real problem, for it sometimes happened that during the hearing of a marriage case, the defendant would marry a third person. In defiance of the law and usually against the court's express order, the defendant would have this second marriage solemnized. The reason for taking this illegal action was simple. It was to discourage the plaintiff from prosecuting his action. The knowledge that one's intended bride has married and had sexual relations with another man must be, in any age, a strong argument for letting the matter drop.[9] As long as plaintiffs could abandon their lawsuits, the

---

[8] See above, p. 58–9.

[9] Conset, *Practice*, 268, notes that one reason a woman would enter such a marriage is 'that she believes her Adversary will not (willingly, however) obtain an adjudicatory sentence for a Woman, who (in his opinion) is known by another Man; and upon this supposition, that he will willingly compound, or desist from the Sute.'

freedom to contract *pendente lite* would cause real difficulty in the correct decision of marriage cases.

The reaction to this problem used by the English Church courts in the thirteenth and fourteenth centuries was an order to the parties not to contract marriage *pendente lite*. The order was customarily issued at the start of a suit.[10] And it was backed by the threat of excommunication. At Canterbury a monetary penalty was occasionally added to the routine menace of excommunication. Fines of forty shillings, one hundred shillings, and forty marks are mentioned in the records.[11] This remedy, however, was plainly ineffective. As multi-party litigation shows, parties too often disobeyed the order, preferring the chance of excommunication to the certainty of an undesirable spouse. Theoretically, excommunication took effect without formal sentence if a party married in contempt of the court's order. But there are few actual prosecutions against such offenders in the surviving records. It is probable, as the seventeenth-century English canon lawyer Henry Conset suggested, that once their matrimonial tangles had been settled, offenders were simply left alone.[12]

The matter might have stood on a slightly different footing had legal practice made a marriage contracted against the order of a court *ipso facto* invalid. There was, in fact, authority for so holding. A decretal of Alexander III gave a judge power to invalidate a marriage contracted *contra interdictum ecclesie*.[13] Had this become the rule, the second marriage would have had no color of validity. Its psychological effect on the original plaintiff might not have been erased, but the rule might have discouraged defendants from acting against the order not to solemnize *pendente lite*. However, there were also two decretals which held that marriages contracted against the edict of the Church were not invalid.[14] Despite being illicit, they were binding marriages all the same, cause only for the imposition of

---

[10] In one instance from Ely, we find the reason for the warning thoroughly spelled out. EDR D/2/1, f. 58v (1376): 'Et quia intelleximus quod dicti Willelmus cum alia muliere et Margaria cum alio viro matrimonium contrahere proponunt et illud in facie ecclesie facere solempnizari ante ipsius cause decisionem, ideo eisdem Willelmo et Margarie ne aliunde contrahant seu quicquam aliud faciant vel fieri procurent quominus dicta causa matrimonialis coram nobis adhuc pendens indecisa effectum debitum sortiatur inhibemus et interdicimus.'

[11] Y.1.1, f. 45r (1373); f. 3v (1372); Y.1.3, f. 36v (1416).

[12] Conset, *Practice*, 268: 'Secondly, that the Judge will not in all probability proceed against the condemner of his mere office, no body urging it, or promoting his office.'

[13] X 4.4.4.

[14] X 4.16.1, 2.

penance. It was the second rule which the canonists and legal practice adopted. The first decretal was limited to cases where the first contract was made by binding words of present consent. And the rule of the second which prescribed penance but left the second marriage intact was adopted.[15] Thus the mere warning not to solemnize, without more, was not strong enough to ensure that the fair hearing of suits heard in the English courts would not be upset by illegal solemnization.

A possible solution to the dilemma was to place defendants out of harm's way. This meant sequestration until the action was over. And this was the remedy adopted by the courts during the course of the fifteenth century. There was authorization of a sort for it in canonical texts. Several decretals gave judges authority to find safe places for girls to be kept during the hearing of their cases if there was fear of abduction, physical harm, or improper influence on them.[16] The texts do not touch directly the problem of illegal solemnization *pendente lite*. They were aimed primarily at cases where violence was threatened to the person of the girl. Plainly this was not the normal dilemma of the English courts. Nonetheless, if authority was needed, the texts did authorize a judge to 'assign a secure place' to women in marriage actions. That permission could be extended; the same remedy could be used to meet a slightly different problem.

In any event, it was during the fifteenth century that the courts of the southern province began to sequester parties to marriage actions, although the practice was never extended to cover men as well as

---

[15] *Gl. ord.* ad X 4.4.4 s.v. *poteris irritare*: 'Interdictum enim ecclesiae non est tantae efficaciae ut separaretur matrimonium contra illud contractum nisi subsit causa perpetua; tamen poenitentia debet semper imponi.' And Raymond of Pennaforte, *Summa* IV, tit. *de matr. contra interdictum*, no. 1: 'Diversi diversa dixerunt, quae ad presens potius sunt silenda quam loquenda; sed ita tenendum est sine aliqua dubitatione quod illi quorum matrimonium interdicitur non debent contrahere, sed si contrahunt, nisi aliud impedimentum impediat, possunt simul permanere et non sunt separandi nisi ad tempus, ut agant poenitentiam.'

[16] X 4.1.14; X 2.13.8; X 2.13.13; X 2.19.14. See also T. J. McNicholas, 'Legislation on Sequestration in Roman Law and in the Decretals of Gregory IX', *The Jurist*, 23 (1963), 311–13. See also *gl. ord.* ad X 4.1.14 s.v. *nihil timere*: 'Est ergo hic argumentum quod ad officium iudicis pertinet locum securum assignare partibus.' Lyndwood also mentions it; see *Provinciale*, 105 s.v. *causis iustis*: 'Dicitur etiam causa justa conservatio virginitatis quando, scilicet, maritus petit uxorem virginem sibi restitui, quae negat matrimonium contractum. Sequestrabitur namque puella quousque causa fuerit terminata.' An early case in which the possibility of sequestration because of violence was raised is found in Canterbury Ch. Ant. A 36 II, 38 (1330). A similar case is found at York C.P. E 259 (1368–9). In Canterbury Y.1.12, f. 143r (1476), the reason was expressly given 'quod timet puellam predictam corrumpi et defloriari'.

women. There is a possible reference to the practice at Canterbury as early as 1416, but the entry is not definite enough to be sure that actual sequestration was meant. No place is mentioned and the language may be simply an expanded version of the normal order to refrain from keeping company 'in locis suspectis'.[17] By the second half of the century, however, sequestration was in regular use. It appears throughout the Act books. We find, for example, entries like this one from Rochester: 'And the judge sequestered the woman, and ordered her to remain in the monastry of Malling until the matter [was] discussed.'[18] The remedy was not always totally effective; a witness in a London case of 1494 told of a jealous suitor who 'had access' to the girl despite the order of sequestration. Perhaps this is explained by the choice of location. It was the girl's own house.[19]

Sequestration was never automatic. It had to be applied for by one of the parties or his proctor.[20] Unless they did so, only the order not to solemnize would be issued. The same Act books contain both cases in which sequestration was ordered and in which only the order not to solemnize *pendente lite* was issued by the court.[21] Probably a case for its advisability had to be made out and passed on by the proctors and the judge.[22] One entry from 1472 specifically states that the sequestration was agreed to 'de consensu procuratorum'.[23] The pur-

[17] Y.1.3, f. 15r: 'Dominus commissarius monebat dictum Laurencium sub pena xx marc' quod in crastino extunc moveret dictam Johannam Frenssh a comitiva sua et quod poneret eam in aliquo loco tuto quousque sentencia fuerit lata pro una parte vel pro alia et quod non accedat ad eam in aliquem locum suspectum.'

[18] DRb Pa 4, f. 212v (1488): 'Et iudex sequestravit mulierem et iniunxit ei ad essendum in monasterio de Mallyng quousque materia sit discussa.' Other examples: DRb Pa 1, f. 362v (1443); DRb Pa 4, f. 257r (1494); Canterbury Y.1.6, f. 21r (1464); London MS. 9065, f. 37v (1487); Hereford I/3, 62 (1500); Lichfield B/C/1/1, f. 279v (1470).

[19] MS. 9065, f. 194v: 'Iudex consistorii sequestravit eam et deputavit domum suam propriam pro loco sequestri.'

[20] E.g. Lichfield B/C/1/1, f. 279v (1470): 'Et incontinenti post pars dicti Johannis certam peticionem per quem peciit dictam Beatricem sequestrari . . .' Lyndwood, however, notes that sequestration could also be used 'quandoque ipsius iudicis officio mero'. See *Provinciale*, 106 s.v. *interpositorum*.

[21] Compare, for instance, Canterbury Y.1.6, f. 21r (1464), where sequestration was ordered, with f. 118r (1466), where it was not. Or compare Hereford I/1, 322 (1498) with Hereford I/3, 62 (1500).

[22] This is supported by a statement of Lyndwood, *Provinciale*, 105 s.v. *et veris*: 'Non solum requiritur causam sequestrationis esse iustam, sed etiam oportet quod sit vera et sic super hoc requiritur causae cognitio saltem ut super hoc iudex de plano inquirat et summarie se informet.'

[23] Canterbury Y.1.8, f. 288v.

pose of sequestration was to ensure that a correct judgment could be made and enforced.[24] Not every case required so harsh a remedy to guarantee that the parties would not subvert the course of the trial by illegal solemnization. But certainly the regular availability of the practice was established by the end of the century.

It should be said that I have found no evidence of the use of sequestration in the northern province. The York Act books are not so full as those of the South, so that it is impossible to be sure. But the practice is not mentioned in the Cause papers, and in a number of York cases we find only the old warning not to solemnize *pendente lite*, without any sign of sequestration. Probably it was only adopted later, for sequestration in marriage cases was used after the Reformation in both provinces.[25] It had doubtless proved an effective instrument in curbing the hurried marriage *pendente lite* which weakened the enforcement of the law of marriage. As a form of confinement without fault, sequestration may seem harsh, perhaps unjustified, to modern tastes. It is nonetheless an example of a useful change in the canon law, one adopted because of the exigencies of actual litigation.

The second example of change in canonical practice can be more readily applauded by modern readers. It is the gradual abandonment of the practice by which the courts imposed upon men and women the abjuration of sexual relations *sub pena nubendi*. This practice has received only passing notice by historians. But it has a claim to their attention both as an historical curiosity and as an example of growth in sophistication of attitude towards marriage during our period.

The custom itself is easily described. A man and woman, caught in fornication, were brought before a court and required to contract a conditional marriage. The man said, 'I here take you N. as my legitimate wife if I know you carnally from this time forward.'[26] The woman replied with similar words. This meant that if they later had sexual relations they were instantly and automatically married. The

---

[24] This is made particularly clear in an explanation given in a case recorded in London, DL/C/1, f. 22v (1500), where sequestration was ordered in a *causa matrimonialis et divorcii*, and where the court also ordered 'neque partes interim habeant accessum ad eandem vel communicandum nisi in presencia procuratorum utriusque partis'.

[25] Conset, *Practice*, 266, no. 9: 'This Practice is very safe, for nowadays, when they are released from their Sequestration, they are wont to contract second Marriages while the Sute depends.'

[26] E.g. Ely EDR D/2/1, f. 40r (1376): 'Hic accipio te in uxorem meam si ex nunc cognoscam te carnaliter.' An earlier treatment of this subject, here revised and corrected, is my 'Abjuration *sub pena nubendi* in the Church Courts of Medieval England', *The Jurist*, 32 (1972), 80–90.

condition was fulfilled, and the words of present consent took immediate effect. No court action or public ceremony was in theory necessary to bind the couple indissolubly in marriage.

As far as I know, the ultimate source of this practice cannot be traced. I have found no sign of it in the basic canonical texts or in the writings of the canonists. Historians who have noted its existence have apparently not been any more successful in finding references in canonists to the practice.[27] We do know that it was introduced into England by a series of synodal statutes enacted in the thirteenth century. The recent edition of *Councils and Synods* provides examples of its formal adoption in the dioceses of Winchester, Coventry, Salisbury, Wells, London, and Exeter.[28] And if it is safe to infer its adoption from cases heard in Consistory courts, almost all the English dioceses formally accepted the practice.[29] However, it was by no means a custom peculiar to England. The Church courts of at least some French and German dioceses used it.[30] It may be that the practice simply spread from one country to another, without leaving any trace in the works of the canonists. But the question of origin must remain, for the moment at least, obscure.

The reason for adoption of abjuration *sub pena nubendi* is clearer. It was to strike at concubinage. The remedy was, as Father Sheehan says, an 'almost Draconian form of contract'.[31] It seems therefore to have been used only when continued concubinage, not casual fornication, was the problem. Some of the statutes adopted required that the fornication be public and customary. Others restricted its use to third-time offenders. The cases show that in practice it was used with discretion. Mechanical rules were not usually applied. For example, a man and a woman admitted before the Consistory court of Ely that they had lived together for three years, and that they had been

---

[27] Esmein I, 145; Sheehan, 'The Formation and Stability of Marriage', 245–55; Weigand, 'Die Rechtsprechung des Regensburger Gerichts in Ehesachen', 422–4; *Councils and Synods* I, 134, n. 1; II, 999, n. 4. It is ascribed to the episcopate of Roger Niger, bishop of London, 1229–41 in one of the statutes. See *Councils and Synods*, I, 631.

[28] See I, 134–5; 213; 385; 410–11, 598; 631; 650; 707; II, 999. And see Wilkins, *Concilia* II, 283.

[29] See below, *passim*, for cases from these dioceses. Its mention in a formulary from the Court of Arches, Inner Temple Library, Petyt MS. 511.3, f. 33r, indicates that it was also probably enforced there.

[30] See the examples cited in Weigand, 'Die Rechtsprechung des Regensburger Gerichts in Ehesachen', 456–9, and those in Esmein I, 145, n. 3.

[31] See his remarks in 'The Formation and Stability of Marriage', 255.

'frequently fined by the official of the lord archdeacon'.[32] They were required to abjure each other under penalty of marriage. In a York case of 1363, the woman cited for fornication claimed that the man had also contracted marriage with her. It happened that the woman had no witnesses to prove the contract. But the combination of a probable contract with the man's admission of sexual relations was enough, so the court felt, to impose abjuration *sub pena nubendi*.[33]

In some instances, the birth of children appears to have been the motive for requiring a man and woman to undergo abjuration *sub pena nubendi*. Two actions from the records in York specifically mention the birth of children as preceding the decision to impose the conditional contract.[34] That this was the determining factor, we cannot be sure. It is, however, one of the few times in which the existence of children was mentioned in the court records. Their existence and their interests played no apparent part in normal suits to enforce marriage contracts.

Occasionally, the idea may have come from the parties themselves. Faced with the prospect of a humiliating public penance, they chose to contract this conditional form of marriage instead. This happened in at least two cases for which records have survived.[35] One cannot, of course, say that abjuration was used only in cases like these. Not least among its faults was a lack of firm guidelines for its application. Too much, perhaps, was left to the discretion of the cleric who administered it. But, where the evidence is full enough to give the details surrounding it, the fornication which resulted in abjuration *sub pena nubendi* was of an aggravated sort.

This, in brief, is the practice authorized by synodal statutes and adopted by English Church courts in the thirteenth century. No reliable estimate of the frequency of its use can be made. We have, for the most part, only records of suits to enforce such contracts. The actual imposition we see only at second hand. But the practice cannot have been rare. It came to be described as *abjuratio sub forma communi* or *sub forma ecclesie*.[36] It was certainly widely accepted. Nonetheless,

---

[32] Ely EDR D/2/1, f. 12v (1374).

[33] York M 2(1) f, f. 6r (1363).

[34] C.P. E 202 (1392–3); D/C C B 1, f. 235r (1489).

[35] Ely EDR D/2/1, f. 72r (1377): 'Et incontinenti ibidem dicti Johannes et Margeria de eorum mera et spontanea voluntate coram nobis pro tribunali sedente matrimonium adinvicem contraxerunt sub conditione et forma infrascriptis . . .' And York M 2(1) f, f. 6r (1363). For a French example, see *Registre de l'officialité de Cerisy*, no. 11a.

[36] Ely EDR D/2/1, f. 55(A)r (1376); York C.P. E 150 (1389); C.P. E 211 (1394); Canterbury Sede Vacante S.B. III, no. 45 (1293); Y.1.1, f. 44v (1373).

the practice was open to several objections. Abjuration caused serious practical problems. These we may trace in the surviving records.

First were difficulties of proof. Proof of sexual intercourse subsequent to the abjuration was the very foundation of most suits to enforce marriages under this heading. It was often understandably difficult to come by. In an early Canterbury case, for example, one man testified that he had 'heard by the noise of the said W. and A. that they were mixing carnally, but he nevertheless did not see them because it was night'. The court held that subsequent sexual relations had not been proved. There was only one witness, and he had not actually seen the sexual relations take place.[37] In a case from Rochester, the man confessed that 'he lay naked with her and others in one bed, but nevertheless he did not carnally know her'.[38] Whether that admission, coupled with the woman's oath that there had been sexual relations, was enough to warrant a sentence of marriage is a hard question. In a Canterbury case, the man admitted that he had lain in the same bed with the girl after abjuration, 'but whether he carnally knew her he says he does not know'.[39] What of that? The judge in that case held that a valid marriage had been proved. This was probably a correct decision. The canon law set up a strong presumption of sexual intercourse from such admitted facts.[40] But the existence of such a case does point to the real problems of proof which abjuration *sub pena nubendi* raised.

In addition, we find cases where the woman deliberately set up a situation to take unfair advantage of the abjuration. A man in York claimed that a woman had twice come to his bed while he was asleep. Her idea was to spread false rumors about relations between them. But his response was (he said) immediate flight. 'And as soon as he realized that she was there, he at once fled from the said room.'[41] In another case, the woman was seen going into a man's house late one night.

[37] Ecc. Suit, no. 272 (1294): 'Et audivit per strepitum dictorum W. et A. quod commiscuerunt se carnaliter adinvicem, non tamen vidit eosdem carnaliter conmiscentes quia nox erat.'

[38] *Reg. Hamonis Hethe*, 922 (1347). See also Ely EDR D/2/1, f. 12r (1374), where the man admitted that 'ab illo tempore per duas noctes solus cum sola nudus cum nuda simul iacuerunt, omnem tamem carnalem copulam inter eosdem a dicti contractus tempore expresse negarunt'. No judgment survives, however.

[39] Y.1.1, f. 66r (1374).

[40] See X 2.23.12: 'violenta et certa suspicione fornicationis'. The result of the case is found at f. 91r.

[41] C.P. E 191 (1392): 'Et quatenus novit vel scivit ipsam ibidem, incontinenti fugit a dicta camera.'

Whether this was in accordance with their plan, or an unwelcome surprise, as the man later claimed, was the question in dispute.[42] In both instances, the judge held against the woman. No sexual relations had actually been proved. But again, it could easily be said that a practice which gave rise to these situations was open to question and challenge.

There were a few cases in which subsequent sexual relations, although admitted, did not in fact lead to marriage. They suggest a further weakness. The penalty was not evenly enforced. It could not be. For example, in one York case, a man told of confessing to his parish priest that he had carnally known a woman he had abjured. For this he received 'maior penitencia' from his confessor. But he was not condemned to marriage in the external forum of the Church. Although legally married, he was saved from its consequences by the woman's lack of proof and the Church's rules about the confessional.[43]

There is also the interesting case of a man and woman who have abjured each other, then had sexual relations while one of them was drunk. Does that make a valid marriage? The situation arose at York in 1418.[44] Even assuming that a drunk man or woman cannot contract marriage if he or she has not the use of full reason, this does not solve the legal question.[45] The marriage had been contracted at the time of abjuration. Only the fulfillment of the condition took place during drunkenness. A fourteenth-century treatise on ecclesiastical discipline, now in the Library of the Inner Temple, gives an answer to the problem. If the drunkenness could be proved and the person had not approved his action after returning to sobriety, the marriage was not valid.[46] The same result was apparently reached in the York case.

---

[42] C.P. E 211 (1394). The man claimed here that he had ejected the woman: 'Dicit quod cepit eam per humeros et expulit [eam] a dicta domo et clausit hostium post eam.'

[43] C.P. E 135 (1387). And see York M 2 (1) f, f. 22r (1394), in which Robert Coupeland and Elena Comyn appeared and confessed to fornication after having abjured each other *sub pena nubendi*. The court's response was this: 'Et dominus auditor, attentis huiusmodi confessionibus, monuit dictum Robertum solempnizare matrimonium huiusmodi inter ipsum et dictam Elenam citra primam diem dominicam Adventus proximi, alioquin proxima die dominica sequente incipiat penitenciam suam.' And see Lichfield, Reg. Le Scrope, f. 40v (1392) for a case in which the woman had not been present at the abjuration, so that although subsequent fornication was admitted, the abjuration had to be repeated and no sentence of marriage could be given.

[44] C.P. F 78: 'dicit tamen quod inebriata fuit illo tempore quo ipsam sic carnaliter cognovit.'

[45] Sanchez, *De Matrimonio*, Lib. I, d. 8, no. 20, wrote that a drunk person could not normally contract marriage, but he cited no medieval canonist on the subject, and I have found no discussion of the matter myself.

[46] Petyt MS. 511.21 f. 111r: 'Dic quod non si constiterit ecclesie de tali ebrietate, nisi quod fecit in tali ebrietate ratum habeat post ebrietatem.'

The defendant 'fecit finem, et composuerunt'. That was, no doubt, a fair settlement. But it does point out again that attacking concubinage through the use of abjuration *sub pena nubendi* brought with it both special difficulties of proof and enforcement.

The second difficulty which inevitably went with abjuration was that its widespread use meant that inferior judges, who did not enjoy jurisdiction over matrimonial causes, could in fact hear them. In law, marriage cases were to be heard only in the courts of bishops or other dignitaries who had, by custom and experience, obtained the right to hear them. But purely corrective jurisdiction over sins was much more broadly spread. And as long as correction could lead to marriage by abjuration, lesser officials were led to impose sentences of marriage. To take one example, the receiver of the exchequer of the Archbishop of York was, as his title implies, primarily an accounting official. But he was sometimes also granted corrective jurisdiction by the archbishop. Thus he came to award abjuration and to give sentences of marriage when subsequent sexual relations were established. In a suit of 1389 his authority to do so was challenged in the Provincial court. But his right 'ad corrigendum excessus subditorum' was shown in court. And to the question of 'whether this judge was expert in law', enabling him to take cognizance of marriage cases, the answer was made, 'Yes, and especially in cases of abjuration *in forma ecclesie*.' The court held this enough to validate his action and to enforce the marriage.[47] But, as an authorization to hear marriage cases, it is not entirely convincing. The receiver had been allowed to do indirectly what he was prohibited from doing directly.[48] In other cases, we hear of abjuration being made before archdeacons without matrimonial jurisdiction, before prebendaries, before rural deans, apparently even before simple rectors.[49]

The third objection raised against abjuration was more fundamental. It was that the practice used marriage as a penal sanction. One of the announced principles of the canon law was that consent to marriage must be freely given. The canonists often repeated it. To

---

[47] C.P. E 150: 'An ille iudex fuit iuris peritus ad cognoscendum in causis matrimonialibus.' 'Sic, et precipue in causis abiurationum in forma ecclesie.'

[48] On this subject see Lyndwood, *Provinciale*, 79 s.v. *nullam causam matrimonialem*: 'Per consequens non possunt audire causas incidentes, nec etiam accessorias, . . . , nam prohibito principali prohibetur et accessorium.'

[49] Canterbury Ecc. Suit, no. 272 (1294) and Ch. Ant. A 36 IV, f. 54r (1341), the archdeacon of Canterbury; York C.P. E 211 (1394), the rural dean of Bulmer; Lichfield B/C/1/2, f. 107r (1473), the rural dean of Stafford; York C.P. E 6 (1312), the prebendary of Bugthorp; Canterbury Sede Vacante S.B. III, no. 45 (1293), the archdeacon's chaplain and the rural dean of Dover. In a case in Sede Vacante S.B. III, no. 56 (1293), the abjuration was recorded 'per registrum rectoris ecclesie de Godmersham'.

force a man and woman, by threat of excommunication, to enter into a contract of marriage, albeit a conditional one, ran directly counter to this principle. As a gloss to one of the synodal statues specifically pointed out: 'Note that this constitution is against right and natural equity, because *de iure* marriages and espousals ought to be free.'[50] Abjuration appears to violate the standards of the law.

The cases show that the objection against abjuration was raised in practice. Defendants claimed that marriages consequent upon abjuration were invalid because they had been coerced. Under the law, as we noted in the third chapter, a marriage contracted under duress sufficient to sway a 'constant man' or 'constant woman' was voidable by the party coerced. Some men argued that abjuration forced upon them by the threat of excommunication met this test. For instance, in one fourteenth-century case from York, a defendant, sentenced to marriage after abjuration, claimed that the contract was void because he had entered into it 'by fear which can affect a constant man and by a penalty condemned by the law'.[51] In another suit to enforce such a contract, the defendant argued that his marriage was invalid because he had been forced to make the contract under compulsion and 'because of the fear of excommunication'.[52]

Two arguments in favor of the legitimacy of the original imposition of abjuration could be raised under the canon law. First, Church courts consistently enforced marriage contracts and sworn espousals under threat of excommunication.[53] Enforcing marriage after abjuration could be said to amount to the same thing. However, this argument is open to an obvious objection. It is one thing to force a man to fulfill a contract he has voluntarily undertaken. It is quite another to force him to make the contract in the first place. Second, a text from the Book of Exodus, incorporated in the Decretals, specified that a man who had seduced a virgin be required to endow her and take her

---

[50] *Councils and Synods* II, 999, n. 4: 'Nota quod hec constitutio est contra iura et naturalem equitatem, quia de iure libera debent esse matrimonia et sponsalia.' For statements of the general principle, see for example X 4.1.29: 'cum itaque libera matrimonia esse debeant . . .' See also *gl. ord.* ad C. 31 q. 2 c. 1 s.v. *quod autem*; Hostiensis, *Summa Aurea* I, tit. *de his quae vi metusve causa fiunt*, no. 6; Durantis, *Spec. Iud.* IV, tit. *de sponsalibus*, no. 3.

[51] C.P. E 150 (1389): 'Per metum qui cadere potest in constantem ac sub pena legibus reprobata.'

[52] York C.P. E 111 (1372): 'Dicit quod non animo contrahendi neque habendi ipsam Johannam in uxorem suam huiusmodi abiurationem fecit, sed compulsus per dictum Thomam Wyles tunc decanum Christianitatis Ebor' et propter timorem excommunicationis per ipsum decanum in dictum Thomam in hac parte tunc ferende et non aliter.'

[53] X 4.1.10; see also Chapter 1, n. 33.

as his wife.[54] On the strength of this text, it could be said that in cases of serious, continued fornication, the same principle should be applied.[55] The difficulty with the argument, however, is that the canonists interpreted the text to give the man a choice. Under their reading he could *either* endow her or marry her. Some said that if he was unwilling to do either, he should only be subject to corporal punishment.[56] The canonists, in other words, stressed the importance of free choice in interpreting the Old Testament text. Rather than supporting the legitimacy of abjuration *sub pena nubendi*, citation of the text might actually be a way of attacking it.

Under this analysis, the original imposition of the conditional marriage of abjuration *sub pena nubendi* by the Church courts was, at the least, questionable legally. However, this is not the end of the matter. The texts quoted deal only with unconditional marriages. And, as noted in Chapter 3, a marriage initially voidable because of duress was converted into a binding marriage through subsequent sexual relations. Canonists held that enough volition was present even in a marriage contracted because of force and fear so that later *carnalis copula* would make it indissoluble.[57] Thus, under the canon law, a sentence in favor of marriage where abjuration had been followed by intercourse appears to have been justified. And this was the result reached in the two York cases: both marriages were upheld. But some judges must have been uneasy about the matter. Their records stated specifically that the parties had been willing to accept the abjuration.

[54] X 5.16.1: 'Si seduxerit quis virginem nondum desponsatam, dormieritque cum ea, dotabit eam et habebit uxorem.' The source of this text is Exodus 22:16. See also Deuteronomy 22:28.

[55] The fault of the man is the reason given by the canonists for the decretal's penalty. The same principle might arguably apply to abjuration. See Hostiensis, *Lectura* ad X 5.16.1, no. 2: 'Dominus autem noster notavit quod hic est specialis casus in quo quis cogitur ad matrimonium contrahendum, . . . , et hoc propter delictum viri.'

[56] Hostiensis, *ibid.*; Antonius de Butrio, *Commentaria* ad X 5.16.1, no. 6: 'Dic quod eam habebit in uxorem, si pater sibi eam dare voluerit, vel si ipse secum contrahere voluerit; alias si nolit secum contrahere, punietur;' Panormitanus, *Commentaria* ad X 5.16.2 no. 3: 'Sed si non vult contrahere, debet eam dotare et etiam corporaliter castigari.' A text from the Decretum might also be used to support this argument. C. 22 q. 4 c. 22 involved a situation where a man was forced to marry his concubine, and this was apparently approved. But the point made by Gratian in using the text was a different one, to show that the other oaths taken at that time were not enforceable. And it received the same modification in favor of free consent at the hands of the canonists as did X 5.16.1. See *gl. ord.* ad C. 22 q. 4 c. 22 s.v. *matrimonium.*

[57] E.g. Jo. And., *Novella Commentaria* ad X 4.7.2, no. 7: 'Et copula facit hoc matrimonium propter voluntatem, quae inest sponsalibus contractis etiam per metum conditionalem.' On this subject generally, see the excellent treatment in J. G. Chatham, *Force and Fear as Invalidating Marriage; the Element of Injustice* (Washington, 1950), esp. 32–6.

This rationalization for imposition of the penalty appears in one York case. The defendant 'at first was held to the aforesaid abjuration by Master Roger under pain of excommunication, and afterwards the same John abjured the said Alice spontaneously and of his own free will.'[58] The obvious purpose of such an entry was to forestall a later attack on the contract as invalid because of duress. Even though abjuration could be defended legally, the coercion it entailed seemed suspect enough under the canon law's announced principles to warrant this sort of safeguard.

Cases drawn from the Church court records thus show that abjuration *sub pena nubendi* was attacked on three counts. It was difficult to prove and sometimes conducive to fraud; it meant extension of matrimonial jurisdiction to judges not entitled to it; and it violated the freedom from constraint that was one of the foundations of marriage. It is hardly surprising, therefore, that the practice did not last. It seems to have been imposed with decreasing frequency as time went on. Court records from Canterbury, for example, produce several examples from the thirteenth and fourteenth centuries. But only one is forthcoming from the fifteenth, when the surviving records are in fact much more complete.[59] From Ely, where only one fourteenth-century Act book remains, several examples can be drawn.[60] But from London and Bath and Wells, where nothing survives from before the fifteenth, I found no examples of abjuration.[61] The Cause papers of the Provincial court at York tell the same story. There are nine cases raising the issue among the remaining fourteenth-century papers. For the fifteenth, when more marriage cases survive in all, there is only one dealing with abjuration.[62] Use of abjuration *sub pena nubendi* was, so far as the records allow for accurate generalization, used only fitfully in the fifteenth century. There is an example from Norwich in

---

[58] C.P. E 150 (1389): 'Primo fuerat inditus per dictum magistrum Rogerum ad abiurationem huiusmodi supradictam sub pena excommunicationis, et postea idem Johannes dictam Aliciam abiuravit sponte et voluntate sua propria.' Ely EDR D/2/1, f. 55(A)r (1376): ' . . . de eorum expresso consensu contraxerunt.' And see *supra*, n. 35.

[59] Sede Vacante S.B. III, nos. 45 (1293), 55 (1293), 348 (1294); Ch. ant. A 36 IV, fols. 16r (1340), 58r (1342), 59v (1342); Y.1.1, fols. 66r (1374); for the fifteenth century, Y.1.11, f. 359v (1471).

[60] EDR D/2/1, fols 12r (1374), 39v–40r (1375), 55(A)r (1376), 72r (1377).

[61] This statement is based on the examination of London MS. 9065 (1489–1516) and MS. 9064/1 (1470–3), MS. 9064/2 (1483–9) and MS. 9064/3 (1475–82); for Bath and Wells on examination of D/D/C Al. (1458–98).

[62] C.P. E 6, 102, 111, 114, 135, 150, 191, 202, 212; F 78.

1429, one from Rochester in 1447, one from Hereford in 1455, and one from Lichfield in 1473.[63] The latest instance I have found comes from 1489, imposed by the court of the Dean and Chapter of York.[64] Probably I have missed a few late examples. But it is clear that by the end of the fifteenth-century abjuration *sub pena nubendi* had virtually disappeared from court practice.

No one, I think, will lament the passing of the custom. Using marriage as a penalty for fornication is inconsistent, at bottom, with the principles of Christian marriage. The story of its abandonment is evidence of a matured thinking about the nature of marriage. It was an institution which seemed, by the end of the fifteenth century, to require a more truly free kind of consent than had been thought in the thirteenth. Abjuration was objectionable on several counts. But the compulsion to marry it entailed was by no means the least of these. Its abandonment is the best example we have of change and growth in canonical marriage practice in later medieval England.

★　　★　　★

Besides these two developments, the court records reveal no major substantive changes in marriage practice over the course of our period. There are a few minor ones which are worth mentioning. One is the increasing use of English in the court records, particularly in the depositions of witnesses. In the thirteenth-century documents at Canterbury the entire deposition was invariably recorded in Latin. There are a few examples from the fourteenth-century York Cause papers in which English was used to record the words of the marriage contract, but not many. Only in the fifteenth century did those words gradually come to be given frequently in English. By the end of the century, they were almost always written in the vulgar tongue.

This change was, I think, a real improvement in the conduct of marriage litigation. Where so much hung on what specific words had been used to contract marriage, it was a real step forward to have the actual language before the judge. Normally, it did not make much difference. To write 'I take thee' instead of 'accipio te' is of little consequence. But distortion sometimes crept in under the old system

---

[63] Norwich Cathedral Archives, Acta et Comperta 6, s.d. 7 July; Rochester DRb Pa 2, f. 79v; Hereford 0/3 35; Lichfield, B/C/1/2, f. 107r.

[64] D/C C B 1, f. 235r.

which used only Latin. An example can be drawn from a York case of 1373. The English phrase 'I am fully paid' had been used to answer one party's *verba de presenti* in a marriage contract. In the Latin of the deposition, this was originally translated as 'plenarie contentor'.[65] No doubt, this is a fair approximation, but the two are certainly not identical. The English phrase suggests an agreement on the terms under which the marriage was to be contracted: the conditions, the settlement of land, etc. The Latin more easily connotes actual consent to the marriage itself. In the case, the translation was challenged by the defendant. That is the reason that we can make the comparison. The result was a verdict against marriage. Whether the opposite result would have been reached had the examiner's Latin translation been allowed to stand is unclear. Perhaps not. But the case does show the real need for recording the actual words used. We should recall that the judge often did not hear the witness's testimony at all. It was taken out of court by a special examiner. The judge sometimes saw only the written record. Under these conditions, and certainly whenever there was an appeal, it was a real advance to have the vulgar tongue used in the record. This was accomplished slowly but irrevocably in the fifteenth century. It is perhaps cause for wonder that it was not done sooner.

Two minor changes in the judicial attitude towards punishment and proof should also be noted. In the thirteenth century, the standard penalty for adultery or fornication included being whipped while going around one's parish church or market.[66] By the fifteenth century, in Canterbury and Rochester, that harsh punishment had been dropped. The usual penance was restricted to walking in the parish procession on successive Sundays, wearing penitential garb and carrying a candle.[67] On the last Sunday, the candle was to be used as an offering, sometimes with money added. Whether this mitigation in punishment was general over all of England is not clear. There are examples of whipping for sexual offenses from York and Hereford towards the end of the fifteenth century.[68] Perhaps these dioceses,

---

[65] C.P. E 131.

[66] E.g. Canterbury Sede Vacante S.B. III, no. 132 (1293): 'Unde nos penitenciam eisdem R. et A. iniunximus infrascriptam, videlicet septem fustigaciones circa forum Cant' et septem fustigaciones circa forum Dovor' et trinas fustigaciones circa quamlibet ecclesiam Dovor' nudis in camisiis (sic) prout moris est peragendam.' This is the most severe instance I have found. Normally three times around the parish church were enough.

[67] See Woodcock, 97–8.

[68] Hereford o/2, 18 (1442); o/6, 78 (1456); o/8, 17 (1468); York D/C C B 1, f. 250v (1473).

in the North and West, found the more severe punishment appropriate even after it had been discarded in the South.

Another sort of relaxation occurred in one instance of the requirements for proof in marriage cases. This was in *ex officio* inquisitions about supposed consanguinity or affinity. In the thirteenth-century records from Canterbury, twelve men were summoned to give evidence in these inquisitions. 'Duodecim vel circiter viri fidedigni' were to be summoned to testify.[69] In the next century, the number had dropped to six.[70] At Ely in 1379, there was a case in which the court summoned eight men to testify to alleged consanguinity.[71] I have found no inquisitions in the fifteenth-century Canterbury records, but there is one from Rochester in 1437.[72] In that case, the inquisition was made up of only three men. It may be that this decline in numbers reflects a more tolerant view of the canonical prohibitions against marriage between kin. The Church became more lenient in granting dispensations for affinity and consanguinity as time went on.[73] This change in attitude may explain why the courts felt that fewer people could be summoned to make up the inquisitions. The records also contain fewer inquisitions in all on questions of consanguinity and affinity in the fourteenth and fifteenth century than in the thirteenth. Perhaps this reflects the same change, although it is also possible that the canonical prohibitions were being better observed, so that fewer inquisitions were necessary.

⋆　　⋆　　⋆

We turn now to the question of differences in the various diocesan courts. Some variations in practice have already been mentioned. Advocates were employed in some places, but not in others. The number of proctors attached to different courts varied. Archdeacons held matrimonial jurisdiction in some dioceses, but not in others. Public whipping for sexual offenses continued to be used in some courts during the fifteenth century, but not in others. These are not, we may think, fundamental differences. They touch externals. But they give a fair characterization of the general situation. There was

---

[69] E.g. Sede Vacante S.B. III, no. 124 (1292).

[70] Y.1.1, f. 34v (1373); f. 74r (1374).

[71] EDR D/2/1, f. 108v.

[72] DRb Pa 1, f. 32r. Note also that in Canterbury Y.1.11, f. 348r (1474) a man cited for having married a girl who was allegedly his *soror spiritualis* was dismissed *proprio iuramento*. No inquisition was called.

[73] J. Brys, *De Dispensatione in iure canonico* (Bruges, 1925), 160.

room for some variation in custom and practice between courts. A Consistory court could have traditions of its own. But the variation, so far as we can tell, was not great enough to warrant speaking of basic differences. Perhaps if the surviving records were fuller, or if we had more compilations of the customs of each court as we do for the Court of Arches, this conclusion might have to be revised.[74] In their absence, the evidence suggests that, rather like synodal statutes, the courts were not identical. But they were recognizably cut from the same mold.

One difference between dioceses lay in the sort of litigation and the specific court which each officer held. In Canterbury, the Commissary General presided over a strictly diocesan court, held in the cathedral. The Official Principal was the Dean of Arches, who heard cases in the Provincial court of appeal in London. At York, the Commissary General and the Official sat in the same court, the latter taking precedence when he was present. And that court heard both appeal and first instance cases. At Hereford, the two officers seem to have held separate courts, except that the Commissary General went on circuit and heard more *ex officio* cases than the Official, who normally sat only in the cathedral. Otherwise, their jurisdiction overlapped, but so far as I can tell from the remaining late-fifteenth-century material, there was no right of appeal from one to the other.

Some differences between courts did not go beyond their habits in record keeping. The Ely Registrum Primum, for example, contains both instance and office cases, together with some miscellaneous diocesan business. The Act book from the same period at Canterbury was devoted exclusively to instance litigation, suggesting a more highly developed system of recording in the latter diocese. In the Ely Act book, it was the practice to record the name of one of the parties in the margin beside each case, as a means of identifying the same suit from one session to the next. At Canterbury during the same period, it was the parish of the parties which was used for the same purpose. The York Act books of the fifteenth century, on the other hand, give the names of both parties in the margin or just above the entry for the case. The York records usually do not, however, give the subject matter of

---

[74] The compilation for the Court of Arches, now Ashmole MS. 1146, fols. 111v–116v, Bodleian Library, Oxford, is titled, 'Consuetudines et observantie non scripte apud Curia de Arcubus London' diutius observate'.

each case under each session entry, as those of Ely and Canterbury almost invariably do. And, to take one more variation of recording practice, in the fifteenth-century Act books at Canterbury and Rochester, it became standard to record all the *acta* of a particular case under the entry for the first hearing of the suit. This made for messy Act books, since subsequent entries sometimes ran over the space available on that folio. They had to be continued in odd spaces on other pages.[75] In other dioceses all through the fifteenth century, the record was kept more chronologically. A new entry for each case, with action taken, was made for each new Consistory session.

One peculiarity of the practice in the Hereford courts is worth noting. It illustrates the discretion vested in the judges to deal with offenses as they thought best, and it shows one instance of how that discretion was used. English courts sometimes imposed fines for relapsed adulterers. That is, men and women convicted of adultery were required to swear not to repeat the offense under pain of a money fine. That money, if required, went to the Church. But in Hereford, the practice was for half of the money to be paid to the secular lord under whose jurisdiction the offenders were. In 1442, for instance, a man abjured his sin 'under penalty of 100 s. to be applied in equal portions to the church of Clone and the lord of the fief there'.[76] No doubt, the aim was to elicit the lord's help in enforcing of the court's sentence, although it seems possible that sometimes the exact opposite must have occurred, since the lord stood to profit from a subsequent offense. I have found no other instances in Church court records of this sort of secular–ecclesiastical cooperation, but Professor Ault has shown that a number of manorial courts used the same device of sharing fines with the parish church.[77] Perhaps the practice at Hereford was a part of such an arrangement.

*   *   *

[75] The cases must be followed by locating the appropriate sign (e.g. //) which is given at the end of one entry and the beginning of the next. Sometimes the entries for one case were spread on as many as four different pages.

[76] o/2, 53: 'sub pena C s. applicand' per equales portiones . . . ecclesie de Clone et domino feodi ibidem.' Other examples: o/2, 18 (1442); o/5, 158 (1454).

[77] W. O. Ault, 'Manor Court and Parish Church in Fifteenth-Century England: A Study of Village By-Laws', *Speculum*, 42 (1967), 53–67; unfortunately, none of the material from which this article is drawn comes from Herefordshire.

In sum, this review suggests that the unitary view of marriage practice in the later middle Ages is largely correct. The major change in practice was the decline in numbers of marriage actions. This tells only of a growing stability in people's attitude towards marriage. It entailed no variation in substantive law or legal practice. At the same time there were a few changes in practice itself. And there were differences among the various Consistory courts. The adoption of sequestration and the abandonment of abjuration *sub pena nubendi* are the most significant of the former. Of the latter, enough examples have been given to show that each court had its own identity and some of its own traditions. Further research on the organization of each court would certainly turn up more evidence of this. Probably it would also suggest modifications of some of the conclusions given above. The variations among the courts and the changes in marriage practice over our period are great enough to warn us that, when dealing with the English Church courts, we must not automatically assume that what is true for one time and place is necessarily true of another time and place. But the variations and changes are not, in my view, enough to upset the notion that English marriage litigation from the thirteenth century through the fifteenth can safely be treated as a unit.

CONCLUSION

To attempt to fit the pieces of any sort of litigation into a coherent picture must be a difficult task. Litigation is diverse and confused, as the aims and motives of the parties to it are diverse and confused. But any searcher in the records of the Church courts cannot avoid an attempt to connect his findings with two problems. One is the relation of canonical theory to actual practice. In particular, this raises the question of the relevance of the writing of the canonists. The other is a substantive evaluation of the Church's jurisdiction over marriage and divorce. Both of these have, in a sense, lain behind much of what has already been said. But they are worth considering directly.

Certainly the broad picture is one of fidelity between the commentaries of the canonists and what went on in the courts. Most of what the canonists wrote was useful and most of their conclusions were observed in practice. The ingenious, and apparently artificial, distinctions they drew between the effects of different words used to contract marriage were actually relevant to real problems. And so far as we can tell, the distinctions were applied by the courts. The difference between a marriage contracted under the words 'I will have' and one contracted under the words 'I will take' seems, at first blush, a matter of purely academic speculation. But the records show that it was in fact an important difference in litigation. There are, we have seen, clear instances where practice diverged from theory. The allowance of compromise in marriage litigation is a good example. But this was surely because the rule was impossible to enforce. Overall, what the canonists had to say about marriage was of real value. They treated problems that arose in practice. The extent to which the lawyers and judges in fact made use of their commentaries is one of the questions it has been impossible for me to answer. The records do not tell us. But to say that the canonists occupied themselves with a world of theory, not tied to actual practice, is clearly wrong.

The second question is less clear. It asks for some conclusions about the effectiveness of the Church courts in exercising their jurisdiction over marriage. On this most historians have spoken harshly. Maitland surveyed the available evidence and wrote, 'It is difficult to believe that the ecclesiastical courts were preeminently fit to administer the law of marriage and divorce.'[1] Most writers have echoed that judgment. To Canon Lacey, the Church 'failed miserably' in upholding the ideals of Christian marriage.[2] To Lady Stenton, it seemed fair to speak of 'the incompetent archaism of the ecclesiastical courts'.[3] Even A. L. Smith, who set out to attack Maitland's treatment, argued only that the Papacy exerted a beneficent influence. He had little or nothing to say for the English courts themselves.[4]

Has the study of the court records themselves given just cause for reversing, or modifying, these verdicts? The answer must depend, in my view, on how one regards the duty of the courts. There are two ways. The first emphasizes the enforcement of principles of Christian law and doctrine on the laity. The second looks at how well the courts settled actual legal quarrels, with less concern for principle. The two overlap, certainly. Courts must use some standards of law to settle disputes. But they nonetheless ask rather different questions. They expect different things from the courts.

The first was the normal method of approach in the nineteenth and early twentieth centuries. It was, perhaps, an easier and more natural attitude in a society where ideas about marriage were more settled than they are in our own. We do not take quite so much for granted about the nature of marriage as our ancestors. I do not say that for this reason there is no validity to the first approach. That it has an old fashioned ring is no reason to discard it. But it is hard to adopt fixed standards. We may dislike the commercial way in which marriage was often treated. 'Though called a sacrament, marriage was in fact treated like a contract.'[5] But can we say that, in so doing, the Church courts destroyed the essence of Christian marriage? If people think of marriage essentially as a matter of contract (and of this there is good evidence in the records), can it be wrong for courts to deal with it accordingly?

Even with this apology, however, the verdict on the first question remains a mixed one at best. The indissolubility of marriages con-

---

[1] Pollock and Maitland, *HEL* II, 396.
[2] *Marriage in Church and State* (London, 1912), 159.
[3] D. M. Stenton, *The English Woman in History* (London, 1957), 49.
[4] *Church and State in the Middle Ages* (repr. London, 1964), 75ff.
[5] S. B. Kitchin, *A History of Divorce* (London, 1912), 70.

tracted by words of present consent, the prohibition of clandestine marriages, the enforcement of conjugal duties between husband and wife, the exclusive competence of the Church courts to deal with marital questions: these were all sufficiently and definitely set down in the law. They were more than ideals. They were rules of law. And the surviving records show that they often went unenforced. We see examples of long-standing noncompliance by the laity. We see the courts themselves making compromises and adjustments in individual cases. For whatever reasons, accommodation to lay habits was often worked out. Perhaps it is true that the Church did 'the best it could', given the unsettled medieval attitude towards marriage. Perhaps we can expect no more than that the Church should require the passage of centuries before its standards could penetrate into the marrow of popular attitudes. But the evidence of widespread and continued disrespect for the standards of the canon law is too great, I think, to allow us to conclude that the Church courts were 'effective guardians' of the holy estate of marriage.

To the second question – which asks how effective the courts were in settling disputed lawsuits – one can give a more favorable response. Here harsh words about practice in the ecclesiastical tribunals should be modified. The courts proceeded swiftly, without long delays or abusive appeals. They worked effectively, without frequent obstruction from contumacy. And they operated flexibly, without rigid adherence to procedural niceties against the interests of the parties. That no improvements could have been made can scarcely be argued. That there were no miscarriages of justice can hardly be maintained. But against this, the records do not indicate the presence of widespread corruption. Nor do they show the courts allowing easy and collusive divorces. And they do show marriage cases moving regularly and smoothly through the courts. Modern lawyers will recognize how important that is. Let us recall, once again, that people in the Middle Ages regarded the making of a marriage as a more private and contractual affair than we do. What they therefore expected from their courts was the settling of disputes about marriage. When we remember this, there is reason to respect, and even to admire, the work of the Church courts in handling marriage litigation.

APPENDIX

Introduction

Transcribed in this appendix are marriage cases drawn from England's ecclesiastical archives. They are meant to illustrate and in a few instances to expand on points made in the text of this study, for it is upon the examination of many cases like these that my conclusions have been based. The cases are here arranged according to subject, using the appropriate heading of the Decretals. I have prefaced each with a brief note about the formal law involved, and occasionally with remarks about the case itself.

A word should be said about the principles of transcription used. I have treated the records as documents illustrating concrete points of law. From this have followed several decisions. The transcriptions do not always include every document or entry available in the original records. I have selected enough to make the facts and legal issues of the case apparent. But purely formal entries and depositions which merely repeat what has already been said are usually not included. Also, I have occasionally added words to the text so that the meaning will be clear, in cases where the scribe has apparently left out a word through carelessness or error. These words are in every instance placed within square brackets. I have standardized the letters 'c' and 't' to conform to modern usage. These letters are sometimes quite indistinguishable in the original record, particularly in those of the fifteenth century. Although no choice is entirely satisfactory, it seemed preferable to have all letters 'c' and 't' treated identically, and in the way most easily recognizable to modern readers. This has, however, sometimes meant turning a letter certainly written as 'c' into 't'. Finally, marginalia and scribal additions above the line have not been specially noted, but incorporated into the transcription to accord with the scribe's intention.

What is lost in fidelity to the original documents through application of these principles will, I hope, be made up for by easier comprehension of the issues involved in each case. The issues and the facts have in no instance (so far as I am aware) been falsified. I have not attempted to 'correct' the Latin of the documents, because of the greater errors to which such a course often leads. Most endings have been extended, except for proper names. The spelling has been left as found in the original documents.

One case, *Lovell* v. *Marton*, is included by way of introduction. This is for three reasons. First, it contains the fullest transcription here given of the documents to a law suit. The libel, the positions with answers, the depositions, a court memorandum, and the definitive sentence are all included. Second, the case contains two interesting legal issues: the interpretation of negative words of marriage in a contract, and the subsequent condition. The legal questions have been discussed at length for Chapter Two. And third, the case records two informal ways in which marriage questions were settled. One was by the advice of friars, who instructed one of the parties on the meaning of the words of the original contract. Another was by a meeting of the important men of a community in the parish church. Only when these failed to resolve the question was resort had to the Consistory court. How often disputes over marriage were thus settled out of court, we cannot be sure. But the case points out how wrong it is to imagine that all questions about marriage went immediately and automatically into the Church courts. Carefully read, *Lovell* v. *Marton* makes an excellent introduction to the problems of matrimonial litigation.

Lovell v. *Marton* (*1328*)[1]

In Domine nomine amen. Coram vobis domine iudex dicit et in iure proponit procurator Elizabeth' filie domini Simonis Lovell militis nomine procuratorio pro eadem contra Thomam filium Roberti de Marton' et quemlibet pro eodem in iudicio legitime comparentem quod predicti Thomas et Elizabeth matrimonium per verba mutuum consensum de presenti exprimencia legitime adinvicem contraxerunt; quod idem Thomas in presencia dicte Elizabeth' et aliorum fidedignorum expresse fatebatur; que sunt publica notoria et manifesta in decanatu de Rydale et locis convicinis; ac super hiis ibidem publica vox et fama laborat. Quare petit dictus [procurator] nomine quo supra, probatis in hac parte de iure probandis, dictum Thomam eidem Elizabeth' domine sue in virum et maritum legitimum per vos domine

---

[1] York C.P. E 18.

iudex sentencialiter et diffinitive adiudicari, eamque maritali affectione pertractare et eidem adherere compelli, et ulterius fieri in omnibus quod est iustum. Hec dicit et petit coniunctim et divisim, iuris beneficio semper salvo.

Has positiones facit coniunctim et divisim Elizabeth filia Symonis Lovell militis contra Thomam filium Roberti de Marton'. In primis ponit dicta Elizabeth quod verba matrimonialia habebantur inter prefatum Thomam et ipsam. Non credit nisi sub conditione.

Item ponit quod tractatus habebatur inter eosdem de matrimonio inter eosdem ineundo. Dependet et non credit nisi sub conditione.

Item ponit quod ipse consensit eam habere in uxorem sicut dixit eidem Elizabeth', et ipsa eadem vice consensit eum habere in virum sicut ipsa dixit. Dependet et non credit nisi sub conditione.

Item ponit quod et matrimonium adinvicem contraxerunt. Non credit ut ponitur.

Item ponit quod legitime. Dependet et non credit ut ponitur.

Item ponit quod per verba de presenti. Dependet et non credit ut ponitur.

Item ponit quod mutuum consensum faciencia. Dependet et non credit ut ponitur.

Item ponit quod tunc Thomas promisit dicte Elizabeth' eam ducere in uxorem suam. Non credit et nisi sub conditione.

Item ponit quod mutue consenserunt adinvicem ut coniuges sicut verbis inter se expresserunt. Non credit nisi sub conditione.

Item ponit quod iterato verba matrimonialia inter eos habebantur. Non credit ut ponitur nisi sub conditione.

Item ponit quod et ibidem matrimonium adinvicem contraxerunt. Non credit ut ponitur nisi sub conditione.

Item ponit quod legitime. Dependet et non credit ut ponitur.

Item ponit quod idem Thomas et ipsa Elizabeth adinvicem ut coniuges consenserunt. Dependet et responsum est supra.

Item ponit quod per verba de presenti. Dependet et responsum est supra.

Item ponit quod idem Thomas in presencia dicte Elizabeth fatebatur se cum eadem matrimonium contraxisse. Non credit ut ponitur et nisi sub conditione.

Item ponit quod et aliorum fidedignorum. Dependet et responsum est.

Item ponit quod expresse. Dependet et non credit nisi ut supra responsum est.

Item ponit quod in presencia predicti domini Symonis Lovell, Roberti patris dicti Thome, Edmundi de Staneley, Willelmi de Apelton', Willelmi de Thornton' et Willelmi de Besingby. Dependet et non credit ut ponitur nisi ut supra responsum est.

Item ponit quod in ecclesia de Homingham. Dependet et non credit ut ponitur nisi ut supra responsum est.

Item ponit quod non est consanguinitas inter dictos Thomam et Elizabeth. Nescit et impertinens est.

Item ponit quod dictus Thomas nunquam cognovit carnaliter aliquam de consanguinitate vel affinitate dicte Elizabeth'. Nescit et impertinens est.

Item ponit quod nec ius ad aliam habuit. Non credit ut ponitur et impertinens est.

Item ponit quod nec habet. Dependet et non credit ut ponitur et impertinens est.

Item ponit quod antequam contraxit cum dicta Elizabeth solutus fuit et nunquam coniugatus. Dependet et non credit ut ponitur.

Item ponit quod premissa sunt publica in decanatu de Rydale. Non credit nisi ut supra est responsum.

Item ponit quod notoria. Non credit nisi ut supra.

Item ponit quod manifesta. Non credit nisi ut supra.

Item ponit quod super hiis ibidem laborat publica vox. Non credit nisi ut supra.

Item ponit quod et fama. Non credit nisi ut supra.

Agnes filia domini Simonis Lovell militis iurata examinata et super articulis huic rotulo appensis diligenter interrogata. Et primo si novit Thomam filium Roberti de Marton' de quo agitur, dicit quod sic per decem annos et Elizabet est soror carnalis ipsius iurate. Requisita si aliquo tempore presens fuit ubi dictus Thomas aliqua verba matrimonialia protulit et fecit cum Elizabet predicta, dicit quod sic. Requisita que fuerunt illa verba, ubi et quando prolata erunt, dicit quod dictus Thomas et Elizabet predicta presentes fuerunt in bracino dicti domini Simonis apud Drokom' in Rydale die Dominica proximo ante Purificationem beate Marie ultimo preteritam post horam cene, bene infra noctis tenebras, ubi ipsa iurata tunc similiter presens, audivit ut dicit dictum Thomam, habentem dictam Elizabet per manum dexteram, dicere verba infrascripta: 'Ecce fides mea quod non ducam aliquam in uxorem nisi te.' Et ipsa statim respondebat: 'Ecce fides mea quod nullo tempore habebo aliquem in virum nisi te habeam.' Et pro ista conventione confirmanda et secure habenda manus simul traxerunt et postmodum adinvicem fuerunt osculati; presente quodam Nicholao Bertelmew conteste suo cum dictis contrahentibus et ipsa iurata et non pluribus quod sciat. Item dicit ipsa iurata quod presens fuit in quadam camera situata ultra portas dicti domini Simonis apud Drokton die Martis in septimana Pasche ultimo preterite ubi ista iurata accessit ad Elizabet predictam cum Eufemia sorore sua; in qua camera dictus Thomas eo tempore nudus in lecto suo iacebat ubi audivit, ut dicit, dictos Thomam et Elizabet loqui de verbis matrimonialibus prius habitis inter eos. Et dictus Thomas tunc dicebat quod a fratribus confessoribus suis eidem fuerat dictum quod prior contractus non valuit; quin licuit utrique cum alio contrahere matrimonium ubi vellet. Et tunc ad voluntatem utriusque verba

infrascripta adinvicem protulerunt, dicto Thoma primo dicente et ipsam
Elizabet per manum dexteram tenente: 'Hic accipio te Elizabet in uxorem
meam fidelem coniugatam, tenendam et habendam usque ad finem vite mee
et ad hoc do tibi fidem meam.' Cui dicta Elizabet respondebat: 'Et hic accipio
te Thomam in fidelem virum meum desponsatum, tenendum et habendum
usque ad finem vite mee et ad hoc do tibi fidem.' Et post ipsum contractum
adinvicem osculabantur. Alia verba matrimonialia non audivit ista iurata
proferri inter eos. Requisita qui fuerunt tunc presentes, dicit quod Eufemia
soror sua, Ricardus Hynman famulus dicti Thome, ipsa iurata cum dictis
contrahentibus et non pluribus quod sciat. Requisita qua hora diei dictus
contractus initus erat, dicit quod cito post ortum solis. Requisita quibus
indumentis dicta Elizabet induta erat, dicit quod una supertunica de viride
cum tunica et capucio de rubeo. Alio modo vel plura super dictis articulis ipsi
iurate expositis et recitatis nescit deponere.

Willelmus de Besingby iuratus examinatus et diligenter [interrogatus].
Et primo si sciat deponere de aliquo contractu matrimoniali inito inter
Elizabet filiam domini Simonis Lovel militis et Thomam filium Roberti
de Merton, dicit quod contractui inito inter eos non interfuit; ipsos tamen
audivit fateri in presencia dicti domini Simonis, Roberti de Marton,
Edmundi de Staneley, Willelmi de Apelton', Willelmi de Thornton', ipsius
iurati et uxoris sue se adinvicem per verba matrimonialia consensisse et
[per] verba matrimonialia adinvicem contraxisse. Requisitus ubi dictas
confessiones enunserunt partes predicte et sub qua forma confessiones
huiusmodi enunserunt, dicit quod in ecclesia parochiali de Hougham dicti
Thomas et Elizabet coram hominibus predictis personaliter constituti die
Martis per octo dies post festum sancti Michaelis ultimo preteritum,
etiam iuramento super librum onerati, fatebatur dicta Elizabet primo et
asseruit dictum Thomam verba infrascripta eidem dixisse primo apud
Drokten' die Dominica proximo ante festum Purificationis beate Marie
Virginis tunc proximo precedentem: 'Promitto tibi quod non ducam
aliam in uxorem nisi te.' Et postea die Martis in septimana Pasche proximo tunc sequente: 'Hic accipio te Elizabet in uxorem meam tenendam et
habendam usque ad finem vite mee et ad hoc do tibi fidem meam.' Et
ut asseruit ipsa Elizabet', consimilia verba utroque tempore dicto Thome
proferebat. Et postmodum dictus Thomas, post huiusmodi confessionem
dicte Elizabet, parum deliberavit cum Willelmo de Thornton et Willelmo
de Apelton et dicta Elizabet'. Et statim rediens ad dictum Simonem et alios
superius nominatos, fatebatur se talia verba matrimonialia in forma per
ipsam Elizabet' recitata eidem Elizabet dixisse et protulisse. Adiecit tamen
idem Thomas quod tempore quo talia verba matrimonialia fecit et protulit
dicte Elizabet, in mente et voluntate cogitavit quod dictum contractum non
adimpleret nisi adesset voluntas amicorum suorum. Et tunc dicta Elizabet
eidem respondebat quod de cogitatione nescivit, sed quod ille contractus

fuerat simplex, sine conditione aliquali. Cui assertioni dictus Thomas nichil in contrarium respondebat.

Memorandum quod iiii kln' Decembris anno etc. xxvi[to] Thomas filius Roberti de Marton coram nobis officiali curie Ebor' et commissario generali in maiori ecclesia Ebor' loco consistorio eiusdem pro tribunali sedente personaliter constitutus prestito prius per eundem iuramento de dicenda veritate super requirendis per nos ab eodem, confessus fuit iudicialiter coram nobis se solempnizasse matrimonium cum quadam Elena filia Jordani de Aneport' commorantis apud Ryngoy in episcopatu Cestr' pendente lite super matrimonio inter Elizabeth' filiam domini Simonis Lovell' militis pendente indecisa; asseruit tamen se precontraxisse cum prefata Elena ante litem inchoatam.

In Dei nomine amen. Auditis et intellectis meritis cause matrimonialis mote coram nobis officiali curie Ebor' inter Elizabeth filiam domini Simonis Lovel militis per magistrum Willelmum de Humermanby clericum procuratorem suum comparentem actricem ex parte una et Thomam filium Roberti de Marton' per magistrum Willelmum de Twyforde clericum procuratorem suum comparentem reum ex altera, dato libello verborum subscriptorum seriem continente: In Dei nomine amen. Coram vobis etc., liteque ad eundem legitime contestata, iuramento a partibus hinc inde prestito de calumpnia et de veritate dicenda secundum ipsius cause qualitatem et naturam, traditis positionibus et secutis plene responsionibus ad easdem, productis testibus iuratis examinatis et eorum dictis publicatis, datis terminis ad dicendum in testes et eorum dicta et ad proponenda omnia in facto consistencia, iurisque ordine que in hac parte requiritur in omnibus observato. Quia invenimus dictam partem actricem intentionem suam coram nobis in iudicio deductam sufficienter probavisse, prefatum Thomam dicte Elizabeth in virum legitimum adiudicamus sentencialiter et diffinitive in hiis scriptis. Lata vi Kaln' Novembris anno etc. xxviii[o].

THE MARRIAGE CONTRACT

The foundation of the establishment of marriage in the Middle Ages and the focus of most litigation was the actual contract of marriage. The following three cases illustrate that point. Canonists discussed at length the problem of how far a marriage could be presumed simply from the conduct of the parties. If the parties live together for years, if the neighbors think they are man and wife, and if they talk to each other as such, does this amount to a marriage enforceable in the Church courts? The answer, in general, is no. It was not an enforceable marriage. At least, as noted in Chapter 2, the standards for establishing a valid marriage from such circumstances were very high. There had to be the conjunction of three things to make an enforceable marriage: (1) long cohabitation, (2) *fama viciniae* that a marriage existed, and (3) other supporting evidence.[2] Without all three elements there could be no valid marriage without an actual exchange of matrimonial consent. In almost all cases there had to be a provable contract.

In refusing to presume marriage from simple conduct, the canon law diverged from the Roman law rules, as the canonists often pointed out. According to a text from the Digest, marriage could be inferred from long cohabitation. But these the canon law rejected.[3] The cases are entirely consistent with the canonists. The first two given here show that marriages were not lightly presumed from conduct. *Colton* v. *Whithand* is the classic case discussed by the canonists. *Cursted* v. *Tournour* is an easier, more frivolous case. But it also shows that talk about marriage plus sexual relations did not, in legal practice, make a marriage. The conduct of the parties in the third case, *Lynch* v. *Holyngbourne*, may not seem much different in substance from that of the other two. But the facts included something not present in either of the first two: words which were at least arguably *verba de presenti*. It was the exchange of present consent which made a valid marriage.

Colton v. Whithand (1398)[4]

Robertus Whithand junior etatis xxii annorum libere conditionis et bone fame consanguineus dicti Roberti Whithand de quo articulatur in iii° consanguinitatis gradu, ut dicit, testis admissus iuratus super articulis presentibus annexis. Super primo articulo examinatus, dicit quod nescit deponere. Super ii° articulo examinatus, dicit quod super aliquo contractu matrimoniali sive sponsalicio inter dictas partes habito nescit deponere nisi secundum aliorum relationem; dicit tamen quod hinc ad triennium ultimo preteritum dicti Roberti et Alicia simul ut vir et uxor in thoro et mensa in una domo, primo in villa de Wigyngton' et postea in quadam grangia de Stakeldon Abbatis et Conventus de Biland moram traxerunt, de visu noticia et sciencia istius iurati, ut dicit. Interrogatus quando primo videbat eos simul in thoro et mensa in dictis locis cohabitare, dicit quod modicum ante Quadragesimam hinc ad triennium ultimo preteritam usque festum Pasche tunc proximo sequentis in villa de Wigyngton videbat eosdem Robertum et Aliciam ut virum et uxorem in thoro et mensa in eadem domo simul stare

---

[2] The best discussion of the problem I have seen is given by Panormitanus, *Commentaria* ad X 2.23.11, nos. 3, 8. On the reason that consent without verbal expression could not constitute marriage, see Innocent IV, *Apparatus* ad X 4.1.25: 'Et hec est ratio, quia sic statuit ecclesia licet sit contra ius naturale quod est, quod solo consensu contrahitur matrimonium, sed fuit iusta causa statuti huius, scilicet ne tantum sacramentum esset in incerto.'

[3] Compare Dig. 23.2.24 with C. 30 q. 5 c. 1 and 2.

[4] York C.P. E 236.

et ad dictum festum Pasche iidem Robertus et Alicia transtulerunt se ad dictam grangiam abbatis de Biland et ibidem per totum illum annum et ultra iste iuratus vidit illos in thoro et mensa tanquam virum et uxorem cohabitare. Et audivit eos diversis vicibus pluribus locis pro veris coniugibus se nominare et pro talibus ab omnibus vicinis suis publice reputabantur. Item interrogatus an dictus Robertus, medio tempore dum sic ut prefertur in locis predictis moram traxerunt, ex dicta Alicia aliquas proles generavit, dicit quod sic, quia unum masculinum generavit nomine Thomam adhuc superstitem modo etatis duorum annorum et ultra, quem bene novit iste iuratus ut dicit. Dicit etiam iste iuratus quod vidit et audivit dictum Robertum eundem Thomam filium suum nominare et reputare et ipsum pro filio suo alimentare. Et quod idem Thomas sit filius eiusdem Roberti ex dicti Alicia per eundem Robertum genitus fuit et est communiter dictum creditum et reputatum in dictis villis de Wigyngton', Whenby, et locis vicinis, ut dicit in iuramento suo. Dicit etiam iste iuratus quod dictus Robertus dum ipse et dicta Alicia sic ut prefertur cohabitarunt genuit ex eadem Alicia post dictum Thomam unam aliam prolem, nomine Johannam, modo defunctam, quam iste iuratus ad rogatum prefati Roberti patris sui de sacro fonte suscepit, ut dicit. Item interrogatus quomodo scit quod idem Robertus dictam Johannam ex dicta Alicia generavit, dicit quod sic fuit et est communiter dictum creditum et reputatum in villis predictis et locis vicinis. Super iii° articulo examinatus, dicit quod nescit aliter deponere quam superius deposuit. Super iiii° articulo examinatus, dicit quod nescit deponere. Super ultimo articulo, dicit quod, ut superius per ipsum depositum, articulus continet veritatem. Et non est conductus instructus vel informatus ad deponendum ut superius deposuit; nec curat que pars victoriam in premissis optineat dumtamen utrique parti fiat iusticia, ut dicit in iuramento suo.

Alice produced one other witness, Thomas Curwen of Wigenthorp, who gave the identical evidence in substance. But the Commissary General gave sentence against Alice and in favor of the defendant Whithand and Agnes, the woman he had married after deserting Alice. That is, he held that the evidence given above did not constitute a valid marriage. The verdict was appealed to the Official, and part of his judgment confirming the Commissary General's decision is given below. This was, in turn, appealed to the papal court.

In Dei nomine amen. Quia invenimus dictum commissarium nostrum generalem iuste rite et legitime sentenciasse, prefatamque Aliciam perperam appellasse, prefatam sentenciam sic per commissarium nostrum latam ut prefertur per hanc nostram diffinitivam sentenciam approbamus et confirmamus sentencialiter et diffinitive in hiis scriptis.

Cursted v. Tournour (1421)[5]

Acta in ecclesia omnium sanctorum Cant' v die mensis Augusti in quadam causa matrimoniali inter Robertum Cursted de Hochfeld ex una et Aliciam Tournour de eadem ex altera, parte dicti Roberti personaliter comparente iuratus et examinatus super contractu matrimoniali inter ipsum et dictam Aliciam, dicit quod [non] contraxit cum ea nisi sub istis verbis: 'Alicia es tu in voluntate dandi mihi terras tuas et ego volo facere sicut vir faceret uxori sue?' Que respondebat quod nollet alienare terras suas. Tamen carnaliter cognovit eandem, et postea idem Robertus contraxit cum Leticia Bett' de eadem per verba de presenti. Deinde vii° die dicte (sic) mensis prefata Alicia iurata et examinata super huiusmodi contractu, dicit quod dictus Robertus tractavit cum ea pro matrimonio inter eos coniungendo infra mensem post mortem mariti, qui affectavit habere certas terras suas vocatas Wynfeld, que respondebat sibi quod nollet sibi dare terras suas. Interrogata qui fuerunt tunc presentes, dicit quod nullus. Interrogata an tempore illo quo primo tractarunt inter se de matrimonio contrahendo carnaliter cognovit eam, dicit quod non, neque secunda vice. Interrogata an illo tempore quo carnaliter cognovit eam fuit ipsa in voluntate habendi eum in maritum suum, dicit quod sic si ipse voluit habuisse eam. Interrogata an aliquo tempore pendente huiusmodi tractatu carnaliter cognovit eam, dicit quod sic ut supra. Interrogata an aliquo tempore quando idem Robertus petiit ab ea quod daret sibi terras suas an ipsa respondebat sibi quod vellet deliberare se super responsione, dicit quod non, ymmo in primo et omni tempore negavit sibi terras suas. Dictus Robertus examinatus super eisdem concordat cum eadem. Igitur commissarius decrevit huiusmodi contractum nullum et invalidum et concessit viro licenciam nubendi alteri mulieri et mulieri alteri viro.

Lynch v. Holyngbourne (1374)[6]

Comparuit Agnes Lynch de parochia de Northgate et petiit Willelmum Holyngbourne de eadem sibi in virum legitimum et maritum adiudicari pro eo quod idem Willelmus promisit dicte Agneti de habendo eam in uxorem, carnali copula subsecuta. Vir de veritate dicenda iuratus, negat omnem huiusmodi promissionem; dicit tamen quod dixit dicte mulieri, 'Ego habebo tecum carnalem copulam,' muliere respondente, 'Non habebis mecum factum nisi velles habere in uxorem,' ipso respondente, 'Si aliquam mulierem volo habere in uxorem, volo habere te in uxorem.' Et ista verba fuerunt prolata per eum in castino (sic) festi Circumsionis (sic) Domini proximo preteriti. Et in nocte sequente iacuit cum eadem et eam carnaliter cognovit. Et ultimo cognovit eam, ut dicit, infra quindenam proximo preteritam. Dicit insuper quod antequam protulit dicta verba mulieri predicte, prefata mulier dixit

---

5   Canterbury Y.1.4, fols. 55r–55v.
6   Canterbury Y.1.1, fols. 64r, 66r.

sibi quod noluit pati se carnaliter cognosci ab eo nisi eam vellet ducere in uxorem. Ad audiendam pronunciationem super premissis. Et iuratus est vir quod non faciat se promoveri ad sacros ordines nec contrahat matrimonium cum alia muliere; et mulier iurata est quod non contrahat matrimonium cum alio pendente causa ista indecisa. Et fatentur peccatum et fustigatus est uterque circa ecclesiam; vir satisfecit pro se.

In causa matrimoniali mota inter Agnetam Lynch de parochia de Northgate Cant' partem actricem et Willelmum Hollyngbourne de eadem partem ream in termino ad audiendam pronunciationem super confessatis per partes predictas, partibus personaliter comparentibus, magister Robertus commissarius predictus confessiones partium predictarum coram eo alias emissam (sic), . . ., et inveniens predictam Agnetam intentionem suam in hac parte deductam sufficienter, ut dixit, fundasse et probasse, predictum Willelmum predicte Agneti in virum legitimum et maritum ipsamque Agnetam eidem Willelmo in uxorem legitimam adiudicavit sentencialiter et diffinitive per decretum.

DE DESPONSATIONE IMPUBERUM

Under the canon law, children below puberty but older than seven who contracted marriage could, on reaching puberty, either ratify or nullify the original contract. In the normal course of affairs, approval was shown by cohabitation and consummation of the union. Dissent was indicated by some sort of public statement. Such a proclamation might be made before the bishop, his court, or perhaps even a group of neighbors. But it was, in any event, a public protestation of disavowal.

The two cases which follow deal with the problem of conduct which fell somewhere between express dissent and approval. Suppose that one party allows years to pass before making any move, either negative or positive. Or suppose that his actions are ambiguous. The medieval canonists did not provide very exact guidelines. The judge was left with a wide area of discretion. The law held that sexual relations made the marriage absolute. But, beyond this, there is support for the argument that simple voluntary cohabitation signified approval. And there is support for the opposite rule, that mere living together created no presumption of consent.[7] And the canon law did not make it clear whether the passage of any particular length of time, without more, could serve to ratify a contract. *Aunger* v. *Malcake* suggests

---

[7] Compare *gl. ord.* ad X 4.2.9 s.v. *consensus*, speaking of consent validly given 'expressus vel presumptus, ut si patienter cohabitet illi', with Innocent IV, *Apparatus* ad X 4.2.10, no. 3: 'Si habitaret cum ea non praesumerem matrimonium.' See also X 4.18.4.

that the passage of a considerable amount of time was a vital factor. There was more evidence of actual consent in that case than in *Draycote* v. *Crane*. But the young boy in the first case acted promptly on reaching his fourteenth year by bringing an action for divorce. In the second case, the boy took no formal action for several years afterwards, although his witnesses testified that he expressed his unwillingness throughout and even the girl's witnesses brought forward no evidence of cohabitation. Whether this is sufficient difference to distinguish these cases satisfactorily may be doubted. But, even if they are inconsistent, they are not necessarily contrary to the law, for the law left considerable discretion to the judge in such cases.

Aunger v. *Malcake (1357–8)* [8]

Willelmus Raynald de Synflet' iuratus et examinatus super premissis articulis, dicit quod omnia contenta in eisdem sunt vera, quia Willelmum et Johannam de quibus agitur novit ab infancia eorundem et parentes eorundem dum vixerunt. Et audivit, ut dicit, quod matrimonium fuit celebratum in capella manerii de Fenwyk inter eosdem quodam die de quo non recolit modicum post Pascham ultimo preteritam fuerunt sex anni elapsi. Et tunc dictus Willelmus fuit etatis octo annorum et amplius, ut dicit, et dicta Johanna fuit duodecim annorum, sed nescit an complete quia de tempore nativitatis eiusdem non recolit. Dicit etiam interrogatus quod statim post matrimonium sic celebratum dictus Willelmus divertebat se ad villam de Elsyn in Northfoch, ubi cum domino Willelmo de Swynflet avunculo dicte Johanne per quatuor annos continuos moram traxit. Et tunc divertit se ad dictam villam de Swynflet, et ibi stetit per unam septimanam causa recreationis. Et cohabitavit cum eadem Johanna per dictam septimanam; credit tamen quod eam tunc carnaliter non cognovit, nec ante nec post. Et post lapsum dicte septimane rediit ad villam de Elsyn et ibi fuit continue per duos annos et ultra usque ad festum sancti Michelis ultimo preteritum. Et tunc fuit plene xiiii[cim] annorum, quo tempore rediit ad dictam villam de Swynflet et ibidem cohabitavit cum dicta Johanna per unam septimanam; et hoc coactus per amicos dicte Johanne, sed de qua vi vel metu vel qui eum astruxerunt nescit deponere. Dicit etiam interrogatus quod una nocte in septimana proximo post dictum festum sancti Michelis ingressus fuit lectum dicte Johanne ad excitationem quorundam vicinorum dicte ville, et sic iacuit in uno lecto cum dicta Johanna solus cum sola, nudus cum nuda, prout audivit iste testis ab aliis referri. Et post duos dies proximo tunc sequentes venit dictus Willelmus ad domum istius iurati in villa de Swynflet et dixit in hunc modum: 'Displicet michi quod uncquam novi dictam Johannam, eo quod me non diligit affectione qua tenetur. Et ideo

---

[8] York C.P. E 76.

pro certo nuncquam intendo consentire in eam quod sit uxor mea nec cum ea cohabitare.' Et post in die sequenti recessit idem Willelmus a villa de Swynflet et comitiva dicte Johanne ad villam de Redeness ubi ad illo tempore usque in hodiernum diem quasi continue moram traxit. Aliter vel plura super premissis articulis et interrogatoriis deponere nescit, nisi quod super veritate premissorum in forma qua deponit laborat publica vox et fama in villis de Swynflet et Reddenness' et locis vicinis.

In Dei nomine amen. Auditis et intellectis meritis cause divorcii mote et pendentis coram nobis domini officialis curie Ebor' commissario generali in dicta curia inter Willelmum filium Ade Aunger de Rednesse per magistrum Edwardum de Cornubia clericum procuratorem suum comparentem partem actricem ex parte una et Johannam filiam Thome Malcake de Swyneflete per magistrum Johannem de Stanton' clericum procuratorem suum comparentem partem ream ex altera; oblato libello eo qui sequitur sub tenore: In Dei nomine amen. Coram vobis domino officiali curie Ebor' vestrove commissario generali etc., factaque litis contestatione ad dictum libellum per procuratorem dicte partis ree sub hac forma: Fateor quod dicti Willelmus et Johanna de consensu suo et parentum suorum verba matrimonialia mutuo protulerunt et matrimonium adinvicem contraxerunt. Ad cetera in dicto libello contenta dico narrata ut narrantur vera non esse et ideo petita ut petuntur fieri non debere. Iuramento de calumpnia et de veritate dicenda hinc et inde prestito, traditis positionibus et responsionibus secutis ad easdem, nonnullisque testibus productis iuratis examinatis et eorum dictis publicatis, datisque terminis et prefixis ad dicendum in testes et eorum dicta et ad proponenda omnia in facto consistencia, demumque in dicta causa concluso et termino ad audiendam sentenciam diffinitivam per nos assignato, quo termino, partibus ut supra per procuratores suos comparentibus, nos commissarius antedictus, invocata Spiritus Sancti gracia, ad sentenciam diffinitivam procedimus in hunc modum. Quia invenimus predictam partem actricem intentionem suam coram nobis in iudicio deductam sufficienter fundasse, matrimonium seu sponsalia predictos inter ipsos Willelmum et Johannam de facto ut premittitur contractos dissolvimus et [adnullamus] eidemque Willelmo ad contrahendum matrimonium cum alia muliere licenciam concedimus sentencialiter et diffinitive in hiis scriptis.

Draycote v. Crane (1332–3)[9]

In Dei nomine amen. Petit Alicia filia Ricardi de Draycote in Croppill Boteler Willelmum Crane de Byngham sibi in maritum adiudicari pro eo quod ipsi matrimonium adinvicem per verba de presenti mutuum consensum exprimencia contraxerunt et postmodum, lapsis sex annis, illum contractum

[9] York C.P. E 23.

ratificarunt, super quibus laborat fama publica in villa de Croppill predicta et locis vicinis. Predicta proponit et petit dicta Alicia coniunctim et divisim, iuris beneficio in omnibus semper salvo.

Johannes de Draycote iuratus examinatus et diligenter interrogatus utrum habeat noticiam Alicie de Draycote in Croppill Botoler et Willelmi Crane de Byngham et a quo tempore, dicit quod mulierem novit a puericia eiusdem, virum novit a tempore octo annorum et amplius. Requisitus utrum sciat de aliquo contractu matrimoniali uncquam inito inter Aliciam et Willelmum predictos, dicit quod sic. Requisitus quid scit super hoc deponere, dicit quod ipse presens fuit, vidit, et audivit ubi dictus Willelmus accepit dictam Aliciam per manum sic dicendo: 'Hic accipio te Aliciam sicut in uxorem meam legitimam habendam et tenendam usque ad finem vite mee si sancta ecclesia hoc permittat, et ad hoc do tibi fidem meam', muliere statim respondente eidem, 'Willelme hic accipio te sicut in virum meum legitimum habendum et tenendum usque ad finem vite mee si sancta ecclesia hoc permittat et ad hoc do tibi fidem meam.' Requisitus de loco, tempore, die, hora diei, presentibus, dicit quod in domo Henrici de Kyketon' apud Croppill Boteler in festo sancti Johannis Ewangeliste iuxta Natalem Domini ultimo preteritam octo anni elapsi infra noctis tenebras illius diei, de die vero quo illud festum accidebat non recolit propter lapsum tanti temporis, presentibus contrahentibus, ipso iurato, Elizabet Crane, Adlina filia Roberti de Roberti de Croppill contestibus cum Henrico de Kyketon' et Felicia uxore sua qui viam universis carnis sunt ingressi. Requisitus cuius etatis dicti contrahentes erant tempore contractus initi inter eosdem, dicit quod vir erat tunc temporis tresdecim annorum et amplius, mulier erat fere quatuordecim annorum. Requisitus qualiter hoc scit, dicit quod hoc didicit ex relatu Alicie de Kyketon' matris Alicie de qua agitur de etate mulieris; de etate vero viri ex relatu commatris sue qui eum de sacro fonte levavit. Requisitus de indumentis contrahentium et ex qua parte domus sic contraxerunt et an erant stantes vel sedentes, dicit quod vir induebatur quadam tunica de tanny et quodam capucio viridi et mulier tunica nigra cum quodam capucio de percio. Et sedebant ex parte australi domus iuxta ignem. Requisitus de causa existencie sue tunc ibidem, dicit quod ibi fuit in domo matris sue sicut unus de familia eiusdem. Requisitus de fama dicit quod super premissis laborat publica vox et fama in villa de Croppill et locis vicinis.

Hugo Wodecok de Byngham iuratus examinatus et diligenter interrogatus utrum habeat noticiam Willelmi Crane de Byngham et Alicie de Draycote de Croppill et a quo tempore, dicit quod virum novit a tempore decem et octo annorum, mulierem vero non novit, ut dicit. Requisitus super primo articulo qui talis est: Inprimis intendit probare dictus Willelmus quod si quis contractus matrimonialis unquam inter ipsum Willelmum et dictam Aliciam fuerat initus, quod non fatetur, prefatus Willelmus tempore huiusmodi contractus minoris etatis quam duodecim annorum extitit et pro tali habitus fuit, dicit quod a quadam Elizabet Crane audivit quod quidam contractus matrimonialis initus fuit inter ipsos Willelmum et Aliciam circa Natalem Domini proximo futuram erunt novem anni elapsi; ipse tamen iuratus huiusmodi contractui nuncquam interfuit. Dicit etiam quod prefatus Willelmus tempore huiusmodi contractus erat undecim annorum et non amplius. Requisitus qualiter hoc scit, dicit quod hoc scit per collaneos suos in villa de Byngham et per quandam filiam suam propriam que est eiusdem etatis et per famam loci publicam que hoc tenet. Requisitus super secondo articulo qui talis est: Item intendit probare dictus Willelmus quod si quis contractus matrimonialis inter ipsum Willelmum et Aliciam predictam aliquo tempore initus fuisse iudicialiter probari videatur per testes ipsius Alicie, quod tamen idem Willelmus non fatetur, prefatus ipse Willelmus a tempore huiusmodi contractus ante et post renitens fuit reclamans ac invitus nec hactenus in dictam Aliciam ut in uxorem suam legitimam uncquam consensiit, sed dissenciit omni tempore, dicit quod audivit a prefato Willelmo et ab aliis qui tunc interfuerunt quod metu fuit ductus ad contrahendum sic cum dicta Alicia per quandam Elizabet Crane, que voluit abcidisse auriculam eius si hoc non fecisset. Ipse tamen hoc non vidit quia non interfuit. Dicit etiam quod a dicto tempore contractus citra semper audivit reclamantem ipsum Willelmum et renitentem, et vidit ipsum consortium illius mulieris in omnibus locis fugientem in quibus ipsos videbat. Et super premissis laborat publica vox et fama.

Simon Couper de Byngham iuratus etc. Requisitus de noticia Willelmi Crane de Byngham et Alicie de Draycote, dicit quod virum novit a tempore viginti annorum et amplius, mulierem non novit. Requisitus super primo articulo, dicit quod continet veritatem et concordat cum primo, hoc excepto quod Willelmus predictus tempore huiusmodi contractus fuit undecim annorum et amplius et hoc scit ex relatu aliorum et ex fama loci que hoc tenet. Dicit tamen quod duodecim annum tempore contractus non attingebat. Ad secundum et tercium concordat.

Willelmus Machon' de Byngham iuratus etc. Requisitus de noticia Willelmi Crane et Alicie de Draycote, dicit quod virum novit a tempore viginti annorum, mulierem per dimidium annum. Super primo articulo requisitus concordat cum primo et super secundo et tercio.

In Dei nomine amen. Auditis et intellectis meritis cause matrimonialis coram nobis domini archidiaconi Notingh' officiali mote inter Aliciam filiam Ricardi de Draycote de Croppille Boteler actricem personaliter comparentem ex parte una et Willelmum Crane de Byngham reum per Adam de Sewale clericum procuratorem suum comparentem ex altera, dato libello verborum subcriptorum seriem continente: In Dei nomine amen etc., lite ad eundem verbis negativis legitime contestata; iuramento a partibus ipsis prestito de calumpnia et de veritate dicenda, productis testibus juratis examinatis et eorum dictis pupplicatis, diebusque datis ad dicendum in testes et eorum dicta et ad proponenda omnia in facto consistencia, ac iuris ordine que in hoc casu requirebatur in omnibus observato. Quia invenimus dictam Aliciam intentionem suam coram nobis in iudicio deductam sufficienter et legitime probavisse prefatum Willelmum in virum legitimum eidem Alicie adiudicavimus sentencialiter et diffinitive.

CONDITIONAL MARRIAGES

The validity of conditional contracts, even by *verba de presenti*, was established under the law. But as noted in the text, the condition must have been inserted 'immediately' or 'in the act of contracting' to be valid. If it were added later, the marriage was binding even if the condition went unfulfilled. *Hokerigge* v. *Lucas* tells the story of an attempt to add a condition after the contract had been made. The defendant here, as usually happened, claimed that she had not meant the original exchange of words to be unconditional. But the court disregarded her explanation. The Church courts adhered to an external standard in deciding the case. Subjective intent, the deciding fact in the 'internal forum' of men's conscience, did not ordinarily figure in the resolution of cases in the ecclesiastical tribunals.

Cheseman v. *Kenot* raised a rather different problem, one not mentioned explicitly in the text. It was at least arguable that a marriage specifically conditioned on one party's return to health had been contracted in that case. The court held against the plaintiff, however. And it may be that the result reflects the same principle at work in the first case: the necessity that the condition be made an unmistakable part of the initial contract. Note also that the case contains one of the rare examples of personal intervention by the bishop in the litigation of his diocese.

Hokerigge v. Lucas (1417)[10]

Facta fuit sequens examinatio testium pro parte Thome Hokerigge de parochia de Cranebroke contra Godelevam Lucas de parochia de Benynden' in quadam causa matrimoniali productorum xxix die Januarii in domo habitationis commissarii Cant' examinatorum.

Ricardus Seynden' de parochia de Cranebroke etatis xxiii annorum et amplius libere conditionis ut dicit iuratus requisitus et diligenter examinatus. Primo interrogatus de noticia partium predictarum dicit quod novit dictum Thomam a nativitate sua et prefatam Godlevam per vii annos proximo

---

[10] Canterbury X. 10.1, fols. 95r–95v; Y.1.3, fols. 8v–9r.

preteritos. Interrogatus super summaria petitione apud acta pro parte dicti
Thome contra prefatam Godlevam ministrata, cuius tenor est talis etc., et
primo an fuit presens in aliquo loco ubi audivit aliqua verba matrimonialia
inter partes predictas, dicit quod sic, et quod quodam tempore circa quindenam ante festum sancti Dunstani anno preterito, videlicet anno domini
m ccc xv°, loquebatur iste iuratus supradicte Godleve sicut transibant simul
quodam die Dominico circa cimiterium ecclesie parochialis de Renyden et
dixit hec verba, 'Godleva, quid dicis de tali viro cognato meo,' nominando
dictum Thomam Hokerygge, 'Numquid possis invenire in corde tuo ad
habendum eum in virum et maritum tuum?' Que respondebat eidem, 'Si ipse
voluerit venire ad loquendum mecum in propria persona, tunc ipse sciat
veritatem.' Et tunc dixit iste iuratus, 'Et ego volo loqui sibi quod veniat ad
loquendum tecum.' Et mulier respondebat, 'Placet michi.' Et extunc accessit
iste iuratus ad prefatum Thomam et adduxit eum ad prefatam Godlevam,
referendo sibi precedencia verba, videlicet quodam die Lune proximo post
festum Pentecoste ultimo preteritum, quando dictus Thomas venit ad domum
Johannis Brinchesley situatam in parochia de Bydynden dicto die contingente
in die Lune predicto. Finxit se habere unum nuncium sive negocium ex-
pediendum cum predicto J. Brychesley. Quo expedito cepit licensiam suam ab
eodem. Et obviavit prefatus Thomas predicte Godleve extra portam antedicti
Johannis. Et ibidem tractarunt inter se de matrimonio contrahendo inter
eosdem, ut prefatus Thomas retulit isti iurato. Et extunc cepit licenciam ab
eadem. Et postmodum adveniente festo quod dicitur Ad Vincula anno predicto, revenit iste Thomas ad prefatam Godlevam et iste iuratus cum eo ad
quandam parvam silvam vocatam 'a grove' iuxta domum magistri dicte
Godleve vocati Johannis Brinchesley, ubi et quando post modicum tractatum
habitum inter predictos Thomam et Godlevam, prefatus Thomas vocavit
istum iuratum ad eos. Et ibidem dixit prefatus Thomas dicte Godleve, 'Vos
estis in voluntate quod iste Ricardus cognatus meus audiat voluntatem
nostram?' Que respondebat quod sic. Et tunc idem Thomas cepit dictam
Godlevam per manum dexteram et dixit hec verba: 'Ego Thomas accipio
te Godlevam in uxorem meam et ad hoc do tibi fidem meam.' Et tunc idem
Thomas osculatus est eandem, et tradidit eidem unum loculum cum xii d.
contentis in eodem, quem loculum vidit iste iuratus; non tamen argentum nisi
ex relatu eiusdem Thome. Et dixit idem Thomas prefate Godleve quod domicella que venit cum ea ad dictum locum haberet iiii d. Interrogatus an dicta
domicella audivit aliqua verba superius recitata inter predictos Thomam et
Godlevam, dicit quod non sed stetit a longo expectans dictam Godlevam.
Et incontinenti post premissa, convenerunt dicti Thomas et Godleva quod
omnia premissa, scilicet conventio inter eos facta et cetera dicta recitata inter
eosdem custodirentur in secretis per i quarterium anni sequentis, ut possit
idem Thomas tractare cum Johanne Brinchesle magistro domini Godleve ad
habendum bonum amorem suum. Interrogatus in quo gradu est iste iuratus

consanguineus prefato Thome, dicit in secundo gradu in linea equali, scilicet filius avunculi sui. Item interrogatus de fama, dicit quod super predicto contractu laborat fama in parochia predicta et locis convicinis. Aliter nescit sed quod non est informatus nec prece vel precio conductus. Aliter nescit etc.

Facta fuit sequens examinatio testis, videlicet Willelmi Wilcok de parochia de Bynynden producti pro parte Thome Hokerygge de parochia de Cranebroke xix die Februarii in domo habitationis supradicti per eundem.

Willelmus Wilcok de parochia de Bynynden etatis xxx annorum et amplius libere conditionis ut dicit iuratus etc. Primo interrogatus super noticia partium, scilicet Thome Hokerygge et Godleve Lucas, dicit quod novit dictum Thomam per iii annos et Godlevam per v annos proximo preteritos, et desponsavit sororem dicte Godleve. Interrogatus an fuit presens in aliquo loco ubi audivit aliqua verba matrimonialia inter partes predictas, dicit quod non; sed quodam tempore inter festum nativitatis sancti Johannis Baptiste et festum quod dicitur Ad Vincula ultimo preteritum ante datum presentium, quodam die de quo certo die non recolit neque de mense, venit iste iuratus ad domum Johannis Brynchesle situatam in parochia de Bydynden', et ibidem alloquebatur prefatam Godlevam sic dicendo eidem, 'Godlef, est michi relatum quod habebis quendam Thomam Hokerig in maritum tuum.' Que respondebat eidem iurato in presencia uxoris dicti Johannis Brynchesle quod sic. Et dicta uxor, magistra prefate Godleve, irancundia mota ut sibi apparuit propter verba predicta per eandem Godlevam prolata, tunc ibidem precepit eidem Godleve transire cum ea. Et sic pariter recesserunt uxor dicti Johannis cum eadem Godleva. Postea tamen per mensem vel ultra, revenit iste iuratus ad loquendum cum dicta Godleva et dixit eidem, 'Quid dicis ad materiam illam de qua alias tibi loquebar de persona Thome Hokerygge, numquid est ita sicut michi pro tunc retulisti?' Que respondebat quod, 'Illa verba que vobis retuli pro tunc referebam vobis ad sciendam voluntatem vestram, quia non consentiebam ad habendum eum in maritum meum nisi amici mei vellent ad illud consentire.' Interrogatus iste iuratus an laborat fama in parochia de Byndynden super contractu matrimoniali inter dictos Thomam Hokerygge et Godlevam Lucas, qui dicit quod sic ac etiam in locis convicinis dicte parochie. Interrogatus an sit informatus prece vel precio conductus vel affectat victoriam pro una parte magis quam pro alia, dicit quod non. Aliter nescit nisi ut supra etc.

In causa matrimoniali inter Thomam Hokerygge de parochia de Cranebroke actorem ex una et Godlevam Lucas de parochia de Benynden ream ex alia in termino ad audiendam sentenciam in dicta causa diffinitivam, partibus ut supra comparentibus, commissarius antedictus in causa memorata sentenciam tulit diffinitivam et adiudicavit pro vero et legitimo matrimonio inter eosdem Thomam et Godlevam contracto, a qua quidem sentencia Adam Body procurator dicte partis ree apud acta illico appellavit ad sedem apostolicam et pro tuitione ad curiam Cant' et apostolos petiit primo secundo tercio instanter instantius et instantissime. Et iudex antedictus antedicto Ade Body ad recipiendum apostolos penultimum diem iuridicum assignavit loco predicto. Presentibus tunc ibidem domino Nicholao Julyan rectore de Sturmouthe et domino Willelmo Staunton' rectore de Henxhull Lincolnienc' dioc' et multis aliis ibidem tunc presentibus.

Cheseman v. Kenot (1440) [11]

Johanna Kenot de Tonnbregg citata est per J. North ad instanciam Johannis Cheseman de Eltham in causa matrimoniali de iusticia responsura. Dictus Johannes constituit procuratorem suum apud acta magistrum Ricardum Letott in causa predicta cum omnibus clausulis necessariis sub forma communi. Partes personaliter comparent, et iurati de veritate dicenda, et predictus Johannes Cheseman interrogatus, virtute iuramenti sui an contraxisset matrimonium cum predicta Johanna dicit quod die Martis in ebdomada Pasche ultimo preterite, convocatis secum amicis suis, videlicet Roberto Cheseman, Thoma Draper, Willelmo Kyng et Alano Typan' in domo prefate Johanne causa contractus fiendi et recitandi coram eisdem; et prefatus Robertus Cheseman interrogavit mulierem an vellet habere ipsum Johannem fratrem suum in maritum. Ipsa dixit quod sic. Et tunc dederunt hinc inde fidem, et matrimonium contraxerunt. Et dicta Johanna interrogata, dicit quod convocatis amicis dicti Johannis ut prefertur, [dixit] quod nunquam vellet sponsare aliquem nisi prius posset gaudere sanitate corporali, et si unquam sponsare aliquem vellet ipsum accipere in maritum. Et ad hoc dedit ei fidem. Et interrogata de carnali copula, negat.

In Dei nomine amen. Auditis et plenius intellectis meritis et circumstanciis cause matrimonialis que coram officiali Roffen' in consistorio Roffen' inter Johannem Cheseman partem actricem ex parte una et Johannam Kenott de Tonnbregg Roffen' diocesis partem ream ex altera aliquandiu vertebatur et pendet indiscussa; quia nos Willelmus permissione divina Roffen' episcopus, rimato per nos primitus et diligenter investigato toto processu in dicta causa habito, invenimus per acta, inactitata, deducta, allegata, et confessata et probata, partem dicti Johannis Cheseman in probatione intentionis sue in dicta causa proposite, qua peciit eandem Johannam eidem Johanni adiudicari in uxorem, omnino defecisse, idcirco Christi nomine invocato, ipsum solum Deum pre oculis habentes, de iuris peritorum cum quibus communicavimus in hac parte consilio, prefatam Johannam ab impetitione predicti Johannis absolvimus et perpetuum silencium eidem Johanni in ea parte imponimus per hanc nostram sentenciam diffinitivam, quam ferimus et promulgamus in hiis scriptis, condempnationem expensarum in hac causa factarum ex causis omittentes.

---

[11] Rochester DRb Pa 1, fols. 145r, 188r.

Lecta et lata et in scriptis promulgata per venerabilem in Christo patrem predictum in capella sua de Trott predicto xxvii die mensis et anni predictorum, presentibus discretis viris magistro Thoma Hanwall officiali Roffen' et magistro Willelmo Middleton ac magistro Willelmo Rowe.

THE IMPEDIMENT OF CRIME

Suardby v. *Wald* tells an interesting, perhaps somewhat implausible, story. Its verdict illustrates the point discussed at some length above, the difficulty of securing a divorce for 'pollution by adultery' prior to a marriage. Under certain conditions a marriage contracted with a second woman during the life of a man's wife was absolutely void. The conditions were (1) the second woman must have known of the existing marriage; (2) there must have been a contract of marriage or a promise to marry later made during the life of the first wife; and (3) there must have been adultery between the man and the second woman. All these conditions were seemingly fulfilled in *Suardby* v. *Wald*. Yet the suit for divorce was not allowed. Whether the result reflects failure of proof or disregard for the impediment is difficult to say. What I can say on the subject is included in Chapter 3.

Suardby v. Wald (1372)[12]

Xii^{mo} die mensis Novembris anno etc. lxx secundo, comparentibus personaliter coram domini officialis Ebor' commissario generali pro tribunali sedente Johanna de Suardby et Thoma del Wald' de Ebor' potter, dicta Johanna petiit prefatum Thomam sibi in virum legitimum adiudicari pro eo quod dictus Thomas promisit eidem Johanne quod ipsam duceret in uxorem, qui postmodum eandem carnaliter cognovit et suscitavit de ea prolem. Habitaque altercatione inter eosdem, prefatus Thomas super requirendis iuratus dicere veritatem, dixit quod contraxit cum dicta Johanna vivente Mariona uxore sua et eam carnaliter cognovit. Interrogatus quot anni sunt elapsi a tempore illo quo primo cognovit eandem, dicit quod circa festum sancti Laurencii ultimo preteritum fuerunt quatuor anni elapsi. Interrogatus in quo loco, dicit quod in quadam camera quam tunc inhabitavit in Walmegat'. Item interrogatus, dicit quod post mortem uxoris sue dictus Thomas coram decano Christianitatis Ebor' in forma ecclesie abiuravit eandem Johannam, videlicet quod si eam carnaliter extunc cognosceret, eam duceret in uxorem. Interrogatus si postea cognovit eam, dicit quod sic. Item xiii° die mensis Novembris anno supradicto, prefatus Thomas coram domino officiali predicto pro tribunali sedente iuratus super requirendis ab eo dicere veritatem, dixit

¹² York C.P. E 111.

quod vivente Mariona uxore sua, carnaliter cognovit dictam Johannam et quod eidem Johanne dixit sub hac forma: 'Ita bene diligo te quod vellem ducere te in uxorem si uxor mea esset mortua.' Interrogatus quomodo dicta Johanna vel qualiter sibi respondit, dicit quod non recolit.

In Dei nomine amen. Positiones et articulos infrascriptos et contenta in eisdem dat et facit ac probare intendit procurator Johanne de Suardby nomine procuratorio pro eadem contra Thomam del Wald potter de Ebor' in causa matrimoniali inter dictos Thomam et Johannam in curia Ebor' mota et pendente. Et si que positiones sint multiplices, eas ponit divisim et sic petit quod per dictum Thomam respondeatur ad easdem.

In primis ponit ac probare intendit dictus procurator nomine quo supra quod predicti Thomas et Johanna sponsalia per verba de futuro, carnali copula inter eosdem postmodum subsecuta ac matrimonium per verba mutuum consensum de presenti exprimencia post mortem Marione quondam uxoris ipsius Thome defuncte adinvicem legitime contraxerunt. Non credit.

Item ponit ac probare intendit quod idem Thomas post mortem dicte uxoris sue prefatam Johannam coram decano Christianitatis Ebor' in forma communi ecclesie, videlicet si dictus Thomas eandem Johannam extunc carnaliter cognosceret, ipsam Johannam in uxorem suam teneret et haberet, in presencia predicte Johanne iudicialiter abiuravit. Dicit quod non animo contrahendi neque habendi ipsam Johannam in uxorem suam huiusmodi abiurationem fecit, sed compulsus per dictum Thomam Wyles tunc decanum Christianitatis Ebor' et propter timorem excommunicationis per ipsum decanum in dictum Thomam in hac parte tunc ferende et non aliter. Et dicit quod ante predictam abiurationem prefatus Thomas constante matrimonio inter ipsum et Marionam uxorem suam legitimam tunc superstitem, predictam Johannam carnaliter cognovit in adulterinis amplexibus, et fidem suam eidem Johanne dedit de habendo ipsam in uxorem suam post mortem dicte Marione tunc superstitis, ut prefertur.

Item ponit ac probare intendit quod prefatus Thomas del Wald eandem Johannam post predictam abiurationem sepius carnaliter cognovit et prolem ex eadem suscitavit. Dicit quod postquam compulsus fuerat iurare ut prefertur, dictam Johannam carnaliter cognovit.

Item ponit ac probare intendit quod dictus Thomas premissa omnia et singula in presencia ipsius Johanne et aliorum fidedignorum tam in iudicio quam extra sepius ex sua certa sciencia sponte est confessus. Non credit ut ponitur.

Item ponit ac probare intendit quod premissa sunt publica notoria et manifesta in civitate Ebor' et locis vicinis; et super hiis ibidem laboravit et adhuc laborat publica vox et fama. Non credit de negat'.

Margereta de Burton moram trahens in Walmgate in Ebor' per xv annos etatis xxx annorum et amplius libere conditionis ut dicit et consanguinea

Thome de Wald, nescit tamen in quo gradu, partis de qua agitur in causa presenti, noticiam habens de eodem Thoma per xx annos ut dicit, et de Johanna Swardby per viii annos ut credit, testis admissa iurata et examinata. Super primo articulo diligenter requisita, dicit quod dictus Thomas habuit quondam mulierem nomine Marionam in uxorem suam, ex qua quatuor vel quinque filios et filias procreavit; non tamen fuerat presens quando dictus Thomas contraxit cum dicta Mariona vel matrimonium solemnizavit, sed fuit eodem die in convivio hora prandii ut dicit. Interrogata in qua domo convivium huiusmodi fuerat factum, dicit quod non recolit. Interrogata quamdiu vixit dicta uxor Mariona cum dicto Thoma, dicit quod per xiiii annos ut credit, et decessit tribus annis elapsis et ultra. Super secundo articulo requisita, dicit quod dictus Thomas, uxore sua Mariona predicta vivente, ipsa Mariona, ista iurata et Johanne Wald conteste suo audientibus, in camera in parte inferiori domus sive hospicii dicti Thome cituati in Walmgate in parochia sancti Dionisii edificata, illis tribus predictis ad hostium dicte camera stantibus, contraxit cum dicta Johanna, sciente illum uxorem superstitem tunc habentem, in hiis verbis: 'Johanna, do tibi fidem meam quod te sponsabo post mortem uxoris mee si tunc vivas,' muliere sibi respondente anglice, 'I hald thar' to.' Et osculati adinvicem fuerunt, cum nota quia audiverunt ad hostium dicte camere. Interrogata qua hora diei et quomodo dictus Thomas intravit cameram et ad instigationem cuius huiusmodi fecit, dicit quod dicta camera habet introitum de aula per unum gradum prope ad hostium cuiusdam celarii; in quo celario iacuit dicta Mariona uxor dicti Thome cum filiis suis. Et alius lectus fuerat supra in camera in quo aliquando iacuit dictus Thomas cum Johanna predicta, ut sepius audivit ista iurata a dicta Mariona tunc vivente. Et uno die non recolit in quo die circa festum sancti Laurencii ultimo preteritum fuerunt quatuor anni elapsi quod dictus Thomas mane circa horam matutinalem venit de orto suo et dictam cameram per aulam intravit, dicta Johanna existenti in dicta camera, Mariona, Johanne conteste suo et ista iurata in aula stantibus et ipsum intrare videtibus. Et tunc dixit Mariona predicta isti iurate et Johanni contesti predicto, 'Eamus ad ostium camere et audiamus verba et facta eorundem.' Et transiverunt usque ad pedem gradus illius camere et audierunt, ut dicit, verba sponsalia predicta. Interrogata quot passus sive gradus continet gradus predictus, dicit quod octo gradus, ut credit. Et dicit interrogata quod tunc dicta Johanna dixit Thome supradicto, 'Si velitis michi concedere quod michi promisistis modico tempore elapso, anglice langare, essem valde letis.' Tunc ait ille, 'Quod fuerat illud?' Respondit illa, 'Quod me duceretis in uxorem.' Tunc dixit verba sponsalia ut prefertur. Interrogata qua de causa tunc dicta Johanna fuerat in camera, dicit quod cum dicto Johanne illa nocte ante pernoctavit et non audebat recedere propter visum aliorum, prout dixit dicta Mariona isti iurate; aliter nescivit. Interrogata an dicta Johanna fuerat tunc serviens et conducta cum dicto Thoma, dicit quod non tunc, sed ante fuit per duos annos cum dimidio. Super tercio articulo requisita, dicit quod dictus Thomas dictam Johannam carnaliter cognovit uxore sua vivente, predictam in adulterio [tenens], quia semel ista iurata invenit dictum Thomam in lecto dicte Johanne. Et notum est quod eam cognovit carnaliter nec diffiteri potest. Interrogata de vestimento viri, dicit quod quando intravit cameram, tunicam stragulatam. Interrogata si fuerat dies festivalis vel laboriosa, dicit quod laboriosa. Interrogata si sepius disponsavit dictam Johannam, dicit quod nisi semel quod novit. Interrogata de ayere illius diei contractus, dicit quod fuerat pulchrum tempus et dies cara (sic). Interrogata qualiter recolit de premissis per tantum tempus, dicit quod nescit sed quia recolit. Interrogata ad instanciam cuius premissa fuerunt facta, dicit quod nescit. Super penultimo articulo requisita, dicit quod de illo deponere nescit. Interrogata quare illo die venit ad locum predictum et quos invenit in eodem loco, dicit quod venit ad dictam Marionam prout fecit in dees communiter causa negociorum, et invenit illam in domo et dictum Johannem contestem suum. Interrogata ubi fuerat ostium dicte camere, an supra vel ad pedem gradus, an apertum vel clausum, et qualiter steterunt et recesserunt quando dicta verba audiverunt. Dicit quod ostium similiter clausura ostii fuerat supra, vocatum a faldure, et apertum. Et dictus Johannes stetit propinquius super primum gradum, et dicta Mariona remotius, ista iurata in medio. Et dicta Mariona, adveniente Thoma predicto, fugit in celarium predictum, . . . , et ista iurata fugit extra in altam viam et dictus Johannes, ut postea dixit isti iurate, in ortum, ubi dictus Thomas ipsum percussiebat cum pugnore. Interrogata si multum habundat in bonis, dicit omnia bona sua non extendunt se ad decem solidos, falcatis falcandis. Super ultimo articulo requisita, dicit quod super contractum et carnalem copulam laboravit et laborat inter notos publica vox et fama. Non est conductus prece precio odio vel timore, ut dicit, consanguinius in tercio gradu.

In Dei nomine amen. Auditis et intellectis meritis cause matrimonialis primo coram reverendo viro domino officiali curie Ebor' et eius commisario generali ac postmodum coram nobis Johanne de Tyverington' rectore ecclesie de Tyverington' diocesis eiusdem officialis commissario in hac parte specialiter deputato mote et pendentis inter Johannam de Suardby de Ebor' primo personaliter et deinde per magistrum Johannem de Rouclyff clericum procuratorem suum partem actricem ex parte una et Thomam del Wald de Ebor' potter primo personaliter ac postmodum per magistrum Henricum de Axiholm' clericum procuratorem suum partem ream ex altera comparentem. Oblato dicto domino officiali et eius commissario generali necnon dicti (sic) parti ree libello cuius tenor talis est: In Dei nomine amen, petit Johanna de Suardby Thomam de Wald de Ebor' potter pro eo quod idem Thomas et Johanna sponsalia per verba de futuro ac matrimonium per verba mutuum consensum de presenti exprimencia carnali copula inter eosdem subsecuta adinvicem legitime contraxerunt. Et habeatur libellus pro lecto, lite ad eundem libellum per partem ream predictam negative contestata, iuramento de calumpnia et de veritate dicenda hinc inde a partibus ipsis prestito, traditis positionibus et articulis, secutisque responsionibus ad easdem positiones, proposita etiam quadam exceptione per viam facti contrarii per partem ream predictam, qua sub modo admissa, nonnullisque testibus per dictam partem ream super exceptione predicta productis, quibus admissis iuratis et examinatis et eorum dictis et depositionibus publicatis, datis terminis et prefixis ad dicendum in testes et eorum dicta necnon ad proponenda omnia in facto consistencia, factisque per dictum dominum officialem ex officio suo dictis partibus pro veritate in hac parte eruenda quibusdam interrogationibus ac responsionibus per easdem partes factis et secutis ad easdem, demum in dicta causa concluso, et termino ad audiendam sentenciam diffinitivam prefixo et assignato, nos dicti domini officialis commissarius specialis in hac parte supradictus, Christi nomine invocato, ad sentenciam diffinitivam procedimus in hunc modum. Quia invenimus prefatam Johannam intentionem suam in iudicio deductam sufficienter probavisse, prefatum Thomam eidem Johanne in virum suum legitimum, prefatamque Johannam eidem Thome in uxorem suam legitimam adiudicamus, ipsumque Thomam ad solempnizandum matrimonium cum eadem Johanna in facie ecclesie canonice fore compellendum et cohercendum non obstantibus exceptionibus per partem dicti Thome partis ree propositis et allegatis, decernimus sentencialiter et diffinitive in hiis scriptis.

Lecta et lata fuit ista sentencia xviii° die Decembris anno etc. lxx secundo, indictione xi, pontificatus domini Gregorii pape xi anno secundo, presentibus Johanne de Kirkalstoun et N. Esingwald, Thoma Fitlyng, Edwardo Flecham, necnon W. Aslkely et aliis.

ERROR OF CONDITION

Canonists distinguished four sorts of errors in marriage: errors as to person, condition, fortune and quality. The first two gave rise to a claim for divorce; the second two did not. Thus, if a man married Titia believing her to be Bertha, or a slave believing her to be free, the marriage could be voided. But if he married a pauper believing her to be rich, or a shrew believing her to be gentle, the marriage was valid. The case transcribed here has to do with the second of these errors, that relating to servile condition. It illustrates, first, the availability of divorce on this ground; and, second, the rule that if the person of free condition had knowledge of the servile status, no divorce would be allowed.[13] It was also the rule that sexual relations after discovery of the fact of the unfree partner's true condition rendered the mar-

---

[13] See C. 29 q. 2.

riage indissoluble. The free partner was held to have ratified the prior contract.[14] The medieval Church went this far in applying St Paul's precept that in Christ there is neither Jew nor Greek, slave nor free. But no further.

Everard v. 'Beneyt' (1376)[15]

Johannes Everard de Ely et Johanna commorans cum Roberto Beneyt de eadem citati coram nobis officiali Elien' ad diem Lune proximum post festum Omnium Sanctorum in ecclesia sancte Trinitatis civitatis Elien' super contractu matrimoniali inter eosdem fama referente inito, uterque comparet personaliter coram nobis et de veritate dicenda iurati ac super dicto contractu requisiti. Dictus Johannes fatebatur ac proposuit et allegavit quod ipse et prefata Johanna matrimonium adinvicem per verba de presenti mutuum consensum eorundem exprimencia contraxerunt, quem quidem contractum uterque eorum in alterius et aliorum fidedignorum presencia fatebantur (sic) et recognoverunt (sic) et super quibus publica fama dinoscitur laborare, quare petiit dictus Johannes prefatam Johannam in uxorem legitimam ipsumque Johannem eidem Johanne in virum legitimum sentencialiter et diffinitive adiudicari. Dicta vero Johanna super predicto contractu requisita fatebatur quod contraxerunt sub forma que sequitur et non alio modo: dictus Johannes quesivit ab eadem sub ista forma, 'Vis tu habere me in virum?' Et ipse respondebat, 'Sic,' et quod placuit sibi. Fatetur etiam dicta Johanna quod postea procurarunt banna edi in facie ecclesie; unde eisdem Johanni et Johanne diem crastinum loco quo supra ad proponendam causam rationabilem si quam habeant quare iuxta dictas confessiones adiudicari non debeat pro matrimonio inter eos prefigimus et assignamus. Quibus die et loco partibus predictis coram nobis Thoma de Glouc' domini officialis Elien' commissario personaliter comparentibus, proposito per dictam Johannam quod idem Johannes tempore dicti contractus ante et post fuit et adhuc est servus et nativus et servilis conditionis; quodque suam ignorans conditionem sic ut prefertur cum eo contraxit, alias non contractura. Allegat etiam quod a tempore quo de dicta conditione servili constituit statim penituit et contradixit ac dissentiit et in presenti penitet contradicit et dissentit. Dictus insuper Johannes fatetur se servum et servilis conditionis, sed dicit replicando quod dicta Johanna novit eum pro servo diu ante dictum contractum et post. Iuratis partibus hincinde de calumpnia et de veritate dicenda ac de malicia, datur dies in proximo consistorio in ecclesia sancti Michelis Cant' partibus predictis ad probandum hinc inde propositum per eos.

In causa matrimoniali mota inter Johannem Everard de Ely partem actricem ex parte una et Johannam commorantem cum Roberto Beneyt de eadem

---

[14] X 4.9.2.
[15] Ely EDR D/2/1, fols. 55(B)v, 58v–59v.

partem ream ex altera partibus coram nobis officiali predicto in ecclesia sancte Trinitatis civitatis Elien' die Mercurii proximo post festum sancte Lucie Virginis personaliter comparentibus, nullis testibus per dictas partes seu earum aliquam productis, sed factis per nos pro informatione consciencie nostre eisdem partibus quibusdam positionibus, videlicet dicto Johanni an tunc fuit et nunc est servus et nativus et servilis conditionis, dicteque Johanne an tempore dicti contractus per eos confessi scivit ipsum Johannem fore servilis conditionis. Iuratisque dictis Johanne et Johanna de veritate dicenda in hac parte ac super predictis positionibus requisitis, dictus Johannes fatetur quod tunc fuit et nunc est servus et servilis conditionis; dictaque Johanna fatetur quod tempore dicti contractus ante et post scivit ipsum esse servilis conditionis et quod non obstante dicta conditione sic ut premittitur adinvicem contraxerunt et banna matrimonialia in facie ecclesie inter eos publice edi fecerunt. Factaque per nos conclusione in dicta causa eo quod dicte partes nichil effectuale proponunt quare pro matrimonio inter eos non debeat adiudicari et partibus predictis horam tercie pulsationis post prandium huiusmodi diei Mercurii loco quo supra ad audiendam sentenciam in dicta causa diffinitivam prefigimus et assignamus. Quibus hora et loco partibus coram nobis officiali predicto personaliter comparentibus et requisitis iterato an quicquam sciant rationabile proponere quare pro matrimonio non debeat adiudicari iuxta confessiones suas coram nobis iudicialiter emissas, dicunt se nescire quicquam deponere nisi dumtaxat quod iam mutarunt suam voluntatem quia credunt quod se invicem non deligunt propter resistentiam per dictam Johannam factam. Auditisque per nos et intellectis meritis cause matrimonialis supradicte, rimato et investigato toto processu in dicta causa habito, habitaque deliberatione sufficiente super eodem de consilio iurisperitorum nobis assidentium, Christi nomine primitus invocato, ad sentenciam diffinitivam in hac parte ferendam procedimus in hunc modum. Quia invenimus dictum Johannem intentionem suam in hac parte deductam bene et sufficienter fundasse et probasse, nec aliquod canonicum obstare impedimentum, ipsum Johannem eidem Johanne in virum legitimum, ipsamque Johannam eidem Johanni in uxorem legitimam sentencialiter et diffinitive adiudicamus in hiis scriptis, decernentes matrimonium fore inter eos in facie ecclesie solempnizandum pro loco et tempore oportunis.

CONSANGUINITY AND AFFINITY

These four cases deal with the canon law's impediments relating to kinship. The first case, *Bello* v. *Bello*, is the earliest surviving document here transcribed. It shows the use of an inquisition to determine a question of affinity in a comparatively primitive form. The *inquisitio* is not clearly separated from the oath of the parties. And there is a collective verdict given by all. At the end of the thirteenth century, the members of the inquisition were treated as witnesses pure and simple.

The second and third cases illustrate the difficulty of proving these impediments, a point discussed at some length in the text. The fourth raises a rather interesting point of law. Did a man disqualify himself as a husband to a woman for cause of spiritual affinity when he had not been present at the private baptism of her sickly child by a former marriage, by the fact that he had held the child at the subsequent solemnities held in church? The people of the community apparently thought so. The Papal Penitentiary determined otherwise, though with an imprecision slightly annoying to the modern reader; it is not clear whether he is settling a doubtful point of law in the couple's favor or simply granting a dispensation in an easy case.

Bello v. *Bello* (c. *1200*)[16]

Nomina iuratorum ad inquirendum de coniugio inter Stephanum de Bello et Agnetem uxorem eius. Asch' scriptor. Stephanus ipse iuravit et uxor eius Agnes, Johannes le Vanur, Robertus filius Brichmer, Gilleb' de Bosco, Thomas Rufus, Organus Curtelier, Wibertus le Wrench, Osmundus Wlvena, Ydonea, Ysabella. Omnes isti de affinitate idem dicunt, videlicet quod Agnes uxor Stephani fuit uxor Helie Coq. Et Ysabel quondam concubina Stephani fuit filia matricere ipsius Helie. Idem attestatur tota vicina et est omnibus notissimum. De commaternitate dixit Agnes uxor Stephani quondam uxor Helie Coq quod Ysabel ad petitionem eius suscepit filium suum de sacro fonte et munus accepit quod Ysabel contulit filio eius baptizato ut commater, et eam ut commatrem semper in osculo soliccitavit.

Johannes le Vanur iuratus dixit quod ipse suscepit filium Helie et Agnetis de sacro fonte et eadem hora predicta Ysabel suscepit eundem ut commater Agnetis; Thomas Rufus iuratus dixit idem per omnia quod Johannes, adiciens quod nomen suum imposuit puero.

Wlvina mulier iurata dixit quod interfuit ubi Johannes le Vanur et Thomas Rufus et predicta Ysabel et quedam alia mulier nomine Arnild susceperunt simul dictum filium Agnetis de sacro fonte baptizatum a capellano nomine Ada' dominica proxima post festum Omnium Sanctorum.

Ysabel' idem dixit quod Wilvena nisi quod de die non recolit, adiciens quod iiii d. dedit puero quos misit Agneti matri pueri.

Tangerton v. *Smelt* (*1294*)[17]

Inquisitio super consanguinitate que dicitur esse inter Henricum de Tangerton' et Symonem dictum Smelt'.

Johannes le Wlf iuratus et requisitus super consanguinitate que dicitur

---

[16] Canterbury Sede Vacante S.B. II, p. 51.
[17] Canterbury Ecc. Suit, no. 188.

esse inter Henricum de Tangerton' et Symonem le Smelt', qui quidem Henricus nunc vellet solempnizare matrimonium cum Johanna relicta dicti Symonis le Smelt, dicit quod quedam fuit Cristina stipes, que habuit duas filias per duos diversos viros:

> de qua Godeleva, de qua Henricus, de quo Johannes, de quo Henricus de quo agitur.

stipes

> de qua Margeria, de qua Symon, qui fuit maritus dicte Johanne de qua agitur.

Requisitus si vidit omnes quos nominavit, dicit quod sic et gerebant se pro consanguineis. Requisitus a quibus didicit sic distinguere gradus, dicit quod a se ipso, quia vidit omnes ut premittitur. Requisitus si sit de consanguinitate vel affinitate partium predictarum, dicit quod non. Requisitus quantum tempus est elapsum quod sic scivit distinguere gradus, dicit quod sexaginta anni sunt elapsi et amplius. Requisitus si iste testis interfuit alicui contractui inito inter dictos Henricum et Johannam, dicit quod non. Requisistus si unquam fuit presens in editione bannorum inter eosdem Henricum et Johannam, dicit quod sic semel tantum in ecclesia de Wytstaple. Requisitus si dictis bannis tunc contradixerit, dicit quod sic. Requisitus si aliqui alii tunc tempore dictis bannis contradixerunt, dicit quod non nisi iste solus. Nec instructus nec corruptus deponit. Requisitus etiam si scandalum foret si dicti Henricus et Johanna matrimonialiter coniungerentur, dicit quod nescit. Requisitus utrum mallet coniunctionem quam separationem inter dictos Henricum et Johannam, dicit quod coniunctionem si fieri posset.

Hamo dictus Eylmer iuratus et requisitus super dicta consanguinitate, dicit quod quidam vel quedam fuit stipes cuius nomen ignorat:

> de qua Godeleva, de qua Henricus, de quo Johannes, de quo Henricus de quo agitur.

stipes

> de qua Margeria, de qua Symon, qui fuit maritus dicte Johanne de qua agitur.

Requisitus si vidit omnes quos superius nominavit, dicit quod sic; nescit tamen si gerebant se pro consanguineis nec ne. Requisitus a quibus didicit sic distinguere gradus, dicit quod a Johanne le Wlf conteste suo preexaminato, qui quidem Johannes isti testi et aliis contestibus suis subsequentibus hac instanti die inquisitionis sive examinationis in ecclesia Christi Cant' dictos gradus exposuit. Requisitus si iste testis sit de consanguinitate vel affinitate dictorum Henrici et Johanne, dicit quod sic. Requisitus si interfuit alicui contractui matrimoniali inter predictos Henricum et Johannam, dicit quod non, sed audivit dici quod contraxerunt adinvicem coram officiali domini archidiaconi Cant', quibus die et loco ignorat. Requisitus si interfuit editioni

bannorum editorum inter eosdem Henricum et Johannam, dicit quod sic in
ecclesia de Wytstaple per sex vices; nec fuit aliquis contradicens nisi tantum-
modo prefatus Johannes le Wlf preiuratus. Et ipse Johannes contestis suus
contradicebat predictis bannis pro quadam contentione mota inter Johannam
filiam suam et Johannam de qua agitur ut dicit. Requisitus utrum mallet
coniunctionem quam separationem dictorum Henrici et Johanne, dicit quod
habet pro indifferente. Requisitus utrum scandalum foret si matrimonialiter
dicti Henricus et Johanna coniungerentur, dicit quod non. Nec corruptus
deponit.

Richardus le Kyng' iuratus et requisitus super dicta consanguinitate, dicit
se nescire de aliqua consanguinitate dictorum Henrici et Symonis. Dicit
tamen quod Johannes le Wlf contestis suus primo examinatus exposuit isti
testi gradus dicte consanguinitatis, quos non credit esse veros quia nullus
alius contradixit bannis dictorum Henrici et Johanne. Et dicit iste testis quod
fama patrie dicit predictos Henricum et Johannam matrimonialiter posse
legitime copulari. Et est iste testis de consanguinitate predicti Symonis de
quo agitur. Nec etc.

In Dei nomine amen. Auditis et plenius intellectis meritis cause matrimonialis et divorcii que coram nobis fratre R. de Clyve commissario Cant'
ex officio procedentes vertitur inter Henricum de Tangertone et Johannam
relictam Symonis le Smelt matrimonium in facie ecclesie solempnizare
volentes, super affinitatis impedimento, [articulo] partibus in iudicio
porrecto, lite ad eundem legitime contestata, partibus de veritate dicenda
iuratis, facta inquisitione super dicto impedimento per viros fidedignos
iuratos et diligenter examinatos, qua quidem inquisitione de consensu
partium publicata et partibus copia inde decreta, terminoque eisdem legitime
prefixo de dicendo in dictam inquisitionem et nichil proposito, concluso in
causa de consensu partium et omnibus rite peractis, quia dictum impedimentum nullatenus esse probatum, famamque super eodem nullam esse, eosdem
Henricum et Johannam matrimonialiter copulari posse sentencialiter et
diffinitive pronunciamus.

Clopton v. Bosco (13th century)[18]

Productio Ricardi super exceptione consanguinitatis inter ipsum et Johannam.
Johannes Bysewod' iuratus et diligenter examinatus de consanguinitate inter
Ricardum filium Ricardi Bysewood et Johannam filiam Johannis Everard,
dicit quod due fuerunt sorores, videlicet Alicia et Sotheta. De Alicia nascebatur Matillida, de Matillida nascebatur Ricardus Bysewode, de Ricardo
Ricardus de quo agitur. De Sotheta nascebatur Ysabella, de Isabella nascebatur Matill', de Matill' Johanna de qua agitur. Requisitus quomodo scit de tali
consanguinitate, dicit per hoc quod Alicia soror Sothete fuit mater patris sui.

18 Canterbury Ecc. Suit, no. 310.

Requisitus si videret alias duas sorores, dicit quod non quia valde antique fuerunt sed filias earundem vidit. Requisitus quis fuerit stipes, dicit quod ignorat quia ille due sorores quesite fuerunt de longinquis partibus et ducte ad Clopton, fuerunt quesite apud Aylescumbe.

Hugo de Wyse iuratus et examinatus, dicit de consanguinitate huiusmodi numerando ut preiuratus. Requisitus quomodo sciebat hoc, dicit quod ex relatu consanguiniorum, sed non vidit duas predictas sorores nec stipitem quia de partibus alienis venerunt. In omnibus concordat cum preiurato preter hoc quod non est ex eorum consanguinitate.

Ricardus Bysewod iuratus et diligenter examinatus connumerat consanguinitatem predictam ut Johannes Bysewod preiuratus in omnibus concordando. Requisitus quomodo scit de tali consanguinitate dicit per hoc quod Matillida filia Alicie sororis Sothete fuit mater sua. Nichil de stipite dicit quia ille due sorores in alienis partibus nascebantur. Nec vidit illas sorores quia ut credit moriebantur ante suam nativitatem.

Decimo Kl' Junii comparuerunt partes personaliter, publicatis attestationibus viri super ultima exceptione, oblata partibus copia, datus est dies ad faciendum quod ius dictabit. Id' Junii conparuerunt partes personaliter. Officialis pronunciavit in hunc modum. In Dei nomine amen. Nos officialis inspectis huiusmodi cause meritis, non obstantibus exceptionibus propositis, in quarum probatione te defecisse pronunciamus, te Ricardum de Bosco Johanne de Clopton in virum et ipsam tibi in uxorem sentencialiter adiudicamus.

Layburne–Stut (1352)[19]

Willelmus etc. dilectis filiis Johanni de Layburne et Alicie Stut mulieri nostre diocesis salutem graciam et benedictionem. Literas venerabilis patris domini Stephani miseratione divina episcopi Ostiensis et Velletrensis domini nostri pape penitenciarii pro vobis nuper recepimus tenorem qui sequitur per omnia continentes. Venerabili in Christo patri Dei gracia archiepiscopo Ebor' vel eius vicario in spiritualibus Stephanus miseratione divina episcopus Ostiensis et Velletrensis salutem et scinceram in Domino caritatem. Ex parte Johannis de Layburne et Anicie (sic) Stutte vestre diocesis nobis oblata petitio continebat quod olim ante contractum inter eos matrimonium, dum quidam puer ipsius Anicie ex alio viro conceptus, propter mortis periculum in domo primo baptizatus, ac postmodum portatus ad ecclesiam pro facienda solempnizatione baptismi fuisset, dictus Johannes interfuit et, sicut moris est, dictum puerum suo nomine nominavit et, capellano respondente, dicebat 'amen' et 'credo'. Dictum tamen puerum nec rem sibi adherentem quando fuit baptizatus in domo non tetegit nec tenuit, set cum solempnitas huiusmodi baptismi in ecclesia facta fuit, et non ante, puerum ipsum tantum tenuit. Sub-

¹⁹ York Reg. Zouche, f. 61r.

sequenter vero iidem Johannes et Anicia matrimonium per verba de presenti inter se contraxerunt, sed dum banna ederentur multe persone ex causa predicta contradixerunt; propter quod ad solempnizationem ipsius matrimonii procedere est omissum. Super quibus ad ora huiusmodi et aliorum si qui fuerint obloquencium obstruenda fecerunt humiliter supplicari sibi per sedem apostolicam misericorditer provideri. Nos igitur, auctoritate domini pape cuius penitenciarie curam gerimus, circumspectioni vestre committimus, quatinus si est ita et aliud canonicum non obsistat, decernatis eosdem Johannem et Aniciam posse libere ad solempnizationem dicti matrimonii procedere et in eo licite remanere. Dat' Avinion' sexto Kl' Aprilis pontificatus domini Clementis pape sexti anno decimo. Quarum quidem auctoritate litterarum inquisita per nos super contentis in eisdem litteris diligentius veritate, quia comperimus suggestionem per vos in hac parte factam veram esse et coram nobis sufficienter et legitime fuisse probatam, decernimus vos Johannem et Aniciam libere posse ad solempnizationem matrimonii inter vos ut dicitur contracti procedere et in eo licite remanere, dumtamen aliud vobis in hac parte canonicum non obsistat. Valete. Dat' apud Cawode vicesimo septimo die mensis Maii anno domini millesimo ccc^{mo} quinquagesimo secundo et pontificatus nostri decimo.

DIVORCE A MENSA ET THORO

There is not much to be said by way of introduction to this case beyond what is contained in the text. *Blare* v. *Blare* illustrates how far separation cases were decided according to the wishes of the parties. Here they were 'reduced to concord'. But that concord gave them the right to live apart. And it is not at all clear from the record that any canonical cause had been shown by John Blare, who had been cited for illegally expelling his wife Joan from his house. The case also contains an interesting instance of the settlement of alimony terms between the separated spouses.

Blare v. *Blare* (*1439*)[20]

Comparet Johannes Blare de Dertford et exhibuit certificatorium vicarii de Dertford penes registrum remanens. Dominus officialis obiciebat eidem Johanni ex officio suo ad promotionem Johanne uxoris eiusdem Johannis in iudicio ibidem personaliter comparentis quod licet ipsi Johannes et Johanna matrimonium adinvicem legitime contraxissent et illud in facie ecclesie solempnizari obtinuissent et ut vir et uxor diutius adinvicem cohabitassent, ipse tamen Johannes Blar' eandem Johannam uxorem suam a consorcio et cohabitatione suis absque iudicio ecclesie seu causa rationabili vel legitima

[20] Rochester DRb Pa 1, fols. 129r, 140r.

quacumque expulsit et eidem vite alimenta denegavit et denegat in presenti, in anime sue grave periculum et aliorum exemplum perniciosum. Et petiit idem Johannes Blar inducias usque ad proximum consistorium et terminum sibi dari ad respondendum super premissis. Et dominus officialis de consensu suo et ad petitionem eiusdem Johannis eidem Johanni ad respondendum super premissis terminum assignavit, ulteriusque ad faciendum et recipiendum quod fuerit iustum in proximo consistorio.

In negocio ex officio promoto per Johannam Blar' contra Johannem Blar'. Comparent partes personaliter et officialis Roffen' reduxit eos ad concordiam sub hac forma, videlicet quod uterque eorum in loco honesto habitaret et continenter viveret quousque aliud inter partes predictas unanimi assensu contigerit ordinari. Et ad relevamen dicte Johanne prefatus Johannes solvet seu solvi faciet annuatim ad quatuor anni terminos xxvi s. viii d. per equales portiones solvendas sic quod prima solutio incipiet in festo Pentecoste proximo futuro. Et pax est inter partes et dimissi sunt.

FORCE AND FEAR

Should a man forced to marry a girl for what society considers to be good and sufficient reason be able to divorce her by pleading force and fear? This is not an easy question. That it was not easy for the medieval canonists we have the witness of Sanchez: 'Quaestio haec difficillima est ob confusionem et brevitatem qua a DD. tractatur.'[21] It is also something of a test case. Is freedom of consent so far the essence of a marriage contract that the law should free a man from its bonds when he has, at least in the sense that he was aware of society's conventions, brought them upon himself? Or must he take the consequences of his foolishness, his recklessness, and his misfortune? The classic case is that of a man caught in compromising circumstances with a young girl. It appears in the Decretals, and it is that of the three cases transcribed here.

The medieval canon law on the subject began with the rule that any fear which a man had brought on himself (*culpa sua*) would not excuse him from obligations undertaken because of that fear.[22] But marriage was an exceptional case. 'Forced marriages usually have unhappy results', the canonists frequently noted. They held that marriage cases did not come under this basic rule. Rather they constituted an exception to it.[23]

---

[21] *De Matrimonio*, Lib. IV, d. 13, no. 1.

[22] See *gl. ord.* ad X 1.40.2 s.v. *coactus*.

[23] *Ibid.*, 'Ab ista doctrina sive generalitate excipiuntur casus in quibus fallit etiam si culpa sua incidisset in metum. Et primo est causa matrimonii, qualiscunque metus interveniat culpa sua vel sine culpa matrimonium contractum non tenet.'

One difficulty for the canonists was that a text from the Decretum and one from the Decretals appeared to give express sanction to the use of force where there was just cause. In the first, a certain Hubaldus was 'taken by fear of death and compelled to swear to take his concubine as his wife'. In the second, a man was compelled to endow and marry a virgin he had seduced.[24] In both, the marriages were apparently held valid. But these texts were explained away by the canonists, and the *communis opinio* was against upholding marriages contracted because of duress, despite the existence of what society considered just cause. Panormitanus gave the true reason for the special treatment accorded marriage: 'Certum est quod in matrimonio contrahendo requiritur liber consensus ut ibi; sed ubi metus intervenit licet non faciat cessare consensum, tamen tollit qualitatem libertatis requisitam.'[25]

The later medieval canonists thus emphasized the 'requisite quality of freedom' over the demands of society. The following cases are consistent with this emphasis. In *Besete* v. *Peper*, it is true that the marriage was upheld. And it is obvious that the young man was far from anxious to marry the girl. But the compulsion in the case did not go beyond the combination of strong words and the natural embarrassment of a man caught in such circumstances. His resistance was also no more than an entreaty for delay coupled with an unsuccessful subterfuge. A constant man, the court may have felt, would have done more to escape. In *Penysthorp* there was an order backed with an unsheathed sword; in *Barkar* one with a threat of legal action and physical punishment. These were enough to sway the constant man. In none of the cases was what society considered to be a 'just cause' enough to require enforcement of the contract.

Penysthorp v. Waldegrave (1334)[26]

Ricardus filius Walteri de Waldegrave iuratus examinatus et super articulis huic rotulo appensis diligenter interrogatus. Dicit quod Johannem filium Radulphi de Penysthorpp' novit a quatuor annis elapsis ac Elyzabeht' filiam Walteri de Waldegrave novit a nativitate eiusdem quia soror sua carnalis est. Requisitus si sciat de aliquibus vi et metu eidem Johanni per dictam Elyzabeht' seu ex parte eiusdem illatis ad contrahendum matrimonium cum eadem prout in articulis continetur, dicit quod idem iuratus audivit referri quod idem Johannes habuit communem accessum ad Elyzabeht sororem ipsius iurati.

---

[24] C. 22 q. 4 c. 22; X 5.16.1.
[25] *Commentaria* ad X 1.40.2, no. 8.
[26] York C.P. E 26.

Et inter cetera audivit dici a quadem muliere quod idem Johannes venire debuit ad domum Walteri patris eiusdem Elyzabeht' apud Wynested nocte proxima subsequente diem beati Petri ad Vincula proximo preteritum. Et cum idem iuratus percepisset adventum eiusdem Johannis infra noctis tenebras dicti diei ad domum patris sui, idem iuratus ivit ad pistrinam in fine orti predicti Walteri situatam et pulsavit ad hostium eiusdem. Et statim cum ingressus fuit, obviavit eidem iurato Johannes supradictus; et petiit ab eodem, 'Veniam', anglice 'Merci'. Ipso iurato interrogante, 'Quis es tu?' et respondit, 'Ego Johannes', et dixit quod vellet facere quicquid idem Ricardus vellet. Et statim idem iuratus extraxit gladium suum ne idem Johannes exiret domum. Et misit famulum suum et contestem suum quod iret pro Elyzabeht' et Alicia sororibus ipsius iurati; quibus ibidem venientibus, idem iuratus dixit prefato Johanni quod caperet dictam Elizabeht' per manum dexteram et contraheret cum ea matrimonium. Idemque Johannes dixit eidem Elyzabeht, 'Hic accipio te Elyzabeht' in uxorem meam habendam et tenendam usque ad finem vite mee et ad hoc do tibi fidem meam;' dicta Elyzabeht' statim respondente, 'Hic accipio te Johannem in virum meum habendum et tenendum usque ad finem vite mee et ad hoc do tibi fidem meam.' Et credit verisimiliter quod idem Johannes predicto modo non contraxisset nisi ipse iuratus fuisset et modo quo premittitur fecisset; sed an idem metus potuisset in constantem virum cadere, qui ut dicitur eidem Johanni fuerat per eundem Ricardum illatus, nescit. Ad hoc dicit quod idem Johannes statim postmodum eadem nocte a dicto loco et habitatione prefati Walteri de Waldegrave discessit et comitiva eiusdem Elyzabeht'; et hucusque seorsum moratus est et adhuc moram trahit ut dicitur ibidem. Aliter super aliquibus vi sive metu eidem Johanni illatis per dictam Elyzabeht' vel partem eiusdem nescit dicere quam supra deposuit. Requisitus qui fuerunt presentes, dicit quod ipse Ricardus et Johannes, Alicia et Elyzabeht' sorores eiusdem Ricardi et Thomas contestis suus et non plures quod sciat. Requisitus an premissa sunt publica notoria et manifesta, dicit quod audivit publice dici in parochia de Wynested et locis vicinis quod idem Johannes per vim et metum compulsus extitit ad matrimonium contrahendum ut premittitur.

Thomas de Hummanby etatis ut dicit xvii annorum iuratus examinatus et super articulis huic rotulo appensis diligenter interrogatus, requisitus si sciat de aliquibus vi et metu illatis Johanni filio Radulphi de Penysthorpp' ad contrahendum matrimonium cum Elizabeht' filia Walteri de Waldegrave prout in articulis continetur, dicit quod presens fuit in manso Walteri de Waldegrave apud Wynested in domo pistrine eiusdem Walteri quadam nocte de qua non recolit infra annum nunc instantem vel modicum plus, ubi et quando vidit Ricardum de Waldegrave contestem suum pulsare super hostium dicte pistrine et ingredi. Ac statim obviavit eidem Johannes predictus a quo idem Ricardus petiit, 'Quid hic agis?' Et ipse respondit, 'Veni huc pro Elyzabeht' sorore tua.' Et statim dictus Ricardus dixit sibi, 'Tu desponsabis eam in uxorem tuam.' Qui respondit, 'Libenter volo sicut tu vis.'

Statim idem Ricardus misit eundem Thomam contestem suum quod quereret Elyzabeht predictam; qua veniente ibidem audivit dictum Johannen dicere eidem Elyzabeht' capiendo eam per manum dexteram, 'Hic accipio te Elyzabeht in uxorem meam habendam et tenendam usque ad finem vite et ad hoc do tibi fidem meam,' dicta Elyzabeht statim respondente, 'Hic accipio te Johannem in virum meum habendum et tenendum usque ad finem vite mee, et ad hoc do tibi fidem meam,' presentibus tunc Ricardo conteste suo, Alicia sorore sua et partibus contrahentibus. Requisitus si dictus Johannes modo quo predicitur fuerat compulsus predicta verba dicere et proferre, dicit quod sic ut credit quia vidit prefatum Ricardum evaginare gladium; et extracto gladio comminabatur eidem Johanni et precepit quod caperet sororem suam per manum et cum eadem contraheret ut predicitur. Dicit insuper quod statim post eadem nocte ab eadem Elizabeht' et comitiva eiusdem idem Johannes descessit et extra comitiva eiusdem adhuc moratur. De aliis vi et metu quam superius deposuit non audivit quicquid dici, nec plura super dictis articulis dicere seu deponere novit, licet diligenter interrogatur.

Quia invenimus dictam partem actricem intentionem suam coram nobis in iudicio deductam sufficienter probasse, contractum matrimonialem inter eosdem Johannem et Elizabeht', quatenus de facto processerat, nullum et invalidum fuisse et esse pronunciamus et declaramus sentencialiter et diffinitive in hiis scriptis.

Besete v. *Peper (1382)*[27]

Robertus Peper fornicat' cum Agnete Besete. Vir et mulier comparent personaliter predicto die Octobris; fatentur articulum et habent pro commissis uterque iii fustigationes coram processione hic. Et mulier petit ipsum sibi adiudicari in virum pro eo et ex eo quod idem Robertus secum contraxit matrimonium per verba mutuum consensum de presenti exprimencia carnali etiam copula inter eosdem postmodum subsecuta. Liteque ad dictam positionem per dictum virum negative contestata, iuratis partibus hinc inde de calumpnia et de veritate dicenda; et quia mulier allegat se habere testem que interfuit in contractu inter eos habito, ideo prefigimus sibi diem crastinum ad producendum testem predictam coram nobis loco isto, et ulterius utrique parti ad faciendum et recipiendum coram nobis eisdem die [et] loco quod iusticia suadebit.

Quibus die et loco partibus predictis coram nobis auditore predicto personaliter comparentibus, productaque per dictam mulierem partem actricem Alicia uxore Ade de Baumburght' de Ebor' que admissa iurata et per nos diligenter examinata super contractu predicto, dicit in sacramento suo quod die Lune ad noctem proximo ante festum Ascensionis Domini proximo preteritum, accessit ad quandam cameram altam infra mansum habitationis dicte iurate situatam ubi invenit, ut dicit, ipsos Robertum et Agnetem simul in

[27] York M 2(1) f, fols. 17r–17v.

uno lecto solos iacentes. Cui quidem Roberto ipsaque iurata dixit, 'Quid facis hic, Roberte?' Cui ipse respondit, 'Iam sum hic.' Cui ipsa iurata dixit, 'Cape ipsam Agnetem per manum, quia affidabis eam.' Dictusque Robertus dixit eidem iurate, 'Rogo vos, expectetis usque in crastinum.' Et ipsa iurata respondens dixit, 'Per Deum non, tu facies iam.' Tandem dictus Robertus capiens dictam Agnetem per manum dixit, 'Ego ducam te in uxorem meam.' Cui dicta iurata dixit, 'Tu dices isto modo: accipio te Agnetem in uxorem meam et ad hoc do tibi fidem meam.' Et dictus Robertus, sic inductus per dictam iuratam, capiensque dictam Agnetem per manum dexteram, contraxit cum ea per verba superius recitata, videlicet, hic accipio te etc. Requisita quid dicta Agnes respondit eidem Roberto, dicit quod dicta Agnes sibi respondebat quod reputavit se contentam. Plura non deposuit nisi quod recessit et dimisit eos solos ubi eos invenit.

Super isto contractu, quibus sic factis, nos auditor prefatus audientes et intelligentes prefatam Agnetem intentionem suam in hac parte probasse, ipsum Robertum virum legitimum eidem Agneti et ipsam Agnetem in uxorem legitimam eidem Roberto sentencialiter et diffinitive adiudicamus in hiis scriptis.

Barkar v. *Waryngton (1417)*[28]

Johannes Gamesby de parochia sancte Elene in Stayngate Ebor' etatis xl annorum libere conditionis nulli partium consanguineus affinis domesticus vel familiaris, ut dicit, testis admissus iuratus et super articulis presentibus annexis diligenter examinatus. Super primo et ii° articulis divisim eidem perlectis requisitus, dicit quod eo tempore et septimana quibus assise et liberacio fuerunt apud castellum civitatis Ebor' de sua certa sciencia, que assise fuerunt, quatenus modo recolit, in prima septimana quadragesime ultimo preterite, videlicet die lune eiusdem septimane quatenus modo recolit, post horam prandii circa horam sextam quasi in crepusculo noctis, accensis candelis in domo habitationis Johannis Bown cordwener de Ebor' in presencia istius iurati, dicti Johannis Bown, uxoris eiusdem, et servientis eorundem nominate ut credit Agnetis, Johannes Waryngton' et Margareta Barkar matrimonii verba proferebant sub hac forma: dicto Johanne Waryngton' primo sic dicente et dictam Margaretam per manum dexteram accipiente, 'Hic accipio te Margaretam in coniugatam uxorem meam pro meliori vel peiori etc., et ad hoc do tibi fidem meam.' Cui Johanni eadem Margareta statim respondens dixit, 'Hic accipio te Johannem in coniugatum maritum meum pro meliori vel peiori etc., et ad hoc do tibi fidem meam.' Que verba uterque eorum proferebat secundum informacionem et previam recitationem Johannis Bown predicti. Interrogatus si dictus Johannes fuit metu vel minis inductus ad contrahendum cum dicta Margareta ut prefertur, dicit quod die dominico proximo precedenti dictum diem lune dictus Johannes Bown magister dicti Johannis Waryngton' in absencia eiusdem Johannis intimavit huic iurato quomodo ipse Johannes Waryngton' serviens suus cognovit carnaliter unam mulierem servientem suam predictam infra domum habitationis sue predicte; et quod ipsum Johannem iurare fecit super librum quod taliter de cetero non dilinqueret cum aliqua serviente sua infra domum suam predictam. Quo iuramento non obstante invenit eundem Johannem Waryngton' noviter in loco suspecto cum dicta Margareta solum cum sola, videlicet in una alta camera ubi fenum iacebat infra domum habitationis sue predicte, et quod credebat ipsum Johannem in eodem loco dictam Margaretam carnaliter cognovisse. Et concilium propterea ipse Johannes Bown petebat ab isto iurato, quomodo ei melius foret facere cum dicto Johanne Waryngton' et si melius tunc esset facere eundem Johannem duci ad carceres de Kydcot vocatos Ebor'. Et tunc iste iuratus consuluit dicto Johanni Bown quod super tali proposito et predicto bene deliberaret, et quod communicaret et videret primo si ipse Johannes Waryngton' vellet dictam Margaretam habere in uxorem suam. Et ita tandem dicto die lune ad noctem ut prefertur coram ipso iurato, dicto Johanne Bown et ipsius uxore in domo habitationis eorundem predicte, presente tunc ibidem dicta Margareta, comparuit dictus Johannes Waryngton' a quo tunc petebat dictus Johannes magister suus si dictam Margaretam carnaliter cognoverat et si eidem promisit eam ducere et habere in uxorem. Qui Johannes Waryngton' tunc dixit quod non cognovit eam carnaliter nec ei promisit vel fidem fecit quod eam habere vellet in uxorem suam, cuius contrarium tunc dicta Margareta asseruit, videlicet quod eam ducere et habere in uxorem dictus Johannes promisit. Et tunc ipse idem Johannes dixit eidem Margarete et dicto magistro suo quod dixit illi Margarete sub hac forma; quod dictus Johannes magister suus potuit ei ita facere et ita bonus et benevolus esse quod ipsam Margaretam vellet facere bonam mulierem et facere ei honorem quatenus in eo fuit. Et ita tandem ex post facto statim dictus Johannes Bown delicta per ipsum Johannem Waryngton' infra domum habitacionis sue ut prefertur commissa eidem Johanni recitavit et quomodo potuit eo pretextu facere ipsum Johannem multipliciter gravari et puniri secundum ius commune, ac dixit quod si dictam Margaretam tunc habere et accipere vellet in uxorem suam quod tunc major pars emendarum ... per eum facta pro delictis predictis. Et ita tandem ab ipso Johanne Waryngton' dictus Johannes Bown magister suus quesivit si dictam Margaretam vellet habere in uxorem suam. Qui Johannes modico tempore stans non respondens, tandem dixit eidem magistro suo, 'Vos potestis esse michi ita bonus et ita benevolus et ita facere michi favorem quod potestis facere me magis benevolum ad affidandum et habendum eam in uxorem meam.' Et tunc eidem Johanni dictus Johannes magister suus dixit, 'Capias eam per manum et dicas ut ego dicam tibi.' Et tunc ipse Johannes Waryngton dixit, 'Per fidem meam si pater meus et alii amici mei iam

essent hic presentes nec eam affidarem nec acciperem in uxorem meam.'
Attamen postea, ut iste iuratus dicit, ipse idem Johannes Waryngton quia
timuit quod dictus magister suus pro delictis suis ei ut prefertur inpositis et
commissis infra domum habitacionis ipsius magistri sui idem magister suus
faceret eum carceribus tradi et committi, propterea et ex nulla alia causa ut
iste firmiter pro veritate credit in consciencia sua, dictus Johannes Waryngton' contra voluntatem consensum suum verba matrimonialia ut prefertur
proferebat et contraxhit ut prefertur. Et aliter super istis articulis nescit
deponere ut dicit. Super ultimo articulo requisitus, dicit quod nescit aliter
deponere quam supra deposuit. Et non est conductus instructus corruptus vel
informatus, sed iusticiam inter partes istius cause vellet fieri ut dicit requisitus in iuramento suo.

Margareta Bown etatis xxx^{ta} annorum et amplius libere conditionis nulli
partium consanguinea vel affinis; Johannes tamen Waryngton' de quo agitur
est serviens Johannis Bown mariti istius iurati (sic) ut dicit, testis admissa
iurata et super articulis presentibus annexis diligenter examinata. Super
primo et ii° articulis ei perlectis requisita, dicit quod uno die lune post horam
prandii, qua certa hora non recolit, post festum Purificationis beate Marie
Virginis ultimo preteritum, per quantum tempus vel quot septimanas post
huiusmodi festum iam non recolit, in domo habitationis istius iurate et
mariti sui predicti, existente in parochia sancti Martini in Conyngstret Ebor',
Johannes Waryngton' predictus et Margareta Barker verba matrimonialia
inter se proferebant et adinvicem contraxherunt sub hac forma: dicto
Johanne primo sic dicente et dictam Margaretam de mandato dicti Johannis
Bown magistri sui per manum dexteram accipiente, 'Hic accipio te Margaretam in uxorem meam ad habendam et tenendam in thoro et mensa pro meliori
vel peiori etc., et ad hoc do tibi fidem meam.' Cui Johanni eadem Margareta
statim respondens dixit, 'Hic accipio te Johannem in maritum meum et ad
hoc do tibi fidem meam.' Et sic manus traxherunt, presentibus et huiusmodi
verba audientibus ista iurata, dicto marito suo, Johanne Gamesby conteste
suo, dictis partibus et non pluribus. Interrogata quomodo dicte partes
descendebant ad huiusmodi contractum et an dictus Johannes fuit compulsus
vel metu inductus ad contrahendum cum dicta Margareta ut prefertur, dicit
quod die et hora predictis Johannes Bown magister dicti Johannis Waryngton'
fecit eundem Johannem vocari et venire de schopa sua in domum et aulam
habitationis sue predicte; cui Johanni tunc dixit ipse magister suus coram
ista iurata dicto Johanne Gamesby et dicta Margareta sub hac forma, 'Tu
dixisti esterva die quando recitavi tibi delicta que commisisti in domo mea et
infra habitationem meam quod voluisti pro emendis faciendis facere sicut ego
volui et ponere te in mea voluntate, et ita te posuisti ad faciendum secundum
voluntatem meam. Et ideo hec est voluntas mea, quod tu accipias et affidas
illam Margaretam Barkar ibidem in uxorem tuam iam hic coram nobis.' Et
tunc ipse Johannes Waryngton' modico tempore stans nichil respondens

tandem dixit, 'Ego habeo amicos, qui essent hic, ego non nuberem nec affidarem ipsam Margaretam in uxorem meam ista vice vel isto tempore.' Et post plura et diversa verba locuta tunc inter ipsum Johannem et dictum magistrum suum, idem magister suus ei, 'Dicas michi, es tu in voluntate habere ipsam Margaretam in uxorem tuam?' Qui Johannes tunc dixit dicto magistro suo, 'Vos potestis ita facere michi quod potestis facere me magis benevolum habere eam in uxorem meam.' Et ita tandem ad preceptum dicti magistri sui ipse Johannes ipsam Margaretam accepit per manum et cum ea matrimonium contraxhit ut prefertur contra voluntatem suam. Et ita ista iurata, ut dicit, firmiter pro veritate credit in consciencia sua; et ita super librum si iam deberet mori bene ausa est iurare, ut dicit in iuramento suo interrogata, quia bene scit quod dictus Johannes Waryngton' timuit si modo predicto cum dicta Margareta matrimonium ad mandatum dicti magistri sui tunc non contraxhisset, quod idem magister suus voluit fecisse eum incarcerari et alio modo puniri secundum ius commune. Et hoc satis constabat dicto Johanni Waryngton' pro certis delictis per eundem Johannem infra domum habitationis dicti magistri sui commissis secundum assercionem eiusdem magistri sui, dicentis quod ipse Johannes cognovit carnaliter mulieres servientes suas infra domum suam predictam, et etiam quod invenit ipsum Johannem cum dicta Margareta solum cum sola in loco suspecto die dominico proximo precedente dictum diem lune, videlicet in una camera ubi fenum iacebat existente in remotiori quodammodo parte domus habitationis sue predicte. Si vero dictus Johannes Waryngton' dictam Margaretam post dictum contractum carnaliter cognovit nescit ista iurata ut dicit, quia ut dicit eadem iurata nescivit suo sensu percipere quod dictus Johannes voluntarius fuit ad ipsam Margaretam, in tanto quod post dictum contractum quasi per septem dies extunc sequentes idem Johannes dixit huic iurate quod dictus magister suus male fecit cum eo ex hoc quod fecit eum affidare dictam Margaretam in uxorem suam et cum ea contrahere matrimonium, et quod credidit firmiter huiusmodi matrimonium non posse stare vel esse, quia nuncquam fuit in mente sua habere eam in uxorem suam. Et aliter super istis articulis nescit deponere, ut dicit, nisi quod dicit super ultimo articulo requisita quod quatenus supra deposuit diu laboravit et adhuc laborat in parochia sancti Martini predicta publica vox et fama. Et non est conducta instructa vel corupta nec aliud in hac causa desiderat nisi quod iusticia fiat, ut dicit.

The definitive sentence in this case has not survived. However, the Consistory Court Act Book from this period has. It records that a sentence was read on 29 July 1422, and that subsequently an appeal was taken for Margaret Barkar (Cons. A B 1, fols. 36v, 38r). Therefore, judgment must have gone in favor of the servant Waryngton; in other words the court held that force and fear was proved here. It should also be said, perhaps, that Waryngton had subsequently married another girl.

THE REQUIREMENT OF TWO WITNESSES

The rule of evidence given by the maxim 'vox unius, vox nullius' was given regular, if not totally consistent, application by the Church courts. It is possible to find a few cases in which an affirmative judgment was based on the testimony of a lone witness. But they are isolated instances. And some of them may be explained under the law itself, which allowed some exceptional cases to be decided on one man's testimony.[29]

The rule was not, in any event, one of those found within the canon law which was almost entirely eaten away by exceptions. *Wylson v. Fox* illustrates this point. It also involves an interesting legal problem. What if there are two or more witnesses, but they testify to two different events, either of which (if sufficiently proved) would be enough to warrant a definitive sentence in favor of the plaintiff? Or suppose that by piecing together the events narrated by different witnesses the judge can construct a valid case for the plaintiff. This was apparently the situation in *Wylson*. Canonists wrote that, if possible, variant testimony was to be reduced to concordance.[30] But that was not always possible. And it does not necessarily cover this case. The judge here apparently took the position that the two witness requirement had not been met. The witnesses must testify to the same underlying facts to meet this rule of evidence.[31]

Wylson v. Fox (1402)[32]

Cristina de Knarsburgh, parochia sancti Martini in Markylgate etatis xxx^{ta} annorum testis admissa et examinata, dicit quod Thomas Fox et Isabella Wylson' inter quos agitur tribus septimanis ante festum sancti Michaelis ultimo preteritum ad duos annos venerunt ad domum istius iurate causa constituendi ipsam Isabellam apprinticiam ipsius iurate in arte sutricia; et ista iurata interrogavit ipsum Thomam quid haberet noticie cum ipsa

---

[29] Guillelmus Durantis gives an exhaustive list of the cases in which the testimony of one witness sufficed. See *Spec. Iud.* I, tit. *de teste* § *de numero testium*, no. 7.

[30] *Gl. ord.* ad X 2.20.16 s.v. *benigne*.

[31] On this situation see Hostiensis, *Summa Aurea* II, tit. *de test.*, no. 10: 'Quando unus dicit de re una et alius de alia re, vel unus de uno facto sive contractu alius de alio, non valet talium testimonium, cum singuli sint in suis testimoniis singulares.'

[32] York C.P. F 22.

Isabella. Ac ipsa Isabella respondit, 'Si fidus homo est, debet esse vir meus.' Et ista iurata, 'Thoma, est hoc verum?' Et ipsa utique, 'Vis ergo habere illam in uxorem tuam?' Et ille, 'Volo quamcito potuero ducere illam.' Et statim comederunt et biberunt cum ista iurata, ut dicit; et videbatur isti iurate quod dicta Isabella consensit idem (sic) Thome habere eum in virum suum. Et dicit quod audivit frequenter ipsos repetere verba predicta multis diebus. Dicit preterea quod dictus Thomas ipsam Isabellam fecit transire cum illo multo-tiens et eam detinuit interdum per duos dies interdum per septimanam, ut credit, carnalis copule causa. Interrogata de presentibus tempore prolacionis dictorum verborum, dicit de quadam Eva cuius cognomen ignorat.

Johanna Bever, parochia Omnium Sanctorum in Fisshargate etatis xxx^{ta} annorum et amplius, dicit quod quadam die cuius non recordatur inter festa Assumpcionis et Nativitatis beate Marie ultimo preterita ad duos annos in domo viri istius iurate in Fisshargate, presente viro suo, accesserunt Thomas et Isabella per contestem suam memorati postulantes hospicium. Cui vir istius iurate, 'Est ista uxor tua?' Et ipse, 'Est futura.' Et vir, 'Non habebitis hospicium mecum nisi contraxeritis in presencia mea.' Deinde dictus Thomas dixit Isabelle, 'Accipio te in uxorem meam,' et illa vice versa Thome, 'Accipio te in virum meum.' Et postea, ut dicit, manserunt ibi in hospicio et in eodem lecto iacentes soli et nudi per sex dies.

XX° die mensis Octobris anno domini infrascripto Johanna Bever testis repetita et ad dicendam veritatem super requirendis ab eadem iterato iam iurata, dicit in iuramento suo quod fama publica laborat in civitate Ebor' et precipue in parochiis Omnium Sanctorum in Fysschergate in qua parochia ista iurata trahit moram ut dicit et Sancti Martini in Mykelgate Ebor' et aliis locis vicinis super omnibus et singulis per istam iuratam infra depositis ut dicit in iuramento suo. Et non est conducta corrupta aut subor-nata ad deponendum ut supra deposuit ut dicit in iuramento suo.

Johannes Fouler examinatus, dicit quod tribus ut credit annis elapsis, mensem et diem non recolit, presens in camera magistri Johannis Schafforth tunc decani Christianitatis Ebor' una cum Johanne Ward, vidit et audivit Thomam Fox et Isabellam Wilson' coram ipso decano presentes de crimine fornicationis impetitos et idem crimen confessatos, ac quod fuerunt ad matrimonium contrahendum affidati. Et propterea, ut fidem implerent, decanus mitius cum illis egit, penitenciam in parte remittendo pro eiusmodi excessu infligendo. Et amplius nescit, ut dicit.

Johannes Ward examinatus, dicit quod audivit magistrum Johannem Schafford referre sibi quod unus cuius nomen ignorat affidavit unam cuius nomen nescit. Et aliter nescit deponere ut dicit.

In Dei nomine amen. Quia invenimus dictam partem actricem intentionem suam coram nobis in iudicio deductam sufficienter non probasse, prefatum Thomam partem ream ab impetitione dicte Isabelle partis actricis in hac parte absolvimus sentencialiter et diffinitive in hiis scriptis.

THE PROBLEM OF BRIBERY

The canon law on bribery of witnesses may be simply stated, but as noted in the text, its application posed difficult problems. A witness's testimony was to be rejected if he had been corrupted by gifts or money.[33] On the other hand, he could lawfully receive the expenses incurred in coming to court and in testifying.[34] There was, however, no firm line between how much he could receive and how much would be too much. What counted was whether it was enough to corrupt him.[35] Canonists, for example, seriously put the question: what if money is given to a witness to corrupt him, but he is not in fact corrupted? Is the gift of money alone enough? They held that it was not enough, that the testimony was valid.[36] Thus, in each case, the court had to decide not simply whether any gift had passed between party and witness, but whether the gift was large enough to corrupt the witness and whether the witness had in fact been corrupted by it. *Chapelayn* v. *Cragg* illustrates the dilemma perfectly.

Chapelayn v. *Cragg* (*1303*)[37]

Alicia filia Willelmi Blanuck de Wyteby iurata et diligenter examinata super hiis que procurator Andree Cragg' de Wyteby intendit per eam probare contra Emmam de Allenmouth et etiam contra Aliciam Colle testes Johanne filie Capellani de Wyteby; videlicet quod heedem Emma et Alicia fuerunt et sunt subornate et muneribus insuper corrupte per eandem supradictam Johannam ad deponendum pro ea que iam deposuerunt in sua siquidem causa matrimoniali que inter ipsam et predictum Andream in capitulo ventilatur. Quo ad subornationem predictarum Emme et Alicie, dicit breviter se nichil scire. Quo vero ad earum munere corruptionem, dicit pro firmo quod bene scit ipsas muneribus esse conductas ad perhibendum eidem Johanne supradicte testimonium contra prefatum Andream Cragg' in illo contractu qui inter illos in capitulo vertitur. Requisita quibus induciis tam constanter asserit se hoc scire, dicit pro eo quod occulata fide conspexit et audivit quando dicta Johanna prefatas Emmam et Aliciam conduxit, unicuique earum solvendo tres solidos argenti et insuper utrique earum capucium unum

---

[33] C. 4. q. 2 & 3 c. 2; X 2.20.1.

[34] See Durantis, *Spec. Iud*, I, tit *de test.* § *que possunt contra testes opponi*, no. 43: 'Expensas tamen potest a producente recipere.' And see Cod. 4.20.11, incorporated into the Decretum as C. 4 q. 2 & 3 c. 4 § 40.

[35] Panormitanus, *Commentaria* ad X 2.20.1, no. 1: 'Nota ibi pretio etc., nihil enim dicit de prece, ex quo argue secundum Hosien' quod preces intervenire possunt, dummodo cesset corruptio.'

[36] See Durantis, *Spec. Iud.* I, tit. *de test.* § *que possunt contra testes opponi*, no. 48.

[37] York C.P. E 1.

contulit de viridi panno ut essent ei previores et efficaciores in premissis. Requisita si tunc cum ipsis in domo extiterat quando talis conductio et etiam solutio inter ipsas facta fuerat, dicit quod bene prope illas tunc erat quia domus in qua ipsa eadem hora erat et domus dicte Johanne in qua omnes ipse res in prefate (sic) tunc fuerant congregate ita deprope sub uno culmine ad modum burgi coniungebantur quod inter eas non erat nisi divisio unius muri lucei valde tenuis, super quo quoddam foramen ad modum caverne tunc habebatur, ad quod eadem hora se inclinaverat et per medium aspexerat omnia et singula inter ipsas sic gesta evidenter vidit et audivit rursum enucleacius. Requisita si tunc aliqua verba subornationis inter ipsas tunc audierat, dicit quod non. Requisita si stando vel sedendo et in qua parte domus facta fuit hec conductio et denariorum solutio, dicit quod sedendo in domo dicte Johanne iuxta quandam fenestram versus viam communem. Requisita de die, de anno et de hora diei, dicit quod die Inventionis Sancte Crucis anno domini m° ccc^mo primo circa horam diei undecimam. Requisita de earum vestibus, dicit quod Johanna de qua agitur tunc fuerat induta de pannis vermiculis cum capucio de blueto et cetere Emma et Alicia tunc fuerunt duabus tunicis de wacheto indute, sed de earum tegimine capitum non meminit ad presens. Requisita de presentibus, dicit quod quedam Agnes Hoggestak cum Matilda filia Ricardi filii Petri contestes et non plures.

Agnes Haggestak de Wyteby iurata et diligenter examinata super excepcione illa quam procurator Andree Cragg' de Wyteby per eius testimonium intendit legitime declarare contra Emmam de Allenmouth et Aliciam Colle testes Johanne filie Capellani, quod heedem Emma et Alicia fuerunt et sunt subornate et insuper muneribus corrupte ad deponendum pro eadem Johanna ea que deposuerunt in illa videlicet causa matrimoniali que inter Andream Cragg' et ipsam Johannam de quibus agitur coram ordinariis in capitulo vertitur. Ipsa siquidem sic affata sub vinculo iuramenti sui ad hec itaque respondit, dicens quod quo ad subornationem earundem E. et A. et etiam donis corruptionem per predictam Johannam filiam Capellani factam se nichil scire nec aliquid aliud sentire, nisi quod patula auri et occulata fide audivit et vidit dictas mulieres Emmam et Aliciam aliquantulum post horam diei nonam domum dicte Johanne subintrare; et post quarum introitum tam ipsa Johanna quam dicte Emme et Alicia protinus renes suos uni banco in domo dicte Johanne adhesere prope fenestram unam que erat versus viam communem. Et sedentibus itaque illis, dicta Johanna in eadem hora cum eis composuit ut eis siquidem certam pecunie summam donaret sub tali convencione ut illi sedulum concederent perhibere testimonium in causa supradicta que inter Andream prefatum et ipsam Johannam promulgatur. Ad quam vero conventionem statim cum consensum dedissent, ipsa vidente, dictis mulieribus E. et A. tres solidos argenti, utrique earum in eadem hora pacavit; et insimul duo capucia de panno viridi eis contulit ut fiducialiter in premissis cum ipsa insisterent. Requisita de hiis eisdem sic impensis, si ea eis pro viaticis vel laboribus seu pro earum expensis secundum suam extimaverat oppinionem eis conferri, dicit quod ob nullam aliam causam intendit predicta exennia eis aliquando contulisse nisi ut premissa testificarent. Requisita diligentius si sperat dictas Emmam et Aliciam prefate Johanne fidele testimonium in sua querela perhibuisse, dicit se nolle hoc affirmare nec reprobare. Requisita ex quo ex visu et etiam auditu hec itaque deponit, si fuerat cum ipsis in domo quando dicta Johanna ut prenotatur cum prefatis Emma et Alicia ita siquidem composuit, dicit quod in eadem domo cum illis non erat, sed erat in quadam domo que est domui ipsius Johanne tam prope coniuncta quod inter ipsas non est divisio nisi parietis unius valde tenuis, super quo tunc quoddam foramen habebatur per cuius medium tunc conspexerat, ita quod omnia que inter ipsas tunc gesta fuerant ab earum introitu et insimul exitu veraciter perpendit. Requisita de die de anno et de earum indumentis, dicit quod die Inventionis Sancte Crucis proximo preterito fuerunt quatuor anni elapsi, et quod sepedicta Johanna fuerat eadem hora induta supertunica et tunica de panno rubei coloris cum capucio de blueto. Et cetere mulieres E. et A. de duabus tunicis de wacheto fuerant tunc vestite; de aliis earum vestibus non recolit ad presens. Requisita de presentibus dicit quod Alicia filia Willelmi Blanuck preiurata cum Matilda filia Ricardi conteste et non plures.

Capitulo celebrato apud Wyteby xv Kaln' Julii anno domini m° ccc^mo tercio comparuit pars actrix personaliter et pars rea per suum procuratorem superius constitutum. Et partes petierunt sentenciam, que lata est in hunc modum: In Dei nomine amen. Auditis et intellectis meritis cause matrimonialis que vertitur inter Johannam filiam Walteri Chapelayn partem actricem ex parte una et Andream Cragg' partem ream ex altera, libello oblato, litis contestatione facta ad eundem negative, partibus iuratis de veritate dicenda et de calumpnia, testibusque productis, eorum attestationibus publicatis ac omnibus aliis rite peractis que requirit ordo iuris, reiecta exceptione proposita per Andream Cragg' legitime non probata; quia constat nobis legitime dictam Johannam suam intentionem probasse, predictum Andream eidem Johanne in virum sentencialiter et diffinitive adiudicamus in hiis scriptis.

BIBLIOGRAPHY

MANUSCRIPT SOURCES

(i) BRITISH MUSEUM

Harl. MS. 2179: Fifteenth-century ecclesiastical court formulary.
Reg. MS. 11 A XI: Fifteenth-century ecclesiastical court formulary.
Add. MS. 11821: Extracts from Act book, Rochester, (1436–44).
Reg. MS. 11 A XV: Fifteenth-century treatise on ecclesiastical procedure.

(ii) PUBLIC RECORD OFFICE

K.B. 27: King's Bench plea rolls.
C.P. 40: Common Pleas plea rolls.
E. 135/7: Exchequer, Ecclesiastical Documents.
C. 47/15/4: Chancery Miscellaneous.

(iii) LAMBETH PALACE LIBRARY

Register of Archbishop Islip, 1349–66.
Register of Archbishop Langham, 1366–8.
Register of Archbishop Whittlesey, 1368–74.
Register of Archbishop Courtenay, 1381–96.

(iv) DEAN AND CHAPTER LIBRARY, CANTERBURY

Ecclesiastical Suits: Suit rolls mainly thirteenth century.
Chartae Antiquae A 36 I, Court of Audience Act book, 1325–8.
Chartae Antiquae A 36 II, Court of Audience Act book, 1328–30.
Chartae Antiquae A 36 IV, Court of Audience Act book, 1340–3.
Sede Vacante Scrapbooks I, II, and III: Cause papers mainly late-thirteenth-century.
Y.1.1: Act book, 1372–5.
U.41: Act book, 1393–5.
X.8.1: Ex officio Act book, 1395–1410.
Y.1.2: Act book, 1398–9.
X.10.1: Deposition Book, 1410–21.
Y.1.3: Act book, 1416–23.
Y.1.4: Act book, 1419–25.
X.1.1: Ex officio Act book, 1449–57.
Y.1.5: Act book, 1454–7.
Y.1.7: Act book, 1459–63.
X.8.3: Act book (Hythe, Romney, and Dover Sessions), 1462–8.

Y.1.6: Act book, 1463–8.
Y.1.8: Act book, 1468–74.
Y.1.11: Ex officio Act book, 1468–74.
Y.1.12: Act book, 1474–9.
Y.1.13: Act book, 1479–85.
Y.1.14: Act book, 1485–8.
Y.1.15: Act book, 1488–92.
Y.1.16: Act book, 1492–6.
Y.1.17: Act book, 1496–9.
Y.1.18: Act book, 1499–1500.
MS. D.8: Fourteenth-century ecclesiastical court formulary from the Court of Arches.

(v) BORTHWICK INSTITUTE OF HISTORICAL RESEARCH, YORK

C.P. E: Cause papers, fourteenth-century.
C.P. F: Cause papers, fifteenth-century.
Cons. A B 1: Consistory Court Act book, 1417–20.
Cons. A B 2: Consistory Court Act book, 1424–7.
Cons. A B 3: Consistory Court Act book, 1428–30.
Cons. A B 4: Consistory Court Act book, 1484–9.
D/C A B 1: Dean and Chapter Court book, 1387–1494.
R I.10: Register of Archbishop William Zouche, 1342–52.
R I.11: Register of Archbishop John Thoresby, 1352–73.
R I.13: Register of Archbishop Alexander Neville, 1374–88.
R I.15: Register of Archbishop Waldby, 1397.
R I.17, 18: Register of Archbishop Bowet, 1407–23.
R I.21: Register of Archbishop George Neville, 1465–76.

(vi) YORK MINSTER LIBRARY

M 2(1) a: Dean and Chapter Court book, 1315–27.
M 2(1) b: Consistory Court Act book, 1371.
M 2(1) c: Consistory Court Act book, 1372–5.
M 2(1) e: Dean and Chapter Court book, 1376–7.
M 2(1) f: Dean and Chapter Court book, 1357–1471.

(vii) SOMERSET RECORD OFFICE, TAUNTON

D/D/C Al: Consistory Court book, Bath and Wells, 1458–98.

(viii) CAMBRIDGE UNIVERSITY LIBRARY

EDR D/2/1, Registrum Primum, Act book, Ely, 1374–82.

(ix) EPISCOPAL ARCHIVES, RECORD OFFICE, COUNTY OF HEREFORD
(TEMPORARY CLASSIFICATIONS)

O/1: Act book, 1442–3.
O/2: Act book, 1442.
O/3: Act book, 1445–6.
O/5: Act book, 1453–4.

O/6: Act book, 1456–7.
I/1: Consistory Court Act book, 1491–9.
I/2: Consistory Court Act book, 1496–9.

(x) JOINT RECORD OFFICE, LICHFIELD

B/C/1/1: Act book, 1464–71.
B/C/1/2: Act book, 1471–9.
B/A/1/2: Register of Bishop Northburgh, 1322–58.
B/A/1/6: Register of Bishop Le Scrope, 1386–98.
B/A/1/11: Register of Bishop Boulers, 1453–9.

(xi) LINCOLN DIOCESAN RECORD OFFICE

Cj/1: Ex officio court book, 1493–1504.

(xii) GUILDHALL LIBRARY, LONDON

MS. 9064/1: Acta quoad correctionem delinquentium, 1470–3.
MS. 9064/2: Acta quoad correctionem delinquentium, 1483–9.
MS. 9064/3: Acta quoad correctionem delinquentium, 1475–7, 1480–2.
MS. 9065: Liber Examinationum, 1489–97.
MS. 9065B: Liber Examinationum, 1488.

(xiii) GREATER LONDON COUNCIL RECORD OFFICE

DL/C/1: Consistory Court Act book, 1496–1505.

(xiv) NORFOLK RECORD OFFICE, NORWICH

REG/5: Register of Bishop Brown, 1436–45.
REG/6. Register of Bishop Lyhert, 1446–72.

(xv) NORWICH CATHEDRAL ARCHIVES

Acta et Comperta 1, 1416–17.
Acta et Comperta 1a, 1417.
Acta et Comperta 2, 1419–20.
Acta et Comperta 6, 1428–9.

(xvi) KENT COUNTY RECORD OFFICE, MAIDSTONE

DRb Pa 1: Consistory Court Act book, Rochester, 1436–44.
DRb Pa 2: Act book, 1445–56.
DRb Pa 3: Act book, 1456–68.
DRb Pa 4: Act book, 1472–5, 1481–1500.

(xvii) DIOCESAN REGISTRY, ROCHESTER

Ecclesiastical Precedents c. 1428: Formulary from the Court of Arches.

(xviii) INNER TEMPLE LIBRARY, LONDON

Petyt MS. 511.3: Fourteenth-century ecclesiastical court formulary.
Petyt MS. 511.21: Fourteenth-century treatise on canon law.

(xix) BODLEIAN LIBRARY, OXFORD

Ashmole MS. 1146, fols. 111v–116v: Consuetudines et observantie non scripte apud curia de Arcubus.

(xx) HUNTINGTON LIBRARY, SAN MARINO

EL 9/H/3: William of Pagula, Summa Summarum.

PRINTED RECORD SOURCES

Anglo-Norman Letters and Petitions, ed. M. D. Legge, Anglo-Norman Text Society (Oxford, 1941).

Child-Marriages, Divorces, and Ratifications etc. in the Diocese of Chester, A.D. 1561–6, ed. F. J. Furnivall, Early English Text Society, Original Ser. 108 (1897).

Civil Pleas of the Wilshire Eyre, 1249, ed. M. T. Clanchy, Wiltshire Records Soc., 26 (1971).

Concilia Magnae Britanniae et Hiberniae, ed. D. Wilkins (4 vols, London, 1737).

Councils and Synods with other documents relating to the English Church, Vol. II, ed. F. M. Powicke and C. R. Cheney (Oxford, 1964).

Depositions and Other Ecclesiastical Proceedings from the Courts of Durham from 1311 to the Reign of Elizabeth, ed. J. Raine, Surtees Soc. 21 (1845).

Dolezalek, G., *Das Imbreviaturbuch des erzbischöflichen Gerichtsnotars Hubaldus aus Pisa, Mai bis August 1230*, Forschungen zur neuren Privatrechtsgeschichte, 13 (Cologne, 1969).

An Episcopal Court Book for the Diocese of Lincoln, 1514–1520, ed. M. Bowker, Lincoln Record Soc., 61 (1967).

Liber practicus de consuetudine Remensi, ed. P. Varin, Archives legislatives de la ville de Reims, Pt. 1 (Paris, 1840).

Norwich Consistory Court Despositions, 1499–1530, eds. E. D. Stone and B. Cozens-Hardy, Norfolk Record Soc., 10 (1938).

The Paston Letters, A.D. 1422–1509, ed. James Gairdner (6 vols, London, 1904).

'Proceedings taken in Winster Church regarding the Consanguinity of the Parties to the Marriage of two of the Staffords of Eyam', ed. C. E. B. Bowles, *Journal of the Derbyshire Archaeological and History Society*, 23 (1907), 83–6.

Recueil de lettres des officialités de Marseille et d'Aix (XIVe–XVe siècles), ed. R. Aubenas (2 vols, Paris, 1937).

Register of Henry Chichele, Archbishop of Canterbury, 1414–43, ed. E. F. Jacob, Canterbury and York Soc., 45 (4 vols, 1937–47).

Register of Thomas Langley, Bishop of Durham, 1406–1437, ed. R. L. Storey, Surtees Soc. (6 vols, 1949–67).

Registre des causes civiles de l'officialité épiscopale de Paris, 1384–87, ed. J. Petit (Paris, 1919).

Registre de l'officialité de Cerisy, ed. M. G. Dupont, Mémoires de la Société des Antiquaires de Normandie, 3rd ser., 10.

Registrum Hamonis Hethe, ed. Charles Johnson, Canterbury and York Soc., 48 (1948).

Statutes of the Realm, Record Commission (London, 1810).

LEGAL TREATIES

Antonius de Butrio, *Commentaria in Quinque Libros Decretalium* (Venice, 1578, repr. 1967).

Ayliffe, J., *Parergon Juris Canonici Anglicani* (London, 1734).

Azo, *Summa Institutionum* (Venice, 1485).

Bergmann, F. C. (ed.), *Pilii, Tancredi, Gratiae libri de iudiciorum ordine* (Göttingen, 1842).

Bernard of Parma, *Glossa ordinaria* to Decretals (Lyons, 1553).

Bracton, *De legibus et consuetudinibus Angliae*, ed. G. E. Woodbine (4 vols, New Haven and London, 1915-42).

Conset, H., *The Practice of the Spiritual or Ecclesiastical Courts* (London, 1708).

Corpus Juris Canonici, ed. E. Friedberg (2 vols, Leipzig, 1879-81).

Corpus Juris Civilis, ed. T. Mommsen, P. Krueger, and G. Kroll, 11th edn (3 vols, new printing Berlin, 1963-6).

Geoffrey of Trani, *Summa in titulis decretalium* (Lyons, 1519).

Glanvill, *De legibus et consuetudinibus regni Anglie*, ed. G. D. G. Hall (London, 1967).

Guido de Baysio, *Rosarium* (Venice, 1577).

Guillelmus Durantis, *Speculum Iudiciale* (Lyons, 1543).

Henricus Bohic, *Distinctiones in V Libros Decretalium* (Lyons, 1498).

Hostiensis, *Lectura in quinque Libros Decretalium* (Venice, 1581).

    Summa Aurea (Venice, 1574).

Innocent IV, *Apparatus in V Libros Decretalium* (Frankfurt, 1570).

Joannes Andreae, *Novella Commentaria in Libros Decretalium* (Venice, 1581).

Joannes Teutonicus, *Glossa ordinaria* to Decretum (Lyons, 1671).

John of Acton, *Constitutiones Legatinae Othonis et Othoboni, cum Annotationibus Johannis de Athona* (Oxford, 1679).

Lyndwood, W., *Provinciale (seu Constitutiones Angliae)* (Oxford, 1679).

Oughton, T., *Ordo Judiciorum* (2 vols, London, 1738).

Panormitanus, *Commentaria in Libros Decretalium* (Venice, 1571).

    Concilia (Lyons, 1555).

Paucapalea, *Summa*, ed. J. F. Von Schulte (Giessen, 1890, repr. 1965).

Quinque Compilationes Antiquae, ed. E. Friedberg (Leipzig, 1882).

Raymond of Pennaforte, *Summa de Poenitentia et Matrimonio* (Rome, 1603).

Ricardus Anglicus, *Summa de ordine iudiciario*, ed. Wahrmund (q.v.).

Sanchez, T., *De sancto matrimonii sacramento* (Venice, 1737).

Summa Parisiensis on the Decretum Gratiani, ed. T. P. McLaughlin (Toronto, 1952).

Swinburne, H., *Treatise of Spousals or Matrimonial Contracts* (London, 1686).

Wahrmund, L., *Quellen zur Geschichte des römisch-kanonischen Processes im Mittelalter* (Innsbruck, 1907-28).

William Hay's Lectures on Marriage, ed. J. C. Barry, Stair Soc., 24 (1967).

William of Drogheda, *Summa Aurea*, ed. Wahrmund (q.v.).

SECONDARY SOURCES

Aston, M., *Thomas Arundel, a Study of Church Life in the reign of Richard II* (Oxford, 1967).

Ault, O., 'Manor Court and Parish Church in Fifteenth Century England', *Speculum*, 42 (1967), 53-67.

Baldwin, J. W., 'Critics of the Legal Professions: Peter the Chanter and his Circle', *Proceedings of the Second International Congress of Medieval Canon Law*, ed. S. Kuttner and J. Ryan (Vatican City, 1965).

Barraclough, G., *Papal Notaries and the Papal Curia* (London, 1934).

Biggs, J. M., *The Concept of Matrimonial Cruelty* (London, 1962).

Bowker, M., *The Secular Clergy in the Diocese of Lincoln, 1495–1520* (Cambridge, 1968).

Brentano, R., *York Metropolitan Jurisdiction and Papal Judges Delegate (1279–96)* (Berkeley and Los Angeles, 1959).

Briegleb, H. K., *Einleitung in die Theorie der summarischen Processe* (Leipzig, 1859, repr. 1969).

Brooke, C. N. L., 'Problems of the Church Historian', *Studies in Church History*, Vol. 1, ed. C. W. Dugmore and C. Duggan (London, 1964).

Browne, A. L., 'The Medieval Officials Principal of Rochester', *Archaeologia Cantiana*, 53 (1940).

Bryce, J., *Studies in History and Jurisprudence* (2 vols, London, 1901).

Brys, J., *De Dispensatione in 'ivre canonico* (Bruges, 1925).

Cam, H. M., 'Pedigrees of Villeins and Freemen in the Thirteenth Century', *Liberties and Communities in Medieval England* (London, 1963).

Cheney, C. R., *English Bishops' Chanceries, 1100–1250* (Manchester, 1950).
  Notaries Public in England in the Thirteenth and Fourteenth Centuries (Oxford, 1972).

Churchill, I. J., *Canterbury Administration* (2 vols, London, 1933).

Corbett, P. E., *The Roman Law of Marriage* (Oxford, 1930).

Daudet, P., *L'Établissement de la competence de l'église en matière de divorce et consanguinité* (Paris, 1941).

Dauvillier, J., *Le Mariage dans le droit classique de l'église* (Paris, 1933).

Dictionnaire de droit canonique (7 vols, Paris, 1935–65).

Donahue, C. and Gordus, J. P., 'A Case from Archbishop Stratford's Audience Act book', *Bulletin of Medieval Canon Law* (n.s.) 2 (1972), 45–59.

Donohue, J. F., *The Impediment of Crime*, Catholic University of America Canon Law Studies, 69 (Washington, 1931).

Duncan, G. I. O., *The High Court of Delegates* (Cambridge, 1971).

Dunning, R., 'The Wells Consistory Court in the Fifteenth Century', *Proceedings of the Somersetshire Archaeological and Natural History Soc.*, 106 (1962), 46–61.
  'Rural Deans in England in the Fifteenth Century', *Bulletin of the Institute of Historical Research*, 40 (1967) 207–13.

Elton, G. F., *England, 1200–1640* (Ithaca and London, 1969).

Emden, E. B., *A Biographical Register of the University of Cambridge to A.D. 1500* (Cambridge, 1963).
  A Biographical Register of the University of Oxford to A.D. 1500 (3 vols, Oxford, 1957–9).

Engdahl, D. E., 'English Marriage Conflicts Law before the time of Bracton', *American Journal of Comparative Law*, 15 (1967), 109–35.

Engelmann, A., *A History of Continental Civil Procedure*, trans. R. B. Miller (Boston, 1927).

Esmein, A., *Le Mariage en droit canonique* (2 vols, Paris, 1891).

Ferraboschi, M., *Il Matrimonio sotto condizione* (Padua, 1937).

Fisher, G. F., *The Archbishop Speaks* (London, 1958).

Floyer, P., *The Proctor's Practice in the Ecclesiastical Courts* (London, 1744).

Fournier, P., *Les Officialités au moyen âge* (Paris, 1880).

Fowler, L., 'Recusatio iudicis in Civilian and Canonist Thought', *Studia Gratiana*, 15 (1972), 717–85.

Fraghi, S., *De Condicionibus matrimonio appositis* (Rome, 1941).

Fransen, G., 'La formation du lien matrimonial au moyen-âge', *Le lien matrimonial*, ed. R. Metz and J. Schlick (Strasbourg, 1970), 106–26.

Freisen, J., *Geschichte des canonischen Eherechts* (Paderborn, 1893).

Gaudemet, J., 'Le lien matrimonial; les incertitudes du haut moyen-âge', *Le lien matrimonial*, ed. R. Metz and J. Schlick (Strasbourg, 1970), 81–105.

Glasson, E., *Du Consentement des époux au mariage* (Paris, 1866).

Graveson, R. H., *Status in the Common Law* (London, 1953).

Guise, L. de, *Le Promoteur de la justice dans les causes matrimoniales* (Ottawa, Canada, 1944).

Hackett, M. B., *The Original Statutes of Cambridge University* (Cambridge, 1970).

Haines, R. M., *The Administration of the Diocese of Worcester in the first half of the fourteenth century* (London, 1965).

Harvey, P. D. A., *A Medieval Oxfordshire Village: Cuxham, 1240 to 1400* (Oxford, 1965).

Hastings, M., *The Court of Common Pleas in Fifteenth Century England* (Ithaca, 1947, repr. 1971).

Haw, R., *The State of Matrimony* (London, 1952).

Helmholz, R. H., 'Bastardy Litigation in Medieval England', *American Journal of Legal History*, 13 (1969), 360–83.

Hill, R., 'The Theory and Practice of Excommunication in Medieval England', *History*, 42 (1957).

Hilling, N., *Die Officiale der Bischöfe von Halberstadt im Mittelalter* (Stuttgart, 1911).

Homans, C., *English Villagers of the Thirteenth Century* (Cambridge, Mass., 1942).

Howard, G. E., *A History of Matrimonial Institutions* (3 vols, Chicago, 1904).

Hudson, W., *Leet Jurisdiction in the City of Norwich*, Selden Soc., 5 (1891).

Jackson, J., *The Formation and Annulment of Marriage*, 2nd edn (London, 1969).

James, M. R., *The Ancient Libraries of Canterbury and Dover* (Cambridge, 1903).

Joyce, G. H., *Christian Marriage: An Historical and Doctrinal Study*, 2nd edn (London, 1948).

Kemp, E. W., *An Introduction to Canon Law in the Church of England* (London, 1957).

Kitchen, S. B., *A History of Divorce* (London, 1912).

Lacey, T. A., *Marriage in Church and State* (London, 1912).
Marriage in Church and State, rev. and suppl. by R. C. Mortimer (London, 1947).

Laribière, G., 'Le Mariage à Toulouse aux XIVe-XVe siècles', *Annales du Midi*, 79 (1963), 335–62.

Le Bras, G., 'Canon Law', *Legacy of the Middle Ages*, eds. C. G. Crump and E. F. Jacob (Oxford, 1926).
'Naissance et croissance du droit privé de l'église', *Études d'histoire du droit privé offertes à Pierre Petot* (Paris, 1959).

Levy, J., 'L'officialité de Paris et les questions familiales à la fin du XIVe siècle', *Études d'histoire du droit canonique dediées à Gabriel le Bras* (2 vols, Paris, 1965), II, 1265–94.

Logan, F. D., *Excommunication and the Secular Arm in Medieval England* (Toronto, 1968).
'An early thirteenth century Papal judge-delegate formulary of English origin', *Studia Gratiana*, 14 (1967), 75–87.

McNicholas, T. J., 'Legislation on Sequestration in Roman Law and in the Decretals of Gregory IX', *The Jurist*, 23 (1963).

Maitland, F., *Roman Canon Law in the Church of England* (London, 1898, repr. 1968).

Makower, F., *The Constitutional History and Constitution of the Church of England* (London, 1895).

Marchant, R. A., *The Church under the Law: Justice, Administration, and Discipline in the Diocese of York, 1560–1640* (Cambridge, 1969).

Milsom, S. F. C., 'Law and Fact in Legal Development', *U. of Toronto L. J.*, 17 (1967).

Morris, C., 'A Consistory Court in the Middle Ages', *Journal of Ecclesiastical History* 14 (1963), 150–9.
'The Commissary of the Bishop in the Diocese of Lincoln', *Journal of Ecclesiastical History*, 10 (1959), 50–65.

Nace, A. J., *The Right of Accuse a Marriage of Invalidity*, Catholic University of American Canon Law Studies, 418 (Washington, 1961).

Neilson, N., 'The Court of Common Pleas', *The English Government at Work, 1327–1336* (3 vols, Cambridge, Mass., 1950).

Owen, D. M., *The Records of the Established Church of England, excluding parochial records* (Cambridge, 1970).

Pollock, F. and Maitland, F. W., *History of English Law*, 2nd edn (2 vols, Cambridge, 1898; reissued, 1968).

Powell, C. L., *English Domestic Relations, 1487–1653* (New York, 1917).

Purvis, J. S., *An Introduction to Ecclesiastical Records* (London, 1953).
A Mediaeval Act Book with some account of Ecclesiastical Jurisdiction at York (York, 1943).

Ritchie, C. A., *The Ecclesiastical Courts of York* (Arbroath, 1956).

Sangmeister, J. S., *Force and Fear as Precluding Matrimonial Consent*, Catholic University of America Canon Law Studies, 80 (Washington, 1932).

'A Satyre on the Consistory Court', *The Political Songs of England*, ed. T. Wright, Camden Soc., 6 (1839).

Sayers, J. E., *Papal Judges Delegate in the Province of Canterbury, 1198–1254* (Oxford, 1971).

Scammell, J., 'The rural chapter in England from the eleventh to the fourteenth century', *English Historical Review*, 86 (1971), 1–21.

Sheehan, M. M., 'The Formation and Stability of Marriage in fourteenth-century England: Evidence of an Ely Register', *Mediaeval Studies*, 33 (1971), 228–63.

Silvestre, H., 'Dix plaidoiries inédites du XIIe siècle', *Traditio*, 10 (1954), 373–97.

Smith, A. L., *Church and State in the Middle Ages* (Oxford, 1913, repr. 1964).

Smith, C. E., *Papal Enforcement of Some Medieval Marriage Laws* (Baton Rouge, 1940).

Stenton, D. M., *The English Woman in History* (London, 1957).

Stone, L., 'Marriage among the English Nobility in the 16th and 17th centuries', *Comparative Studies in Society and History*, 3 (1961).

Storey, R. L., *Diocesan Administration in the Fifteenth Century* (York, 1959).

Thomas Langley and the Bishopric of Durham, 1406–1437 (London, 1961).

Stubbs, W., 'Report of Ecclesiastical Courts, 1883', Historical Appendix No. I to Vol. I of *Parliamentary Papers*, 1883, Vol. XXIV.

Thompson, A. H., *The English Clergy and their Organization in the Later Middle Ages* (Oxford, 1947).

'Diocesan Organization in the Middle Ages', *Proceedings of the British Academy* 39 (1943), 153–94.

Timlin, B. T., *Conditional Matrimonial Consent*, Catholic University of America Canon Law Studies, 89 (Washington, D.C. 1934).

Turlan, J. M., 'Recherches sur le mariage dans la pratique coutumière (XIIe–XVIe siècles)', *Revue Historique de droit français et étranger*, ser. 4, 35 (1957), 477–528.

Vinogradoff, P., *Villainage in Medieval England* (Oxford, 1923).

Wahl, F. X., *The Matrimonial Impediments of Consanguinity and Affinity*, Catholic University of America Canon Law Studies, 90 (Washington, 1934).

Weigand, R., *Die bedingte Eheschliessung im kanonischen Recht* (Munich, 1963).

'Die Rechtsprechung des Regensburger Gerichts in Ehesachen unter besonderer Berucksichtigung der bedingten Eheschliessung nach Gerichtsbuchern aus dem Ende des 15. Jahrhunderts', *Archiv für katholisches Kirchenrecht*, 107 (1968), 403–63.

Woodcock, B. L., *Medieval Ecclesiastical Courts in the Diocese of Canterbury* (Oxford, 1952).

Worsley-Boden, J. F., *Mischiefs of the Marriage Law* (London, 1932).

Yunck, J. A., *The Lineage of Lady Meed: The Development of Mediaeval Venality Satire* (Notre Dame, 1963).

INDEX

abjuration *sub pena nubendi*, 172–81, 208–12

'acceleration' of marriage cases, 121 n.

Act books, 7–11, 22, 72, 142, 172; recording of, 20, 80, 100, 114, 116, 134–5, 184–5

Acton, John of, 67 n., 78 n., 128 n., 142 n.; *see also* canonists

Adam of York, 45

adultery, 63, 65, 71, 94–8, 104, 208–12

advocates: duties of, 149, 153; role of in English Church courts, 16, 134, 150, 183

affinity, impediment of, *see* impediments; consanguinity and affinity

age: of witnesses, 83, 131, 155; proof of, 99; *see also* impediments, *infra annos nubiles*

Alexander III, Pope, 27, 46, 169

alimentatio prolis, 108–9

alimony, 67–8, 106, 219–20

Alne, Robert, 142 n.

Alta Ripa, Thomas de, 148 n.

amici, 47 n.

annulment, meaning of, 74

answers: by defendants, 13, 15–16, 125, 164; examples of, 192–3, 209

Antonius de Butrio, 34 n., 37, 56 n., 108 n., 179 n., *see also* canonists

apparitors, 118, 147

appeals, 1, 92 n., 116, 119–20, 139, 184; tuitorial, 206–7

Appelby, Thomas, 120 n., 148 n.

arbiters, 103, 135–7

archdeacons, jurisdiction of, 144–5, 177

Arches, Court of, 1, 20 n., 23, 128 n., 148, 150, 184

argument, legal, 134–5, 149

Arnall, Richard, 142 n.

articles, 17–18, 19, 131; example of, 209

Attestations, *see* depositions

Augustine, St, 81

Ault, W. O., 185

Austin, J. L., 27

Ayliffe, J., 15; *see also* canonists

Baldwin, J. W., 77 n.

banns, publication of, 27, 30, 65, 107–8

Barton, Thomas, 148 n.

bastardy, 3

Bath and Wells: diocesan court at, 150; records at, 9, 12, 180 n.

Bere, John, 148 n.

Bere, Martin, 148 n.

Biggs, J. M., 105 n.

Bishops' registers, 12, 22–4

Body, Adam, 206–7

Bologna, School of, 26

Bowker, Margaret, 6 n., 167 n.

Bracton, Henry de, 110

breach of faith, suits over, 106

Brede, John, 148 n.

bribery, 65, 146–7, 157–8, 230–2

Brooke, C. N. L., 2 n., 87 n.

Burbaych, James, 148

Burgh, Richard, 142 n.

Byllys, John, 148 n.

Calton, William, 148 n.

Cam, H. M., 84 n.

Cambridge, University of, 120 n., 142, 148

Candour, John, 142 n.

canonists, 21, 87–8, 121; development of the law by, 43, 69, 100 n., 104, 179, 221; disagreement among, 37, 41 n., 42, 43, 56, 199; opinions of, 14, 34, 52, 63, 88–9, 91, 93, 97–8, 128, 177–8, 220–1, 228; relation to practice, 2, 21, 47, 134, 173, 187

canon law, extent of enforcement, 95–8, 103–4, 108, 113, 135–8, 150, 155, 168–9, 188–9, 219–20

Canterbury: cases heard at, 25, 58, 74, 77, 115, 116, 128, 166, 180; Consistory court at, 16, 118 n., 120 n., 135–6, 142, 144, 148, 150, 182–3, 184; procedure at, 25 n., 89–90, 169, 183; records at, 6, 9–10, 12, 80, 185

Causa matrimonialis et divorcii, 57–8, 68, 76

Cause papers, 11–22, 172

cautio, 102, 105

Cawode, William, 142 n., 143

Chaucer, 147

children, 47, 51, 61 n., 98–9, 108–9, 132, 154, 174; *see also* parents

Church courts: behavior in, 22, 119–20; contemporary attitude towards, 117–18, 119 n., 138, 162; differences among, 9, 183–6; fees and costs, 23, 161–2, 207; jurisdiction of, 1–2, 3, 110, 117–8, 138, 141–2, 143–6, 177, 184; modern views of, 111, 113–4, 147, 188; records of, 6–22; terms of, 122–3, 127, 134

Churchill, I. J., 23, 128 n., 151 n.

civil law, 142–3; *see also* Roman law
Clanchy, M. T., 137 n.
Clement V, Pope, 120–1
Cleveland, archdeacon of, 146
Clyve, Richard de, 217
coercion, *see* impediments, force and fear
collusion, 162–3; dangers of, 64–5, 82 n., 88
Colt, Thomas, 148 n.
common Law, *see* courts, royal
compromise, 101–2, 104, 119–20, 135–8, 176
compurgation, *see* oaths, use of
concubinage, 34, 132, 173
conditions: against indissolubility, 55;
    classification of, 50–1; impertinent, 54–7;
    sexual, 51–4, 172–81; *see also* marriage
    contracts, conditional
confessions by parties, 15, 96, 104, 162
consanguinity and affinity: judicial attitude
    towards, 69, 71 n., 82–4; popular attitude
    towards, 69, 79–80, 87; *see also*
    impediments, consanguinity and affinity
conscience, role of, 63, 65, 71, 80, 129,
    163–4
consent, necessity for in marriage contracts,
    43, 91, 177–81, 199–201, 220–1
Conset, Henry, 8 n., 13 n., 121 n., 169;
    see also canonists
'constant man' test, 91, 93, 105 n., 178, 221
consummation, 27, 32, 140; *see also* sexual
    relations, effect on marriage contracts
contumacy, 113 n., 115, 125–6, 139
Conyngton, Richard, 142 n.
costs, *see* Church courts, fees and costs
Councils: Fourth Lateran, 8, 78, 81; Trent,
    72–3
Couper, John, 148 n.
courts: royal, 6, 11, 24, 61, 109–10, 117,
    130, 146; secular, 5, 137, 185; *see also*
    church courts
Croftes, John, 148 n.
cruelty, as grounds for divorce *a mensa et
    thoro*, 100–1, 105

deaf and dumb, marriages of, 34
defendants: affirmative defenses by, 13 n., 67,
    79, 126; personal summoning of, 16,
    124–5, 126, 134
defensor vinculi, 137, 162
definitive sentences, 12 n., 20–2, 114–15,
    125–6, 134–5
delays, *see* procedure, speed of
Delegates, High Court of, 21 n., 127 n.
depositions: generally, 19–20; publication of,
    127; recording of, 12 n., 129–30, 159,
    181–2; value of, 7
Derby, archdeacon of, 145

Digest, 134; *see also* Roman law
dispensations, papal, 24, 85–7, 183, 215,
    218–19
divorce: *a mensa et thoro*, 74, 100–7, 219–20;
    medieval definition of, 74; popular attitude
    towards, 3–5, 59–62, 75, 168; proof of,
    62; suits for, 25, 67, 74–100, 167
dower, 24, 110, 124
Driffeld, William, 120 n., 121 n., 148 n.
Drogheda, William of, 125 n.
drunkenness, effect on marriage contract,
    176–7
Durantis, Guillelmus, 13, 17, 41 n., 121 n.,
    129 n., 143 n.; *see also* canonists

East Riding, archdeacon of, 65
ecclesiastical sanctions, 21–2, 25, 35 n., 61,
    92 n., 114, 115–16, 125, 128, 139, 169,
    170 n., 180, 185
Egerdon, John, 148 n., 150 n.
Elton, G. R., 9 n.
Ely: cases heard at, 116, 167 n., 180;
    Consistory court at, 57, 150–1, 183;
    records at, 10, 130 n., 135 n., 184–5
English, use of, 119, 124–5, 131, 181–2
error of condition, *see* impediments, error of
    condition
Esmein, A., 2, 67 n., 85, 106
Esyngwald, Roger, 142 n., 148 n.
ethical standards, 146–7, 152–4
evidence, 127–34, 139, 157–8, 196; hearsay,
    81–3, 132; nature of, 93
examiners, *see* witnesses, examination of
excommunication, 63, 178; *see also*
    ecclesiastical sanctions
ex officio prosecutions, 25 n., 63, 70–2, 85–6,
    95, 138, 145–6
Exodus, Book of, 178
external forum, 43, 63, 176

fama publica, role in litigation, 46, 71, 83,
    132, 196
family, *see* parents; *amici*
force and fear, *see* impediments, force and fear
formularies, 12, 22–4, 113
fornication, 116 n., 145, 173–4, 182, 223, 229
Fowler, L., 146 n.
Fox, John, 143 n.
France: Church courts of, 17 n., 36, 92 n.,
    136 n., 173; marriage customs in, 32 n., 66 n.
French, use of, 119
friars, 191, 193
frigidity, *see* impediments, impotence

Geoffrey of Trani, 32 n., 134; *see also*
    canonists

Germany: marriage cases in, 51 n., 52 n., 173; marriage customs in, 66 n.
gifts, 46–7, 147, 162, 205; as evidence, 127 n.; in consideration of marriage, 48–9, 110–11
Glanvill, 110 n.
Gratian, 26, 179 n.
Green, Hugh, 120 n., 148 n.
Gregge, William, 148 n.
Guido de Baysio, 91 n., 143 n.; see also canonists
Gyles, Hugh, 148 n.

Halsnoth, William, 148 n.
Hamo of Hethe, bishop of Rochester, 24 n., 82 n., 84 n., 109 n.
handfasting, 40 n., 45
handwriting, of court records, 11
Hanwell, Thomas, 208
Haw, R., 75 n.
Hay, William, 63
Henricus Bohic, 37 n.
Hereford: cases heard at, 181; Consistory court at, 120, 147 n., 148 n., 150, 182, 184, 185; records at, 9
Hide, John, 120 n.
Hisham, John, 120 n.
Homans, George, 30
Hostiensis, 37 n., 43 n., 56 n., 63, 88, 91 n., 134, 143 n.; see also canonists
Hudson, William, 148 n.
Hughes, John, 148 n.
Humana Concupiscencia, 27 n.
Humermanby, William de, 195
Hyde, John, 148 n.

impediments: generally, 62, 75, 100, 108; consanguinity and affinity, 4, 60, 70, 71–2, 77–87, 183, 214–9; crime, 94–8, 208–12; error of condition, 100, 160, 212–14; force and fear, 7, 18, 60, 69, 70, 90–4, 99, 178–81, 220–8; impotence, 53–4, 69, 70, 87; infra annos nubiles, 60, 69, 70, 98–9, 199–204; pre-contract, 60, 67, 69, 76–7; public honesty, 78
indissolubility of marriage, 4, 27, 55, 74, 164, 188–9
inheritance, 61, 92, 94, 97
Inner Temple, Library of, 176
Innocent III, Pope, 42–3
Innocent IV, Pope, 7 n., 14, 67 n., 89 n., 143 n., 196 n.; see also canonists
inquisitiones, 71–2, 82, 85, 183, 214–15
internal forum, 43, 204
interrogatories, 18–19, 129, 131
ius commune, 141, 143–4

Jacob, E. F., 117 n.
Joannes Andreae, 37, 67 n., 143 n., 179 n.; see also canonists
Joannes Bononiensis, 131 n.
Jones, Hugh, 120 n., 148 n.
Jonys, David, 148 n.
judges, 141–7; action by, 19, 21, 66, 71, 113, 128–30, 170–3; as mediators, 101, 103–4; discretion of, 18, 21, 37–8, 94, 105, 125 n., 131 n., 133–4, 171, 173–4, 185, 199–200; training and legal knowledge of, 142–3, 177; uncertainty of, 40, 45, 54, 57
jurisdictional disputes, see Church courts, jurisdiction of

Kemp, E. W., 3 n.

Lacey, Canon T. A., 62, 111, 188
Lancaster, William, 148 n.
Latin, use of, 119, 131, 181–2
law and fact, 93, 130–1
lawyers, 147–54; see also advocates; proctors; ethical standards
Leek, John, 146
Lepyngton, 148 n.
Letot, Richard, 120 n., 207
Leverton, William, 151
libels, 13–14, 88, 121, 162 n.; examples of, 191–2, 201–2
libraries, cathedral, 143
Lichfield: bishop of, 144; cases heard at, 25, 68, 167, 181; Consistory court at, 143, 148, 150; records at, 69 n., 80
Lincoln: bishop of, 167 n.; sequestrator of bishop of, 146
litigants, see parties
Logan, F. D., 22 n.
Lombard, Peter, 26–7
London, Consistory court at, 16 n., 20, 118, 119 n., 180 n.
Lord Hardwicke's Marriage Act, 64 n.
love, 7, 32, 91, 131
Lovelich, William, 143 n.
Lyde, Nicholas, 148 n.
Lyndwood, W., 27 n., 107 n., 121 n., 141–2, 143, 170 n.; see also canonists

Maitland, F. W., 3, 75, 77, 79, 188
Major, John, 148 n.
Malling, monastery at, 171
Mareys, David, 151
maritagium, 110; see also gifts, in consideration of marriage
marital affection, 13, 102
marriage: by proxy, 2; canonical definition of, 26–7; clandestine, 27–31, 48, 66,

71, 167, 189; multiple, 57–66, 107, 169–70, 208; place of contracting, 29, 49, 154; popular attitudes towards, 5, 27–30, 31–3, 51, 72–3, 97–8, 118, 138, 167–8, 172, 180–1, 188–9; Roman law of, 4; solemnization of, 29–30, 35 n., 67, 167

marriage contracts: ambiguous words used in, 42–4; conditional, 38, 44–5, 47–57, 172–3, 191, 192–5, 204–8; interpretation of, 36–46, 72, 96, 125–6, 182; multiple, 35–6, 57–66, 74–5; necessity for exchange of words, 45–7, 195–9; negative words used in, 41–5, 191, 193–4; objective validity of, 43–4, 50, 204; specific enforcement of, 35–6; suits to enforce, 25–6, 31–3, 64–6, 166–8

Mersh, Thomas, 137
Middleton, William, 208
Milsom, S. F. C., 109, 130 n.
Mortimer, R. C., 62 n.

negative words, see marriage contracts
Niger, Bishop Roger of London, 173 n.
Northumbria, archdeacon of, 146
Norwich: bishop of, 57 n., 144, 161; dean of, 144; records at, 6, 180–1
notaries public, 7, 128 n., 149

oaths: effect of, 154, 164; use of, 61 n., 71, 88–9, 95 n., 102, 109, 152, 154
officials principal, see judges
Oughton, Thomas, 14, 68 n., 121 n., 134
Overay, Thomas, 137
Owen, D. M., 6 n., 10 n.
Oxford, University of, 142–3, 148

pact of mutual separation, 103–4
Padua, University of, 142 n.
Pagula, William of, 88 n.
Panormitanus, 37, 55, 82 n., 88, 98 n., 104, 108, 221; see also canonists
Papal collector, 86 n.
Papal court, 86, see also appeals
Papal penitentiary, 215, 218–9
parents, 48, 63; duty to support children, 108–9; role in marriage contracts, 47–8; 90, 92–3, 98; see also children
Paris: episcopal court at, 17 n.; Masters of, 26
parties, initiative of, 70–1, 125, 137–9, 163, 171; parishes of, 80–1; presence in court, 119, 124, 134; sequestration of, 168–72; social status of, 132–3, 160–1
Paston Letters, 161, 163–4
Paynell, John, 148 n.

Pennesby, Thomas, 148 n.
perjury, 15, 96, 155–9
petitory actions, 67–8; see also marriage contracts, suits to enforce
Piers Plowman, 147
placet mihi, used in contract of marriage, 38–9, 213
plea rolls, 6, 11, 24; see also courts, royal
positions, 14–16, 112; examples of, 192–3, 209
positive law, 82, 97–8
possessory actions, see restitution of conjugal rights
possessory assizes, English, 67, 69
poverty, pleas in forma pauperum, 158, 161
pre-contract, see impediments, pre-contract; marriage, multiple
presumptions, canonical, 35, 44, 44 n., 47 n., 175, 196
procedure: generally, 71, 112–40, 154–5; abuse of, 23, 65–6; effectiveness of, 115–17, 159, 169–70, 189; flexibility of, 104, 111, 189; oral, 14, 121, 134 n.; recording of, 8–10; speed of, 113–15, 122–3; 126, 138–9; summary, 120–2, 171 n.
proctors, 119, 147–54; duties of, 149–50, 152–3; fees of, 150–1; numbers of, 120; regular employment of, 124, 147, 149; role in litigation, 16, 39 n., 119, 136, 171; training of, 148–9
prohibition, writ of, 110
proof, 127, 182–3; burden of, 67, 82; in divorce a mensa et thoro, 104–6; necessity for, 62, 77, 81–5, 96, 158; problems of, 33, 51, 88, 157–8, 175–7, 228–9, 230–2
public fame, see fama publica
Purvis, Canon J. S., 11

quadruplications, 23
Quynton, John, 148 n.

Ragenhill, John, 120 n., 148 n.
Raulyn, Robert, 143 n.
Raymond of Pennaforte, 32 n., 43, 170 n.; see also canonists
reclamation against marriage, 98–9, 107–8, 199
recusatio, 146
Reformation, effect of, 3, 11 n., 64, 118, 172
repudiation, see divorce, popular attitude towards
res judicata, 66
restitution of conjugal rights, 25 n., 67–9, 103, 161

reverential fear, 94
Reynolds, Thomas, 143 n.
Richmond, archdeacon of, 145
Rochester: archdeacon of, 144; bishop of, 207–8; cases heard at, 25, 58, 68, 74, 115, 116, 166, 181; Consistory court at, 120, 142, 144, 146, 148, 150, 182–3; procedure at, 14; records at, 12, 23, 185
Roman law, 4, 26 n., 46, 49, 134, 142 n., 143 n., 196
Roucliff, John, 211
Rowe, William, 208
rural deans, 143, 145, 177
Ruthyn, Eliseus, 148 n.

Saepe, see procedure, summary
saevitia, see cruelty
Sanchez, Thomas, 36, 56 n., 98 n., 176 n., 220; see also canonists
Sayers, Jane, 6 n., 166 n.
Schefford, John, 142 n.
Scotsmen, 130
secular arm, invocation of, 114, 125
Selby Abbey, custos spiritualitatis of, 145
sentences, see definitive sentences
separation, see divorce a mensa et thoro
sequestration, see parties, sequestration of
Sewale, Adam de, 203
sexual relations, 35 n., 109, 173–4, 198–9; creating impediment of affinity, 77; effect on marriage contracts, 26, 34–5, 41, 51, 55–6, 67, 91, 179, 212–3; jurisdiction over, 2, 70, 145–6, 177
Sheehan, M. M., 6 n., 28, 173
Shirlawe, Walter de, 142 n.
Smith, A. L., 188
social mobility, 80
sponsalia de presenti, 32
Stafford, archdeacon of, 144, 146
Stanton, Thomas, 148 n., 201
statutes, English, 64, 109
Stenton, Lady D. M., 114 n., 188
Stone, Lawrence, 87 n.
Stratford, John, Archbishop of Canterbury, 27 n.
'Stubbs–Maitland Controversy', 3
Sturneton, John, 120 n., 148 n.
subtractio uxoris, 109–10
suspension ab ingressu ecclesie, see ecclesiastical sanctions
Swan, William, 120 n.
Swinburne, H., 34, 37, 55, 96 n.; see also canonists

synodal decrees and statutes, English, 27 n., 141 n., 173, 184

Tametsi, see Councils, Trent
terminology, 8 n., 12
terms, legal, see Church courts, terms of
testimony: perjured, 65, 156–9; publication of, 20; variant, 156–7, 228
trespass, writ of, 109
triplications, 23
Twyforde, William de, 195
Tyverington, John, 211

upper classes, 24, 86–7, 176–1

verba de futuro, 34–40, 55–6, 125 n.
verba de presenti, 31, 34–40, 55–6, 66, 125
viis et modis, citation, 124
villeins, 100, 155, 160, 212–4
violence, 90, 92, 105–6
Virgin Mary, marriage of, 26
volo, used in contracting marriage, 36–40, 125, 187, 198–9

whipping, 182, 223
Wilkhous, Henry, 120 n.
Willyngham, John, 120 n., 148 n.
Witnesses, 15, 83–4, 93, 108, 154–59, 228–9; compulsion of, 128; de auditu, 81; examination of, 17–8, 18–9, 83, 112, 128–31, 182; numbers of, 82, 127–8, 154; payment of expenses, 128, 154, 158, 230–2; qualifications of, 133–4; reliability of, 18–19, 81–2, 129–30, 156–8; status of, 154–5; see also inquisitiones
Wodham, John, 152 n.
Wolffe, Richard, 120 n., 148 n.
women, treated differently from men, 69, 88–90, 106, 170–2
Woodcock, Brian, 2, 6, 166
Wyles, Thomas, 209

Year Books, 135
York: archbishop of, 145, 177, 218–9; archdeacon of, 92 n., 144; cases heard at, 58, 59 n., 68, 74, 115, 116, 180; Dean and Chapter of, 181, 182 n.; Exchequer court at, 145, 177; procedure at, 25 n., 89–90; Provincial court at, 1, 118 n., 120, 128 n., 142, 144, 148, 150, 177, 184; records at, 6, 9–10, 12, 17, 80, 157, 172, 181, 184
Yunck, John, 147 n.